From Media Systems to Media Cultures

In *From Media Systems to Media Cultures: Understanding Socialist Television*, Sabina Mihelj and Simon Huxtable delve into the fascinating world of television under communism, using it to test a new framework for comparative media analysis. To understand the societal consequences of mass communication, the authors argue that we need to move beyond the analysis of media systems and instead focus on the role of the media in shaping cultural ideals and narratives, everyday practices, and routines. Drawing on a wealth of original data derived from archival sources, programmes and schedule analysis, and oral history interviews, the authors show how communist authorities managed to harness the power of television to shape new habits and rituals yet failed to inspire a deeper belief in communist ideals. Their analysis in this book contains important implications for the understanding of mass communication in non-democratic settings and provides tools for the analysis of media cultures globally.

Sabina Mihelj is Professor of Media and Cultural Analysis at the Centre for Research in Communication and Culture at Loughborough University. She has written extensively on issues of media and nationalism, comparative media research, television studies, Eastern and Central European media, and Cold War media and culture. Her books include *Media Nations: Communicating Belonging in the Modern World* (2011) and *Central and Eastern European Media in Comparative Perspective: Politics, Economy and Culture* (2012). Her research was funded by the Arts and Humanities Research Council, the Economic and Social Research Council, the British Academy, and the Leverhulme Trust.

Simon Huxtable is Visiting Fellow in Media and Cultural History at Loughborough University. His research focuses on the social and cultural history of late socialism. His research has been published in journals including *Contemporary European History, Cahiers du Monde russe*, and *Media, Culture and Society*, and in a number of edited volumes. He is currently writing a monograph on the Soviet press and the public sphere after 1945, based on his doctoral research. His latest project focuses on the notion of the 'Socialist Way of Life' in the USSR and GDR.

Communication, Society and Politics

Editors

W. Lance Bennett, University of Washington

Robert M. Entman, The George Washington University

Politics and relations among individuals in societies across the world are being transformed by new technologies for targeting individuals and sophisticated methods for shaping personalized messages. The new technologies challenge boundaries of many kinds – between news, information, entertainment, and advertising; between media, with the arrival of the World Wide Web; and even between nations. Communication, Society and Politics probes the political and social impacts of these new communication systems in national, comparative, and global perspective.

Other Books in the Series

Erik Albæk, Arjen van Dalen, Nael Jebril, and Claes de Vreese, *Political Journalism in Comparative Perspective*

Eva Anduiza, Michael James Jensen, and Laia Jorba, eds., *Digital Media and Political Engagement Worldwide: A Comparative Study*

C. Edwin Baker, *Media Concentration and Democracy: Why Ownership Matters*

C. Edwin Baker, *Media, Markets, and Democracy*

W. Lance Bennett and Robert M. Entman, eds., *Mediated Politics: Communication in the Future of Democracy*

Rodney Benson, *Shaping Immigration News: A French-American Comparison*

Bruce Bimber, *Information and American Democracy: Technology in the Evolution of Political Power*

Bruce Bimber, Andrew Flanagin, and Cynthia Stohl, *Collective Action in Organizations: Interaction and Engagement in an Era of Technological Change*

Lynn S. Clark and Regina Marchi, *Young People and the Future of News*

Murray Edelman, *The Politics of Misinformation*

Frank Esser and Barbara Pfetsch, eds., *Comparing Political Communication: Theories, Cases, and Challenges*

Myra Marx Ferree, William Anthony Gamson, Jürgen Gerhards, and Dieter Rucht, *Shaping Abortion Discourse: Democracy and the Public Sphere in Germany and the United States*

Hernan Galperin, *New Television, Old Politics: The Transition to Digital TV in the United States and Britain*

Tim Groeling, *When Politicians Attack: Party Cohesion in the Media*

(*continued after the Index*)

From Media Systems to Media Cultures

Understanding Socialist Television

SABINA MIHELJ
Loughborough University

SIMON HUXTABLE
Loughborough University

CAMBRIDGE
UNIVERSITY PRESS

CAMBRIDGE
UNIVERSITY PRESS

University Printing House, Cambridge CB2 8BS, United Kingdom

One Liberty Plaza, 20th Floor, New York, NY 10006, USA

477 Williamstown Road, Port Melbourne, VIC 3207, Australia

314–321, 3rd Floor, Plot 3, Splendor Forum, Jasola District Centre,
New Delhi – 110025, India

79 Anson Road, #06–04/06, Singapore 079906

Cambridge University Press is part of the University of Cambridge.

It furthers the University's mission by disseminating knowledge in the pursuit of education, learning, and research at the highest international levels of excellence.

www.cambridge.org
Information on this title: www.cambridge.org/9781108422604
DOI: 10.1017/9781108525039

First published 2018

Printed in the United States of America by Sheridan Books, Inc.

A catalogue record for this publication is available from the British Library.

Library of Congress Cataloging-in-Publication Data
NAMES: Mihelj, Sabina, author. | Huxtable, Simon, 1980– author.
TITLE: From media systems to media cultures : understanding socialist television / Sabina Mihelj, Loughborough University ; Simon Huxtable, Loughborough University.
DESCRIPTION: Cambridge, United Kingdom ; New York : Cambridge University Press, 2018. | Series: Communication, society and politics
IDENTIFIERS: LCCN 2018003690 | ISBN 9781108422604 (hardback)
SUBJECTS: LCSH: Communism and mass media. | Mass media – Political aspects. | Mass media – Economic aspects. | Mass media and culture. | BISAC: POLITICAL SCIENCE / Government / International.
CLASSIFICATION: LCC HX550.M35 M54 2018 | DDC 335.4–dc23
LC record available at https://lccn.loc.gov/2018003690

ISBN 978-1-108-42260-4 Hardback

Contents

Figures

Tables

Acknowledgements

While working on this book, we have accrued many debts. First of all, a comparative project of this kind would not have happened without substantial institutional support. This book represents the culmination of a research project entitled *Screening Socialism: Popular Television and Everyday Life in Socialist Eastern Europe* (2013–2016), which was generously funded by the Leverhulme Trust. Despite frequent expressions of commitment to interdisciplinarity and blue-skies research in contemporary academia, funding bodies that consistently and systematically fund interdisciplinary research are few and far between. The distinct mission of the Leverhulme Trust sets it apart from many other funding bodies in this respect, and we are immensely grateful that the reviewers and the panel found it worthwhile to invest in what must have seemed, at the time, a rather risky project on a relatively obscure topic. From the very start, Loughborough University and the Centre for Research in Communication and Culture have provided an inspiring and supportive home for our research, and we are indebted to many colleagues, old and new, who have supported us with criticisms, suggestions, and encouragement.

We are especially indebted to the many colleagues who participated in the *Screening Socialism* project and helped us make it a success. These include, first of all, Alice Bardan and Sylwia Szostak, who played a major role in acquiring the materials for two of the five countries we investigate in the book. Many other researchers assisted us with acquiring some of the materials, transcribing and translating interview data, or supporting the project in other ways: Alex Boican, Magdalena Bugajska, Marijana Grbeša, Emily Harmer, Polina Kliuchnikova, Ivan Kozachenko, Antonios Kyriopoulos, Aleksandra Milovanović, Cristina Preutu, David Smith, and Mila Turaljić. Finally, advisory board members Anne

Gorsuch, Ann Grey, Thomas Lindenberger, and Michael Pickering offered invaluable advice on different aspects of our research as well as provided comments on our publication plans and drafts.

The launch of the *Screening Socialism* project happily coincided with the formation of the European (Post) Socialist Television History Network, led by Dana Mustata, which helped us establish and sustain an ongoing conversation with several colleagues with expertise in state socialist television history, including Cristine Evans, Ferenc Hammer, Anikó Imre, Lars Lundgren, Alexandru Matei, Mari Pajala, Cristina Preutu, and Irena Reifova. We would also like to express our gratitude to the following, who have, with their valuable criticism, suggestions, and encouragement, supported the development of the *Screening Socialism* project and this book in a variety of ways: Catherine Baker, Jérôme Bourdon, Paulina Bren, Deborah Chambers, Christoph Classen, Nevena Daković, David Deacon, John Downey, Kirsten Drotner, Igor Duda, Astrid Erll, Andreas Fickers, Heather Gumbert, Karol Jakubowicz, Nadia Kaneva, Emily Keightley, Judith Keilbach, Gholam Khiabany, Yuliya Komska, Stephen Lovell, Kati Lustyik, Julia Obertreis, Susan Reid, José Ricardo Carvalheiro, Ann Rigney, Kristin Roth-Ey, James Schwoch, Joes Segal, Marsha Siefert, James Stanyer, Liz Stokoe, Petr Szczepanik, Ana Tominc, Ekaterina Vikulina, Rolf Werenskjord, Odd Arne Westad, Liesbet Van Zoonen, and Barbie Zelizer.

Like any book reliant on historical sources, ours would not have been possible without the support of numerous archivists working in both national and local archives and libraries as well as broadcast archives across Eastern Europe and beyond. Many of them have gone well beyond their call of duty to accommodate our many requests. We are also indebted to the 171 interviewees who agreed to share their memories of television with us and thereby enabled us to reconstruct the experience of life with the small screen from the perspective of audiences. In particular, we would like to acknowledge those individuals who helped facilitate interviews with friends and family members and extended hospitality to the book's authors and other researchers.

Many of the arguments presented in this book were previously aired at conferences and symposia organized by national and international associations, and we have benefited greatly from the comments received and questions asked by the participants. These include the European Communication Research and Education Association conferences in Istanbul in 2012, in Lisbon in 2014, and in Prague in 2016; the European Network for Cinema and Media Studies conferences in

Prague in 2013, in Milan in 2014, and in Łodż in 2015; the International Communication Association Communication History pre-conferences in Seattle in 2014 and in San Diego in 2017; the Association for Slavic, East European and Eurasian Studies conventions in San Antonio in 2014 and in Washington, DC, in 2016; and the British Association for Slavonic and East European Studies conference in Cambridge in 2015. We have also had the fortune of receiving invitations to many thematically more focused international conferences and workshops, including the workshop 'Radio – das Medium der Ideologie' in Konstanz in 2013, the conference 'Television in Europe beyond the Iron Curtain' in Erlangen-Nürnberg in 2013, the 'Third Annual Screen Industries in East-Central Europe Conference' in Olomouc in 2013, the inaugural meeting of the European (Post) Socialist Television History Network in Stockholm in 2013, the conference 'Cold War and Entertainment Television' in Paris in 2014, the conference 'Media and the Cold War, 1975–1991' in Volda in 2014, the workshop 'Transnational Media Relationships during the Cold War' in Potsdam in 2014, the conference 'The Pleasures of Backwardness' in Berkeley in 2015, the 'Symposium on Late Socialism' in Tallinn in 2015, the COST Action ISTME workshop 'The Audiovisual Production of Transcultural Memory in Europe' in Dubrovnik in 2015, the workshop 'Comparative Studies of Communism' in Sofia in 2015, the conference 'Material Cultures of Television' in Hull in 2016, and the workshop 'Cold War Mobilities and Immobilities' in Budapest in 2017. Finally, we have also presented our work at departmental seminars and similar events organized in the United Kingdom, including at the University of Cambridge, Loughborough University, and the University of London.

The support of Cambridge University Press has been impressive throughout, particularly the assistance of Sara Doskow and her team, and the editors of the Communication, Society and Politics series, Lance Bennett and Robert Entman. We are also grateful to the three anonymous reviewers who commented on the book project at various stages of its evolution.

Finally, we owe special thanks to our partners and children, who have gracefully endured all the side effects of our passion for state socialist television: Clara, Emma, Jovan, and Chrysi.

Abbreviations of Archival Sources

AHRTV	Arhiv Hrvatske radio televizije/ Archive of Croatian Radiotelevision, Zagreb, Croatia
AJ	Arhiv Jugoslavije / Archives of Yugoslavia, Belgrade, Serbia
AMDTR	Arhiva Media şi Documentare, Televiziunea Română/ Romanian Television Media Archive, Bucharest, Romania
ANR	Arhivele Naţionale României / The National Archives of Romania, Bucharest, Romania
DRA	Deutsches Rundfunkarchiv / German Broadcasting Archive, Potsdam- Babelsberg, Germany
FFN	Fototeka Filmoteki Narodowej / Photo Collection of the National Film Archive, Warsaw, Poland
Fortepan	Fortepan Online Photo Archive, Hungary
GARF	Gosudarstvennyi arkhiv Rosiiskoi Federatsii / State Archive of the Russian Federation
HDA	Hrvatski državni arhiv / Croatian State Archives, Zagreb, Croatia
NAC	Narodowe Archiwum Cyfrowe/ National Digital Archives, Poland
NARA	National Archives and Records Administration, Washington, DC, USA
RGALI	Rossiiskii gosudarstvennyi arkhiv literatury i iskusstvo / Russian State Archive of Literature and Art

RGANI	Rossiiskii gosudarstvennyi arkhiv noveishei istorii / Russian State Archive of Contemporary History
RTS-CIJMPA	Radio televizija Srbija, Centar za istraživanje javnog mnenja, programa i auditorijuma / Radio Television of Serbia, Center for Public Opinion, Programme and Audience Research, Belgrade, Serbia
RTS-PATVB	Radio televizija Srbije, Programski arhiv Televizije Beograd / Radio Television of Serbia, Programme Archives of Television Belgrade, Belgrade, Serbia
SAPMO-BArch	Stiftung Archiv der Parteien und Massenorganisationen der DDR im Bundesarchiv / Foundation Archives of Parties and Mass Organizations of the GDR in the Federal Archives, Berlin, Germany
TsAOPIM	Tsentr khraneniia dokumentov obshchestvenno-politicheskoi istorii Moskvy – Fondy byvshego Tsentral'nogo arkhiva obshchestvenno-politicheskoi istorii Moskvy / Center for Preservation of Records of Socio-Political History of Moscow – Holdings from the former Central Archive of Social-Political History of Moscow, Moscow, Russia
TNS OBOP	Dział Dokumentacji Aktowej, Ośrodek Badania Opinii Publicznej / Archive of Reports, Center for Public Opinion and Broadcasting Research, Warsaw, Poland.

1

Introduction

The advent of the Cold War coincided with the rise of a new medium that came to occupy a central place in the everyday lives of citizens on both sides of the Iron Curtain. While the historical growth and social impact of television in the West have long attracted substantial and sustained scholarly attention, the medium's trajectories elsewhere in the world have taken longer to reach the academic radar.[1] The development of television in countries under communist rule, in particular, has been of marginal relevance to mainstream media and communication research – an object of interest to media historians and area specialists perhaps, but of limited significance to central debates in the field.[2] At first glance, the lack of interest in state socialist television may seem warranted. State socialist television, so the story goes, was a grey vehicle of propaganda which viewers ignored as much as possible, tuning into signals from their glamorous capitalist neighbours wherever and whenever they could. Yet this story is challenged by the sizeable audiences that state socialist television attracted throughout its existence and the fondness with which viewers remember many socialist-era television programs. To be sure, many viewers complained and even joked about the content of television programs. Even so, television's presence in viewers' living rooms ensured a constant means of contact between party and citizen,

[1] Research on television beyond the West started gaining momentum only around the turn of the century, with volumes such as Abu-Lughod (2005); Mankekar (1999); Rajagopal (2001).

[2] The majority of recent book-length studies of state socialist television have come from historians or area specialists rather than media or cultural studies experts. The first major exception to this in the English language is Imre (2016). See also notes 25 and 26.

and acted as an important source of shared sociality, aligned with communist values and goals. Yet, as shown in this book, television achieved all this while largely failing to engender a sense of unqualified adherence to communism. Thus, the history of state socialist television has much to tell us about the complex relationship between state and society during state socialism and, in doing so, has the capacity to challenge long-standing convictions about media and communication under totalitarian rule.

The experience of state socialist television we discuss in this book is not only of historical relevance. Rather, we use this foray into the long-dead era of Cold War broadcasting to advance a number of general arguments relevant to communication and media research. First and foremost, we seek to reorient the focus of comparative media research from media systems to media cultures. The comparative study of media systems and their relationships with political systems has received a substantial amount of attention in recent years and made significant strides in explicating the diversity of mediated communication around the world Yet, while important, this systemic approach offers only a partial insight into the social implications of mediated communication and, more generally, into the diversity of global media landscapes. To gain a fuller grasp of this diversity, we need to acknowledge that socially significant communication extends well beyond the traditional domains of politics, and encompasses the mediation of basic cultural ideals and narratives, as well as the structuring of everyday practices and routines. These include the perceptions of private and public life, the understanding of the nation and its position in the world, the modes of organizing daily routines and everyday spaces, and the historical events remembered and celebrated on a mass scale. To investigate these dimensions, we develop an analytical framework that conceives of media cultures as patterns of ideas and practices that enable mediated meaning formation, and that have distinct spatial and temporal characteristics. These media cultures, we argue, can vary on a number of dimensions, from the extent to which they seek to serve public or private goals, the degree to which they are open to transnational exchanges, and to their modes of engaging with the past, present, and future. This framework can be applied to different media and cultural forms, in diverse political and cultural contexts.

Second, we use the historical experience of socialist television to unsettle some of the key concepts in contemporary communication and media research, and question their global relevance. For instance, although talking of a socialist public sphere may seem a contradiction in terms, there is no doubt that socialist policymakers and television professionals had a clear sense of public mission and explicitly sought to use television as a means of stimulating public engagement and even social critique. What does this mean for our established ways of conceptualising television's involvement in the public sphere, or for our understanding of public service broadcasting? Or, to take another example: how are we to interpret the transnational ambitions of socialist television, and how do they relate to the much-debated processes of Americanization, cultural imperialism, and cultural globalization? To make sense of socialist television's trajectory, and situate it vis-à-vis its counterparts elsewhere in the world, we suggest a number of revisions to established concepts and arguments. Drawing on recent debates in sociology and history, as well as in media and cultural studies, we also propose a new theoretical agenda for comparative media research, anchored in the notion of entangled modernities. Following this approach, the different trajectories of media development around the world can be seen as resulting from multiple, yet connected, visions of modernity and modern society. The different modern visions evident in Cold War TV in many instances engaged with and responded to each other. This created a discourse that both reinforced the distinctions between varieties of modernity and also created the conditions for their mutual entanglement. This understanding of modernity and television chimes with proposals put forward by several other authors examining media cultures beyond the Western world, and offers a particularly suitable frame for conceptualizations that are sensitive to the diversity of media trajectories globally.

Third, this book enhances our understanding of the specificities of mediated communication in non-democratic settings. This is not of marginal importance to our discipline. When we began to think about this project, over a decade ago, it was still possible that the liberal media world was here to stay, and that its historical competitors, state socialist media systems included, had been consigned to the dustbin of history. Even then, of course, we felt that the study of state socialist television was important and relevant: it served as a reminder that the liberal media world that seemed so entrenched at that point was not the only one possible, but had historically evolved in competition with very different arrangements of mediated communication. Today such a reminder is no longer needed. As the 'illiberal turn' sweeping through democracies both old and new attests, it would be wrong to think that the liberal democratic approach to media governance possesses a universal and lasting appeal, or that it is inseparable from the global advance of commercial media ownership. Studying the bygone era of state socialist television in Eastern Europe is therefore not merely of historical relevance, but helps address some of the key questions that face media researchers in the present. How do media systems and cultures emerging in non-democratic contexts differ from those familiar in democratic environments? In what ways do the media in non-democratic contexts seek to affect audiences, and how effective are they in their endeavour? What is the role of new communication technologies in cementing the status quo, but potentially also in disrupting prevailing beliefs and routines, and existing relationships of power? The contemporary onslaught on the liberal media order is of course taking place in a political and media landscape that is rather different from the one that prevailed during the Cold War. Nonetheless, it is only through a better understanding of the differences and similarities between various media systems and cultures, both old and new, near and far, that we will be in a better position to appreciate where the current developments are heading. Understanding the historical experiences of socialist television is an important prerequisite for this endeavour.

The remainder of this introduction first provides a brief outline of the methodological and theoretical framework adopted in the book and explains how it departs from existing practices in comparative media research. The second part of the chapter looks more closely at the reasons that make the historical formation of state socialist television a particularly attractive object of comparative media cultures research. Central to this is the importance of understanding television's relationship with the communist political project: did communist authorities during the Cold War manage to harness the potential of television to advance their revolutionary ideas, or did television set in motion a revolution of its own, contributing to developments that in the long run proved detrimental to the communist project? As we shall see, the answer lies somewhere in the middle: television was immensely successful at weaving communist ideals into the very texture of everyday life, providing a basis of shared rituals and other forms of sociality, but did so without necessarily inspiring a commitment to the communist agenda. As such, television had an ambiguous relationship with the communist project: it served as an anchor of normality and thereby contributed to the stability and longevity of communist rule, while at the same time allowing the ideological message to become ever more blurred.

FROM MEDIA SYSTEMS TO MEDIA CULTURES

Comparative media research has advanced considerably over the past two decades, evolving from a marginal preoccupation to a well-established subfield of media and communication research. As Sonia Livingstone notes, the conduct of research within a single country can no longer be taken for granted, and has to be accompanied, at the very minimum, by asking whether the findings are limited to that country or are part of a wider transnational trend.[3] In the process of achieving greater recognition in the field, comparative research has also reached a considerable level of methodological and theoretical sophistication, and enlarged its substantive and geographical scope. As a result, it is now possible to identify a significant body of comparative work across all the major subfields of communication and media research, ranging from political communication to social interaction, and from media policy and regulation to audience reception.[4]

Yet if we look more closely at which kinds of substantive questions, geographical areas, and units of analysis have received the most attention, it is clear that existing research focuses primarily on Western media, is marked by a preference for national media systems as the sole units of analysis, and is heavily biased in favour of political communication and news genres. These tendencies are clearly evident in what is presently the most influential study in the field, namely Hallin and Mancini's *Comparing Media Systems*.[5] In this landmark book, the authors examine eighteen countries in Western Europe and North America, focusing on news media and regulation, conceived as parts of national media systems. Although the choice of the term 'system' implies comprehensiveness, the focus on news media and regulation effectively means that what are being compared are, for the most part, political communication systems, rather than media systems in general. The authors readily acknowledge that their analysis could be expanded to encompass other cultural industries, including television, but admit that this would 'involve other literatures and require very different sets of concepts'.[6]

The shortcomings of existing comparative work are often noted in the literature, but the various critiques and suggestions for improvements have not yet coalesced into a substantive new framework. For instance, several scholars have sought to expand and amend existing media typologies and comparative frameworks by looking at cases beyond those of Western Europe and North America.[7] Yet, despite some notable

[3] Livingstone (2012), p. 415. [4] For an overview see Esser and Hanitzsch (2012).
[5] Hallin and Mancini (2004). [6] Ibid. p. 7.
[7] E.g. Dobek-Ostrowska et al. (2010); Downey and Mihelj (2012); Guerrero and Márquez-Ramírez (2014); Hallin and Mancini (2012a); Voltmer (2013).

theoretical and methodological advances, this body of work typically consists of country-by-country compilations or comparative treatments that zoom in on narrowly defined aspects of media systems. Likewise, some authors have pointed to the need to reorient the attention of comparative research from systemic to cultural aspects of mediated communication, yet these discussions have given rise neither to a shared approach, nor to a firm understanding of what comparing media cultures actually involves.[8] Finally, many scholars have highlighted the inherent methodological nationalism of existing research and proposed methodological solutions designed to make comparative work more sensitive to transnational exchanges and influences.[9] However, these solutions are yet to be tried and tested on a substantive body of empirical materials.

The subject matter examined in this book required us to make methodological choices very different from those adopted by Daniel C. Hallin and Paolo Mancini. It also offered us the opportunity to take on board diverse suggestions for improvements developed since the publication of *Comparing Media Systems*, integrate them into a new analytical framework, and test their usefulness empirically. The framework we propose differs from those prevailing in existing work in a number of ways. Apart from the obvious shift in geographical focus, and the fact that we examine a set of communist-ruled countries rather than liberal democracies, our concern with television required us to move beyond news and encompass a considerably more varied range of genres and modes of communication, including fiction and entertainment. At the same time, our intention to combine institutional and programme analysis with audience history also meant that the focus of analytical attention moved from the vertical relationships between media systems and political systems to the horizontal processes of meaning-formation that tie together producers, programmes, and audiences.

This reorientation can best be conceived in terms of a shift in focus from comparing media *systems* to comparing media *cultures*. Systemic aspects are of course not absent from our investigation; in fact, we argue that a comparative inquiry into media cultures cannot proceed without

8 E.g. Couldry and Hepp (2012); Hanitzsch (2007). A more comprehensive survey of existing research that deals comparatively with cultural aspects of communication is provided in Chapter 1.

9 E.g. Esser (2013); Hardy (2012); Livingstone (2003).

a parallel consideration of media systems, which constitute one of the major contextual factors that help explain why media cultures are the way they are. The vast majority of the analysis presented in the empirical sections of this book, however, focuses on media cultures themselves, the specific patterns of practices and meanings that constitute them, and the ways in which these patterns are negotiated in processes that tie together the circuits of media production, texts, reception, and use.

The emphasis on culture may leave the impression that our intention is to link the diversity of media cultures to ethnocultural or civilizational differences, and distinguish between 'French', 'Polish', 'British', and 'Russian' media cultures, or between 'European', 'Asian', 'African', or 'Latin American' media cultures. This is not how the relationship between media cultures and global contexts is conceptualized in this book. Reducing media cultures to cultural differences runs the risk of adopting an essentialist understanding of culture and cannot fully explain the diversity of media cultures. Instead, our analytical move from media systems to media cultures is coupled with a novel theoretical approach to comparative media research, anchored in the notion of entangled varieties of modernity.[10] This approach helps us situate socialist television trajectories vis-à-vis their counterparts around the globe, as well as understanding intra-regional variation in the socialist world itself. As such, analyzing the entangled varieties of modernity also serves to advance the agenda of 'de-Westernizing' or internationalizing communication and media research.[11] However, this de-Westernization is achieved in a manner that steers away from the culture-centricity often advocated as an alternative to West-centred approaches – namely, the tendency to explain differences between Western and non-Western media cultures as results of ethno-cultural or civilizational diversity.[12]

This is not to say that cultural differences should be ignored. As shown in our analysis, state socialist television cultures differed depending, among other factors, on the character of gender relations, the level of acceptance of religious traditions, and the nature of national historical narratives in a particular context. Yet, such cultural differences are not all that mattered; they constituted pieces of a much larger puzzle. State socialist television cultures also differed depending on the foreign policies

[10] E.g. Arnason (2000); Dirlik (2003); Eisenstadt (1974); Schmidt (2006); Therborn (2003).
[11] Curran and Park (2000); Thussu (2009); Wang (2011).
[12] E.g. Chen (2007); Miike (2007).

of the country and the transnational orientations of broadcast infrastructure, on the relative core-periphery position of the country and its television system, on the extent and forms of party-state control over the media, and on the timing of infrastructural developments they were tied to. To unpack these multiple factors, we approach different media cultures as rooted in different visions of modern society, all stemming from similar core assumptions about the nature of human beings and their relationship to the world, and sharing a tendency towards structural differentiation, but articulated through different constellations of modern institutions, including different models of media systems. By foregrounding the shared traits of the different varieties of modernity, this approach avoids reducing the diversity of global media landscapes to a narrow range of cultural differences, and enables us to theorize the shared traits and also the distinctive qualities of media cultures within a common conceptual framework.

WHY STATE SOCIALIST TELEVISION?

State socialist[13] television provides a particularly apposite testing ground for a comparative framework centred on media cultures and anchored in the notion of entangled varieties of modernity. As part of the communist propaganda apparatus, socialist television formed an integral part of a political, economic, and cultural system that set out self-consciously to develop an alternative form of modernity, one premised on communist rule and the planned economy and designed to give rise to a classless society. Culture – including media culture – formed an essential part of this revolutionary endeavour. The good life anticipated by communist rulers promised not only education, health, and social security for all, but also a genuinely common 'mass culture', one that would extend its appeal beyond educated elites, erase differences of taste between classes, and involve individuals of all backgrounds not only as audiences, but also as cultural producers.[14] In such a context, culture in all its

[13] In this book, we chose to use the epithet 'state socialist' rather than 'communist' when referring to television, as well as when talking of societies and countries. In contrast, we use the label 'communist' when referring to the form of rule, the party elite, and values and visions of progress. This decision to talk about 'socialist' television was in part influenced by the fact that this is the preferred label in most of existing literature on the topic (but see Bren, 2010, for a notable exception). We also felt that this terminological choice reflected the dual nature of our object of investigation, and more generally the tension between the communist vision and politics on the one hand, and the historical reality of societies and cultures on the other.

[14] See Fitzpatrick (1992); Mihelj (2011b).

manifestations, including those embodied in the mass media, was endowed with a tremendous burden of responsibility, but also with a sense of prestige and authority. As Stephen Lovell points out in his plea for a 'media-centred' approach to Soviet history, culture was 'not simply the handmaiden of politics; it was more akin to a valued senior employee'.[15] As we shall show further on in the book, this elevated status meant that the state socialist media and cultural industries enjoyed some independence and could on occasion offer their own interpretations of the party line.

While endeavouring to foster an alternative form of modern society and culture, state socialist television was not entirely different from its relative in the West, or completely isolated from it. Television in the state socialist world in many ways shared the trajectory of its Western cousin and became involved in some of the central processes of transformation that marked the post-World War II era. Television offered tangible proof of a country's ability to master modernity, as well as promising access to education, culture, and information for all, and thereby acted as a means by which post-war welfare regimes could deliver the dream of a good life to all of their citizens. It represented powerful means both of national integration and of globalization, and also responded to the thirst for cheap entertainment among the fast-growing urban populations which enjoyed increasing amounts of leisure time and income. As Christine Evans rightly points out, these shared traits of television both East and West were in no small part generated by the nature of the Cold War contest in which the Soviet Union and the United States, along with their allies, competed over the inheritance of the Enlightenment, more specifically over the best ways of delivering a good life to all.[16] To put it differently, the similarities between television trajectories on both sides of the Iron Curtain testify to their shared participation in the project of modernity, and act as a reminder that 'the story of modernity is not just the story of liberal capitalism; it is the story of liberalism and socialism and their relationship to one another'.[17]

Understanding state socialist television, then, requires us to approach it as a specific subtype of modern television, in many ways similar to its Western cousin, but also designed to promote an alternative vision of progress and belonging – one premised on a teleological vision of history centred on the revolution and culminating in a socially equal, worker-led society. A central question of this book concerns the extent to which communist authorities and TV professionals managed to use the medium

[15] Lovell (2015), p. 1. [16] Evans (2016), pp. 30–31. [17] Gumbert (2014), p. 4.

to further their revolutionary goals. How exactly, and to what extent, did the alternative vision of progress advanced by the party translate into actual patterns of television production, forms of programming, and audience use? Were these patterns successful in promoting the communist cause?

At first sight, television technology offered a uniquely powerful means of furthering the revolution. As with radio, its social reach was not tied to the advance of literacy, and its gradual institutionalization as a domestic medium meant that messages produced centrally could reach citizens in the comfort of their homes, removing the need for an intricate network of local propagandists. In addition, its ability to offer an instantaneous, 'live' connection with unfolding events also held the promise of engendering shared participation in the onward march of revolutionary progress. But television went even further than radio. The ability to couple sound with moving image had the potential to make messages both more accessible and appealing to a wider range of audiences, and also significantly broadened the range of forms and genres that could be transmitted. This included not only the possibility of broadcasting propaganda films or the latest theatre performance of Chekhov's *Three Sisters*, but also the opportunity to capture popular participation in the communist project in its full splendour, transmitting live images of mass rallies and showcasing the achievements of model workers. Finally, the combination of the medium's visual nature with its liveness and the domesticity seemed to provide television with an ability to create a uniquely intimate, authentic, and truthful insight into the inner world of individuals otherwise unavailable to the naked eye. This 'new vision' (*novoe zrenie*), as the 'prophet' of Soviet television Vladimir Sappak called it, could generate a 'revolution in perception ... through which man might be jolted out of his quotidian routine and caused to see the world in a new, more authentic way'.[18] Television, then, was an inherently revolutionary medium, seemingly perfectly suited to advance the communist project.

This was the theory, but the practice of socialist television suggests a more complicated picture. As recent research indicates, every advantage brought by television also harboured a disadvantage. It quickly became obvious that the addition of the moving image did little to increase the appeal of political speeches, not least because professional propagandists were often reluctant to embrace the new medium and preferred to stick to traditional methods of direct oral agitation.[19] By contrast, cultural

[18] Quoted in Evans (2016), pp. 236–238. [19] Roth-Ey (2011), pp. 192–196.

industry professionals were quicker to realize the potential of the new medium and used the addition of the visual to expand the roster of entertainment genres, both through arranging live broadcasts and through creating programs expressly made for television. As a result, paradoxically, socialist television was better at entertaining than at propagandising. Surveys conducted in Yugoslavia in the 1960s repeatedly found that the popularity of entertainment genres and transmissions of football matches exceeded the appeal of news programs and also showed that Yugoslav audiences viewed television primarily as a means of relaxation and entertainment.[20] This was not simply a Yugoslav peculiarity: a survey conducted among employees in Moscow in 1967 likewise revealed that the top three programs watched by respondents were soccer, boxing, and the variety show *Little Blue Flame*, while programs with more explicit political messages ranked further down.[21]

The promise of television as a means of staging live events involving ordinary people also proved far trickier in practice than on paper, for it unsettled the precarious balance between participation and control. The most striking example of this is provided by Nicolae Ceauşescu's speech on 21 December 1989, broadcast live and delivered in front of a large crowd gathered in front of the Presidential Palace in Bucharest. As usual, many spectators were bussed in from across the city, yet rather than following the usual protocols of participation, complete with applause and pro-communist chants, they began to shout and scream, demanding that Ceauşescu step down. This uncontrolled behaviour caused the broadcast to be cut short and marked the beginning of the 'live Romanian revolution' that we examine more fully in Chapter 9. Similar examples of live broadcasts derailed by disruptive participants can be found in earlier decades of communist rule. During the live transmission of a Soviet quiz entitled *Evening of Merry Questions* (*Vecher veselykh voprosov*) in 1957, more than 600 viewers turned up in the studio, some of them drunk, and many of them poorly dressed and unruly, one even carrying a live chicken. The show was thrown into disarray, the host lost his bearings and soon disappeared from the stage, and after some delay the director of the show finally decided to cut the transmission.[22] Paradoxically, the very traits that promised to make television the ideal medium of the communist

[20] Mihelj (2013), p. 255. [21] Evans (2016), p. 84.
[22] Roth-Ey (2011), pp. 246–253; Evans (2016), pp. 37–42.

revolution – namely its liveness and its capacity to showcase popular participation – also embodied a potential threat to the communist order.

The establishment of television as a domestic medium was another stumbling block for the communist project. While it had the ability to deliver political messages to socialist citizens in the comfort of their homes, television also restricted the ability of communist authorities to control how these messages were received – if they were received at all. As Kristin Roth-Ey notes in her study of Soviet television, broadcast media enabled audiences 'to interact with mass culture on their *own* terms' rather than in a collectively organized fashion, and allowed them to make choices that were not necessarily the ones envisioned by the elites.[23] A related challenge posed by domestic consumption was its potential to lure citizens away from collective forms of leisure and public life, ultimately diminishing the ability of the medium to promote mass mobilization. Thus, the rise of domestic media was strangely at odds with Soviet cultural and political ideals: 'Where Soviet tradition was geared to mass political and cultural mobilization, TV looked like immobilization; where Soviet tradition privileged collective, public settings, TV broadcasting reached individual and anonymous viewers in their homes.'[24] If the essence of the communist ideal of mass communication lay in marrying authority with participation, the domesticity of television appeared to undermine both.

Yet, we should be wary of assuming that these negative examples rendered television inimical to the communist project. Communist elites and television professionals across Eastern Europe were well aware of both the opportunities and the dangers ingrained in the new medium and worked hard to embed television technology in an alternative cultural form, one that capitalized on the potential of broadcasting sound and images while adapting it to communist goals. For instance, although the audience preference for entertainment over education and information often prompted consternation among elites, it also gradually led to a range of successful attempts to mobilize entertainment for political goals. An important aim of this book is precisely to map out the different points of contact and tension between, on the one hand, the cultural forms of television as developed in the West and, on the other hand, the nature and goals of the communist project. To do so, the book performs a balancing act between media-centrism and social determinism, or

[23] Roth-Ey (2011), p. 15. [24] Ibid. p. 181.

between what Raymond Williams has termed 'technological determinism' and 'determined technology'.[25] In line with this, television is treated both as a set of technological solutions with their own possibilities, and as a distinct cultural form, complete with particular public functions, conventions of representation, and personal uses. The same – or closely similar – set of technological solutions we now recognize as 'television' could therefore give rise to a host of different cultural forms of the medium depending on the context in which it was embedded.

Existing research on socialist television offers much that is of relevance to the discussion developed in this book, yet this body of work largely consists of single-country studies.[26] In the few cases where a more transnational perspective is adopted, the focus remains on transnational cooperation and exchanges, selected policy aspects, or programme analysis, without developing a more systematic comparative overview of shared traits, cross-country differences, or changes over time.[27] The existing literature is also largely concerned with the analysis of institutional infrastructures, elite views, professional practices, and TV programmes, while having relatively little to say about audience practices and perspectives. This raises the question of whether trends noted in individual countries appeared elsewhere, and whether the intended social impact of particular programming was borne out by audience response. The comparative approach adopted in this book helps overcome these weaknesses. Applied to five countries that embody the main dimensions of variation

[25] Williams (2007 [1974]), p. 133.

[26] The most important contributions include book-length studies focusing on a single country, and a handful of edited volumes comprising single-country studies from different parts of Eastern Europe. For a selection of studies of Soviet TV see Evans (2016); Prokhorova (2003); Prokhorova and Prokhorov (2017); Roth-Ey (2011). Studies of East German television include Dittmar (2010); Gumbert (2014); Meyen (2003a, 2003b); Pfau et al. (2010); Steinmetz and Viehoff (2008). Finally, for a sample of literature on Czechoslovak TV see Bren (2010) and Štoll (2018) and for Romanian TV, Mustata (2011) and Matei (2013). The most important edited volumes include Goddard 2013; Imre et al. 2013; Bönker et al. 2016.

[27] For some examples of research focusing on transnational cooperation and exchanges within and beyond the socialist world see Badenoch et al. (2013); Bönkers et al. (2016); Lundgren (2012). The only comprehensive book-length treatment of socialist television covering more than one country is Anikó Imre's (2016) *TV Socialism*, which offers an insightful and in many ways ground-breaking analysis of shared traits across a wide range of television programmes and genres, but does not seek to develop systematic cross-country comparisons or investigate the broader context of TV production, reception, and use. Some of the early research on East European television, most notably Burton Paulu's (1974) work, also provides valuable information from a range of countries, but is mostly descriptive rather than analytical in its approach.

in socialist television, it enables us to identify both the shared traits and the distinct trajectories of socialist television in the region. The weaving together of institutional and programme analysis with audience history, on the other hand, makes it possible to ascertain how the hopes and anxieties surrounding television played out on the ground and to answer the question whether, ultimately, socialist television managed to advance the communist cause.

As we show over the course of the book, the state socialist context did give rise to a cultural form of television that was in many ways distinct from its Western cousin, clearly aligned with communist ideals not only at the level of elite discourse and editorial policies but also at the level of programme output and audience use. Yet at the same time, television largely failed to engender the kind of active adherence to communist ideals it aspired to: it gave rise to new practices attuned to communist agendas, but did not necessarily create new loyalties. In this sense, television helped sustain the paradoxical duality of communist ideology as theorized by Alexei Yurchak, contributing to its 'hegemony of form' while leaving much of its content indeterminate. According to Yurchak, Soviet public life after Stalin's death in 1953 was characterized by a disjunction between form and content, or more precisely between the significance of official speeches, parades, and public events as performances, and their literal meanings. People thus participated in such acts and events not because they endorsed the ideological content, but because participation allowed them to partake in various forms of sociality, creativity, and self-fulfilment that were not necessarily determined by the literal meaning of these acts and events. At the same time, the disjunction between performance and literal meanings did not mean that people were opposed to the communist project. Rather, it allowed them to develop a differentiated relationship with this project, selectively adopting or rejecting particular meanings, norms, and values depending on context, and even creating new meanings. As a result, argues Yurchak, this duality of Soviet public life paradoxically contributed to the perceptions of both the stability and the immutability of the Soviet system, as well as of its creative and unpredictable possibilities.

State socialist television, we argue, was a key institution that helped embed this interplay of form and content, stability and creativity, into the daily lives of millions. It aligned the everyday lives of state socialist citizens with the communist agenda, and presented daily reminders of communist ideals and goals, but also generated modes of viewing, shared habits, and rituals not necessarily determined by the content of programming, let alone by the intentions of policymakers or television producers. Through that, communist ideology became taken for granted as part of the texture of everyday life, as well as providing a basis for common reference points and shared experiences for families and communities. In tandem with the repetitive, predictable structures of television scheduling and viewing, these shared experiences imbued the revolutionary project with a sense of comforting normality and stability, regardless of whether or not one actually endorsed the ideological messages. At the same time, television also injected the communist project with a new sense of vibrancy: as a new medium, it instituted new habits, offered new ways of retelling the story of the communist revolution, and brought the excitement of new experiences. Ultimately, however, the disjunction between performance and meaning took its toll: a political project geared for revolutionary change could not survive on normality and stability alone, and the novelty brought by television did not always work to the advantage of the communist agenda.

OUTLINE OF THE BOOK

The book is divided into three main parts. Part One opens with a chapter that lays out the overall analytical framework in greater detail. It develops a definition of media culture, and introduces time and space as its two key dimensions, building on a long tradition of theorising the distinguishing characteristics of mediated communication with regard to the temporal and spatial qualities of communication technologies. The majority of Chapter 2 is taken up by a discussion of the key dimensions of variation among media cultures, with a focus on television. Seven such dimensions are introduced: publicness, privacy, gendering, transnationalism, temporal orientation, extraordinary temporality, and secularization. The last part of the chapter turns to methodological issues. It considers the sources and methods that can be used for the purpose of comparative media culture analysis, and presents the specific materials and techniques used in the book. The chapter concludes by discussing two major methodological obstacles facing comparative media culture research: the danger of methodological nationalism and the challenge of researching change over time.

To help explain how and why television cultures in state socialist Eastern Europe differed along the seven dimensions introduced in Chapter 2, the third chapter offers a broad overview of the historical conditions in which they arose. Particular attention is paid to the five countries at the forefront of analysis – the Soviet Union, Yugoslavia, East Germany, Poland, and Romania – and to the four main characteristics of their broadcasting systems: the timing of infrastructural developments, the transnational orientation of broadcasting systems, their relative core-periphery position, and television's relationship with the party and the state. The last section of Chapter 3 builds on these characteristics to develop a typology of state socialist television systems. Three major types are identified: market state socialist, reformist state socialist, and hard-line state socialist TV systems. To conclude, the chapter considers how these three types of systems relate to the cultural dimensions of variation introduced in Chapter 2 and discusses further contextual factors to be taken into account when explaining state socialist television cultures.

Building on the historical overview and the typology developed in the previous chapter, Chapter 4 seeks to situate socialist television cultures vis-à-vis trajectories of television development elsewhere in the world. To this end, this chapter lays out a framework for thinking of the diversity of media trajectories as rooted in varieties of modernity, building on three strands of existing literature: general debates about multiple modernities, existing discussions of alternative modernities in the context of mediated communication, and comparative media systems research. The first part of the chapter summarizes general arguments about multiple modernities and explains how and why state socialism should be approached as a variety of modernity. The second part applies this framework to the media, and uses it to situate the state socialist television trajectories examined in Chapter 3 vis-à-vis models of broadcasting elsewhere in the world, with a particular focus on those that evolved in Western Europe and North America after World War II. In this context, the chapter also revisits Hallin and Mancini's three Western models of media systems – the Polarised Pluralist, the Democratic Corporatist, and the Liberal Model[28] – and suggests how their analytical framework can be modified and extended to account for the specificities of state socialist television.

Parts Two and Three of the book turn to the empirical investigation of socialist television cultures and thereby offer an example of how the analytical and theoretical framework for comparing media cultures can be applied in practice. Following the conceptualization of media culture introduced in Part One, television is conceived as a medium with distinct

[28] Hallin and Mancini (2004).

spatial and temporal characteristics that participate in shaping basic assumptions about the world. In line with this, the empirical chapters are divided into two groups: one investigates socialist television from a spatial perspective and the other from a temporal perspective. Each chapter focuses on one of the dimensions of variation introduced in Chapter 2, identifies the shared features and main differences between the countries, and where relevant, outlines some of the key developments over time. Each chapter also reflects on how these patterns of difference and similarity relate to the systemic and contextual features discussed in Chapters 3 and 4.

Part Two starts with an investigation of the medium's involvement in the public realm. To capture the different aspects of this involvement, Chapter 5 distinguishes between two dimensions of television's publicness: the *public sphere* and the *public mission*. The first section considers how state socialist television acted as a provider of public goods and compares its public mission with that of public broadcasting in Western Europe at the time. The second section zooms in on entertainment programming and the disjunction between audience preferences and elite views on the matter, as well as highlighting the key cross-country differences and changes over time in this area. The third and final section considers the specificities of public life under communism and discusses whether and to what extent something resembling a public sphere could emerge in such a context. While it is argued that the direct application of the Habermasian model to the state socialist world is misguided, the analysis presented also suggests that the state socialist media, television included, helped establish a truncated, semi-public sphere.

Chapter 6 shifts the focus towards the other side of the 'grand dichotomy', and explores television's involvement with the private sphere.[29] Two dimensions of television's engagement with privacy are considered. In the first part of the chapter, the focus is on the *domestication* of television, namely the gradual adoption of television as a domestic medium. The chapter examines how television as a material object gradually entered domestic life and became an essential part of a modern home, as well as how it came to be integrated into family life. In the second part of the chapter the analysis turns to *privatization* as visible in television programming. The chapter examines a range of fictional serial

[29] The designation of the public-private distinction as one of the 'grand dichotomies' is borrowed from Bobbio (1992).

programmes that dealt with personal relationships or were set within the domestic living spaces of ordinary citizens. In examining these issues, the chapter also asks whether and to what extent the processes of domestication and privatization of state socialist television resembled those familiar in the West at the time, as well as how they varied within the region. Particular attention is paid to the distinctly hybrid, semi-public character of privacy in the state socialist context, and to the ways in which this 'public privacy' became articulated through television cultures in the region. While discussing television's engagement with the private realm, Chapter 6 also examines how the processes of domestication and privatization of television in state socialist countries interacted with gendered practices and assumptions specific to the region.

The final chapter in Part Two looks at another key dimension of variation between television cultures, namely its involvement with transnational exchanges and ties. As we show, state socialist television cultures shared a commitment to transnationalism: as elsewhere in the world, television schedules included substantial proportions of imported material, and audiences often thought of the small screen as a means of connecting with distant corners of the globe. Yet, the exact forms of transnationalism varied considerably across countries and over time, both within the region itself and with regard to television cultures elsewhere in the world. To investigate this variation, the chapter examines the relative *openness* of state socialist television cultures to transnational exchanges and ties, and the *origins* of these cross-border interactions and links. Did television succeed in establishing a cross-border television culture that was specifically pan-socialist and focused on other state socialist countries? Or, rather, did it give rise to a form of transnationalism oriented primarily to the West? To answer these questions, the chapter first analyses the balance of domestically produced and imported TV materials and the origin of foreign programming across the five countries, outlining key differences and similarities and considering explanatory factors that can account for this variation. In the second part, the analysis turns to audiences and uses oral-history interview materials to examine what foreign television programmes meant for state socialist audiences and their perceptions of their country and the world.

Part Three shifts attention to temporal aspects of television cultures, focusing primarily on their temporal orientation. The key question addressed across all three chapters in this part concerns the relationship between the present-centeredness of television, arising from its ability to establish an instantaneous, live connection with the unfolding present, and the distinctly teleological, future-oriented understanding of the passage of time characteristic of the communist vision of modern progress. Chapter 8 tackles this question from the perspective of everyday television programming and viewing. To this end, the chapter first examines how TV elites in Eastern Europe sought to organize schedules in order to capture and transform viewers and ensure that audiences remained attuned to the rhythms of revolutionary progress. In the second part, the analysis draws on oral-history interviews to investigate how and whether these scheduling techniques shaped viewers' everyday practices, thus seeking to reconstruct the lived experience of daily television viewing and the extent to which it instilled a sense of participation in revolutionary movements. Throughout the analysis, attention is also paid to cross-country differences and to how the patterns of everyday temporal organization found in state socialist television cultures resembled or departed from those seen in the West. In doing so, the chapter also highlights further aspects of the gendered structures of state socialist television culture and shows how the distinct organization of everyday television functioned as a means of secularization. As shown in the chapter, gendering and secularization are two aspects in which the temporal logic of everyday television in state socialist countries differed from patterns found in the West.

Chapter 9 studies yet another aspect of television culture where the link with temporal orientation becomes apparent – namely, its engagement with history. As shown in the chapter, socialist television cultures were inherently bound up with history: many of the most popular TV programmes from the state socialist era revolved around historical events, and television was often singled out as a particularly effective means of shaping historical awareness, even being explicitly tasked by the authorities with history education. The chapter first investigates how and why state socialist television became so steeped in history. On the one hand, it considers the distinct teleological, future-oriented understanding of time underpinning the communist project and shows that this understanding demanded a constant engagement with revolutionary achievements of the past. On the other hand, the chapter points out that the prominence of televised history in the state socialist world needs to be interpreted also as an integral part of transnational trends, especially the coming of age of the first post-World War II generation, and the rise of new forms of expression tied to the medium of television. The second part of the chapter examines the depictions of history on screen themselves, paying particular attention to serial fiction. It identifies the shared elements of historical narratives found in the region, as well as some of the key points of variation across countries, and considers the factors that can explain this variation.

The last chapter in Part Three asks how the distinct teleological, future-oriented vision of time became articulated on extraordinary occasions, when television abandoned the routines of everyday programming and viewing. In doing so, the chapter also considers the differences and similarities in ways of engendering a sense of special occasion, both within and across different television cultures. The first part of the chapter examines state socialist television holidays, paying particular attention to major festive occasions such as Labour Day and New Year's celebrations. The chapter first outlines key characteristics of the festive media schedules across the five countries, noting relevant intra-regional differences as well as considering how they differed from festive schedules in the West. This is followed by a comparative analysis of two major types of media holidays that appear across all countries: those linked to a distinctly communist vision of modern progress and society and those without a marked communist identity. The second part of the chapter turns to a different category of television's involvement with extraordinary time, namely media disruptions. The analysis tackles some of the most dramatic events from the state socialist era: the deaths of major communist leaders such as Yugoslavia's Josip Broz Tito in 1980 and the Soviet Union's Leonid Brezhnev in 1982, the proclamation of martial law in Poland in 1982, the ousting of Ceausescu in Romania, and the fall of the Berlin Wall in 1989. Unlike the festive occasions examined in the first part of the chapter, these disruptive events were at odds with the teleological temporality of the communist project and raised anxiety over the ability of communist-led societies to master the future, or simply stopped revolutionary progress in its tracks. As shown in the chapter, the five examples of media disruptions also offer a suitable basis for reflecting on the involvement of television cultures in the gradual disintegration of the communist order.

The concluding chapter takes stock of the arguments and analysis developed over the course of the book and reflects on their significance both from the perspective of the role of the media under communist rule and from the perspective of comparative media research more generally. It starts by laying out the key characteristics of state socialist television cultures as revealed in the book and considers whether they amount to a distinct form of modern television culture, rooted in communist modernity and geared to advance the communist revolutionary agenda.

It then moves on to examine developments in Eastern Europe after 1989, discussing some of the continuities and discontinuities between socialist and post-socialist television cultures in the region. Finally, it reflects on the relevance of the comparative framework developed in the book for understanding media landscapes beyond Eastern Europe: it emphasizes the importance of cultural and comparative analysis for advancing the understanding of mediated communication in non-democratic settings, discusses the applicability of key findings to the surviving communist states, such as China, and considers the applicability of analytical tools developed in the book to communication and media developments globally. To avoid burdening the body of the text with a detailed explication of methodological procedures and sources used, this information is provided in the Methodological Appendix.

PART I

CONCEPTS AND CONTEXTS

2

Comparing Media Cultures

The idea of focusing comparative efforts on cultural features is not a new one in media research. A significant body of existing comparative, cross-country research in the field deals with aspects of mediated communication that concern culture. Particularly voluminous is the literature examining journalistic values and practices across several countries and the body of cross-country research on news, which focuses either on the general conventions and trends in news reporting or on patterns in the coverage of particular topics such as EU affairs.[1] Other media genres have received their share of attention too, and a sizeable comparative literature now exists on a range of forms of representation across different media platforms, including soap operas, reality television formats, and advertising.[2] Audience habits and reception have also been examined comparatively, both from the perspective of the changing media environments of selected social groups such as children and with regard to the reception of globally successful programmes such as *Dallas* or *The Lord of the Rings*.[3]

It is only very recently, however, that scholars interested in comparative approaches have begun to conceptualize these cultural aspects in a more concerted manner and to consider the best ways of comparing them. Several useful theoretical and methodological suggestions have been put forward but so far have neither coalesced into a shared approach nor given rise to a firm understanding of what comparing media cultures

[1] E.g. Chalaby (1996); de Vreese et al. (2001); Esser (1999).

[2] E.g. Allen (1995); Furnham and Mak (1999); Van Keulen and Krijnen (2014).

[3] E.g. Barker and Mathijs (2008); Liebes and Katz (1990); Livingstone and Bovill (2013).

actually involves. In this chapter we build on these recent efforts to develop a more fully fledged conceptual and analytical framework for comparing media cultures. The first part develops a definition of media culture, understood as distinctive patterns of ideas and practices tied to specific forms of mediated communication, which shape processes of meaning-formation across instances of production, reception, and use. This is followed by a discussion of the key dimensions of variation among media cultures, with a focus on television. We consider seven such dimensions: publicness, privacy, gendering, transnationalism, temporal orientation, extraordinary temporality, and secularization. In the last part of the chapter, we turn to methodological issues. We first consider the sources and methods that can be used for the purpose of comparative media culture analysis and present the specific materials and techniques used in the book: archival sources, schedule and programme analysis, and oral history interviews. We conclude by discussing two major methodological obstacles facing comparative media culture research: the danger of methodological nationalism and the challenge of researching change over time.

DEFINING MEDIA CULTURE

A closer look at recent literature on media cultures reveals that the field of comparative media culture research – if indeed it can be called a field at this point – lacks a shared understanding of what such work should focus on. In that sense, the current state of comparative media cultures research is similar to that described by Jay G. Blumler and Michael Gurevitch half a century ago in relation to comparative political communication research: 'It is not merely that few political communication studies have yet been mounted with a comparative focus. More to the point, there is neither a settled view of what such studies should be concerned with, nor even a firmly crystallized set of alternative options for research between which scholars of diverse philosophic persuasions could choose from.'[4] Although the volume of existing comparative research on media cultures is significantly larger than the volume of comparative work in political communication at the time Blumler and Gurevich wrote their book, a shared sense of what such work should examine, and of the different methodological and theoretical approaches available, is still lacking.

[4] Blumler and Gurevitch (1995 [1975]), p. 75.

The first question we need to address, then, is one of definition: What do we mean by media culture? Two broad approaches can be identified in the existing literature, and they differ in the way they conceive of the relationship between media and culture: one sees culture as either internal to, or in large part determined by, the media, while the other approaches culture as an external force that influences the media. In the first group we find studies that understand culture as shaped by a specific mode of mediated cultural transmission; in this sense, we can talk of 'television culture', 'news culture', 'journalistic culture', 'reality TV culture', 'fan culture', or simply, in generic terms, 'media culture'. A shared trait of these studies is that they think of media culture as a complex of practices and/or ideas (meanings, discourses, etc.) tied to a distinct media genre, or to a distinct medium, or to modern communication media in general. For instance, Thomas Hanitzsch understands 'journalism culture' as 'a particular set of ideas and practices by which journalists legitimate their role in society and render their work meaningful'.[5] In this sense, journalism culture is a form of culture linked to a particular media genre, namely news. In their discussion of media culture, Nick Couldry and Andreas Hepp follow a similar logic, albeit at a more general level. Defining 'media culture' as 'any culture whose primary resources of meaning are mediated or provided by technologies of media communication', they go on to conceptualize such culture as 'a thickening of classificatory systems and discursive formations on which the production of meaning in everyday practice draws'.[6] In this case, media culture is simply any form of mediated culture. A closely similar conception of media culture emerges from the work of social theorists such as Douglas Kellner and Nick Stevenson, both of whom use the term to refer to culture that is transmitted through, and hence in some fundamental way shaped by, modern means of communication.[7]

A very different notion of culture is found in comparative work on cross-cultural communication, where culture – often termed communication culture or cultural communication – refers to communication practices, patterns, or codes unique to particular cultural groups.[8] While also conceived as a complex of practices and/or ideas, communication culture is not tied to a particular medium or genre, but to specific cultural groups, typically defined in ethnic or national terms. Even though such work can occasionally investigate the shared cultural meanings engendered by

[5] Hanitzsch (2007), p. 369. [6] Couldry and Hepp (2012), pp. 253, 256.
[7] Kellner (1995); Stevens (2002).
[8] E.g. Gudykunst and Mody (2002); Kim (2012); Ting-Toomey and Chung (2012).

a particular medium or genre regardless of context, the main emphasis is on divergent features that arise from the production or consumption of this medium or genre among different cultural groups. To put it differently, communication cultures exist relatively independently from the media, are seen as rooted in cultural traditions established over time, and are in large part dependent on modes of interpersonal communication that do not necessarily require media technologies. Understanding the relationship between media and culture in this way implies that the diversity of media cultures can be explained solely or primarily with reference to cultural or civilizational differences. As argued in the Introduction, such an approach runs the risk of essentializing culture and does not offer sufficient breadth for the kind of comparative analysis we develop in this book.

In this book, our focus is on *media cultures*, understood as *patterns of ideas and practices tied to specific forms of mediated communication, which shape processes of meaning-formation across instances of production, reception, and use*. More precisely, this book focuses on television culture – that is, the distinct patterns of ideas and practices linked to television. Furthermore, we are particularly interested in television culture as it developed within a specific political system – state socialism – and in a particular geo-cultural context – Eastern Europe. We are seeking to establish whether and why this environment produced a distinct form of television culture, different from the ones familiar in Western Europe and North America, while also paying attention to the diversity of state socialist television cultures themselves.

Having clarified what we mean by media culture, it is now time to consider how we can examine it empirically. Which of the many patterns of ideas or practices should we focus on in order to ensure both a measure of commonality, and hence comparability, and sufficient variety, and hence differentiation? One solution, particularly common in existing comparative work on media culture, involves finding a shared theme or object at the level of media texts, such as a theme or feature appearing in news coverage internationally, or a media format or programme adopted globally.[9] Another popular approach focuses on practices or values across different social groups involved in mediated communication, such as foreign correspondents, or audiences.[10] Both of these approaches have

[9] E.g. Allen (1995); de Vreese et al. (2001); Esser (1999); Furnham and Mak (1999); Liebes and Katz (1990); van Keulen and Krijnen (2014).

[10] Hannerz (2004); Livingstone and Bovill (2013).

their distinct advantages, but they offer only partial insight into the diversity of media cultures. To start with, they often result in work that fragments the process of communication into moments of production, texts, and reception and use, and focuses on one of them. At the same time, the emphasis on themes and groups also tends to distract attention from the medium or form of communication itself and the particular ways in which it shapes the whole process of meaning-making from production to reception and use.

The analytical framework we apply in this book builds on these established approaches to comparing media cultures but embeds them in an approach that also pays attention to how they interact with the inherent qualities of the medium. To paraphrase Marshall McLuhan, the investigation of the messages conveyed in media 'content' is complemented by the study of the medium itself as a message and of the way it embeds itself both in the content of communication and in the particular practices and perceptions shared among producers or audiences.[11] In practical terms this means that our empirical analysis covers the televised representations of particular themes and events, the practices and preferences of audiences, and the views of television professionals and political elites, but it ties them to a consideration of the specific affordances ingrained in television technology and infrastructure. In doing so, we are also drawing inferences about the impact of particular media technologies and forms on the societies and cultures in which they become embedded.

Attempts to link different communication technologies to the characteristic features of the societies and cultures using them have a long history. An early example is found in the distinction developed by Canadian political economist Harold Innis between space-biased and time-biased media.[12] According to Innis, communication technologies dominant before the rise of print, such as parchment or clay tablets, were time-biased: they were hardy and durable and hence easily weathered the passage of time, but they also proved difficult to replicate and were therefore resistant to dissemination over space. As such, they were conducive to forms of governance that operated on spatially delimited territories, were reliant on the reproduction of tradition over time, and were typically associated with societies and cultures that were relatively conservative and stable. In contrast, modern communication technologies such as print, radio, and television are space-biased: they are ephemeral

[11] McLuhan (1994 [1964]). [12] Innis (2007 [1950], 2008 [1951]).

and perishable and hence less well suited for the transmission of messages over time, but at the same time they are also light and easily transportable or replicable and therefore have the capacity to reach large audiences over long distances. As such, they tend to facilitate the extension of control and authority across space, have an elective affinity with secular forms of governance that are less dependent on the maintenance of continuity over time, and are typically found in societies and cultures prone to social change.

Approaches such as Innis's, which focus on the significance of the medium of communication rather than on its content, have been adopted by a range of other authors. Marshall McLuhan, Jack Goody, Ian Watt, and Walter Ong, among others, focused on the shift from oral to written communication, arguing that the introduction of literacy affected social organization and stimulated the rise of a different mode of consciousness as well as a new conception of the individual.[13] In a related manner, Elizabeth Eisenstein examined the consequences of print technology, showing its involvement in the growth of modern science, nationalism, and the rise of the Protestant Reformation.[14] General discussions of modern means of communication likewise pay attention to the affordances of new communication technologies and typically see them as instrumental in the restructuring of human relationships to time and space, and thereby in fostering the particular temporal and spatial orders characteristic of modern societies.[15] Most recently, such general arguments about the social consequences of the modern media of communication have been rejuvenated by the fast-growing literature on 'mediatization', which likewise seeks to capture the interrelationships between media change on the one hand and social and cultural change on the other.[16]

Existing theories of broadcasting and television, too, tie the distinctive qualities of the medium to its technological characteristics and examine their affinities with broader social and cultural processes. As even a cursory look at the titles of some of the classic writings in the field attests – from Joshua Meyrowitz's *No Sense of Place* (1985) and Roger Silverstone's *Television and Everyday Life* (1994) to Paddy Scannell's *Television and the Meaning of 'Live'* (2013) – television is

[13] Goody and Watt (1963); McLuhan (1994 [1964]); Ong (1982). [14] Eisenstein (1979).
[15] E.g. Morley (2007); Thompson (1995).
[16] E.g. Couldry and Hepp (2013); Deacon and Stanyer (2014); Lundby (2009); Mazzoleni and Schultz (1999).

often seen as a medium defined by its distinct relationship to space and time: its liveness, its ability to cross vast distances in the blink of an eye, and its close association with domestic, everyday life. These ways of relating to time and space are, these authors suggest, enabled by the affordances of broadcast technology and have an impact on the way individuals and societies relate to space and time.[17]

This body of work, especially the writings on television and modern media, contributes to the analysis developed in this book. In particular, the focus on the medium's engagement with time and space offers a convenient basis for organizing the comparative analysis of television cultures developed in Parts II (dedicated to space) and III (dedicated to time). Yet our analysis also departs from this literature in fundamental ways. By and large, writers from Innis to Scannell tend to treat the distinct spatial and temporal characteristics of a particular medium as universal, paying limited consideration to how these traits may vary with respect to social and historical contexts. The only context-dependent variation that does receive some recognition is the one arising from audience reception and use; in this sense, growing numbers of scholars are arguing that the spatial and temporal qualities of communication technologies, television included, do not have the capacity to fully determine the social uses of space and time. Instead, the analysis also has to take into account the role of human agency and the ways in which the experience of space in time is formed through media use, a process potentially affected by other, alternative modes of temporality and spatiality.[18] Our analysis acknowledges the variations arising from individual media use, but it also goes a step further and seeks to describe how and why the general temporal and spatial aspects characteristic of television vary with social, cultural, and political contexts, thereby producing distinct varieties of television culture. To develop a comparative framework aligned with these aims, we first had to identify the key dimensions of variation between television cultures, outlined in the pages that follow.

[17] Meyrowitz (1985); Silverstone (1994); Scannell (2013).

[18] For a sample of literature examining the temporality of media use alongside the inherent temporal qualities of communication technologies, see Green (2002); Hörning et al. (1999); Keightley (2013); Nansen et al. (2009). A similar shift from the study of the inherent traits of communication technology to the examination of use has occurred in relation to the spatial qualities of the media.

DIMENSIONS OF VARIATION

In our analysis we considered a set of seven key dimensions of variation between television cultures: publicness, privacy, gendering, transnationalism, temporal orientation, extraordinary temporality, and secularization. While some of these are tied primarily to one particular spatial or temporal dimension of TV cultures, others capture diversity across both spatial and temporal plains. We introduce each of these dimensions here and then elaborate on them in Parts II and III of the book through the discussion of empirical materials.

Publicness: Public Sphere and Public Mission

The first dimension of variation concerns television's openness to the public realm, which arises from its ability to bring public life into the private lives of millions of citizens. At first sight, it is tempting to argue that the distinctive quality of state socialist television cultures in this respect is their shared hostility to television's publicness: in a context where the media were subjected to close scrutiny by the communist party-state, possibilities for using television as a means of publicly exposing and criticising the failures of communist politics were severely limited. To use the language familiar to communication and media scholars: the existence of a public sphere, understood in the Habermasian sense as a realm of debate independent both from the imperatives of the market and from the encroachments of the state,[19] was next to impossible. It also follows from this that journalists working in the context of state socialist broadcasting would most likely see themselves as supporters or partners of those in power, actively involved in the pursuit of the communist mission, rather than as detached observers who act as agents of the Fourth Estate and openly challenge the ruling elites. That said, we should acknowledge that state socialist television cultures differed in their openness to criticism and hence the extent to which they enabled the formation of at least a semblance of a public sphere. Indeed, as we argue in Chapter 5, state socialist television was certainly not wholly hostile to public criticism, but such criticism had to stop short of challenging the legitimacy of communist rule, which inevitably restricted its scope. As a result, we argue, the state socialist public sphere was distinctly truncated and in a sense only semi-public.

[19] Habermas (1989).

Yet, to limit the discussion of the public nature of television cultures to this aspect would be insufficient. As both historical and contemporary debates surrounding the introduction of public broadcasting remind us, the public remit of television cannot be restricted to its exposure of those in power to public scrutiny. It also encompasses television's capacity to provide access to a range of shared, and hence public, goods: typically, information, education, culture, and entertainment.[20] Scannell' s discussion of publicness in relation to broadcasting offers a good example of this duality. On the one hand, he sees publicness as 'that which is not concealed, not hidden, not covered up, not covered over . . . in short, not secret', but he also contends that publicness is linked to 'the availability of things *as* common, public things'.[21] The latter can of course encompass the former: television's ability to make things visible to everyone, and hence open to public scrutiny, can be conceived as a part of its public mission, and hence as one of the public goods it needs to deliver. Nonetheless, in and of itself, television's contribution to visibility and public critique does not exhaust its public remit – which means that television can be seen as in some sense 'public' even if it does not fulfil its watchdog role.

To capture the full scope of television's relationship with the public realm, it is therefore important to distinguish between two dimensions of television's publicness, which we refer to as the *public sphere* and the *public mission*. Both of these need to be taken into account when developing a comparative assessment of TV cultures. We can differentiate between television cultures depending on the extent to which they enable the public scrutiny of power – in other words, the extent to which they give voice to opinions contrary to, or critical of, those promoted by the ruling elite or official policies, or reveal information that sheds critical light on officially promoted practices or views. Further, more detailed criteria can be added here, derived from the different normative conceptions of the public sphere beyond the one developed by Habermas.[22] It is also important to add that the examination of the public sphere dimension of publicness need not be limited solely to news or current affairs programmes; following the notion of the 'cultural public sphere' we can trace different degrees of publicness in educational, entertainment, and fictional programming.[23]

[20] For a selection of literature surveying the history and normative principles of public broadcasting, see Blumler (1992); Bourdon (2011); Tracey (1998).

[21] Scannell (1996), pp. 165–172.

[22] E.g. Ferree et al. (2002); Butler Breese (2011); Downey et al. (2012).

[23] E.g. McGuigan (2005).

With regard to the second dimension of television's publicness, namely the public mission, we can compare different television cultures depending on their definition of the medium's public remit. As Jérôme Bourdon argues, the notion of public broadcasting is often discussed in unitary terms, yet empirical research shows that this is far from the truth.[24] Rather than being a clearly defined concept, the notion of public broadcasting often emerged as a vaguely defined ideal, and even when it was specified more precisely, the exact formulation and the relative emphasis put on different aspects of the public mission could vary considerably. To mention but one example: as formulated in a document issued in 1964, the rationale for public broadcasting in France echoed the trio of functions familiar from British public broadcasting – to inform, to educate, to entertain – but also added a fourth one, culture, and listed it *before* education and entertainment.[25] This suggests that we can differentiate between television cultures depending on how they articulate their public mission, specifically depending on the emphasis they put on different public functions.

Privacy: Domestication and Privatization

The second dimension of variation captures television's involvement with the other side of the dichotomy, namely privacy. Arguably, television's connection with privacy is inseparable from its link with the public realm. As noted earlier, television's publicness is predicated on the ability of the medium to bring public life into private homes, a characteristic that also makes physical travel into the outside world unnecessary, thereby enabling TV viewers, as Shaun Moores puts it, to combine 'staying at home' and 'going places'.[26] The hybrid nature of television, a medium at once private and public, is captured also in Raymond Williams's discussion of 'mobile privatization', a term coined to describe a situation in which humans, while living in a world of unprecedented mobility, increasingly function in self-enclosed family units, removed from places of work and government. This particular condition, argued Williams, created a need for new kinds of communication capable of bringing news or entertainment from otherwise inaccessible sources into private homes – a need fulfilled first by radio, then by television.[27]

[24] Bourdon (2011), pp. 26–34. [25] Ibid. p. 33. [26] Moores (2000), p. 96.
[27] Williams (2007 [1974]), pp. 19–22.

As with publicness, we consider two sub-dimensions of television's privacy. The first of these is *domestication*, which refers to the gradual adoption of television as a domestic medium, viewed primarily in the context of one's home. The second is *privatization*, which denotes the extent to which television's programming focuses on private life, mimics intimate modes of communication when addressing the audience, or otherwise becomes adapted to the domestic context of reception. These two sides of television's involvement with the private are tied to what are considered to be some of the key distinguishing features of television: on the one hand, the fact that it is intended primarily for viewing in a domestic environment, and hence becomes closely intertwined with domestic and family life, and on the other hand, its propensity for intimate modes of address, for programmes dedicated to private life, and for genre conventions designed to fit with domestic rhythms.[28] The viewing context and the aspects of TV form and content are of course closely related: in many respects, the tendency to privacy and intimacy in television programming emerged in direct response to its domestic viewing context. John Corner called this television's 'domestic aesthetic' and argued that television developed an 'institutional persona' in which 'home-friendly attributes' are key.[29] Of course, many of the 'privatized' features of content and form are discernible also in radio programming, but they have arguably become exacerbated in the context of television, due to its visual nature.[30]

Television's propensity to be viewed in a domestic setting, inclination towards narratives of private life, and intimate modes of address do not mean that the medium's engagement with privacy has taken the same form everywhere. Rather, we argue that the processes of the domestication and privatization of television assumed different shapes depending on the normative, political, and economic contexts. As we suggest in Chapter 6, privacy held an uncomfortable position in state socialist countries. According to the communist vision of progress, the need for privacy was a by-product of the inequality and alienation generated by capitalism and hardly something worth protecting. Though official attitudes to privacy changed significantly during the last decades of state socialism, a measure of suspicion persisted, at least in so far as private matters were seen as a threat to citizen investment in public life. It is feasible to expect that television's engagement with privacy reflected these suspicions and

[28] Chambers (2016); Silverstone (1994), pp. 24–51; Spigel (1992).

[29] Corner (2000), p. 16. [30] E.g. Meyrowitz (1985), p. 100.

that, as a consequence, state socialist television cultures were, by and large, less 'privatized' and 'domesticated' than their counterparts in the West, or at least that privatization and domestication took different shapes, aligned with the pronounced public thrust of the communist project. Again, we should be careful not to exaggerate the differences between state socialist and Western television. Anxieties over the potentially detrimental effect of television on public life were not unique to state socialist countries; similar fears were common in the West, too, including in the United States, where scholars have repeatedly warned of the detrimental effects of television for the quality of public life and civic engagement in the country.[31]

Gendering

Closely intertwined with television's engagement with publicness and privacy is the medium's involvement with gender relations. In this respect, television plays an ambiguous role and can be seen as a medium that both undermines and reinforces traditional gender roles. This ambiguity is rooted in the hybrid spatial location of television, namely its ability to function both as a means of which public life enters private life, and as a vehicle that privatizes or domesticates public matters, making them attuned to the exigencies of home life. On the one hand, as Meyrowitz points out, television's ability to bring the outside world into the home exposed women – as a social group traditionally consigned to domestic space – to a range of issues and experiences they would not otherwise have had access to. At the same time television, as a medium featuring both men and women and used by all members of the family regardless of gender, simultaneously increased exposure to the other sex, perhaps relativizing traditional gender divisions.[32]

Yet on the other hand, due to its domestic and privatized character, television can also be regarded as a distinctly 'feminine' medium, one that often reproduces existing gender inequalities and divisions. For instance, practices of scheduling common in the West in the post-World War II era were premised on the existence of a predominantly male labour force and targeted much of daytime programming at a female viewership engaged in household chores, while designing evening schedules around a more diverse family audience.[33] Assumptions about the gendered structure of

[31] See, for instance, Putnam (1995). [32] Meyrowitz (1985), pp. 208–222.
[33] Paterson (1980); Spigel (1992).

audiences also informed the production process and genre conventions established at that time. Soap operas, in particular, have been identified as a distinctly feminine genre, and their tendency to represent public issues through a personal lens has been described as a means of 'colonizing the public masculine sphere, representing it from the point of view of the personal'.[34] Finally, gendered patterns are also apparent in audience practices and discourses surrounding TV viewing, from the amount of viewing and control over programme choice to perceptions of the technical competence needed to manipulate TV technology.[35]

This is not to say that the intertwining of gender relations and television cultures follows the same patterns everywhere. Even within the same political and cultural context, significant internal variations and changes over time can be discerned. For instance, US and UK series from *Crossroads* (ITV, 1964–1988) to *Ally McBeal* (Fox, 1997–2002), among many others, have been examined from the perspective of how they depict the tensions between women's personal and professional lives and interpreted in light of broader developments in gender equality and feminist politics at the time.[36] The range of possible entanglements between gender relations and television cultures increases even further once we broaden our view to other political and cultural settings marked by different gender relations. As we shall see, political elites in state socialist Eastern Europe all professed a commitment to women's emancipation, and even though realities on the ground often remained far from the idyllic visions of equality painted by official discourse, the heavy emphasis on women's involvement in waged labour nonetheless disrupted traditional configurations of gender relations and the private–public divide. It is to be expected that television cultures, too, were affected by these developments.

For the purpose of comparison, it is therefore useful to ask whether and to what extent particular television cultures contribute to aligning gender relations with the public–private divide and specifically to reinforcing the division between the feminine private sphere and the masculine public sphere.

Transnationalism: Openness and Origin

The relative openness to transnational exchanges and influences, and the origin of such transnational links, forms another crucial dimension of

[34] Brunsdon (1997), p. 15. [35] Morley (1986); Parks (2000).
[36] Hobson (1982); Moseley and Read (2002).

variation. These connections can take a variety of forms, from programme exchanges and co-productions to professional contacts, cross-border television viewing, and the borrowing of foreign formats and conventions. The growing transnationalization of television began attracting scholarly attention from the late 1960s,[37] but became a particularly prominent topic since the proliferation of cross-border satellite channels and the rise of global, profit-seeking media conglomerates from the late 1980s onwards.[38] The close association between TV transnationalism and recent technological changes highlighted in the literature can obscure the fact that the transnational circuits of television cultures have a long history. From the contemporary vantage point, the era of terrestrial television may seem overwhelmingly national: television signals were largely contained within state boundaries, and television ownership and regulation were tied to nation states. Yet this perception is misleading; television was a profoundly transnational medium from its inception, well before the proliferation of cross-border satellite channels and digital broadcasting.[39]

The theoretical frameworks used to interpret television's defiance of state and national borders have shifted considerably over time. The early wave of scholarly discussion on the topic, which emerged in the 1960s and the 1970s, centred on notions of cultural imperialism and Americanization and was marked by a critical perspective which saw the transnational flow of television programming as a vehicle of unequal power relations in the international arena. In the post-Cold War context, the terrain of scholarly debate was transformed. The thesis of cultural imperialism came under attack on multiple fronts, because it overstated the link between economic power and cultural forces, overestimated the centrality of the United States, underrated the resilience of national cultures, or assumed that audiences were passive victims of transnational flows.[40] Several attempts have been made to develop alternative conceptualizations of transnational TV and its impact, typically with an emphasis on the diffuse and multipolar character of cross-border television traffic and the importance of cultural proximity, local institutional conditions and other factors mitigating the influence of

[37] Much of this early discussion emerged in conjunction with debates in the United Nations and UNESCO, fuelled by growing concerns over the impact of transnational media flows and especially US programming on local cultures and tradition. See, for instance, Nordenstreng and Varis (1974); Schiller (1992[1969]); Tunstall (1977).

[38] E.g. Chalaby (2005); Collins (1992).

[39] See Fickers and Johnson (2012); Hilmes (2011).

[40] See Golding and Harris (1996); Tomlinson (1991).

transnational flows, especially their alleged detrimental impact on cultural diversity.[41] Recent research has also shifted attention from the transnationalization of TV content and audience reception to a broader set of arenas of TV transnationalism, ranging from global TV business cultures to the transnational borrowing and adaptation of genre conventions, technologies, and professional practices.[42]

This wide-ranging literature has thrown into relief a vast array of aspects through which we can explore the transnationalism of television cultures and which can potentially be used as a basis for comparison. Two key aspects of variation can be discerned across these various arenas of TV transnationalism: one has to do with the general *extent of openness* to products and practices originating beyond the borders of state and nation, wherever they come from; the other involves the *origin* of foreign materials and practices. The first aspect offers a measure of the relative balance of the national and the transnational in a particular television culture. The second provides insight into the possible transnational cultural and political affinities and influences, as well as the relationships of dependence and domination, articulated through television culture. Distinguishing between these two aspects is important: television cultures may be overwhelmingly reliant on imported programmes, genres, and professional practices, yet there is a significant difference between the transnationalism resulting from exchanges from a single source and those resulting from exchanges from politically and culturally diverse contexts.

Temporal Orientation

The fifth dimension of comparison between television cultures considered in this book concerns temporal orientation, understood as the mode of engagement with the passage of time and specifically the extent to which a particular television culture is oriented towards the past, present, or future. Television of course has, along with radio, a privileged bond with the present; what distinguishes broadcasting from older media is the ability to make events, programmes, and experiences available to dispersed audiences in the blink of an eye and thereby engender

[41] E.g. Norris and Inglehart (2009); Straubhaar (1991); Tunstall (2008).
[42] See Havens (2006); Oren and Shahaf (2013).

a shared, *live* connection with the unfolding present.[43] The wider cultural and social effects of this particular bond with the present, enabled by broadcasting, form part and parcel of a broader reconfiguration that affects not only human engagement with time but also with space: by virtue of its ability to transmit messages over distances at maximum speed, in fact virtually instantaneously, broadcasting enables people to experience the flow of events and time together, yet without being present in the same space. From this point of view, television and radio can be seen as involved in a longer process that has been variously conceptualized in terms of the 'speeding up' of time, 'time-space compression', and the 'separation of time and space', and associated either with (late) modernity or with postmodernity.[44] This process has been shown to be intimately bound up with successive inventions in modern technologies of communication and has arguably reached a new stage with the advent of digital and mobile media.[45]

For several authors, television's live bond with the present effectively renders the medium timeless. In effect, television operates in what Fredric Jameson has called the 'perpetual present', which he associates with 'the disappearance of a sense of history', the loss of capacity to retain one's own past, and the obliteration of traditions characteristic of late capitalist postmodernity.[46] It would be wrong, however, to assume that television's tie with the present eliminates its engagement with the past or the future altogether. Rather, this engagement is folded into the present and adapted to fit with the medium's present-centred character. Television dramas and films, and even reality TV shows, often take viewers on a virtual journey into the past, real or imagined, or invite them to imagine the future. Historical serial fiction, in particular, has been shown to exploit the distinct affordances of television, such as its visual nature and the intimate bond with viewers' everyday lives, to encourage a personal, emotionally involved engagement with the past.[47] Major festive occasions celebrated through the small screen, including some of the major media

[43] This bond with the present, and the associated 'liveness' and 'dailiness' of broadcasting have been discussed particularly extensively by Scannell (1996; 2013). Other important discussions on the issue include Bourdon (2000); Ellis (1982), pp. 132–133; Ellis (2000), pp. 31–37; Marriott (2007).

[44] See Giddens (1990); Harvey (1989).

[45] See Rosa (2013); Thompson (1995), pp. 31–37; Tomlinson (2007), pp. 94–193.

[46] Jameson (1985), p. 125. For an example of theorizing that links television's temporality to the perpetual present see Hoskins (2001).

[47] Creeber (2001).

events that punctuate the broadcast year, serve as reminders of major historical events and rely for their effectiveness on television's ability to establish a live connection with the passage of time as it unfolds.[48] News broadcasts, too, employ historical analogies as means of interpreting the present or incorporate speculation about the future effects of a particular course of events.[49]

This coexistence of different temporal planes within the same medium also means that despite television's fundamental temporal orientation to the present, television cultures differ in the modes and extents to which they engage with the past and the future, and the levels of such engagement over time. Systematic comparative research that investigates such differences and changes is in its infancy, but existing studies suggest that this dimension of variation offers a promising venue for comparative work on media cultures. For instance, a longitudinal analysis of US print news between 1894 and 1994 showed that the proportion of articles including references to the past or the future, as opposed to the present, increased considerably over time,[50] while another study showed that print news more often refers to future events, in contrast to online news, which is more commonly oriented to recent past events.[51] A similar approach can be applied to a variety of other media genres, including fiction. In Chapter 9, for instance, we examine the temporal orientation of historical serial dramas and the ways in which it fostered a distinctly communist sense of the passage of time. It is also possible to analyse, as we do in Part Three of this book, the different articulations of television's temporal orientation across a range of aspects that involve production and reception.

Extraordinary Temporality: TV Holidays and TV Disruptions

Much like television's temporal orientation to the present, its involvement with extraordinary time is often theorized in relation to liveness, namely the ability of television (alongside radio) to link millions of people to a monumental event happening *right now*. In line with this, studies of extraordinary TV temporality mostly focus on what Daniel Dayan and Elihu Katz have called media events, namely live broadcasts of celebratory

[48] For a classic study of media events and the 'live broadcasting of history' see Dayan and Katz (1992).

[49] E.g. Edgerton and Rollins (2001), pp. 230–243, 207–299.

[50] Barnhurst and Mutz (1997). [51] Tenenboim-Weinblatt and Neiger (2015).

events such as mass rallies, sports competitions, or major achievements such as the landing on the moon. The key features of these extraordinary occasions, as defined by Dayan and Katz, include the fact that they monopolize the attention of all TV channels, involve live transmission of events organized outside of the media, and are pre-planned, presented with reverence and ceremony, aimed at large groups, and celebrate reconciliation rather than conflict.[52]

Although such media events are important, they capture only a very small segment of the extraordinary temporality of television cultures. There are two key reasons for this. First, the production of live, pre-planned events constitutes only one strategy in a much wider range employed in broadcasting to create a sense of extraordinary time. For instance, many of the key media festivities in state socialist countries examined in our analysis did not include a live broadcast at all, and yet there is no doubt that they departed from the routine temporalities of television. Second, several extraordinary occasions involving television, both in the state socialist world and beyond – coverage of major natural disasters, terror attacks, protests, or revolutions – are a far cry from the ceremonial events foregrounded in Dayan and Katz's model: they are either partly or wholly unexpected, often catch audiences off-guard, and typically foreground conflict rather than unity, or at least raise a sense of anxiety over the future. Such disruptive occasions are of particular interest to our analysis of state socialist television, because they are at odds with the teleological temporality of the communist project. Rather than serving as periodic reminders of the ongoing march towards the bright communist future, they threaten to stop revolutionary progress in its tracks.

To capture the full range of television's involvement in engendering a sense of extraordinary occasion, we therefore need to move beyond the focus on media events and investigate the full range of strategies involved in disrupting the routine. To this end, we distinguish between two different modes of extraordinary temporality that television can engender: *media holidays* and *media disruptions*. Both work within a different temporal economy from media events in terms of duration and in terms of their relation to liveness: while media events are centred on a single event, transmitted live, media holidays and media disruptions are temporally more diffuse, extend over a longer period of time, and include both live and pre-recorded programming. Media events can form part of media

[52] Dayan and Katz (1992).

holidays and media disruptions, but they are neither a necessary nor a sufficient element of extraordinary temporality.

The two modes of extraordinary temporality differ significantly in their degree of unexpectedness and preplanning, as well as in their relationship with the existing social order. Media holidays are expected by all parties involved – authorities, media producers and audiences, are typically pre-planned and even pre-produced to the most minute detail, and affirm the status quo or include a limited degree of managed, pre-planned transformation. Media disruptions, on the other hand, involve occasions that are to a large degree unexpected and unplanned (or at least in some sense uncontrollable) and present a challenge to the status quo. In some cases, media professionals, usually in conjunction with the authorities, manage to maintain control and reinstitute the old order; in others, the disruption is so fundamental that it requires a complete reshuffling of the existing relations of power and social arrangements, as well as a shift in the established media order.

Ours is, of course, not the first attempt to revisit the theory of media events. The various strengths and shortcomings of Dayan and Katz's original model have attracted much attention, and several proposals have been put forward for how the theory should be amended.[53] Some of the criticisms and proposals aired in this context have been taken on board in our own analysis. We agree with those who have argued that the original model of media events is unduly limited to pre-planned ceremonial events, and we also concur with those who point out that extraordinary media occasions are not always socially integrative and do not necessarily reaffirm the existing social order. Finally, the key differences between media holidays and media disruptions largely coincide with the distinctions between ceremonial and disruptive media events, as discussed by Simon Cottle, Tamar Liebes, and Elihu Katz.[54]

Yet, while these existing criticisms and alternative proposals highlight important shortcomings of the original media events theory, they fall short of offering a suitable framework for the kind of analysis we develop in this book. The key reason for this is that the alternative proposals often remain locked in the language of 'events' and as such miss the full range of strategies contributing to a sense of extraordinary occasion, many of

[53] E.g. Cottle (2006); Couldry (2003); Katz and Liebes (2007); Mitu and Poulakidakos (2016).

[54] Cottle (2006); Katz and Liebes (2007).

which do not fit the event format.[55] Furthermore, much of the recent discussion on media events is written from the perspective of recent media developments. From this vantage point, the key problem with the original model is its outdatedness: namely the fact that it can no longer account for the nature of media events in the post-broadcast, globalised, digital, and mobile media world. In contrast, the framework proposed here, focused on the different modes of extraordinary temporality engendered by the media, has broader applicability. As such, it can serve as a basis for a more general reflection on the diverse modes of involvement of the media, both historically and today, in shaping how societies relate to the passage of time, manage disruptions to routine, and deal with social change.

Secularization

The seventh and last dimension of comparison considered in our investigation is the degree of secularization, understood here as the extent to which a television culture helps reproduce ideas and practices of religious origin – beliefs in supernatural powers, narratives based on sacred texts, or religious rituals such as prayers and annual religious festivities. The choice of secularization as a key dimension of comparison between television cultures may come as a surprise. Official policies in state socialist Eastern Europe were generally hostile to religion, and it is feasible to expect that television cultures reflected such attitudes. Explicitly religious content also seems to constitute a relatively marginal proportion of contemporary media output in Western Europe and North America. Moreover, the relationship between the media and religion is at best a marginal concern in existing comparative media research, and when it appears, it is bundled together with the discussion of the relationship between media and politics.[56]

Yet as recent research shows, religion continues to have a notable presence in media cultures globally. Even the media in the West are not as devoid of religion as one may think: by and large, mainstream media still observe religious festivities, report on religious developments, and

[55] An exception is Nick Couldry (2003, p. 13) who calls for an approach that avoids 'isolating particular moments and elevating them to 'special', even magical significance'.

[56] Hallin and Mancini (2004: 263–267) talk of secularization in semi-metaphorical terms, as a process that encompasses not only the decline of religious institutions and beliefs, but also the decline of institutions and beliefs tied to ideological 'faiths', including political parties and trade unions.

produce religious content, while beliefs in transcendental powers continue to play an important role in popular culture, especially fictional genres. Several authors have examined religious television and the phenomenon of TV evangelism in the United States, as well as the many ways in which religious institutions and audiences have responded to and appropriated modern media technologies for their own purposes,[57] while others have investigated the persistence of religious themes, narratives, and beliefs across different media genres.[58] The importance of religion for understanding contemporary television and media cultures becomes even more obvious when we broaden our comparative scope beyond the West. In many countries of the Middle East, as well as in Malaysia and parts of Latin America, religion forms a prominent feature of media cultures, including television cultures, and religious institutions often have considerable influence over mediated content.[59]

The extent of secularization clearly constitutes an important dimension of comparison when looking at television cultures globally. In some cases, modern means of communication are successfully mobilized by religious organizations, old and new, to advance their cause; in other cases, they can help diminish the relative influence of institutionalized religion while still sustaining a degree of diffuse religiosity, spirituality, and the observance of religious traditions among the population. Several aspects of television culture can be considered when estimating the extent of secularization. The first, and perhaps most obvious, is the amount of explicitly religious programming, but also the extent to which such programming privileges some forms of religion over others and either sustains or challenges existing religious beliefs and belonging. The second option involves tracing the more diffuse forms of religion, including references to the sacred, narratives based on sacred texts or beliefs in supernatural forces, across a range of otherwise 'secular' genres, from news to fiction, as well as in the context of audience reception. Finally, religion also intervenes in the temporal arrangements of TV broadcasting, in relation to routine daily and weekly scheduling, as well as television's involvement in creating a sense of extraordinary, festive occasions. It is this last aspect that will be most relevant in our analysis of state socialist television cultures in Part Three of this book.

[57] E.g. Abelman and Hoover (1990); Hoover and Schofield Clark (2002); Sa Martino (2013).

[58] E.g. Hoover (1998); Knott et al. (2013).

[59] E.g. Lewis et al. (2016), pp. 157–195.

SOURCES AND METHODS

The success of any comparative project stands and falls with the quality of the data. When setting out to investigate the television cultures in state socialist Eastern Europe, we knew that the amount of available data was limited and that this project would require us not only to develop a synthesis of existing work but also to engage in empirical research and to generate a substantial amount of new data sets, while navigating the obstacles created by the multiplicity of languages. In this sense, our endeavour was rather different from much comparative work on the media in Western Europe and North America, which can rely on a greater range of existing research, much of it accessible in English, and focuses on synthesis rather than on new empirical research. At the same time, we should note that it was not easy to locate relevant comparative material from the West that would help us situate state socialist television trajectories in their transnational context. Quite the contrary: especially when looking at the early stages of television development, gaining a solid overview of developments beyond the United Kingdom and the United States was often difficult. This reminds us that we need to take the frequent complaints about the West-centred nature of existing research on television with a pinch of salt: 'the West' here often boils down to the English-speaking world, and while nationally bounded research may be plentiful, comparative data-sets and overviews are a rarity everywhere.

The situation improves as we move closer to the present. Over the course of the late twentieth century, the collection of information on issues such as the frequency of television viewing, types of programming, and international programme flows became more common, standardised, and centralised. Compilations of comparative data sets drawn from several countries became more widely used, too, especially in the European context. When assessing television use, for instance, researchers can rely on comparative quantitative data gathered through the Eurobarometer survey since 1970, while comparative work on television, film, video/DVD, and new audiovisual media in Europe can benefit from the extensive information gathered by the European Audio-visual Observatory, established in 1992. The rise of digital media and the adoption of digitalization in archives, as well as the creation of digital platforms offering remote access to audiovisual heritage, have helped make historical materials more widely available.[60] Researchers interested in extending our study of television cultures into the present, or those keen to amend our framework for the purpose of investigating other media cultures, will have a much wider range of existing materials to draw on and will hopefully be able to access them with greater ease than we did.

A couple of general points are worth noting before we move on to outlining the methods and sources we have used. First, this book is a product of an interdisciplinary endeavour: as scholars trained in very different disciplinary traditions – sociology on the one hand, history on the other – we have drawn on rather different literatures and techniques and had to acknowledge the strengths but also the limitations of our own disciplines. The product of this exercise is a genuinely hybrid piece of work, one that will hopefully appeal to audiences across different disciplines, while demonstrating the value of interdisciplinary collaboration. Second, although the materials we work with are often qualitative in nature, we do not shy away from employing quantitative data. That said, we believe that quantitative data sets should be approached with caution and recognized for what they are – imperfect and superficial measurements of complex processes. In the vast majority of cases, the information derived from quantitative measurements alone was of limited use without both an in-depth understanding of context and qualitative examples that illustrated particular context-dependent processes.

One would hope that the arguments about the relative advantages and disadvantages of qualitative and quantitative methods, and about the productiveness of combining them for the purpose of researching communications, have by now been well established.[61] However, as our experiences with a variety of academic audiences attest, both qualitative and quantitative methods still have their vocal supporters who rarely see eye to eye, and attempts to combine diverse methods in a single study can generate a great deal of misunderstanding and suspicion on both sides. We hope that our work will help allay some of these suspicions and demonstrate the usefulness of methodological eclecticism in comparative media research. In this spirit, the analysis presented in the chapters that follow uses multiple sources and methods and combines

[60] At the same time, we should also be mindful of the inherent biases and the lack of contextual information that often plague such collections. See Strandgaard Jensen (2015).

[61] See, for instance, Deacon et al. (2007).

historiographic techniques with those commonly used among social scientists.

Archival Sources and Paratexts

Archival sources, drawn from a range of archives in eight East European countries as well as the United States and the United Kingdom, form one important point of reference for the study. Wherever possible, we have sought to use both sources produced by relevant state and party institutions and those originating from broadcasting organizations. This allowed us to gain insight into the opinions of political and cultural elites as well as the views of TV professionals in relation to a variety of issues, from the public mission of television (Chapter 5) to questions of the temporal organization of TV programming (Chapter 8) and television's role in nurturing awareness of the shared past (Chapter 9). Also relevant were documents relating to historical audience and programme research which – provided we take into account the usual limitations of methodology and sampling – offer a useful insight into the characteristics of broadcast output and the viewing preferences of television audiences.

Also invaluable for the analysis were various published primary sources, ranging from books and articles written by contemporary media scholars and cultural critics to various 'paratexts' surrounding particular TV programmes or TV in general – ranging from interviews with TV personalities to adverts for TV receivers and programme descriptions in published TV guides. The use of paratexts originates from literary studies, where the term was originally used to refer to various 'texts' that surround the literary text and orient its reading,[62] but has since been adapted for use in various branches of communication and media studies, including television history.[63] These sources have been important in gaining insight into shared modes of imagining television beyond the views of cultural and political elites, and in obtaining insight into the processes of the domestication of state socialist television, among others (Chapter 6). We should note, however, that these representations should not be treated as direct reflections of audience responses to the medium. Instead, they 'reveal a general set of discursive rules that were formed for thinking about television'.[64]

[62] Genette (1997). [63] E.g. Boddy (2004); Penati (2013); Spigel (1992).
[64] Spigel (1992), pp. 8–9.

Programme and Schedule Analysis

Of course, archival sources and paratexts can only get us so far, especially when it comes to assessing patterns of difference and similarity in programming and scheduling across countries. Due to this, it was imperative to generate a number of original datasets that could serve as skeletons for comparison and as anchors for insights derived from the analysis of paratexts and other published and archival sources.

The first such dataset was derived from the analysis of published TV schedules in five-year intervals, using a sample week in early October (Monday–Sunday) and two major holidays celebrated across all the countries in our sample: 1 May (Labour Day) and 31 December (New Year's Eve). While the week in October was chosen as representative of everyday programming (Chapter 8), the two holidays served to assess the characteristics of festive TV (Chapter 10). The data set for the week in October was also used to investigate the relative prominence of imported programming (Chapter 7), and to examine the relative proportions of information and educational, cultural, and entertainment content and thereby assess the relative emphasis put on the different public functions of television (Chapter 5). Schedule analysis combined both quantitative and qualitative techniques. (Details of sampling and coding are provided in the Methodological Appendix.)

The second main data set related to broadcast output consists of all serial fiction broadcast in the five countries – a genre that was popular among audiences and therefore offers a particularly effective means of investigating the involvement of socialist television in fostering the communist agenda.[65] Information about serial dramas was derived primarily from published TV guides, which offered a sufficient basis for a basic quantitative assessment of the genre. Selected dramas, taken from different countries and historical periods, were then chosen for in-depth qualitative analysis. This data set is employed at several points in the book, to investigate the extent and forms of privatization (Chapter 6), the extent and forms of transnationalism (Chapter 7), and the temporal orientation of state socialist TV cultures (Chapter 8).

[65] Established terms for serial fiction, used in the literature dealing with Western European and North American television (series, serial, mini-series, *telenovela*, anthology series, soap opera, etc.), do not always translate well to the state socialist environment. Such discrepancies between Western and state socialist genre structures and terminologies form an integral part of our analysis at different points in the book and help us reflect on the specificities of socialist television.

Further particulars regarding sampling and coding are included in the Methodological Appendix.

Schedule analysis and the analysis of serial fiction do not exhaust the range of programming examined in the book. Other programmes occasionally investigated include news, educational and cultural content, sports and music programmes, and others. A quantitative examination of TV news akin to the one conducted for TV schedules and TV series would of course be extremely valuable. However, due to the incompleteness of archival records and the difficulties with access, the creation of such a data set proved impossible. In most cases, few TV news bulletins have been preserved, and criteria for preservation varied, precluding the creation of comparable data sets for all countries covered.

Life-Story Interviews

Archival sources and paratexts offer only partial insight into audience history. To compensate for the partiality ingrained in historical audience research and other sources, the analysis of audience habits and preferences in this book relies heavily on qualitative, life-story interviews. More than 170 interviews were conducted in a total of eight post-socialist countries between 2014 and 2015. The sample covers three generations, chosen to roughly coincide with different periods in socialist history and different stages in communication history: the pre-socialist/ radio generation born 1935–1945; the first socialist/ black-and-white TV generation, born 1945–1955; the last socialist/ colour TV generation, born 1965–1975. The interview protocol was divided into two parts. The first drew on established procedures of life-story interviewing, which have been successfully applied in media research on a number of occasions and involve inviting the interviewees to tell the stories of their lives while focusing on the role of the media at each point in the life cycle.[66] The second part of the interview used the method of photo-elicitation,[67] meaning that the interviewees were invited to comment on selected excerpts from a number of programmes of particular interest to the study: news, children's programming, and selected dramas of both domestic and foreign origin. Details on the interview sample and interview protocol are included in the Methodological Appendix.

[66] E.g. Bourdon (2003).
[67] On photo-elicitation as an interviewing method see Clark-Ibáñez (2004).

Oral history interviews may well seem a rather unreliable source of information on historical audience cultures, especially if used to investigate an intensely contested historical period such as the state socialist era. Apart from the general unreliability of memory, the analyst needs to contend with the fact that recollections of life during communist rule are inevitably coloured by normative judgments, both of the past and the present, as well as by interviewees' personal experiences and the nature of the post-socialist transformation. It is worth keeping in mind that our interviewees grew up in countries where there were strong normative ideas not only about politics, but also about the 'proper' way to watch television. They then lived in countries where a new set of norms concerned the communist past emerged, within a context where, on the whole, television was becoming commercialized and, to some viewers' minds, vulgarised. These facts cannot but be reflected in the memories of our interviewees, and so the memories presented in interviews cannot be read as uncomplicated windows onto the past. Considered against primary and secondary source material, the recollections provided by our interviewees were frequently wide of the mark. It was common, for instance, for our participants to underestimate the amount of foreign material on state socialist television or to associate fundamental changes in TV programming primarily with the 1990s – both of which were proved wrong by our schedule and archival analysis. Testimonies were also frequently coloured by retrospective re-evaluation or inextricably tied up with reflections on the state of television in the post-socialist present. Yet those discrepancies are in themselves interesting: they show how present-day narratives and the fallibility of memory have intruded upon subjects' understanding of the past.

That said, our interview materials nonetheless display several shared patterns that are difficult to brush away as instances of misremembering or as products of retrospective reinterpretation. When examined alongside other historical sources and evaluated with an awareness of contemporary perspectives on the socialist past, audience testimonies offered invaluable insights into the nature of historical audience cultures. In this sense, our experience with oral history confirms the value of the method for the purpose of investigating audience history, as established by other researchers in the field.[68] Of particular importance were the recollections of practices and preferences that were not perceived as particularly politicized or contentious from the present perspective, but rather constituted

[68] See Dhoest (2015); Reifova (2015).

neutral aspects of everyday life, and were taken for granted. These included early experiences of television viewing in domestic, public or semi-public locations and the characteristics of TV sets and their locations in the home, which we have used to examine the process of domestication of television (Chapter 6). They also encompass viewing routines and preferences, both of everyday television and of extraordinary occasions such as media holidays, which we drew upon to investigate the temporal orientation of TV cultures (Chapters 8 and 10).[69] Also valuable were the recollections of individual programmes and TV personalities, which offered important insights into past viewing preferences, especially when evaluated alongside the results of historical audience research. By investigating the types of content remembered (or forgotten) by interviewees, we were able to draw tentative conclusions about the prominence and types of imported programming in historical viewing diets and use those to assess the transnationalism of socialist TV cultures (Chapter 7).

THE CHALLENGES OF METHODOLOGICAL NATIONALISM AND STUDYING CHANGE OVER TIME

Apart from dealing with incomplete and often only partly reliable sources, comparative research on media cultures also has to contend with two methodological challenges of a more general nature, namely methodological nationalism and the difficulties of combining a comparison across countries with an account of changes over time. Here we briefly outline the nature of each of these obstacles and explain how we sought to overcome them in our own analysis.

Methodological nationalism, rooted in the assumption that media cultures coincide with national cultures as well as with state borders, constitutes a widespread and problematic aspect of media research. Following this logic, comparative work is often conceived as involving comparisons between national media systems or national media cultures.[70] By contrast, the approach adopted in this book does not see

[69] As Jérôme Bourdon (2003) notes, past viewing routines – or what he calls 'wallpaper memories' – tend to constitute a rather minor proportion of viewers' recollections, as they are considered to be too banal to be worth mentioning in an interview. The interview protocol used in our study was designed with an awareness of this in mind and included prompts that encouraged interviewees to elaborate on such routine aspects even if they thought they were unimportant or self-evident.

[70] For a critique, see Livingstone (2003); Hardy (2012).

television cultures as unequivocally 'national', even though it recognizes that they are tied to particular states. Two of the five countries examined in depth here, Yugoslavia and the Soviet Union, departed rather markedly from the nation-state ideal: both were conceived as multinational federations, and their television was designed to appeal to an internally diverse, rather than a homogeneous, national audience. Romania, too, had sizeable national minorities, which were recognized in its broadcast output. The link between state and nation was also problematic in East Germany, since the country's national status was problematized by its notional belonging to a supranational Germany. More generally, as is evident from our earlier discussion of transnationalism, television was a border-crossing medium from its inception, and even though it was often mobilized for the purpose of state- and nation-building, it simultaneously fostered transnational integration, for instance through organizational and technological infrastructure, through programme exchange, through transnational TV events, through fictional narratives of a shared history, or through cross-border viewing.

While the main units of analysis adopted in this book – namely television cultures – are tied to states, they coincide neither with state borders nor with national boundaries. To emphasize this, we avoid referring to a cross-national comparison and instead use terms such as synchronous, horizontal, or cross-country comparison. Apart from that, the transnational plane of analysis also emerges in our analysis of the factors that shape the diversity of television cultures. As James Schwoch points out in his study of Cold War television, the tensions and resolutions that influenced the rise of global television from the mid-twentieth century 'were more often than not manifest beyond the borders, landmasses, and other traditional defining characteristics of nation-states'.[71] The trajectories of television cultures under communist rule were no exception: they were closely intertwined with other state socialist countries but also defined in conversation with their counterparts on the other side of the Iron Curtain. These cross-border entanglements took many forms, ranging from shared histories of infrastructure, cross-border viewing, and personnel and programme exchanges to the mimicking of organizational and legal solutions. Failing to attend to these transnational entanglements can give rise to what is known as Galton's problem, namely mistaking the results of transnational borrowing for an outcome of purely domestic factors.[72] To avoid this problem, we pay attention to contextual factors

[71] Schwoch (2009), p. 5. [72] Hanitzsch and Esser (2012), p. 503.

that go beyond the framework of a single state, and consider how particular traits of television cultures may have been shaped by the transnational orientation of a particular broadcasting system, including its incorporation into international broadcast infrastructures and openness to cross-border signals. That said, we should also acknowledge that television cultures are frequently treated by their key actors – policymakers, producers, and audiences – as national and often become more homogeneous as a result of nation-building efforts. Avoiding the challenge of methodological nationalism therefore does not mean denying a measure of national homogeneity altogether; rather, it requires us to avoid assuming that such homogeneity is given, uncontested, or permanent, or that it precludes transnational ties and similarities.

The second methodological challenge encountered in our analysis was the need to combine a comparative analysis with an account of change over time. Even though our analysis covers a historical period that now appears relatively stable and uneventful, the television systems and cultures we examine underwent significant changes. They grew from a rather marginal ingredient of mass communication to its dominant element and became integral to both everyday routines and political life, and their relationships with the state, communist elites, social structures, and cultural processes changed accordingly. This meant that the balance of differences and similarities between television cultures also shifted, which required us to adopt a mode of analysis that oscillated between cross-country comparison and longitudinal analysis.

Such a combination of synchronic and diachronic comparisons was not without its challenges. As Winfried Schulz notes in his discussion of longitudinal designs in political communication research, relationships between changing political institutions on the one hand, and changing forms of communication on the other, defy a neat distinction between the independent and dependent variables required by standard models of social science research.[73] This applies even in the communist context, where the autonomy of the media was considerably more circumscribed than in a liberal democratic context. For instance, in many of the countries examined here, the intensification of political control following the Soviet invasion of Prague in 1968 was in part motivated by the recognition that the media, including television, played an important role in amplifying domestic dissent. To put it differently, the status of television shifted over

[73] Schulz (2014), pp. 66–67.

time from being a relatively independent causal factor to being a force that was subjected much more firmly to party-state control.

Apart from complicating a neat causal account, the introduction of a diachronic comparison can risk undermining the credibility of synchronous comparisons. As Michael Werner and Bénédicte Zimmermann note in their critique of comparative history, delving too deeply into the analysis of historical processes may make it difficult to justify why, in the comparative analysis, one aspect of the historical process is chosen over another.[74] For instance, when comparing our five countries, the politics–television dynamics in Yugoslavia emerges as the most liberal, given its less pervasive mechanisms of party-state control. Yet at the same time, such a classification glosses over the fact that in the early 1970s, extensive purges took place among the country's media elites, and party control over television increased significantly.

While such tensions were certainly felt at various points in writing this book, we nonetheless believe that the benefits of combining the two planes of analysis are too great to be jettisoned solely on the basis of such obstacles. Quite the contrary: a more complex account of causality, which defies a neat separation of causes and consequences and challenges attempts to fit the reality of communication into static typologies, is precisely why longitudinal comparison should become more widely adopted among communication scholars. Another benefit brought by combining synchronic and diachronic planes of analysis is that this increases the scope of comparison. In addition to comparisons between countries, the longitudinal span opens up opportunities for several within-case comparisons, which make it possible to explore the relationship between context and outcome by looking not only at how they co-vary across cases but also longitudinally. In technical jargon, the addition of historical comparison multiplies the opportunities to test a hypothesis about a causal relationship and thereby increases the number of cases within what may initially seem like a single case.[75]

Finally, it is also important to note that the logic and aims of the comparative techniques adopted in this book differ significantly from familiar quantitative approaches; instead of using comparison to predict the average effects of particular causes, the intention here is to employ comparisons to account for particular outcomes in particular contexts. In following this logic, our approach is aligned with the qualitative

74 Werner and Zimmermann (2006). 75 Collier (1993), p. 115.

approach underpinning historical comparative analysis in sociology and political science, where researchers 'do not look for the net effect of a cause over a large number of cases but rather for how causes interact in the context of a particular case or a few cases to produce an outcome'.[76] To put it differently, while both approaches to comparison are interested in causal relationships, the emphasis of quantitative approaches is on harnessing the potential of comparison to enable prediction, while the primary focus of the qualitative approach followed here is to use comparison as a means of enhancing understanding.

CONCLUSIONS

The conceptual and methodological framework outlined in this chapter has been developed primarily with the view of comparing television cultures and also with the intention of focusing on a particular historical period and geographic area. Nonetheless, we contend that this framework has more general applicability: the seven dimensions of variation cover most of the major variables relevant to the comparative analysis of television cultures in general, as well as providing a solid starting point for comparing media cultures linked to other forms of mediated communication. Similarly, the key sources, methods, and methodological challenges discussed are relevant to comparative media cultures research more generally. We will return to these issues in the concluding chapter, when discussing the evolution of East European television cultures after 1989 and the broader relevance of our comparative framework.

The seven dimensions of variation discussed here should be seen as interrelated and will hence co-vary to some extent. For instance, we shall see that state socialist television cultures that are more open to public scrutiny of power as a part of the medium's public mission will also tend to offer a less idealised depiction of communal and family life, be more open to privatization, more receptive to transnational links with the West, and more oriented to the present rather than to the future or the revolutionary past. Nonetheless, such correlations are never perfect, as the seven dimensions also vary independently – which also means they are not reducible to one another. This, as we shall see, has to do with the different systemic and contextual factors that influence the formation of television cultures, which we introduce in the following two chapters.

[76] Bennett and Elman (2006), p. 262. See also Mahoney and Larkin Terrie (2008).

A final note of clarification is in order at this point. Covering such a broad theoretical terrain, combining such a wide variety of sources and methods, and using them to trace developments over five countries and over several decades is a double-edged sword. Experts concerned with the distinct theoretical debates we draw on, proponents of the different methods and approaches we combine, and specialists in national television histories will no doubt notice blank spots and simplifications and miss the level of detail that a more circumscribed study would afford. At various points in writing this book, we have ourselves bemoaned the inevitable loss of nuance and detail and regretted the many in-depth examinations of individual programmes, archival documents, or audience reactions that we have so painstakingly reconstructed yet could not fit into the final manuscript. Nonetheless, we believe that what is lost in detail is more than made up for in the general patterns this book reveals and in the broader insights these patterns afford into the role of television in the communist project, the position of the medium in global media developments, and the importance of everyday life and culture in the mediation of power in the modern world.

3

State Socialist Television in Historical Context

To understand how and why the television cultures in state socialist Eastern Europe differed along the seven dimensions introduced in the previous chapter, it is important to understand the particular historical conditions in which they arose. Of particular relevance in this respect are the characteristics of the broadcasting systems to which these cultures were linked. When did TV broadcast signals reach the homes in state socialist Eastern Europe, and how quickly did television turn into a truly mass medium? To what extent did state socialist broadcasters participate in transnational networks of cooperation and exchange? In what ways did the communist elites exercise control over television, and how did they seek to mobilize the medium to serve the goals of the communist revolution? What kinds of programmes were on offer, and who watched them? Finally, how did these aspects of state socialist television systems differ across the region, and how did they change over time?

In this chapter we focus most of our attention on the five countries at the forefront of our analysis – the Soviet Union, Yugoslavia, East Germany, Poland, and Romania – but we situate them within the broader regional context. The overview starts from early experiments in television technology in the late nineteenth century and the first experimental broadcasts in the interwar period, then charts the gradual building of a fully fledged broadcasting infrastructure over the post-war decades, noting developments at both the national and transnational levels. In doing so, this section also maps three key dimensions of variation between broadcast systems in the region: the timing of infrastructural developments, the transnational orientation of broadcast systems, and their relative core-periphery position. In the second section, this is followed by a discussion of the medium's relationship with the party and the state, which forms another dimension of variation between broadcast systems in the region. The third section of the chapter turns to developments at the level of programmes and audiences that are important in contextualising the characteristics of the television cultures explored in the rest of the book: it describes the gradual expansion of broadcast hours and the parallel shifts in the size and structure of TV audiences.

The last section builds on the four systemic dimensions of variation introduced over the course of the chapter to propose a typology of state socialist television systems. We distinguish between three major types: market state socialist, reformist state socialist, and hard-line state socialist TV systems. We conclude by considering how these three types of system relate to the cultural dimensions of variation introduced in Chapter 2, and discuss further contextual factors that need to be taken into account when explaining state socialist television cultures.

FROM EARLY EXPERIMENTS TO A FULLY FLEDGED BROADCASTING INFRASTRUCTURE

Transnational Entanglements

From its earliest days, television in Eastern Europe was part of a collective process of technological and cultural innovation operating on a transnational scale. By the end of the nineteenth century, several applications for television patents were recorded in Eastern Europe, with the Polish physicist Mieczysław Wolfke and Russian engineer Alexander Apollonovich Polumordvinov submitting their applications in Russia only a few years after similar devices were developed by Paul Nipkow in Germany, Giulielmo Marconi in Italy, Lazare Weiller in France, Henry Sutton in Australia, and Jan Szczepanik in Austria, to mention just a few.[1] In the early twentieth century, the Russian scientist Boris Rosing, working in his laboratory at St Petersburg University, was the first to use the cathode ray tube as a receiver; he patented the system in 1907 and had transmitted 'very crude images' by 1911.[2] Rosing's inventions also paved the way for the development of an electronic camera, a step accomplished in the 1930s by his student, Vladimir K. Zworkin, who emigrated to the United

[1] Abramson (1987), pp. 16–22.

[2] Dizard (1966), p. 39; Burns (1998), p. 119; Iurovskii (1998), p. 55.

States after the October Revolution and worked at the Radio Corporation of America.[3]

A similar transnational entangling of technological innovation continued throughout the 1920s and the 1930s, when the first test transmissions of still and then moving images took place not only in London, Paris, Berlin, and several US locations, but also, among others, in laboratories in Ljubljana, Zagreb, Bucharest, and Warsaw.[4] The introduction of intermittent regular broadcasting in the United States in 1928 and in the United Kingdom in 1929–1930, and especially the start of regular broadcasting by the BBC in 1932, provided the next benchmarks for technological development and prompted the start of regular transmissions in Germany in 1935 and in the Soviet Union in 1939.[5] At this stage, not only ideas but also devices and personnel circulated transnationally. The Hungarian Dénes von Mihály and the Scotsman John Logie Baird were both invited to Berlin to work in the laboratories of Telefunken AG, while the aforementioned Russian scientist Zworkin, who spearheaded developments in the United States, regularly travelled around Europe to keep abreast of the latest developments.

These transnational developments and exchanges were stopped in their tracks by the onset of World War II. In Britain BBC Television went off the air in 1939 and returned only in 1946; broadcasts in the Soviet Union were stopped in 1941 and did not resume until 1945; and in Poland, the introduction of regular transmissions, originally scheduled for 1941, had to be postponed until 1953.[6] In Germany, broadcasting continued, but almost entirely for military purposes; the production of sets for civilians ceased, and research focused on the application of television technology for missile guidance systems, or as a means for entertaining wounded troops.[7]

The devastating consequences of the war had a lasting effect on the trajectories of television development across the European continent. In the immediate post-war years, broadcasting capacity lay in ruins, and with the exception of Britain and the Soviet Union, which restarted regular broadcasting within about a year from the end of the war, the

[3] Abramson (1995).

[4] Ciontu and Gheorghe (2012), p. 289; Galić (1986), p. 24; Grzelewska et al. (2001), pp. 264–265; Iurovskii (1998), pp. 57–58; Paulu (1974), p. 326.

[5] Paulu (1974), p. 37; Iurovskii (1998), p. 59.

[6] Dizard (1966), p. 39, Grzelewska et al. (2001), p. 264, Pikulski (2002), pp. 7–10.

[7] Uricchio (1990), p. 116.

rest of the continent needed considerably longer to renew its investment in the medium.

It would be tempting to think that the onset of the Cold War effectively blocked the transnational circuits of exchange and cooperation in television broadcasting. Yet as Christian Heinrich-Franke and Regina Immel have pointed out, in a context where agreement between East and West was often strained, technology seemed to offer a more neutral ground for cooperation and exchange.[8] In the mid-1950s, for instance, a group of TV professionals from Yugoslavia toured the United States and Europe to ascertain which technical equipment to import.[9] In Romania, Silviu Brucan, a key personality of early television history in the country, was inspired by British television and developed a close relationship with the BBC, which became an important source of technical, organizational, and editorial know-how.[10] Arguably, these enhanced contacts between specialists in the East and the West allowed for the transfer of signals between the two blocks, creating a practically unified communications space that transcended the Cold War divide.

This is not to say that technical cooperation eschewed the logic of Cold War confrontation. Rather, the Cold War conflict itself demanded a measure of transnational exchange across the East–West divide. Acting on a transnational scale offered a convenient way of showcasing the superiority of communist rule over its capitalist rival, in front of a global audience. This was clearly a motivation for Soviet involvement in global TV events, as well as a reason for the withdrawal of cooperation if a particular transnational cooperation threatened to undermine Soviet superiority. As Lars Lundgren and Christine Evans show in their analysis of the preparations for the transnational *Our World* broadcast, the fact that Moscow was conceived as a minor node in a much larger (London-dominated) transnational network played a major role in its withdrawal from the project.[11] The Soviet Union considered itself a global hegemon and was determined to be treated as such.

The peculiar Cold War logic of transnational broadcasting can also be glimpsed in the relationship between the Soviet-dominated International Radio and Television Organisation (OIRT), set up in 1949 to facilitate the discussion of issues relating to broadcasting within socialist countries, and

[8] Heinrich-Franke and Immel (2013).

[9] AJ, f. 130, k. 566–942, 'Informacija o sastanku kod potpretsednika SIV-a druga Čolakovića po pitanju daljeg rada na uvodjenju televizije dana 10.I.1957,' 1957, p. 1.

[10] Mustata (2013a), pp. 51–53.

[11] Lundgren and Evans (2017).

its 'capitalist' counterpart the European Broadcasting Union (EBU), established in 1950.[12] Both OIRT and EBU also established separate branches dedicated to programme exchanges among members: Intervision, set up in 1954, and Eurovision, established in 1960. While each organization aimed to foster transnational cooperation among its own members, this arrangement was not meant to create wholly separate broadcasting worlds. From the late 1950s, OIRT and EBU members were involved in technical and personnel exchanges and, as we shall see in Chapter 7, the two organizations facilitated programme exchanges not only within but also between the two blocs. This institutional set-up therefore gave rise to competing, yet nonetheless connected, audiovisual realms and formed an integral part of the cultural Cold War waged through television screens.

Not all European countries fit neatly into the bipolar division of the broadcast space. Indeed, the extent to which individual broadcasting systems were open to cooperation with ideological rivals constituted a crucial dimension of systemic variation within the blocks. Finnish television, for instance, was a member of both the OIRT and the EBU, while Yugoslavia, in an assertion of independence from the Soviet Union and an expression of sympathy for the West, opted to join the EBU. Later on, Yugoslav television also sought to develop close ties with members of the Non-Aligned Movement, an organization bringing together states not formally aligned with any major power bloc, founded in the Yugoslav capital in 1961. A major festival of non-aligned broadcasters was held in Yugoslavia in 1979, with participants from forty-seven states.[13] Although these developments never gave rise to a fully fledged rival broadcasting association, they attest to the complexity of the cultural Cold War, which cannot be fitted into a simple, black-and-white confrontation between East and West.

The story of the technological battles that accompanied the introduction of colour television offers another good insight into the transnational entanglements of TV technology during the Cold War. The initial standard for colour broadcasting, NTSC, was developed in the United States and adopted across most of the Americas. Due to the inherent weaknesses of the system, European countries sought an alternative standard. France, in particular, was keen to instrumentalize technology for ideological purposes and used its own colour system as a symbol of its

[12] Eugster (1983), pp. 39–46.

[13] D. Milanović (1979). 'Korak ka novoj televiziji,' *TV Novosti*, 19 October 1979, p. 7.

international status, as well as a vehicle of foreign policy, aimed at establishing Europe as a 'third force' in the competition between the Soviet Union and the United States.[14]

As a result, two separate standards were adopted in Europe – first the SECAM standard, developed in France and promoted across Eastern Europe, parts of Southern Europe, the Middle East, and Africa, and then the PAL standard, initially developed in West Germany and gradually adopted across most of Western Europe, as well as parts of Africa and Asia. The Soviet Union, eager to put one over on its Cold War rival and needing assistance to develop colour television domestically, enthusiastically signed up for the SECAM initiative and pressured other socialist countries to do the same. In the cases of Romania and Yugoslavia, the refusal to adopt the SECAM standard became a means of demonstrating their pro-Western sympathies and independence from the Soviet Union.[15] Together with the politics of relationships between the OIRT and the EBU, decisions over the choice of the colour TV standard thus offer another important indicator of differences in the transnational orientations of television infrastructures between socialist broadcast systems.

Infrastructural Developments

As the continent was emerging from the ruins of World War II, the Soviet Union was eager to use television as a sign of its position in the pecking order of nations. In 1945, it boasted of being 'the first in Europe to renew its programs' after the war, relegating its main continental rival, Britain, to second place. Regular television broadcasts started in East Germany in 1952, in Poland in 1953, in Czechoslovakia in 1954, in Romania and parts of Yugoslavia in 1956, in Hungary in 1957, in Bulgaria in 1959, and in Albania in 1960.[16] Yet, despite patriotic chest-thumping and an eagerness to participate in the global techno-diplomacy, television in much of Eastern Europe took a long time to become a fully 'national', mass medium. The building of a statewide network of stations and transmitters could take years and even decades to complete, producing a daily programme often proved costlier than initially imagined, and the adoption of TV receivers among the population was regularly hampered either by exorbitant costs or by insufficient supply, both characteristic

[14] Fickers (2013). [15] Mustata (2013b); Preutu (2017).
[16] Gumbert (2014), p. 23; Mustata (2013a), p. 49; Paulu (1974), pp. 326, 370, 438; Pokorna-Ignatowicz (2003), p. 43; Vončina (1999).

products of planned economies. The diffusion of TV receivers offers a particularly good indicator of television's slow transformation into a genuinely mass medium (Table 3.1).

Even in the Soviet Union, the rhetoric of pride surrounding the reintroduction of broadcasting in 1945 did not immediately translate into concrete investment in television infrastructure; it was only after the reconstruction of the Television Centre in 1948–1949 that Central Television broadcasts could resume in earnest.[17] Although Soviet television continued to grow across the late 1950s and early 1960s, with the number of stations rising to 121 by 1965, and the number of countrywide channels reaching four by 1967, the supply of TV receivers remained insufficient into the 1960s, limiting the reach of television signals among the population.[18] In the southern corner of socialist Eastern Europe, the problems were even more acute. In Romania, daily broadcasts became a reality only in 1970, more than thirteen years after the introduction of regular broadcasting in the country. In Yugoslavia, the commitment to federalism and linguistic diversity further hampered the building of a statewide television network. While broadcasters in the three northernmost republics of Slovenia, Croatia, and Serbia established their own production facilities and started regular broadcasting between 1956 and 1958, it took more than a decade for locally produced content to start airing in the remaining republics.[19]

Yet, as the data in Table 3.1 indicates, we should avoid presenting the history of infrastructural developments in the region uniformly. In East Germany and Czechoslovakia, and also in Hungary, statewide signal coverage was reached considerably earlier than elsewhere in the region, in part because these countries could build on fairly advanced broadcast infrastructure developed before the war, but perhaps also because of the lure of cross-border broadcasts from West Germany and Austria, which encouraged the acquisition of TV receivers among the population. To be sure, all three countries also encountered significant obstacles; in East Germany, television authorities initially struggled both with the effects of trade embargoes that limited their ability to import modern TV technology and also the phenomenon of so-called republic flight: the defection of qualified cadres to the west.[20] In Czechoslovakia, the Slovak part of the federation lagged significantly behind its Czech counterpart in both

[17] Paulu (1974), p. 37.
[18] Iurovskii (1998), p. 65; Paulu (1974), p. 37; Roth-Ey (2007), pp. 283, 285.
[19] Galić (1986), pp. 139–140. [20] Gumbert (2014), pp. 24–25, 74.

FIGURE 3.1 TV receivers on sale in Budapest, Hungary, in 1976. *Source*: Fortepan/ Urbán Támas. Along with East Germany and Czechoslovakia, Hungary was one of the state socialist countries that experienced a rather fast diffusion of TV sets among the population.

signal coverage and the diffusion of TV sets.[21] These internal disparities and initial stumbling blocks aside, however, it is clear that television in these three countries reached a point of saturation by the mid-1960s, several years before the rest of the region: TV receivers became widely available in department stores and specialist shops, and the number of inhabitants per TV set dropped into the single digits (Figure 3.1).

Core-Periphery Position

Closely intertwined with the two key themes examined so far – namely, the timing of infrastructural developments and the transnational orientation of broadcast infrastructures – is the relative core-periphery positions of the individual countries and their broadcasting systems. By this we mean the extent to which a particular broadcasting system serves as a model for other systems, or alternatively models itself on foreign systems. Among the systems studied in this book, the Soviet system clearly had a core position. Continued attempts by the Soviet Union to lead the way in the

[21] Paulu (1974), p. 326.

development of broadcasting – from the introduction of regular broadcasting to the setting-up of a second channel and colour TV – were important not only as means of demonstrating its technological prowess to capitalist rivals, but also as an assertion of its dominance of other communist-led countries. As documents from the era attest, these attempts were often successful, and many – but not all – broadcasters in the region did indeed look up to the Soviet Union as a leading light in the sector and a model to emulate.[22] However, Romania and especially Yugoslavia preferred to measure themselves against advances in the West and looked to Western Europe, and especially Britain, as sources of professional expertise and technology.

Transnational cooperation constituted another arena within which core-periphery relations, and the tensions surrounding them, became apparent. The organizational structure of Intervision serves as a case in point: as a federal entity, the Soviet Union was represented by each of its European republics (the three Baltic states, plus Ukraine, Belarus, and Moldova, each had its own member), which allowed it to dominate the agenda.[23] In this context, it is hardly a surprise that Yugoslavia, in a bid to assert independence from the Soviet Union and its sphere of influence, opted to join the EBU and Eurovision instead. Not only that; as we have seen, Yugoslavia sought to establish a rival form of cooperation among broadcasters from the Non-Aligned movement, thus aspiring to become an alternative 'core' socialist country itself. As we have seen, a similar dynamic drove decisions over the choice of the colour TV standard: again, the two usual suspects, Romania and Yugoslavia, opted for the technological solution associated more closely with the West.

THE CHANGING FORMS OF POLITICAL CONTROL: FROM MEDIUM TO MESSAGE

Cross-Country Similarities and Differences

Across Eastern Europe, television became part of the 'propaganda state' and was expected to serve the goals of the party and help realize the aims

[22] For instance, an article published in a Polish radio and TV magazine in 1961 praised the technological advances of Soviet broadcasting and asserts its superiority over commercial television in the United States. 'Televizja ZSSR i Postep,' *Radio i Telewizja*, no. 45, 1961, p. 1.

[23] Paulu (1974), pp. 59–61.

of the communist revolution.[24] The legal framework underpinning these checks was broadly similar across the region, testifying to the influence of the Soviet Union as a model for broadcasting arrangements elsewhere. This framework typically included limitations on freedom of expression, such as sanctions against attempts to challenge the established political order, and requirements for production plans to be approved by the relevant committees or dedicated censorship bodies. All countries also established a dedicated state committee that was in charge of regulating television broadcasting, to ensure compliance with the party line. [25] In the Soviet Union, the committee comprised a central group of decision makers, led by a chairman, to whom were answerable a number of departments in charge of producing programmes in various areas.[26] Republic-level and regional broadcasters were structured on a similar model, albeit on a smaller scale.

An exception to this pattern was Yugoslavia, where a state committee was initially set up in 1958, but then abolished in 1966, with its functions transferred to the Yugoslav Radio-Television.[27] This shift towards self-regulation was consistent with the country's relative independence from the Soviet model and with its liberalization of media policy in the 1960s, which granted television professionals greater organizational and financial independence, the freedom to elect their own top management, and a growing reliance on advertising revenues.[28] We should also note, however, that a dedicated radio and television committee continued to operate within the Socialist Alliance of the Working People of Yugoslavia (SAWPY), a semi-independent mass organization sponsored by the party, established with the aim to further mass involvement in the party agenda, but without direct party control. This arrangement ensured a measure of continued party oversight, albeit in a more indirect way than in other state socialist countries.

While the Yugoslav case is fairly straightforward, existing sources offer less guidance as to how the relative influence of the party-state on the broadcasting system differed within other countries. Comparative insights provided by contemporary Western observers offer useful clues. US broadcasting scholar Burton Paulu visited most countries in the region in the later 1960s and early 1970s. He found that programmes tackling social and political issues were more daring in Hungary, Czechoslovakia,

[24] The term comes from Kenez (1985).
[25] Fischer (2001), p. 24; Grzelewska et al. (2001), p. 405. [26] Paulu (1974), pp. 53–54.
[27] Pustišek (1987), pp. 172–173, 191. [28] Robinson (1977), pp. 44–45.

and Poland than elsewhere, suggesting that party control over television was more limited than it would later become.[29] Other sources from the era also attest that journalists and writers in these three countries achieved a degree of autonomy and succeeded in exerting pressure on the party elite, particularly so in periods when the strength of the party leadership declined, as for instance in the aftermath of Stalin's death or during the 1960s.[30] In Poland, the organizations representing media professionals were rather actively committed to establishing a level of autonomy for the profession; they stressed its public value, publicly pressured government officials to provide information to journalists, and regulated the activities of their members in order to minimize the need for external interference.[31] Although often criticised for being too subservient to the party-state, these associations came to play a vital role during the Solidarity movement protests in the early 1980s.

The strong influence across the region of the state and the party went hand in hand with the reliance on state-controlled funding sources. Exact and comparable figures on the structure of funding in broadcasting are not available, but existing literature offers a basis for a broad overview. In the early 1970s, the main source of funding came from licence fees, with the exception of the Soviet Union where from 1962 licence fees were replaced by a levy on television sets.[32] Advertising existed in all countries but did not constitute a major source of funding. The only exception to this rule was, yet again, Yugoslavia, where advertising income grew rapidly during the 1960s as a result of policy changes and reached 23.1 per cent of the total television budget in 1971.[33] It is quite possible that this reliance on advertising helped enhance television's relative independence from party control at the time, although it should also be noted that the share of advertising income fell rapidly over the course of the coming years, dropping to a mere 5.5 per cent in 1983.[34]

The existing general literature on advertising under state socialism likewise suggests that Yugoslavia, while not alone in experimenting with market mechanisms – Poland, East Germany, the Soviet Union, and Hungary did that, too – went furthest in their implementation.[35] These conclusions resonate broadly with the literature on market socialism, a type of economic system in which the state retains control over

[29] Paulu (1974), pp. 373–374, 481. [30] Mond and Richter (1966).
[31] Curry (1990), pp. 117–160. [32] RGANI, f. 5, op. 60, d. 28, ll. 29–30, 38–43.
[33] Milošević (1984), p. 140. [34] Ibid. p. 162.
[35] Gumbert (2014), p. 151; Hanson (1974); Patterson (2011).

firms but allows elements of market competition, typically by enabling producers to sell their goods to consumers in a competitive market environment.[36] Yugoslavia is often mentioned as a country where such a model of the economy was implemented, effectively promising to offer 'a middle way between capitalism and Soviet-style central planning'.[37]

Changes Over Time: From the Early Years to the 1970s

While noting these cross-country differences, we should also acknowledge that the extent of party control in broadcasting varied considerably over time. In all five countries, television was less tightly controlled in its early years, with supervision typically increasing alongside its growing audience and in response to international crises. In the Soviet Union, for instance, a number of amateur stations run by enthusiasts cropped up around the country in the early period (mirroring the development of radio, both in the Soviet Union and worldwide), before the increased government scrutiny of both the quality and ideological content of such broadcasts brought these experiments to an end in the 1960s.[38] We should also acknowledge that the forms and targets of control changed over time. Initially, communist authorities were concerned primarily with the technical and infrastructural aspects of the medium rather than with the broadcast content. As Heather Gumbert has argued in relation to East Germany, the main goal for television in the early years was not the development of programming but rather the occupation of bandwidth which would otherwise be relinquished to other countries.[39] Likewise, Yugoslav authorities spent much of the early period debating the best ways of organizing the federal structure of the broadcasting system.[40] In short, for communist authorities, early television was more about the medium than the message.

The situation changed considerably as the medium's social reach and impact grew, and especially when episodes of domestic dissent or international crisis revealed its potentially detrimental effects on the stability of communist rule. Due to differences in the speed of infrastructure development and the dissemination of TV receivers, and

[36] See e.g. Miller (1990); Shleifer and Vishny (1994). [37] Estrin (1991), p. 187.

[38] Roth-Ey (2007), pp. 285–288. [39] Gumbert (2014), p. 30.

[40] AJ, f. 130, k. 566–942, 'Idejna skica perspektivnog razvitka radiodifuznog programa,' 1985.

differences in the timing of domestic developments and waves of popular discontent, the ebbs and flows of political control over television differed somewhat from country to country. In East Germany, for instance, the first two waves of tighter controls were associated with the Hungarian invasion of 1956 and the Second Berlin Crisis in 1961,[41] but in states such as Yugoslavia and Romania, television was still far too weak as a medium to merit serious political consideration at the time. By the late 1960s and the early 1970s, these diverse trajectories begin to coalesce: by this point, television had established itself as an influential medium in most of the region and become closely involved both in the growth of domestic public contestation characteristic of the 1960s and in the mediation of key shifts in foreign policy agendas and international crises, such as the Soviet invasion of Czechoslovakia in 1968 and the easing of relationships between the United States and the Soviet Union from 1971 onwards. This coincidence of television's coming of age as a truly mass medium and domestic and international developments created a perfect storm that pushed communist elites across the region to reconsider their relationship with television and shift their attention decisively from the medium to the message.

In the Soviet Union, the strained ideological climate of the post-1968 period meant that the authorities were heavily involved in both the composition and the editing of content, while the ability to pre-record shows provided additional security from ideological slip-ups.[42] Television productions were verified at a number of levels before being broadcast. Workers who were deemed to have failed in their duty of care were subject to sacking, demotion, or at best, reprimanding, particularly after the arrival of Sergei Lapin as President of the State Committee on Radio and Television in 1970. In Poland, too, the character of the television–politics relationship began to change in the late 1960s, first in response to the wave of anti-communist protests involving students and intellectuals that swept the country in March 1968, and then in reaction to the 1968 events in Prague. The 1970s saw a growing politicization of television content, and of news in particular, which now became part of the battle against the early workers' movements that later coalesced into the Solidarity movement.[43]

[41] Gumbert (2014). [42] Iurovskii (1998), p. 76.
[43] Grzelewska et al. (2001), pp. 286, 292.

Romania and Yugoslavia took a slightly different course and initially continued with a relatively laissez-faire approach to the media, a stance aligned with their denouncing of the Soviet invasion of Czechoslovakia and, in the case of Romania, the only Warsaw Pact member to do so at the time, also a refusal to contribute troops to support the invasion. Nonetheless, both countries gradually adopted a more stringent approach, albeit for different reasons. In Yugoslavia, the fear of a Soviet invasion akin to the one seen in Prague in 1968 was compounded by the growth of domestic discontent and outbursts of nationalist fervour in 1971, which threatened to tear apart the country's delicate multinational fabric. In response to this, the aging president Tito initiated wide-ranging purges. In Croatia, key media professionals were demoted from their roles and expunged from the League of Communists.[44] In a decree issued in December 1971, the republican branches of the party and the Socialist Alliance were instructed to 'critically and self-critically analyse its functioning to date' and revise their forms of collaboration with the media to ensure more effective oversight.[45] In the years that followed, television professionals were subjected to closer scrutiny than ever before, with party members embedded in the production processes and annual TV production plans scrutinized by the republican branches of the Socialist Alliance.[46]

In Romania, too, party approaches to culture and the media started shifting in the 1970s, though the initial impetus came not from domestic dissent or the Soviet threat but from Ceauşescu's newly found sympathies for China and New Korea.[47] In a series of speeches delivered in 1971, inspired by Mao Zedong's cultural revolution, Ceauşescu called for much stricter conformity in the cultural sector and explicitly demanded that all cultural and media institutions return to their primary goal of raising socialist consciousness.[48] Earlier in the same year, a National Council on Radio and Television was established, headed by a high-ranking party member who approved all basic broadcasting plans and fed policy guidance to the committee of the Council of Ministers mentioned earlier.[49] Despite these shifts however, actual changes to cultural life took a while to materialize, in part due to the initial staunch opposition among cultural

[44] Novak (2005), pp. 725–736.

[45] HDA, f. 1228, d. 1807, 'Stenografski zapisnik sa sastanka Radne grupe Republičke konferencije Socijalističkog saveza Hrvatske sa predstavnicima Radiotelevizije Zagreb, održanog 24.I.1972. u Zagrebu, u Republičkoj konferenciji SSRNH,' 1972.

[46] For examples of such reports and debates see HDA, f. 1228, d. 2749, d. 3188, d. 3731, d. 3737.

[47] Deletant (1995), pp. 184–186. [48] Mustata (2011), p. 23. [49] Paulu (1974), p. 405.

elites in the country.[50] On Romanian television, too, relatively daring content continued to be produced until the late 1970s; for instance, the popular programme *Reflektor* (*Reflector*) reported on specific cases of social injustice, ranging from thefts to political corruption.[51] It was only in the late 1970s that the programme came under scrutiny; it was temporarily suspended in 1977 and then launched in a completely different, more politically obedient form – a development that marked the beginning of the more exhaustive political control over Romanian television that was to intensify over the course of the 1980s.[52]

In East Germany, party interest in the media increased as well in the early 1970s, albeit for a slightly different set of reasons, only tangentially related to the events of 1968 in Prague. In the aftermath of the leadership handover from Walter Ulbricht to Erich Honecker in 1971, East German television underwent a reform that reflected the changing foreign policy position introduced by the new leadership. The combined effects of the détente between the United States and the Soviet Union and the softening of relationships with West Germany led Honecker to adopt a dual politics of moderate openness towards its Western neighbour, coupled with a stronger relationship with the Soviet Union and a tightening of domestic control.[53] This two-pronged approach was designed to ensure that the citizenry, despite the thawing of relationships with West Germany, also appreciated the benefits of living in a communist-ruled state. In this context, in 1972 Honecker called on East German television 'to improve the structure of the programming, to overcome a certain dullness, to take the requirements of good entertainment into account, to create more forceful television journalism and to meet expectations of those members of the population whose working day began very early and therefore wanted to view good quality television programmes in the early evening hours'.[54] Disillusionment with party control over media increased in the late 1970s, which led dozens of employees of the state broadcaster to leave the country.[55]

Changes Over Time: The 1980s

If the 1970s were marked by a notable confluence of developments across Eastern Europe, with television in all countries coming under increased

[50] Deletant (1995), pp. 184–186. [51] Mustata (2013a), pp. 54–55.
[52] Mustata (2013a), pp. 55–56. [53] Dittmar (2004).
[54] Quoted in Steinmetz and Viehoff (2004), p. 320.
[55] E.g. SAPMO BArch DY 30 / vorl. SED 25945, 25946, 30113.

scrutiny by the party elite, in the 1980s national trajectories diverged once more. At one end of the spectrum we find countries where party interference increased. Following the rise of tensions with Solidarity and the introduction of Martial Law on 13 December 1981, Polish viewers saw broadcast hours and entertainment content reduced drastically, a situation that started improving only after the lifting of restrictions in 1983.[56] In Romania, too, the volume of broadcasting was reduced to no more than two hours on weekdays and four to five hours over the weekend, and the content was tailored to flatter Ceauşescu and his family.[57] With regard to East German television, the 1980s are perhaps best described as stable but stale; the medium went through its final decade under communist rule with a personnel and programme roster viewers were familiar with from the 1970s, and the situation started changing only in 1989, shortly before the end of party control.[58]

In the Soviet Union, in contrast, the second half of the 1980s was a period of profound transformation brought about by Gorbachev's reforms, known as perestroika (reconstruction). Television started broadcasting parliamentary debates and congresses, which had previously remained off limits to the Soviet people, allowing the public to see and hear their representatives in action.[59] Several current affairs shows were introduced that began to uncover social problems that had rarely, if at all, been discussed in official mass media outlets.[60] Reflecting the transformed international climate, Soviet television also became increasingly open to the outside world, offering 'bridges' that linked the Soviet Union and the United States and invited citizens to debate international issues, and introducing a greater range of imported dramas from the West. As a result, the fall of communist rule did not bring a sudden transformation of television culture but rather continued a process that had started several years before.

A similar pattern occurred in Yugoslavia, where changes to television culture and public discourse started occurring even earlier in the decade. The death of president Tito in 1980 marked the start of the gradual opening of public debate, with issues considered taboo in previous years now being addressed in the public realm, first in fringe cultural publications and then increasingly in the mainstream.[61] This gradual decoupling of party control and the media, however, was paralleled by a rise in

[56] Grzelewska et al. (2001), p. 314. [57] Mustata (2013a), pp. 56–57.
[58] Wolff (2002), pp. 276–286. [59] Mickiewicz (1997), pp. 83–97. [60] Ibid. pp. 65–82.
[61] Wachtel (1998).

nationalist discourses and sentiments. The Yugoslav media system, like other institutions in the federation, was segmented along national lines, which encouraged the creation of separate and increasingly hostile publics.[62] The republic-level broadcasters served their audiences diametrically opposed interpretations of the same events, aligned with the views of respective nationalist-minded elites, thereby laying the groundwork for the disintegration of the country in the 1990s.[63]

In sum, although television across communist-led countries was subordinate to the party's goals, the extent of control over the medium varied from country to country as well as changing markedly over time. Broadly speaking, we could argue that the 1960s were a period of relative liberalism, followed by a tightening of control in the 1970s and a final softening of party-state oversight towards the end of the 1980s. It is feasible to expect that the ebbs and flows of political control over the medium also coincided with changes in programming and audiences. Indeed, as the next section shows, the 1970s were not simply a period of greater political scrutiny over television but also a time of rapid expansion and the diversification of both the viewing public and television programming.

PROGRAMMES AND THEIR AUDIENCES: FROM ELITE TO MASS MEDIUM

In common with early television everywhere in the world, the first broadcasts in socialist Eastern Europe had very small audiences. In Poland, the inaugural programme, broadcast on 25 October 1952 at 7 PM and lasting thirty minutes, was received by twenty-four Leningrad television sets with 12x18 cm screens located in the dayrooms of the biggest workplaces around the country.[64] In East Germany in July 1952, there were so few viewers that the country's broadcaster was able to inform them personally by telephone about technical problems.[65] In Yugoslavia, too, audiences for the first broadcasts consisted of small groups watching the transmission in the streets and other public or semi-public spaces (Figure 3.2).

For several years, television remained a medium for the elites, not least because TV receivers were rather costly. In 1960s Poland, for instance, the cost of a new black-and-white receiver was equivalent to almost three

[62] Snyder (2002), pp. 213–217. [63] Mihelj et al. (2009).
[64] Grzelewska et al. (2001), p. 264. [65] Gumbert (2014), p. 26.

FIGURE 3.2 Passersby watching the early TV broadcasts on the streets of Belgrade, 23 August 1958. *Source*: RTS-PATVB.

average monthly salaries.[66] This also meant that early television viewers were disproportionally highly educated and typically held white collar jobs. A survey conducted in the late 1960s in several locations on both

[66] Paulu (1974), p. 279.

sides of the Iron Curtain revealed a positive correlation between viewing times and levels of education in communities where TV set ownership was below 50 per cent.[67]

Both editorial priorities and elite discourses were attuned to the cultural tastes and expectations of a predominantly educated audience: they privileged information and education over entertainment and gave pride of place to cultural genres with an established pedigree, such as literature, theatre, and classical music. In all of the countries, one of the most important tasks for television was to put forward a distinctly socialist world view through its news coverage. From the Soviet *News Relay* (*Estafeta novostei*, 1961–1970) and *Time* (*Vremia*, 1968 to date) to the East German *Current Camera* (*Aktuelle Kamera*, 1952–1990) and the infamous *The Black Channel* (*Der Schwarze Kanal*, 1960–1989), state socialist television paid particular attention to news and current affairs programmes, which accounted for a sizeable proportion of domestic production.[68] In parallel, television also sought to acquaint audiences with cultural achievements and enable people to participate in what were considered the key cultural events of the country. In Poland, the emphasis on such programming was so strong that one commentator referred to television in the early years as 'an artistic phenomenon'.[69] This is not to say that entertainment was absent from programming. As we show in Chapter 5, most countries actually broadcast a substantial volume of entertainment, fiction, and sports programmes during the early 1960s (Figure 5.4), yet these were not programmes that attracted particular praise among elites.

Towards the second half of the 1960s, however, it was becoming increasingly obvious that the programmes considered most valuable by the political elites and by TV professionals did not necessarily satisfy viewers and often fell short of achieving their task of persuading, mobilizing, or educating the audience. From the Soviet Union to Yugoslavia, these were seen as television's main functions, yet surveys showed that audiences regarded television primarily as a medium of entertainment.[70] The situation was particularly acute in areas where TV and radio signals from the West were most readily available. In East Germany, where the vast majority of the population (except for those

[67] Robinson and Converse (1972), p. 208.
[68] Evans (2016), pp. 169–171; Engelmann-del Mestre (2013); Leandrov (1986), p. 231.
[69] Quoted in Grzelewska et al. (2001), p. 268.
[70] Evans (2016), pp. 58–61; Mihelj (2013), p. 255.

residing in the so-called Valley of the Clueless in the far northeast and southeast of the country) could watch West German television, audiences could easily switch from a boring current affairs show or a high-minded educational programme to an entertainment-filled variety show or an action-packed film broadcast from the West.[71] Furthermore, they could also contrast the messages of GDR news with its Western counterparts, such as *Daily View* (*Tagesschau*, 1952–). In this context, East German information and current affairs programmes did not fare well, with *The Black Channel*, in particular, achieving low ratings and a certain notoriety for its one-sided commentaries on West German news reports.[72]

Elsewhere in the region, too, the pull of television signals from Western European broadcasters pushed authorities and broadcasters to reconsider established views and practices and pay more attention to audience tastes. Yugoslav authorities worried about the impact of Austrian and especially Italian TV in the border regions,[73] audience research was used in Soviet Estonia to ensure that the most popular domestic shows were scheduled to coincide with peaks in audience rates for broadcasts from Finland, and communist elites in Czechoslovakia raised the alarm over the appeal of Austrian and German television.[74] In countries further east the pull of Western European television was weaker, yet even here, authorities could not ignore the fascination with Western media entirely, though the threat came in the form of radio rather than television.[75]

The authorities' growing acknowledgment of a rift between audience preferences and elite expectations coincided with the gradual establishment of television as a truly mass medium. As is evident from trends in the diffusion of TV sets (Table 3.1), the late 1960s and early 1970s were the period when the number of inhabitants per TV set dropped into single figures across the region. Assuming that an average family owning a set had four members, we can estimate that in this period, over half of the population in state socialist Europe had access to television, meaning that television had become a dominant medium and at least potentially a key source of both information and leisure. Such large numbers were hard to

71 Dittmar (2004). 72 Engelmann-del Mestre (2013).

73 These worries were particularly common during the 1960s, when large parts of the Yugoslav coast were out of the reach of domestic broadcast signals. See, for instance, HDA, f. 1220, d. 670, 'Aktuelni problem prosvjete, kulturnog života I propagandne aktivnosti u Istri,' 1963.

74 Roth-Ey (2011), p. 168; Bren (2010), pp. 120–121. 75 Roth-Ey (2011), p. 191.

TABLE 3.1 *Diffusion of TV sets: trends in the number of inhabitants per TV set, 1960–1990*

	GDR	Cze	Hun	Pol	USSR	Yug	Rom	Bul	Alb
1960	16.8	17.1	95.8	69.9	44.1	612	338	1577	-
1965	5.3	6.6	12.2	15.0	14.4	34.3	37.9	44.5	-
1970	3.8	4.6	5.8	7.7	6.9	12	13.5	8.2	1000
1975	3.2	4.0	4.4	5.2	4.6	7.7	7.9	5.8	526
1980	2.9	3.6	3.9	4.5	3.5	5.9	5.9	5.3	27.8
1985	2.5	3.5	3.6	3.9	3.5	5.7	5.7	5.3	12.8
1990	3.2	3.2	3.6	3.9	3.1*	5.7*	6.2	5.3	11.8

Note: Calculations based on the total number of television licences (or equivalent) and population estimates based on nearest census figures.
Sources: For USSR, see Miasoedov (1982). *Strana chitaet, slushaet, smotrit: statisticheskiĭ obzor*. Moscow: Financi i statistika. East Germany, Czechoslovakia, Hungary, Poland, Yugoslavia, Romania, Bulgaria, and Poland, see Mitchell (2007).
*Based on data from 1989.

ignore: what point was there having a medium capable of addressing millions, if the content provided fell on deaf ears?

The rapid growth of audiences meant that it was becoming increasingly difficult to satisfy viewers' diverse tastes with a single channel. As a result, a second countrywide channel was introduced in most countries, which increased broadcasting hours and opened doors to more variety while greatly increasing the demand for programming. This growth in broadcast output is regularly mentioned in the existing literature,[76] but as the datasets are limited to single countries, are often incomplete, and rely on different methodologies, obtaining a sense of regional trends is difficult. To compensate for that, we have generated original data for the five countries that are at the forefront of analysis in the book, based on the analysis of published TV schedules, using a sample week at five-year intervals (Figure 3.3).

In the interests of comparability, the sampling procedures were devised in a way that underestimates the total volume of broadcast hours produced in the two federal countries, because our sample does not include channels from all republics. Even with that in mind, a clear upward trend is evident across the region throughout the 1960s as well as

[76] E.g. Fischer (2001), pp. 17–18; Mustata (2013a), p. 53; Pokorna-Ignatowicz (2003), p. 185.

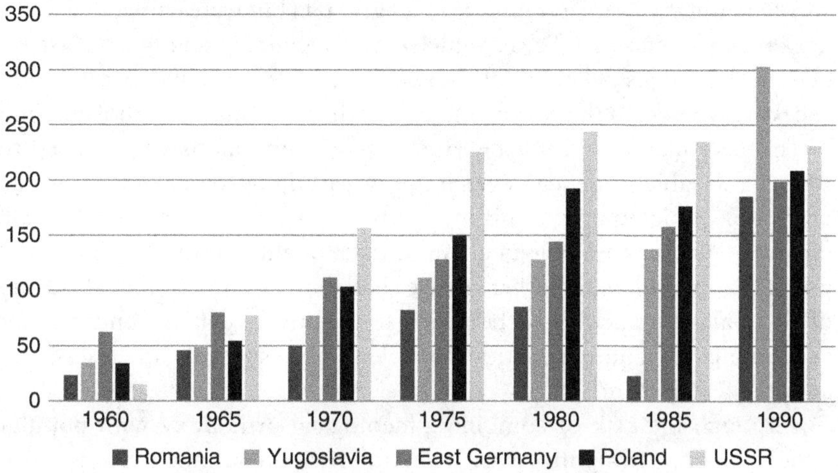

FIGURE 3.3 Growth of broadcast hours in a sample week, 1960–1990.
Note: Data based on the analysis of TV schedules for a sample week, at five-year intervals, from 1960 to 1990. For further details see the Methodological Appendix.

the 1970s. This trend slows down, or even reverses, in the early 1980s, before the final expansion in most countries (except the Soviet Union) in the late 1980s. These results confirm that in terms of broadcasting, the 1970s were not a period of stagnation; rather, the tightening of the party's grip went hand in hand with the further growth of the medium.

The expansion of the viewing public was accompanied by a qualitative shift in social composition. Television was now increasingly a medium watched not only by better-educated white-collar workers, but also by less-educated blue-collar workers. Commenting on the changes in Yugoslavia in 1966, Igor Leandrov, one of the key actors in the early television years in Serbia, argued that the growth of blue-collar workers among TV viewers brought with it 'certain contradictions' and made the task of improving the cultural and educational level of the audience particularly challenging.[77] In the short run, speculated Leandrov, the growth of blue-collar viewers meant that television would be confronted with an audience that was for the time being less educated, but in the long run, once TV reached the whole population, the educational structure of the audience would improve.

[77] RTS-CIJMPA, Report 161, Igor Leandrov, *Programska politika TV u 1967. godini: Teze*, 1966, p. 4.

Such thoughts were not unique to Yugoslavia but were embedded in the notion of the mass media as vehicles of a genuinely common, classless mass culture. This belief underpinned television's relationship with audiences everywhere in the region and meant that communist authorities and TV professionals could not be satisfied with programmes that failed to attract a sizeable audience – even if they were adjudged to be ideologically correct or of high quality. This meant that television had to learn to walk a tightrope between ideological and artistic quality on the one hand and popular approval on the other. As we shall see in Chapter 5, the difficulty of this balancing act could be heard frequently in debates and policies concerning the public functions of television, especially in discussions about entertainment.

Although the task of combining ideological orthodoxy with popular appeal was not straightforward, the authorities' continued efforts eventually bore fruit. The 1970s, in particular, were a period when state socialist television produced a wide range of shows that may be derided today for ideological reasons but were watched enthusiastically at the time. Many of the programmes produced in this period are at the forefront of the analysis in the book. Because entertainment content – unlike news, for instance – was not only widely watched, but also popular, genres belonging to this category offer a particularly good venue for investigating how socialist television sought to co-opt audiences to participate in the communist revolution.

This book focuses in particular on one highly regarded category of entertainment programming: fictional television series. Community dramas such as *Day After Day* (*Den' za dnem,* the Soviet Union, 1971–1972), police procedurals such as *Police Call 110* (*Polizeiruf 110*, East Germany, 1972–1990), war dramas such as the *Four Tank Men and a Dog* (*Czterej Pancerni i Pies*, Poland, 1966–1970) and comedy dramas such as *Theatre in the House* (*Pozorište u kući*, Yugoslavia, 1973–1984), dominated prime-time schedules across the region and typically ranked highest in audience surveys. Alongside these domestically produced drama serials, this book also examines festive programming, ranging from variety shows broadcast on New Year's Eve to live broadcasts of parades and similar festive events marking the broadcast year. Together with television series, such festive programmes are among the most vividly and fondly remembered aspects of socialist television in the post-socialist era. Few of our Russian interviewees failed to mention celebrating the arrival of the New Year while watching the *Little Blue Flame/Little New Year's Flame* (*Goluboi ogonek/Novogodnii ogonek*, 1962–1985), and the same is true for many other interviewees across the region, including those who otherwise scorned and derided the offerings of socialist-era television.

Other genres of socialist TV entertainment should be at least briefly acknowledged here. In the Soviet Union, a particularly successful solution to the demand to balance ideological correctness with entertainment was the development in the 1960s and 1970s of Soviet quiz shows such as *The Club of the Merry and Resourcesful* (KVN – Klub Veselykh i Nakhodchivykh, 1961–1972, 1986 to date) and *Come on, Girls!* (*A nu-ka, devushki!*, 1970–1987), which pitted teams against each other in performing tasks to win prizes.[78] Similar programmes were produced elsewhere in the region, including for instance the game show *Stars of the Stage* (*Gwiazdy Estrady*) and the quiz show *TV Guessing Game* (*Tele-Zgadula*), in Poland, and the game show *Adriatic Encounters* (*Jadranski susreti*, 1978–1980) and the quiz show *Quizcotheque* (*Kviskoteka*, 1980–1995), in Yugoslavia.[79] By and large, however, TV quizzes and game shows were a somewhat less prominent and constant feature of socialist TV programming, and information about them is also less well preserved, which is why they receive only a passing mention in this book. Similar limitations apply to other prominent and widely watched entertainment genres known from socialist television screens, including variety shows and comedy shows, such as for instance the *Cabaret of Elderly Gentlemen* (*Kabaret Starszych Panow*, 1958–1966) in Poland or *A Kettle of Colour* (*Ein Kessel Buntes*, 1972–1990) in East Germany.[80]

THREE MODELS OF STATE SOCIALIST TELEVISION SYSTEMS

Having outlined the key developments over time and identified four key dimensions of variation between state socialist television systems – infrastructural developments, party-state control, core-periphery position, and transnational orientation – it is now time to reflect on this more systematically, situating our five countries with regard to each of the four dimensions then considering whether it is possible to identify distinct types or models of socialist broadcasting based on this.

[78] Evans (2016), pp. 208–215.
[79] Grzelewska et al. (2001), pp. 273–274; Goluža and Novaković (1990).
[80] Dittmar (2010), p. 307; Haltof (2002), p. 140.

Infrastructural Developments

These patterns are easiest to discern with regard to infrastructural developments, not only for the five countries examined in this book, but for the region as a whole. This is largely thanks to the availability of comparable quantitative measures such as the number of TV receivers per capita and collated data on the introduction of regular broadcasting. Based on this, we can distinguish three groups of countries. The Soviet Union, East Germany, and to a lesser extent Czechoslovakia, stand apart from the rest as early adopters, albeit on two slightly different measures: East Germany and Czechoslovakia were the only communist-governed countries where there were fewer than ten inhabitants per TV receiver by the mid-1960s, while the Soviet Union led the way in introducing regular broadcasting in the region, having already done so before World War II. Poland and Hungary rank in the middle on both measures, having introduced regular broadcasting in 1953 and 1957 respectively, where the number of inhabitants per receiver dropped below ten in the late 1960s. Yugoslavia, Romania, Bulgaria, and Albania form the group of late adopters that introduced regular broadcasts in the second half of the 1950s or later and saw the number of inhabitants per TV receiver drop into the single figures in the early 1970s or later. The two aspects of infrastructural development – the start of regular broadcasting and the speed of technology dissemination – are both partly dependent on state regulation and investment in television. In Romania, for instance, both regular broadcasting and the second nationwide channel were introduced earlier than in other late adopters, and even earlier than in East Germany and Poland. Yet, the dissemination of TV receivers lagged behind, demonstrating that state investment can only go so far, and prior infrastructural, scientific, and technological developments impose limitations in their own right.

Party-State Control

With regard to party-state control, distinctions between countries are less clear-cut, not least because, as we have seen in Chapter 3, both the intensity and forms of political control over broadcasting changed considerably over time. Nonetheless, the overview provided in the previous chapter enables us to distinguish between three main types of arrangements and group the countries accordingly. At one end of the spectrum we find Yugoslavia, where the arrangements were most liberal: the dedicated state broadcasting committee was abolished in the late 1960s, and broadcasting professionals also gained greater organizational and financial independence, at least temporarily. At the same time, Yugoslavia also went furthest in introducing market mechanisms, best evident from a relatively high proportion of advertising revenue, a trait aligned with the country's commitment to economic policies known in the literature as market socialism. At the other end of the spectrum we find countries such as the Soviet Union, East Germany, and Romania, where political control over broadcasting was, on average, most extensive and hard line and the presence of market mechanisms was very limited. In the middle lie countries such as Poland, Hungary, and Czechoslovakia, where a reformist state socialist political system coexisted with elements of market socialism, meaning that broadcasting was subjected to less stringent controls and was typically somewhat more reliant on advertising revenue.

Core-Periphery Position

The core-periphery position here refers to the extent to which a particular broadcasting system serves as a model to other systems or, alternatively, models itself on foreign systems. As Afonso de Albequerque points out in his discussion of Latin American media systems, the distinction between central and peripheral media systems should form an important part of global comparisons and is particularly useful when examining former colonies.[81] As shown through our analysis, the distinction also works well in the context of state socialist countries, where broadcasting systems across the region were, at least in part, modelled on Soviet arrangements. That said, a peripheral position does not mean that countries classed as peripheral simply opted for a wholesale adoption of the Soviet model. Even when the peripheral counties sought to mimic the model faithfully, their interpretations of what the model involved may have differed from the self-understanding produced internally within the Soviet Union. Ultimately, then, these peripheries adapted the model in a way that, as Johann Arnason argues, may well have facilitated reinvention rather than a straightforward transfer.[82] As we have seen, Yugoslavia went furthest in this appropriation, seeking to develop a form of broadcasting that also incorporated selected elements found in Western broadcasting systems, including advertising and elements of self-regulation. We could even argue

[81] de Albuquerque (2012). [82] Arnason (2003), p. 308.

that Yugoslavia aspired to establish itself as an 'alternative core' to the Soviet Union and sought to promote its broadcasting production as a model for members of the Non-Aligned Movement.

Transnational Orientation

As far as transnational orientation is concerned – including specifically openness to the West – it is worth noting that we approach this dimension in two distinct ways: we examine these countries in relation to competition from Western cross-border television signals but also with regard to the orientation of institutional and technological ties, as can be perceived from the country's membership in either the EBU or the OIRT and from the country's decision to opt either for the West German PAL or the Franco-Soviet SECAM. While institutional and technological ties help define the extent of Soviet influence (in the sense that countries more closely subjected to Soviet interference were likely to be more hostile to ties with the West), exposure to Western signals was dependent on the country's geographical position and cultural (especially linguistic) proximity, and therefore partly free of political oversight. East German television, for instance, may have been subjected to fairly rigid control but was also affected by the competition with West German television, which was close to local audiences in both geographic and cultural terms. As a result, we can assume that on this measure, East Germany was not as far removed from other countries as the levels of Soviet oversight may appear to suggest.

Taking this into consideration, we can offer the following typology of the five television systems in our sample. At one end of the scale is Yugoslav television as the most pro-Western in the region: the country was exposed to broadcasting from Italy and Austria, was a member of the EBU, and adopted PAL over SECAM. In the middle of the spectrum we find East Germany and Romania, which were either exposed to Western signals (East Germany) or opted for PAL over SECAM (Romania). Poland and the Soviet Union are situated towards the opposite end of the spectrum as countries that were least open to the West both geographically and in terms of institutional and technological ties. We should also note, however, that the Soviet Union, as the core country of the socialist world, had an added motivation to keep the West at arm's length. Unlike the peripheral countries in the region, including Poland, it had to act as a model for others and use its television as a means of demonstrating its superiority vis-à-vis the

West. It is therefore feasible to argue that the combination of the core-periphery dynamics and the country's geographic position and institutional ties meant that Soviet television was systemically the least open to the West.

Based on these four dimensions, we can identify three broad subtypes of state socialist television systems in Eastern Europe: market state socialist, represented in our sample by Yugoslavia; reformist state socialist, represented by Poland, and hard-line state socialist, represented above all by the Soviet Union, but also largely by Romania and East Germany. As evident from Table 3.2, the market state socialist model is characterized by moderate party-state control, a high level of openness to the West, late infrastructural development, and an aspiration to act as an alternative to the Soviet core. The hard-line state socialist model, on the other hand, is marked by almost complete party-state control, low levels of openness to the West, a combination of early and late infrastructural development, and location either in the Soviet core or in a country strongly influenced by the core. The reformist state socialist model falls midway between the two on all dimensions.

Several qualifications are in order at this point. Much as Hallin and Mancini do with regard to their typology of media systems in Western Europe and Northern America,[83] we offer this typology with some hesitation: the three models are not meant to provide a faithful description that fits every single case perfectly; rather, they should be treated as ideal types in the Weberian sense and hence as analytical tools that can help us reflect on the internal diversity of socialist broadcasting and on how the different dimensions of diversity related to one another. In line with this, the five countries we examine approximate the three models to different degrees: while Yugoslavia and the Soviet Union match their type more or less perfectly, the three other countries featured in our sample each diverged from their type in one or more dimensions, suggesting that they combined elements of more than one model. Romanian and GDR television fit the hard-line state socialist model in most dimensions, but were considerably more open to the West than were other countries in this group, while Polish television largely matched the reformist state socialist model, but was systemically less open to the West than were other countries in this category. Although not discussed

[83] Hallin and Mancini (2004), pp. 69–73.

TABLE 3.2 *State socialist television systems in Eastern Europe: three models*

	Market State Socialist System *Yugoslavia*	Reformist State Socialist System *Czechoslovakia, Hungary, Poland*	Hard-line State Socialist System *Albania, Bulgaria, the GDR, Romania, the USSR*
Timing of Infrastructural Developments	Late adoption	Early and mid-range adoption	Early and late adoption
Extent of Party-State Control	Moderate party-state control, with pronounced elements of self-regulation and/or commercial system	Strong party-state control, with some elements of self-regulation and/or commercial system	Almost complete party-state control, self-regulation and commercial elements limited to non-existent
Transnational Orientation/ Openness to the West	High: EBU membership, PAL system, exposure to Western TV signals	Medium: OIRT membership, SECAM system, exposure to Western TV signals (except Poland)	Low to medium: OIRT membership, SECAM system (except Romania), little or no exposure to Western TV signals (except the GDR)
Core-Periphery Position	(Aspiring) alternative core	Periphery, moderately influenced by the Soviet core	Soviet core, or periphery heavily influenced by the Soviet core (Albania until 1960, Romania until 1965)

in depth here, Hungary and Czechoslovakia largely fit the reformist model, while Albania and Bulgaria embodied the hard-line model.

Furthermore, although we have allocated countries to the three types of broadcast systems, we should note that this obscures significant changes over time. As noted in the previous section, the 1960s were marked by less stringent party controls, whereas all countries in our sample experienced a tightening of party control over the medium at some point in the 1970s. From this perspective, Yugoslavia moved closer to the reformist state socialist model, while Czechoslovakia and Poland moved from a reformist to a more hard-line model. The nature and focus of control changed too: the early years of television were characterised by concerns over the infrastructural aspects of the medium, while later, the focus of interest shifted towards the message. The relative core-periphery position could also change considerably. While virtually all countries initially followed the Soviet model, several gradually broke away from it in more or less radical ways – most notably Yugoslavia, but also Albania after 1960 and Romania after 1965. These nuances suggest that the typology should not be treated as static, but as temporally dynamic, with individual broadcast systems moving closer to or further away from a particular model over time or even embodying different models at different points in time.

Finally, the decision to use countries as key units of analysis masks important internal differences. Both Yugoslav and Soviet broadcasting infrastructures were marked by large disparities, with republics in the northwestern parts of the two countries (Slovenia and Croatia in Yugoslavia, and the Baltic republics in the Soviet Union) reaching a full saturation of TV receivers much earlier than did regions located further south and east. The same republics were also more exposed to Western broadcasting.

As we demonstrate in Parts Two and Three of the book, the three types of state socialist television systems gave rise to distinct types of television cultures, which varied reasonably systematically along four of the seven dimensions introduced in Chapter 2: publicness (Chapter 5), privacy (Chapter 6), transnationalism (Chapter 7), and temporal orientation (Chapters 8–10).

Other Contextual Factors

The three types of TV systems, and the four dimensions of systemic variation they are based on, are of course insufficient to explain all of the differences and changes among state socialist television cultures examined in the book. In addition, five further dimensions need to be brought into the picture: (a) gender relations, (b) the extent of secularization (c) the size of the economy, (d) ethno-cultural diversity, and (e) the historical trajectory of state- and nation-building and especially the role of communist rule in this context. These five aspects differ in several important respects from the four systemic dimensions examined earlier. First, they are sociocultural or economic in nature rather than belonging to the political ream. As such, they have shaped the trajectories of state socialist television in a more partial manner and typically help explain only limited aspects of variation between television cultures. Second, these factors are external to the media, and information on how they affected media systems is scarce to non-existent. Third, even where the corresponding media systemic dimensions can be reconstructed, they do not co-vary with the four dimensions of television systems examined so far. It is due to this that we did not include these dimensions in the typology of television systems. Rather than thinking of them as core aspects of systemic variation, it is better to understand them as intervening forces, which modify television systems and cultures without changing their core architecture.

Gender Relations

The first additional dimension brought into play in our analysis concerns gender relations. State socialist countries all shared a commitment to women's emancipation, which was seen – in line with communist ideals – to reside in economic independence and participation in the labour force. As a result, all communist-led countries implemented policies designed to facilitate women's employment, which far outstripped the industrialized economies of the West. As shown by a quick comparison of available data from the late 1980s and early 1990s for a selection of Eastern and Western European as well as North American countries, the female share of the workforce in most state socialist countries came close to 50 per cent, while the share in most of those west of the Iron Curtain hovered around 40 per cent.[84]

It is feasible to expect that these differences in women's participation in the labour force had counterparts in media employment; comparative data from the state socialist era do not exist, but available studies from the early post-socialist years confirm this expectation: in the mid-1990s, women's share in the broadcast workforce in Eastern European countries stood at 45 per cent or more, higher than anywhere else in Europe, and several countries in the region also had higher than average shares of female production executives.[85] High levels of women's employment of

[84] For comparative figures for Eastern Europe see Łobodzínska (1995), p. 23. For Western Europe and North America, Johnston (1991), p. 119.

[85] Pajnik (2012).

course did not mean that state socialist countries succeeded in overcoming obstacles to gender inequality. Despite their participation in waged labour, women continued to shoulder the bulk of household work and equal participation in political life also proved difficult to achieve.[86] As we shall see, these distinct gendered structures of state socialist societies had an impact on the gendered patterns of TV cultures in the region, including domestic viewing practices and the representations of women on screen (Chapter 6), as well as scheduling patterns (Chapter 8).

Extent of Secularization

The second additional dimension of variation to consider is the extent of secularization, understood broadly as the extent of tolerance for religious traditions in a particular society. Official communist policies were of course hostile towards religion throughout the region, with religious beliefs considered to be a superstitious and atavistic remnant of workers' false consciousness. This hostility also had its counterpart in daily and weekly patterns of broadcasting, which were completely detached from a religious temporality (Chapter 8). Yet, despite a shared animosity towards religion, the five countries differed with regard to the amount of religious expression they were prepared to allow citizens. Soviet society was the most militant in terms of prohibiting religious symbols in public life, followed by Romania and Yugoslavia, while the churches in Poland and East Germany were allowed more leeway and played a role in the regime's downfall.[87] These differences were reflected in the nature of the festive calendars adopted in the five countries and consequently also in the character of media holidays celebrated on screen (Chapter 10).

Size of the Economy

The *size of the economy*, closely related to the scale of investment in broadcasting, has received considerable attention in the existing literature on international broadcasting flows in different parts of the world, where it has been shown to play a role in shaping the relative dependence on foreign imports and the volume of domestic production.[88] As demonstrated in Chapter 7, this factor also played a role in shaping the transnational flows of TV programming in state socialist Europe.

[86] Corin (1992); Lapidus (1982); Łobodzínska (1995).
[87] Mojzes (1992); Ramet (1984).
[88] E.g. Dupagne and Waterman (1998); Picard (2011); Štětka (2012b).

Ethno-Cultural Diversity

The third additional contextual factor we take into account concerns ethno-cultural diversity, specifically the extent of ethno-cultural homogeneity characteristic of different countries in the region. Two broad groups can be distinguished: one comprises highly diverse countries with large, well-established ethno-cultural minorities, or even without a clear ethno-cultural majority, such as Yugoslavia and the Soviet Union; the other includes countries that are ethno-culturally more homogeneous and include only a relatively small proportion of ethno-cultural minorities, such as Poland, East Germany, or Romania. These two patterns of diversity tend to give rise to different structures of media systems: countries belonging to the first group typically have a federalised broadcasting system, where each major ethno-cultural group is served by a separate television channel, while countries in the second group tend to have a single, countrywide broadcasting system, which mostly caters to the ethno-cultural majority but also incorporates some dedicated programmes for ethno-cultural minorities.[89] As we shall see, this dimension of variation helps explain some of the cross-country differences in the public mission of television broadcasting (Chapter 5), as well as some aspects of everyday scheduling practices and media holidays (Chapters 8 and 10).

The Role of Communist Rule in the Trajectory of State- and Nation-Building

Finally, the role of communist rule in the trajectory of state- and nation-building is a factor we consider when seeking to explain the different ways of dealing with the communist past. Here, the key distinction is between countries that achieved independent statehood and the current form of nation-state arrangement independently from the arrival of communist rule, typically before the twentieth century, and those countries where the arrival of communist rule played a key role in attaining the current territorial shape, national composition, and form of statehood. In the first category we find Poland and Romania, while Yugoslavia, the Soviet Union, and East Germany all belong to the second category. As we shall see, this distinction can be linked to different patterns of historical narratives on screen (Chapter 9).

[89] Mihelj (2012).

CONCLUSIONS

In this chapter we have provided a broad historical overview of key developments in state socialist broadcasting and used this account to introduce the key contextual factors needed to understand why state socialist television cultures developed in the ways they did. To this end, we also introduced a typology of state socialist television systems, which vary on four key dimensions: the timing of infrastructural developments, the extent of party-state control, transnational orientation (and specifically openness to the West), and core-periphery position. In addition, we have also considered five further aspects of context that influenced the formation of television cultures in state socialist Eastern Europe: gender relations, the extent of secularization, the size of the economy, ethnocultural diversity, and the role of communist rule in the historical trajectory of state- and nation-building.

We would suggest that the contextual factors outlined here also offer a good basis for situating state socialist television trajectories vis-à-vis their counterparts elsewhere in the world, specifically in the West. To be able to explain that, however, we first need to discuss the relationship between television and modernity and introduce the notion of entangled varieties of modernity. It is to this task that we turn in the following chapter.

4

Television and Varieties of Modernity

The mass media are among the central institutions of the modern world, indispensable for the functioning of modern societies. Although means of spreading messages to large audiences have existed throughout human history, mediated communication became much more important during the modern epoch. In the world of politics, ideas of popular sovereignty and democratic representation meant that political decision-making could no longer be the sole domain of small elites but rather had to involve, and hence be communicated to, a mass electorate. The rise of new technologies of reproduction – initially the invention of print and then the inventions of photography, telegraphy, and broadcasting – made it possible to transmit messages to large audiences with relative ease. At the same time, the commercialization of cultural production meant that mass communication was not only technologically viable and politically necessary but also constituted a lucrative business. And finally, in the cultural realm, the belief in the human capacity for reason and the parallel decline of religious beliefs set the stage for forms of mass communication governed by rational thought and oriented to secular problems.

This story of mass communication as an integral element of modern developments is a familiar and compelling one. But it is also very narrow: it assumes that the rise of modern media is dependent on the co-presence of liberal democracy, a capitalist economy, and often also secularization. In short, it is a story modelled on a particular constellation of modern developments that began evolving in the late Middle Ages and the early modern period and became dominant in Western Europe and North America in the eighteenth century. As Wagner points out in a recent discussion of theories of modernity, this common narrative also often entails a belief in the superiority of the West and an assumption that the twin advent of democratic and industrial revolutions transformed the West into a leading force of progress, providing a template that 'would diffuse worldwide because of its inherent superiority'.[1]

This narrow, West-centred understanding of modernity dominated social scientific thinking well into the second half of the twentieth century.[2] In line with this, several of the classic post-World War II studies of mass communication were underpinned by the assumption that the rise of modern media inevitably implies a progression towards the forms of arrangements known in the West. For instance, in their influential discussion of four theories of the press, Fredrick Siebert and colleagues offered an analysis of the different political ideas that governed mass communication around the world at the time – authoritarianism, libertarianism, social responsibility, and communism – yet did so in a way that not only privileged the solutions adopted in the West but also implied that the alternative set-ups were somehow less modern and ultimately caught in traditional, outdated beliefs that had to be overcome for truly progressive forms of communication to take root.[3]

From the mid-1960s onwards, these entrenched views of modernity began to be challenged on different fronts. They were criticised for their value-laden nature, as well as for the lack of firm empirical support and insufficient attention to context.[4] More recently, their links with Cold War politics, including the need to provide legitimacy for Western intervention abroad, has also come under scrutiny.[5] What emerged from these critiques was the acknowledgment that the form of modernity associated with liberal democracy, a capitalist economy, and secularization is only one among many and that the pursuit of progress inspired by the Enlightenment has given rise to different visions of modern society, articulated in a variety of political programmes and embodied in a range of economic, political, and sociocultural structures.

The varieties of modern media systems and media cultures encountered around the world can likewise be thought of as articulations of different notions of modern society, designed to promote divergent visions of progress. This chapter lays out a framework for thinking of the diversity of media trajectories as rooted in varieties of modernity, building on three strands of the existing literature: general debates about multiple

[1] Wagner (2012), p. 1. [2] See Sztompka (1993), pp. 101–112.
[3] Siebert et al. (1969 [1956]). [4] E.g. Moore (1993 [1966]); Eisenstadt (1974).
[5] E.g. Gilman (2007).

modernities,[6] existing discussions of alternative modernities in the context of mass communication,[7] and comparative media systems research.[8] The first part of the chapter summarizes general arguments about multiple modernities and explains how and why state socialism should be approached as a variety of modernity. The second part applies this framework to the media and uses it to situate the state socialist television trajectories examined in the previous chapter vis-à-vis models of broadcasting elsewhere in the world, with a particular focus on those that evolved in Western Europe and North America after World War II.

FROM A SINGLE MODERNITY TO ENTANGLED VARIETIES OF MODERNITY

Embracing the notion of varieties of modernity does not mean rejecting the universal nature of modernity altogether or denying the European roots of some of the core ideas and institutional arrangements of modernity. Despite marked differences in the understanding of what it means to be modern and widely disparate conceptions of what modern progress should entail and aim for, the varieties of modernity all emanate from a shared set of core assumptions. The first of these is what Göran Therborn calls a particular time orientation, that is, a conception of time that sees the future as 'open, novel, reachable and constructable', the present as 'a possible preparation for a future', and the past 'as either something to leave behind or as a heap of ruins, pieces of which might be used for building a new future'.[9] The second shared ingredient involves the belief that human beings are inherently free, capable of reasoning, and able to use reason to understand the world.[10] A third shared premise comprises a particular dynamics of identity construction, based on the opposition between the modern, civilized 'self' and the underdeveloped, backward, and primitive 'other'.[11] Taken together, these core assumptions come together in the notion of human-led progress, grounded in rational thought, oriented towards the future, and constructed in opposition to the past.

6 E.g. Arnason (2000); Dirlik (2003); Eisenstadt (1974); Schmidt (2006); Therborn (2003).
7 E.g. Abu-Lughod (2005); Khiabany (2009); Kraidy (2010); Lau (2002); Lewis et al. (2016); Mihelj (2011a); Pertierra and Turner (2013).
8 E.g. Dobek-Ostrowska et al. (2010); Guerrero and Márquez-Ramírez (2014); Hallin and Mancini (2004, 2012a); Voltmer (2013).
9 Therborn (2003), p. 294. See also Koselleck (2004).
10 Wagner (2012), p. 2.
11 Pickering (2001), pp. 51–53.

Did this shared set of ideas also give rise to a common core of institutional arrangements? Here, the existing literature offers limited guidance, largely because the vast majority of discussion revolves around the cultural features of modernity. Nonetheless, authors writing about multiple modernities or varieties of modernity do identify some shared institutional developments or, at least, constellations of developments. One of these is structural or functional differentiation between social spheres, and consequently their growing autonomy: the differentiation of science and education from religion, the differentiation of the economy, culture, and the mass media from politics, etc. Such differentiation is seen as a key ingredient of modernization already in a range of classic theories, from Émile Durkheim's *The Division of Labour in Society* to Talcott Parsons's work on the functional differentiation of modern social systems.[12] Proponents of multiple modernities take this argument on board but emphasize that differentiation can occur in different ways. According to Shmuel N. Eisenstadt, 'a general trend towards structural differentiation' between different social arenas appeared in versions of modernity around the globe, yet 'the ways in which these arenas were defined and organised varied greatly'.[13] Johann P. Arnason develops a compatible argument, suggesting that the institutional frameworks of modernity are best approached 'as a loosely structured constellation rather than a system'.[14] From this perspective, every version of modernity will include some of the characteristic infrastructural developments associated with modernization – such as industrialization, the rise of a capitalist economy, the formation of a modern state, or the separation of church and state – but will not necessarily encompass all of them. In line with this, Arnason also suggests that these diverse constellations of modern developments are associated with distinct forms of differentiation.[15]

The core assumptions of modernity outlined earlier were originally developed in the context of the European Enlightenment, and several of the institutional developments mentioned so far can also be traced back to Western Europe. In this sense, modernity can be seen as originating in the West. Yet, we should be wary of assuming that this origin of modernity's core premises also led to a single vision of Western modernity, which was applied uniformly and exported as such worldwide. This is an important point, not least because the historical actors involved in different

[12] Durkheim (1984 [1893]); Parsons (1971). [13] Eisenstadt (2000), pp. 1–2.
[14] Arnason (2000), pp. 64–65. [15] Ibid. pp. 71–55.

modernizing projects – including those we will encounter over the course of our book – often spoke of the West in homogenous terms. Such language is misleading: Western societies have historically served as battlegrounds for competing modernizing visions and followed different trajectories of institutional modernization.

The twentieth century in particular was marked by a struggle between three main rival political ideologies – liberalism, fascism, and communism – that differed markedly in their interpretations of the modern condition, in the transformative ideas they pursued, and ultimately also in the institutional set-ups they became associated with.[16] These three rival ideologies can also be linked to the distinct constellations of socio-economic and political arrangements they arose from. In his *Social Origins of Dictatorship and Democracy*, Barrington Moore distinguished between three 'routes to modern society' – the bourgeois revolution, the revolution from above, and the revolution from below – that eventually led to the formation of three main types of modern political regimes – liberal democracy, fascism, and communism or state socialism. In Moore's analysis, the three routes varied considerably in the extent of commercialization and industrialization and, as a consequence, in the relative strength of the class with an independent economic base, namely the bourgeoisie. Together with the constraints of the state bureaucracy, this factor was influential in determining the roles played by the other two key actors in the modernizing process, namely the peasantry and the landed upper classes, and the extent to which the bourgeoisie, when seeking to subvert existing hierarchies of power, would have to seek alliances either with the former (which would lead to the communist route) or with the latter (leading to the fascist route).[17]

Once we look beyond the West, the diversity of modern trajectories proliferates: transposed onto a global stage, the modern pursuit of progress became entangled with a wide variety of historical legacies, political traditions, economic arrangements, social divisions, and cultural sensitivities that contributed to a further diversification of competing visions of modernity, as well as to a proliferation of modern institutions designed to facilitate their realization. One of the most important implications of this diversity, as Eisenstadt argues, is that modernization does not equal Westernization, even though Western patterns of modernization 'enjoy historical precedence and continue to be a reference point for others'.[18]

[16] For overviews see Delanty (2016); Mihelj (2011a).
[17] Moore (1993 [1966]).
[18] Eisenstadt (2000), pp. 2–3.

Again, it is important to remember that the diverse trajectories of modernization that evolved beyond Western Europe and North America cannot be reduced to cultural or civilizational differences alone. This tendency is often found among proponents of the multiple modernities thesis, including Eisenstadt, who derive the multiplicity of modernities primarily from cultural or civilizational differences, and in that sense also talk of 'Asian', 'Arab', 'Chinese', 'Japanese', or 'Indian' variants of modernity as if they were internally homogeneous, stemming from a stable, shared cultural core. Instead, as Arif Dirlik argues, we should acknowledge that contestations over modernity 'cut across national and civilizational boundaries' and take place 'within the cultural, civilizational, national or ethnic spaces' that are often adopted as units of analysis taken for granted.[19] Cultural differences do of course matter, but they are insufficient to explain the diversity of modern trajectories of development. To emphasize this, our analysis avoids the term 'multiple modernities' and instead refers to 'varieties of modernity'.

The need to treat the different routes into modernity as sharing in the same global process of modernity is not self-evident, not least because some are championed by political movements and groups that style themselves as distinctly anti-modern. This is particularly evident in the case of fascist political projects, which saw industrialization and especially democratization as major threats to the established social and moral orders and promised to restore old certainties and sources of stability and unity. Crucially, none of these projects rejected modernity wholesale but rather advocated a vision of the future that involved a selective adoption and recombination of existing responses to the challenges of progress.[20] German Nazis, for instance, were opposed to liberal democracy and saw it as a major cause of social fragmentation and the moral decay of the Weimar Republic, but promised to overcome the chaos and anomie it caused by using distinctly modern means – modern technologies and a modern state apparatus – put into the service of the German nation.[21] Likewise, Italian Fascism offered a vision of the future that would purportedly allow Italians to enjoy the benefits of modernity while circumventing its alleged detrimental effects on the cultural traditions and moral order.[22] Both German Nazism and Italian Fascism also embraced some of the key tenets of economic liberalism, but in the

[19] Dirlik (2003), p. 295. [20] Griffin (2007). [21] Bauman (1989); Herf (1986).
[22] Ben-Ghiat (2004).

absence of a strong bourgeoisie, the implementation of a capitalist economy was reliant on support from the landed classes and the state apparatus.[23]

The various political projects associated with communism are also often treated as anti-modern.[24] Lenin was well known for his disparaging attitudes to 'bourgeois liberalism' and was also vocal in his criticisms of the slow workings of democratic institutions and the bureaucracy-heavy 'bourgeois legality'.[25] Yet, much like liberal democracy and fascism, communism too was rooted in Enlightenment ideals, including the belief in an autonomous human being, capable of enlisting the powers of reason and science for the purpose of social advancement.[26] Furthermore, communist leaders explicitly saw themselves as modernizers and conceived of their project as being more advanced than that of their capitalist rivals. Propelled by the Marxist vision of human progress, they sought to create a post-capitalist modernity – one in which 'free associations of producers' would take centre stage and ultimately dispense not only with the market, but also with the state.[27] Even though the stateless vision was never achieved in practice, it continued to play a central role in communist visions of modernity, from Mao Zedong's notion of 'neither plan nor market' to the Yugoslav project of 'self-management', the latter of which was premised on the ideal of self-managing collectives of workers that exerted full control over social development, without being subjected either to state or to market.

The modernizing impetus of communism also fuelled a number of far-reaching processes of economic, political, and sociocultural transformation which are commonly found in Western European and North American pathways to modernity. As Arnason points out, the introduction of communist rule from the Soviet Union to North Korea went hand in hand with industrialization, the building of a modern state complete with a modern organizational and military apparatus, the introduction of compulsory education and mass literacy campaigns, and an increasing reliance on science as a basis of development.[28] A range of other modern developments, institutions, and cultural traits can be added to the list, including the social welfare state, mass culture and mass politics, surveillance, and the distinctly modern discipline of the self, based on the internalization of authority.[29] Taken together, these processes and

[23] Moore (1993 [1966]). [24] Lenoe (2004); Poe (2003). [25] Burbank (1995), p. 33.
[26] Furet (1999), p. 63; Kotkin (1995), pp. 6–8. [27] Arnason (2000), p. 69.
[28] Ibid. pp. 66–68. [29] E.g. Hoffmann (2003); Holquist (1997); Kotsonis (2000).

traits clearly suggest that communism constituted a modern political project and set in motion a range of modernizing processes, although it did so in ways that differed from the varieties of modernity found elsewhere in the world.

One fundamental objection to the inclusion of communism as a variety of modernity is its apparent lack of structural and functional differentiation between different social spheres. This is an important objection to consider, not least because notions of differentiation also underpinned classic debates on media and modernization and the early work on comparative media research in the first decades after World War II[30] and remain central in recent comparative work on media systems.[31] Indeed, the amalgamation of political, economic, and cultural power and its concentration in the hands of a party-state seem to be at odds with the logic of differentiation. Yet we should equally note that this peculiar 'de-differentiaton' of economy, politics, and culture vis-à-vis the party-state was designed to ensure their differentiation from other social spheres and forces, most notably the imperatives of the market, the interests of the bourgeoisie, and the principles advanced by religious institutions. As we shall see in the chapters that follow, notions of differentiation and autonomy were at the core of ideas advanced by media theorists and policy makers in state socialist countries. In their view, Western media were trapped in the logic of the market and subjected to the interests of the bourgeoisie, while state socialist media, thanks to party-state oversight, were insulated from the encroachment of the market and served the welfare of the working class. Despite obvious misconceptions and exaggerations, such self-understandings make clear that societies rooted in communist notions of modernity were not hostile to differentiation as such but rather sought to implement it differently than in the West.

Such a view, which rejects a single route of modern differentiation, is compatible with theories developed by Jürgen Habermas and Pierre Bourdieu, which have played an important role in influencing recent debates about social differentiation, autonomy, and power with regard to the media. Although Habermas saw the initial rise of the bourgeois public sphere and its separation from the private realm as dependent on the formation of a free market and the growth of the bourgeoisie, he also argued that the subsequent advent of consumer capitalism and commercialization led to a blurring of the distinction between the private

[30] Lerner (1958); Pye (1963). [31] Hallin and Macini (2004), pp. 76–84, 287–294.

and the public, leading to the destruction of the public sphere as such.[32] Put differently, the factors that initially fostered the process of differentiation later contributed to its demise. Bourdieu approached issues of differentiation from a different theoretical perspective, grounded in field theory, but reached a similar conclusion. In his view, the relationships between different 'fields' or spheres of social action – including the media or journalism – do not evolve in a unilinear fashion. A field that is relatively autonomous at one point in time can later become heteronomous, or subjected to the influence of other fields.[33] If we conceive of the media as a field, we could therefore argue that its relative autonomy or level of differentiation from other fields can shift over time, as well as varying from context to context: in one setting, the media can be autonomous from the sphere of politics but subordinated to the logic of the economy, while in another setting, the reverse can occur. Although neither Habermas nor Bourdieu associated their arguments with notions of varieties of modernity, it is clear that their understanding of differentiation is broadly compatible with the approach to modernity and media adopted in this book.

So far, we have discussed communist modernity in generic terms, emphasizing the shared elements across state socialist countries without paying attention to significant differences between them or changes over time. Furthermore, although we have acknowledged the shared roots of the key varieties of modernity, our account has proceeded as if these varieties, once constituted, evolved largely independently from one another. This may have left a false impression of how we intend to apply the framework of multiple modernities to the comparative investigation of media systems and cultures, leading the reader to expect that our analysis will effectively amount to a static, binary distinction between liberal-democratic and state socialist-authoritarian media. This is not our intention; rather, the analysis we develop in this book also seeks to use the framework of multiple modernities to map the internal diversity of the media (and specifically of television) during communist rule, both across countries and across time, and to show how this internal diversity evolved, in part, out of a set of exchanges and conversations with specific local conditions as well as with alternative visions and developments in other locales, both within and beyond state socialist countries.

[32] Habermas (1989). [33] Bourdieu (1984).

This approach to the diversity of modern media is inspired by recent debates that foreground the idea of entangled modernities. This notion is based on the recognition that no vision of modernity evolves in isolation, but always with reference to, and influenced by, other ideas and social arrangements. There are two basic forms of entanglement in play: entanglements with local conditions and historical legacies, and entanglements with alternative modern visions and institutions developed elsewhere.[34] Both of these forms of entanglement influence the ways in which a particular project of modernity develops.

The most obvious examples are found in the mutual exchanges and influences between the most starkly opposed visions of modernity. For instance, the evolution of communism in Russia and nazism in Germany cannot be understood fully without taking into account the history of economic, political, and cultural exchanges between the two countries, and the mutual misperceptions generated through these encounters, from German beliefs in the inherent 'Asianness' and backwardness of Russia to critical remarks by Russian observers about the German obsession with order.[35] Likewise, some of the key distinguishing tenets of Soviet communism, including the command economy, the fusion of the party and the state, and ideological orthodoxy in education and science, evolved not just from principles inherent to Marxist thought or from local conditions and historical legacies but also out of the global rivalry with Western European and especially North American versions of liberal modernity.[36] Such reciprocal influences persisted throughout the state socialist era and became particularly pronounced during the 1960s, when they spilled over into several arenas of culture and everyday life, from consumption and fashion to interior design and popular culture, where rival visions of modern life were promoted and contested.[37]

Transnational entanglements of this kind also gave rise to internal diversification among visions of modern life associated with the same political principles and economic arrangements. The varieties of state socialism that evolved historically around the globe offer a case in point. Rather than following a single, invariable model of development, each state socialist country adopted its own variety, shaped in response to local conditions and historical legacies and emerging out of a conversation both

[34] Arnason (2003), p. 308; Therborn (2003), p. 295. [35] David-Fox et al. (2012).
[36] Arnason (2003), pp. 71–72; David-Fox (2012); Kotkin (1995).
[37] Gorsuch and Koenker (2013); Reid (2002).

with communist-led projects and non-communist alternatives. The Chinese model of modernity, as advocated by Mao Zedong, was in part conditioned by the country's largely rural population but also relied on a radicalization of the Soviet model, including the attempt to abolish the party-state and replace it with a union of the leader and the people, and the effort to create an advanced socialist economy that functioned independently from both market mechanisms and state planning and relied instead on intensified mass mobilization.[38] The state socialist countries of Eastern Europe likewise departed from the Soviet model and developed their own varieties of state socialism, partly inspired by projects of modernity developed elsewhere. This was most evident in Yugoslavia, Romania, and Albania, which all openly proclaimed their independence from the Soviet Union at different points in time and either developed closer relationships with the West or turned to China for inspiration. Even countries that remained closely allied with the Soviet Union throughout the state socialist period did not mimic Soviet arrangements wholesale: both Hungary and Poland experimented with elements of market competition and implemented economic policies resembling those found in Yugoslavia.[39] Furthermore, different visions of communist modernity often coexisted within the same country, and occasionally erupted into major political, social, and cultural upheavals, as was the case with several state socialist countries in the late 1960s.[40]

As we argue in the following section, the notion of entangled varieties of modernity offers a useful theoretical framework for understanding the varieties of modern media systems and media cultures globally. We first consider existing attempts to bring the notions of multiple or alternative modernities to bear on the analysis of media systems and cultures and then discuss how this framework can be connected to comparative media research. In the first step, we show how the entangled varieties of modernity relate to the different trajectories of media development in the state socialist world. In the second step, we discuss how the framework can be extended to enable a comparison between state socialist and Western media cultures.

VARIETIES OF MODERNITY, VARIETIES OF MODERN MEDIA

In recent literature, there is no shortage of criticism of the Euro- or west-centric nature of debates on media and modernity. Several authors have

[38] Arnason (2003), pp. 323–324. [39] Kornai (1992). [40] Arnason (2005).

sought to draw on the notion of multiple modernities to account for the diversity of media developments around the globe, from East Asia to Latin America and the Arab world. What emerges from this body of work is an understanding of different media as 'instruments' or 'tools' of modernity,[41] with specific media genres treated as 'technologies of modern self-making' or as 'social laboratories' in which varieties of modernity are contested.[42] As noted in the preceding chapters, references to multiple modernities are also common in recent work on state socialist media, from Evans's point about Soviet television history as shaped by the global contest over the inheritance of the Enlightenment,[43] to our own arguments about state socialist television as an alternative form of modern television.[44]

This body of work has two shared traits. First, it typically deals with examples drawn from beyond Western Europe and North America. Second, it is focused primarily on cultural rather than systemic or political aspects of the media. Most often, the notion of a variety of modernities is applied to interpret media texts – such as television programmes, films, or popular songs – and to show how they promote different understandings of modern life and the modern self or serve as fora where different visions of modernity are articulated and contested.[45] In some cases, cognate arguments are employed in the study of communication technologies as material objects, drawing attention to how iconic objects such as TV towers have become involved in the global contest over modernity. The Berlin TV tower offers a good case in point: as evident from tourist brochures and memorabilia from the era, the tower featured among the key iconic buildings in East Germany and acted as a material symbol of socialist modernity (Figure 4.1).[46]

In contrast, the notion of multiple or entangled modernities is virtually never taken up in discussions of Western media or in comparative work on media systems. Arguably, this is partly due to a lack of elective affinity between the multiple/entangled modernities approach on the one hand and the media systems debate on the other: while the former focuses primarily on cultural and philosophical aspects of modernity, the latter

41 Lau (2002), p. 3; Pertierra and Turner (2013), p. 123.

42 Abu-Lughod (2005), pp. 111–134; Kraidy (2010), p. 18.

43 Evans (2016), pp. 30–31.

44 Mihelj and Huxtable (2016a).

45 E.g. Abu-Lughod (2005); Kraidy (2010).

46 See Standley (2011). See also the collection of commemorative plates and other memorabilia (including a puzzle) featuring the Berlin TV tower, held in the collection of the Wende Museum in Los Angeles.

FIGURE 4.1 Berlin TV tower, 1970. *Source*: Fortepan / LHM.

privileges institutional and political aspects of communication. As a result, comparative media systems research either avoids discussing the notion of modernity altogether, discusses it in terms of developments that occurred in the West,[47] or deploys theories that help make sense of the diversity of media systems without recourse to notions of modernity, such as the theory of 'multiple democracies'.[48]

The entangled modernities approach that we have adopted is of clear relevance to this book's focus on non-Western media cultures, but this framework can also provide a useful basis for examining the diversity of global media systems. To demonstrate this, we shall revisit the dimensions of variation between television systems introduced in the previous chapter, discuss how they relate to different articulations of modernity, and consider how they can be used to situate state socialist media systems vis-à-vis their Western counterparts. The arguments we develop here should be read as suggestions, and we shall therefore abstain from offering a fully fledged global typology of television systems. Such a typology would require a considerably more elaborated analysis and draw on a much wider range of research and literature than we have space for here.

The most obvious starting point for a global mapping is the **extent of state control** over broadcasting, not least because differences in the role of the state vis-à-vis the media are repeatedly used in existing comparative media systems work. In line with the notion of structural and functional differentiation as a shared trait of all varieties of modernity, it is useful to think of the state-media relationship as one possible form of differentiation and hence compare different media systems with regard to the extent to which they are differentiated from the state. From this perspective, state socialist systems are marked by much lower levels of differentiation than are their Western counterparts. This set-up was aligned with a vision of modern progress that required the leadership of the communist party in all areas of social life. This leadership was exercised through the amalgamation of party and state structures. In the realm of the media, the party-state was expected to insulate mass communication from the imperatives of the market and hence the interests of the bourgeoisie, thereby ensuring that the media advanced the interests of the working classes.

[47] E.g. Hallin and Mancini (2004), pp. 62–63, 76–84, 261ff.

[48] This is the solution adopted by Karin Voltmer, who builds on Paul Blokker's notion of multiple democracies to account for the various roles media play in transitional democracies globally. See Voltmer (2013), pp. 17–20.

Yet, as shown in Chapter 3, this did not mean that the degree and forms of party-state control over the media were everywhere identical. Marked differences could be observed both across countries as well as over time. In this sense, state socialist broadcasting systems implemented subtly different forms of differentiation between the media, the state, and the market: some preferred to keep the media completely severed from market mechanisms and more or less entirely subjected to the will of the party-state, while others saw a measure of market competition and media autonomy as beneficial. Hence the contrast between Western and state socialist media should not be considered solely in terms of high vs. low levels of state-media differentiation. Rather, it makes more sense to arrange the three state socialist models of television on the same continuum as the three Western models of broadcasting outlined in Hallin and Mancini's media models, with the market-dominated liberal systems, characterized by limited state control and the prevalence of commercial broadcasting, at one end of the spectrum and hard-line state socialist systems, marked by virtually complete state control and the absence of commercial broadcasting, at the other.

Both state control and market influence can take different forms which are not necessarily correlated and hence cannot be captured fully by this linear arrangement of the six models on the state-market axis.[49] For instance, greater state control does not necessarily also mean a lower presence of market mechanisms in broadcasting. In socialist Yugoslavia, broadcasting was controlled by the state yet also relied heavily on advertising revenue – market mechanisms were not excluded altogether but were regulated in a way that effectively secured state broadcasting's monopoly over advertising revenue. A different version of such an alliance between state control and market forces can be found in contemporary China and Russia, where the authoritarian state and commercial media are involved in a mutually supportive, symbiotic relationship.[50] This suggests that a more fully fledged global comparative framework might require the introduction of the extent of market control, or media-market differentiation, as a separate dimension of variation.

Another dimension of comparison not accounted for by the linear arrangement of the six models on the state-market axis is the nature of the relationship between broadcasting and political life. This dimension requires us to attend to the ways in which states relate to heterogeneous

[49] Cf. Hallin and Mancini (2004), p. 44.

[50] Vartanova (2012); Zhao (2012).

political actors and their impact on broadcasting, both in terms of representations and access to the airwaves. In Hallin and Mancini's scheme, this aspect is in part covered by **political parallelism**, namely the extent to which divisions in the media sector mirror divisions in the political sector. In the realm of broadcasting, one can thus distinguish between systems where broadcasting is formally autonomous from established political divisions and systems where such divisions are incorporated into the structure of broadcast governance, either in a way that privileges the current political majority or in a way that ensures that all political parties (and sometimes other social groups) participate in broadcasting decisions.[51] When comparing state socialist broadcasting systems, the need for a separate dimension of this kind did not arise, as the three models are largely identical in this regard: they are all characterized by party-state control and hence embody a high degree of political parallelism.

When extending the comparative frame beyond state socialist systems it seems appropriate to look at political parallelism anew and think about how it could be modified to encompass both state socialist and Western media models.[52] Clearly, the three models of state socialist broadcasting are each marked by a high degree of political parallelism and in that sense resemble the polarized pluralist media. What distinguishes them is not the extent of parallelism as such but rather the extent of **political pluralism**: while the polarized pluralist model combines high political parallelism with party pluralism, the state socialist models combine it with a single party monopoly. To fully assess the extent of media-politics differentiation we should therefore consider both the degree of political parallelism and the degree of political pluralism.

A further aspect of differentiation worth including in the global comparative analysis of media systems has to do with the **degree of secularization**, namely the extent to which the modern media function independently from religious organizations. From this perspective, as we have seen, state socialist broadcasting is (notwithstanding a degree of internal variation) highly secularized and differentiated from the field of religion. In contrast, Western broadcasting systems are less secularized

[51] Hallin and Mancini (2004), pp. 30–33.

[52] The need to rethink the concept of political parallelism for the purpose of creating a more globally applicable framework for comparative media systems analysis was highlighted also by several other authors seeking to apply Hallin and Mancini's framework to cases beyond the West. See, for instance, de Albuquerque (2012), pp. 80–82.

and hence less differentiated in this respect. While particularly widespread in the United States, broadcasters with an explicit religious mission exist in most Western countries, although restrictions may be placed on the territorial reach of such outlets. Several public broadcasters, while formally detached from religious institutions, also broadcast religious content and are sometimes legally obliged to do so, as is the case with the BBC.[53]

The inclusion of secularization as a separate dimension of comparison also enables us to situate state socialist and Western media vis-à-vis Arab media, including the so-called Islamic media model, found in Iran.[54] On this dimension, state socialist media and Arab media are positioned at opposite ends of the spectrum; while the former are formally detached from the religious sphere or even hostile to it, and at best tolerate only very limited aspects of established religious traditions, the latter are in most cases closely aligned with religious traditions and institutions and in some cases institutionally subordinated to them. Western European and North American media systems are situated towards the middle of the spectrum, meaning that they are neither wholly opposed to affiliations with religion nor systemically subjected to religious control. In this context, religious institutions are typically allowed to form media outlets, including radio and television stations, to promote their religious beliefs, while public broadcasters are either expected to avoid explicit religious content or cater to diverse religious preferences.

Taken together, the dimensions of variation consider thus far – the degree of state-media and market-media differentiation, the degree of political parallelism and pluralism, and the degree of secularization – allow us to map the diversity of approaches to modern mass communication. More specifically, these dimensions show that different varieties of modernity, and hence different varieties of modern media systems, can foreground different forms of structural and functional differentiation: some will emphasize the autonomy of the media vis-à-vis the state, some will give primacy to their independence from the broader political field, some will stress their independence from the field of the economy, and some will privilege freedom from religious authority.

As the entangled varieties of modernity approach reminds us, different visions of modernity, and hence different approaches to modern differentiation, should not be seen as isolated but as mutually constitutive. To acknowledge these mutual influences, two further, interrelated

[53] Viney (1999). [54] Khiabany (2009).

dimensions of variation between media systems must be considered: **transnational orientation** and **core-periphery position**. In line with this, much of the internal variation between state socialist media systems can be seen (in part) as the result of entanglements with competing versions of modern broadcasting. Socialist television systems oriented towards the West tended to borrow from the West, while systems subordinated to the Soviet Union tended to adopt the Soviet model. For instance, Yugoslavia, which was systemically most open to engagement with the West as well as most removed from Soviet influence, went furthest in limiting the extent of communist control and in experimenting with elements of a market economy in broadcasting.

The same framework can be used to examine the transnational entanglements of Western European and North American television systems. With regard to transnational orientation, a provisional mapping can be established on the basis of the three criteria used for the purpose of socialist broadcasting, with some amendments: EBU and OIRT membership, choice of colour broadcasting standard (SECAM, PAL, or NTSC), and openness to TV signals from Eastern Europe. With this in mind, we can distinguish between three groups of countries, ranked from least to most open to state socialist broadcasting. At one end are Canada and the United States, which were not active members of either the EBU or the OIRT, adopted the NTSC colour standard, and were geographically far removed from state socialist countries. At the other end are those Western European countries that were, at least on one of the criteria, more open to state socialist television: Finland, which was a member of both the EBU and the OIRT as well as being exposed to cross-border broadcasting from the Soviet Union; France, which opted for SECAM over PAL; and West Germany, which was particularly open to socialist TV signals due to both linguistic and geographical proximity to East Germany. The remaining Western European broadcasting systems are positioned in the middle: their membership in the EBU, which had formal exchange agreements with OIRT, meant that they were systemically more open to state socialist broadcasting than were North American broadcasters, but less so than were French, Finnish, or West German broadcasters.

Following the entangled modernities perspective, it is feasible to expect that the development of broadcast systems in the three Western countries most open to state socialist television was significantly shaped by the encounter with the alternative approach to modern broadcasting seen in the East. As Woo-Seung Lee shows in his analysis of broadcasting in divided Germany, ideological competition went hand in hand with extensive exchange and cooperation, ranging from bilateral programme exchange and acquisition to the sharing of facilities for news reporting and programme production.[55] The development of Finnish broadcasting was likewise closely intertwined with the trajectory of its Soviet neighbour: both public and commercial broadcasters in Finland cooperated with their Soviet counterparts, undertook co-productions and programme exchanges, and produced programmes that presented the Soviet neighbour in a relatively positive light.[56] Let us also note that similar forms of East-West cooperation could be found in other Western European countries, typically in conjunction with foreign policy shifts. From the late 1960s, Swedish broadcasters started developing close links with GDR television, which received a boost following Sweden's diplomatic recognition of East Germany in 1972. Over the course of the 1970s and the 1980s, firm networks of exchange, co-production and friendship were established between broadcasting professionals from the two countries, which gave rise to complex reciprocal patterns of influence.[57]

While the impact of such East-West entanglements on broadcasting in state socialist countries has already attracted scholarly attention, the consequences for developments west of the Iron Curtain have not yet been exposed to the same level of scrutiny. Did these encounters simply reinforce the commitment to existing professional practices and policies established in one's own country, or did they also prompt selective borrowing from practices and policies followed by state socialist colleagues? If the latter is the case, how should such borrowings be interpreted if we are to avoid the trap of one-sided normative evaluations grounded in familiar Cold War dichotomies? In post-Cold War Finland, commentators have voiced criticisms over the conduct of Finnish media professionals before the collapse of state socialism, accused them of engaging in self-censorship, being overly subservient to the state and its foreign policies, and even damaging Finnish democratic traditions. Yet, a more comprehensive empirical investigation of mutual influences between broadcasting systems and cultures east and west of the Iron Curtain is likely to reveal a more nuanced picture.[58] As Marie Cronquist's research into transnational exchanges between East German and Swedish broadcasters shows, patterns of reciprocal exchange and influence can be found across a range of TV content,

[55] Lee (2003). [56] Pajala (2017). [57] Cronquist (2014). [58] Browning (2002).

from children's and educational programmes to news programming.[59] It is likely that the factors that attracted Swedish professionals to East German productions varied and included not only political and ideological motivations but also the inherent quality of GDR programmes.

Similar questions can be raised with regard to the impact of the **core-periphery position** of broadcasting systems in the West. Unlike state socialist countries, which initially used the Soviet template when developing their own broadcasting systems, the core-periphery relationships among Western European and North American broadcasting institutions are less immediately evident. Although US broadcasting undoubtedly exerted an influence over Western European broadcasting, the long history of anxieties surrounding Americanization attests that this influence was rarely accepted wholeheartedly and often encouraged the development of alternative solutions and protective measures. Several Western European countries also strove to use broadcasting, alongside other measures of cultural diplomacy, in their own efforts to exert international influence and often saw these explicitly as a counterweight to Americanization. We have already mentioned the techno-diplomacy surrounding France's decision to adopt the SECAM colour TV standard instead of PAL, and its links with the country's aspiration to act as a third force in the Cold War confrontation between the Soviet Union and the United States,[60] but there are many other examples. For instance, West Germany and the United Kingdom both invested heavily in radio broadcasting targeted at state socialist countries, rivalling the impact in the region of Voice of America and Radio Free Europe.[61] In addition, the BBC also functioned as an attractive source of organizational expertise and technological know-how for broadcast professionals in Eastern Europe.[62] This indicates that even though US broadcasting indisputably constituted the main Western core, several Western European broadcasters aspired to act as alternative cores and often succeeded, leaving their own imprint on broadcast developments transnationally.

The transnational exchange and influences generated by this core-periphery dynamic in Western Europe tend to be explored from the point of view of their impact on state socialist broadcasting, rather than

[59] Cronquist (2014). [60] Fickers (2013).

[61] E.g. Johnson and Parta (2010); Mansell (1982); Nelson (1997); Rawnsley (1996).

[62] Mustata (2013a).

of their consequences for Western broadcasting. As we have already suggested, the history of public broadcasting has much to gain from exploring these entanglements with state socialist developments. This is not the case only with respect to the traditions of public broadcasting in Europe, but also the public broadcasting provision in the United States. As Laurie Ouellette's analysis suggests, the approach to cultural diversity characteristic of US public broadcasting was in part informed by a Cold War vision of the United States as a pluralistic society, starkly opposed to the uniformity of communist enemies; in this context, the spectre of the 'vast wasteland' of commercial television could be presented as a threat that had to be counteracted by the introduction of public broadcasting as a guarantor of greater diversity.[63]

In light of the greater openness to state socialist experiences and practices among Western European broadcasters, the shared, pan-European concern over the detrimental impact of US broadcasting, and the existence of formal exchanges and collaboration between the EBU and OIRT, it is also appropriate to ask whether these factors contributed to a partial convergence of broadcast systems – and perhaps also of broadcast cultures – across both sides of the European continent. To put it differently, did the Cold War rivalry between the Soviet Union and the United States, and the core-periphery dynamics it generated on both sides of the Iron Curtain, stimulate the creation of a shared, pan-European realm of professional practices and perhaps also programme features that in part transcended Cold War divisions?

While the consideration of transnational orientation and core-periphery dynamics enables us to understand the transnational entanglements of broadcasting developments in the West, the remaining dimensions of variation examined in the previous chapter shift our attention to the impact of local conditions and historical legacies. The first and most prominent among these are **infrastructural developments**, a term we believe better captures global diversity than the notion of 'media markets' used by Hallin and Mancini in their comparative analysis of Western media systems.[64] With regard to state socialist television systems, we have highlighted the pace of broadcast infrastructure development as a key factor. Arguably, the pace of development in this sector inevitably

63 Ouellette (2002), pp. 142ff.

64 Hallin and Mancini have themselves acknowledged that the term 'media markets' is too narrow, because 'it implies that the media are distributed as commodities to individual consumers'. See Hallin and Mancini (2012b), p. 289.

depended on the extent to which a particular country could rely on communication infrastructures established before the onset of communist rule and especially before the disruption caused by World War II. As noted in Chapter 3, the timing of infrastructure developments can be linked to the timing of some key changes in television cultures in the region, including in particular the transition from television as an elite medium to television as a mass medium. Is it also possible to link the timing of infrastructural developments to cross-country differences? Here, the patterns of influence are less clear, but it is feasible to expect that state socialist countries that developed their broadcast infrastructure early on had more leeway in adopting solutions that departed from the Soviet model. Although the Soviet Union led the way in terms of introducing regular broadcasting, it lagged behind in terms of the speed of diffusion of TV receivers among the population, which meant that it encountered some of the dilemmas of socialist broadcasting – for instance, how to square the popular demand for entertainment with party preferences for education, information, and propaganda – slightly later than countries such as East Germany or Czechoslovakia.

Similar reasoning could be applied to the impact of the pace of infrastructural developments in Western Europe and North America. Here, too, the timing of key infrastructural milestones varied considerably across countries, with parts of Southern Europe lagging significantly behind early adopters such as West Germany, the United Kingdom and the United States. Given the early introduction of regular broadcasting and the fast proliferation of TV receivers in the United Kingdom, it is not a surprise that British broadcasting served as a model for broadcast developments elsewhere and presented the most significant challenge to the influence of US broadcasting both in state socialist countries and in Western Europe. In contrast, late adopters in Western Europe and North America – much like late adopters in Eastern Europe – had little choice but to mould their broadcasting in response to existing practices and models developed by early adopters.

Other dimensions of the comparison used in the analysis of state socialist broadcasting – including the size of the economy, gender relations, ethno-cultural diversity, and the trajectory of state- and nation-building – could usefully be extended to the rest of the world. From the point of view of entangled modernities, all of these dimensions involve the specificities of the local context, historical legacies, and traditions, which became entangled with modernizing visions and projects and inflected them in distinct ways. They can help alert us to the fact that significant differences between broadcasting systems sometimes cut across the East-West division. It is feasible to expect, for instance, that in both the East and the West, the two largest economies – the United States and the Soviet Union – would be least dependent on foreign programme imports, and existing comparative data on international broadcast flows confirms this.[65] Likewise, it may be the case that the broadcasting arrangements in Western countries with a high proportion of ethnic minority populations or without a clear ethnic majority, such as Switzerland or Belgium, in some aspects resembled the patterns found in Yugoslavia, the Soviet Union, or Romania.

CONCLUSIONS

In this chapter we have introduced the notion of entangled varieties of modernity and explained how it relates to the main dimensions of variation between modern media that evolved over the course of the second half of the twentieth century. Our discussion in this chapter has largely limited itself to a discussion of systemic dimensions of variation between media trajectories (with a particular focus on television). Over the six chapters that follow, we delve into cultural aspects in much greater detail. We reveal several interlocking dimensions of similarity and differences between TV cultures, both within and across the East-West divide, and show how they were shaped by the systemic and contextual dimensions outlined in this chapter.

[65] As the analysis of international TV flows conducted in the early 1970s showed, the United States and the Soviet Union were very similar in this respect and relied overwhelmingly on domestically produced instead of imported content. See Nordenstreng and Varis (1974).

PART II

THE SPACES OF STATE SOCIALIST TELEVISION

5

Publicness

Talking about the public realm in relation to state socialist television may seem counterintuitive. Among communication and media scholars, the term 'public' invokes the idea of a Habermasian public sphere, a realm of rational debate independent from the imperatives of the market and the private sphere and also from the encroachments of the state. In a political context where the mass media were subjected to close scrutiny by the state socialist elites and were expected to serve the goals of the party, possibilities for the establishment of such a sphere were severely restricted. Yet as argued in Chapter 2, to limit the discussion of the public nature of television solely to the question of the public sphere would be misleading. There is little doubt that state socialist television was expected to perform a range of roles that made it ostensibly public. It was seen as a powerful means of education and cultural refinement, one that would enable state socialist citizens from all walks of life to partake in the best the country had to offer. It would also mobilize the masses, deflecting them from petty personal concerns and instead inspiring them to contribute to the ongoing effort to build a better future.

To capture the ways in which television was involved with the public realm, we distinguish between two dimensions of television's publicness: the *public sphere* and the *public mission*. With regard to the first, we differentiate between television cultures depending on the extent to which they enable the public scrutiny of power. With regard to the second, we compare different television cultures depending on their definition of the medium's public remit and on the relative emphasis they put on different public functions, such as information, education, entertainment, nation-building, the public scrutiny of power, or other matters conceived as being in the public interest.

These two dimensions of publicness rely on two distinct notions of 'the public' which derive from the 'protean' nature of the public-private distinction – namely the fact that it is embedded in a complex web of conceptual oppositions that are 'neither mutually reducible nor wholly unrelated'.[1] Two key scholarly conceptualizations are of particular relevance for our analysis. The first associates the public with collective goods, which need to be guarded against private interests and protected or guaranteed by the state. Here, the public-private distinction coincides with the boundary between the market and the state, with the latter acting as the protector – or even embodiment – of the public interest. From this perspective, the key ideological battle lines are drawn between those who call for greater privatization of the public sector, with limitations on state intervention into economic affairs, and those who are concerned about private interests colonizing the public realm, who therefore demand greater state intervention for the common good. In the second conceptualization, which underpins Habermas's theory of the public sphere, the public is understood as a shared realm existing relatively independently from both the state and the private sphere of family life and economic interests.[2]

The distinction between the public sphere and the public mission, as well as the two-fold conceptualization of the public and the private it is based on, gives us a much fuller grasp of the ways in which state socialist television intersected with the public realm. It also offers a strong foundation for comparing state socialist television cultures with their counterparts elsewhere in the world. In the first section of this chapter, we show how state socialist television acted as a provider of public goods and compare its public mission with that of public broadcasting in Western Europe at the time. The second section zooms in on entertainment programming and the disjunction between audience preferences and elite views, as well as highlighting the key cross-country differences and changes over time. In the third and final section we consider the specificities of public life under communism and discuss whether (and to what extent) a public sphere could emerge. While the direct application to the state socialist world of the Habermasian model would be misguided, we contend that the state socialist mass media, television included, nonetheless helped establish a truncated, semi-public sphere. This sphere held

[1] Weintraub (1997), p. 2; see also Sheller and Urry (2003). [2] Habermas (1989).

the authorities in check, but did so without undermining the legitimacy of single-party rule.

TELEVISION AS A PROVIDER OF PUBLIC GOODS: A PUBLIC BROADCASTING SERVICE, COMMUNIST STYLE

The relationship between state socialist television and the public realm was underpinned by an understanding of 'the public' in relation to the common good. Communist parties, and by extension the state, were seen as providers of the public good and were entrusted to protect it against the encroachment of private interests. Broadcasting was identified as one of the key vehicles of this public provision, akin to the institutions of public education, transport, and health systems, but with the added ability to deliver goods directly to citizens' homes. In the eyes of state socialist elites and media theorists, the main beneficiaries of this televised provision would be the working class, who were expected to gain education, cultural refinement, and political awareness, thus enhancing their ability to contribute to the building of a communist future.

This understanding of state socialist broadcasting evolved in opposition to an image of capitalist media as means of reproducing existing relations of power and exploitation resulting from the media's subjection to the interests of the wealthy. As early as 1905, Lenin had argued, 'In capitalist usage freedom of the press means freedom of the rich to bribe the press, freedom to use their wealth to shape and fabricate so-called public opinion.'[3] Communists, by contrast, would construct a system of mass communication in which 'genuine freedom and equality will be embodied' and 'in which there will be no opportunity for amassing wealth at the expense of others, no objective opportunities for putting the press under the direct or indirect power of money, and no impediments in the way of any working man ... for enjoying and practicing equal rights in the use of public printing – presses and public stocks of paper'.[4] The solution was clear: to ensure that the press would serve the interests of the working class, it had to be insulated from the corrupting influences of private ownership and commercial gain. The road to a better and more equal society required a media system subjected to the party and the state and insulated from the logic of the market.

The starkly Manichean vision in which state socialist media were contrasted with their capitalist counterparts persisted throughout the

[3] Quoted in Paulu (1974), p. 39. [4] Ibid. p. 39.

Cold War – regardless of the fact that countries in the industrialized West and elsewhere had created publicly funded media systems which were expected to deliver a public service. Much like state socialist broadcasting, public broadcasting in Western Europe was seen as an alternative to commercial broadcasting. In the United Kingdom, Lord John Reith successfully insisted on changing the status of the BBC from a that of a private company to that of a public corporation, which he saw as indispensable for ensuring the BBC's freedom from commercial pressures and ability to pursue public service ideals.[5] The perception of public media as insulated from the market was also echoed in public discourse and scholarly reflections, which repeatedly contrasted public broadcasting with commercial broadcasting.[6] State socialist television and the public broadcasting service of Western Europe thus operated in similar discursive and normative universes, in which public goods were pitched against private interests and the market was seen as a distorting force requiring state intervention to be kept at bay.

It is therefore not a surprise that the functions assigned to broadcasting in the state socialist world were remarkably similar to those familiar to Western European public broadcasting. As Jérôme Bourdon argues in his history of Western European television, public service television across the western half of the European continent was funded on three key principles – to inform, to educate, and to entertain – with particular emphasis on the first two.[7] State socialist elites and television professionals across Eastern Europe saw the key goals of broadcasting in similar terms. The exact phrasing differed from country to country and changed over time – as was also the case in Western Europe – but the similarities are undeniable. When discussing the main tasks of Polish television in 1960, the chair of the Polish Party Committee for Radio and Television, Włodzimierz Sokorski, argued that 'it is our responsibility to not only inform quickly and objectively, and deepen human knowledge about the world, scientific discoveries and most recent phenomena in the domain of social, economic and political tendencies, but also to give people decent entertainment, develop their taste in culture and art, and develop their ethical and worldview needs'.[8] Similarly, a programmatic Yugoslav document issued in 1965 highlights information and politics, education and

[5] Scannell and Cardiff (1991), pp. 7–9. [6] E.g. Blumler (1992); Murdock (1992).

[7] Bourdon (2011), p. 13.

[8] Włodzimierz Sokorski, 'Najbliższe zadania,' in *Radio i Telewizja*, Issue 38 (787), 18 September 1960, p. 1.

upbringing, and culture and entertainment as the media's three main activities.[9]

Political and cultural elites and TV professionals on both sides of the European continent also shared didactic views of broadcasting, which were combined with an elitist view of culture that prized opera and literature over comedy and popular music. As Kees Brants and Els De Bens put it, unlike the commercial logic of private broadcasting, which was based on producing popular programmes to attract advertising money, the ethos of public broadcasting in Western Europe was marked by a 'cultural-pedagogic logic' where public service broadcasters sought to provide programs which were 'in the public interest', but 'not necessarily what the public is interested in'.[10] BBC founder Lord Reith was notorious for his belief in broadcasting as a means of education and cultural elevation, as well as for his disdain for popular entertainment: audiences would receive what they needed rather than what they wanted.[11] In Italy, too, much early television programming was didactic in tone and consisted of educational programming and live transmissions of plays, operas, and classical music concerts.[12]

Much the same could be said about the ethos of broadcasting in state socialist Eastern Europe. In 1965, Aleksandr Iakovlev, then deputy head of the Department of Agitation and Propaganda, described television as 'a people's university at home' and emphasized its roles in furthering the acquisition of scientific knowledge and widening people's horizons.[13] Such views on television were mirrored across the region and resonate with the notion of state socialist regimes as what Dorothee Wierling has called 'educational dictatorships'.[14] This pedagogical ethos, coupled with an insistence on established cultural hierarchies, extended into all aspects of life, and one could argue that it was far more pronounced than in the West. It may even have contributed to a sense of superiority: in the Soviet Union, for instance, the deputy head of Gosteleradio quoted with pleasure the words of the Moscow correspondent of the *Washington Post*, who said: 'From the point of view of cultural level, Soviet television is rising above American television like a giant mast. Which American TV station would stand to broadcast evening after evening a symphony by

[9] AJ, f. 142, k. 207, 'Teze o mestu, ulozi i zadacima štampe, radija i televizije u našem društvu,' 1965, p. 1.

[10] Brants and De Bens (2000), p. 16. [11] Crisell (1997), p. 29.

[12] Monteleone (2006), pp. 302–306.

[13] A. Iakovlev, 'Televidenie: problemy, perspektivy,' *Kommunist* 7 (1965), 67–81, p. 73.

[14] Wierling (1994).

Tchaikovsky or Beethoven, an opera by Bizet or Mozart, the plays of Chekhov or Turgenev ... Which? And not just American, but French, British, or Japanese?'[15] In Romania, a television professional likewise spoke proudly of the accomplishments of Romanian television as an educational tool, comparing it favourably to the Swiss and American television she had had an opportunity to watch during recent trips abroad.[16]

Parallels between state socialist television and Western public broadcasting television were reflected in broadly comparable programme structures. The global UNESCO survey of television programmes conducted in 1971–1972, based on a sample week of programming, illustrates this in an interesting way.[17] When we divide programming into its key functions – information, education, cultural elevation, and entertainment – it becomes evident that the key difference lies not between state socialist and Western broadcasters but between commercial broadcasters, on the one hand, and public and state socialist broadcasters, on the other (Figure 5.1). On commercial television, the majority of the broadcast output – ranging from 53 per cent in Argentina to a staggering 84 per cent in Australia – was taken up by entertainment, fiction, and sports, with only limited provision of educational and cultural programming. In contrast, public broadcasters in Western Europe and Australia, much like broadcasters in state socialist Eastern Europe, dedicated significant proportions of their output to culture and education. These figures confirm that similarities between state socialist and Western public broadcasting were not only a matter of elite discourse but actually translated into similar diets of broadcast content.

Similarities between Western public broadcasting and state socialist television extend to its role in promoting nation-building. From Spain to Britain, Poland to Romania, broadcasting institutions were named after the nations they served: the British Broadcasting Corporation, Televisión Española, Televiziunea Românеă, and Telewizja Polska. Policy documents and reports likewise routinely referred to 'the nation' as the assumed beneficiary of broadcasting. It was not uncommon for the

[15] TsAOPIM, f. 2930, op. 2, d. 851, ll. 20–21, 23–24. 'Stenogramma sobraniia aktiva partiinoi organizatsii Gosudarstvennogo komitete SM SSSR po televideniiu i radioveshchaniiu: O dal'neishem uluchshenii ideino-politiheskoi raboty partiinykh organizatsii Goskomiteta SM SSSR po televideniiu i radioveshchaniiu, usilenii bor'ba s proiavleniami burzhuaznoi ideologii i morali,' 8 April 1975.

[16] ANR, f. CC PCR-SPA, d. 18/1970, p. 26.

[17] Nordenstreng and Varis (1974), pp. 15–29.

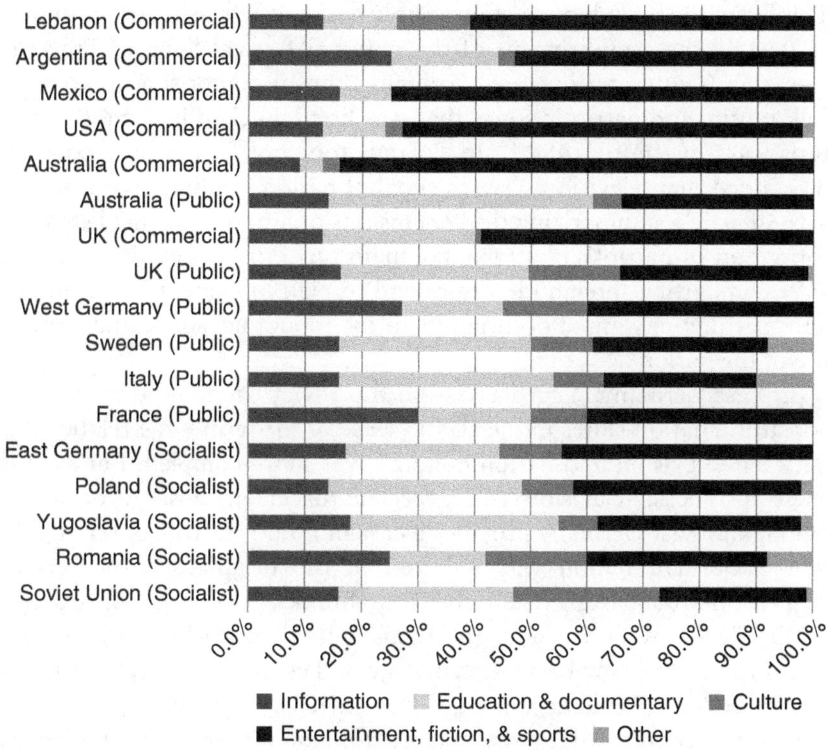

FIGURE 5.1 Programme structures of selected broadcasters globally, 1971–1972. *Note*: The results are based on recoded data derived from the 1971–1972 UNESCO survey, using the following procedures: 'Information' comprises daily news and current affairs, 'Education & documentaries' comprises educational, documentary, and children's programming, 'Culture' comprises TV drama, pure music, religious and folk traditions programming, and 'Entertainment, fiction and sports' includes series, films, sports, and entertainment shows. For original UNESCO survey data see Nordenstreng and Varis (1974), pp. 15–29.

nation-building function of television to be discussed in more explicit terms, especially in the context of official pronouncements and elite debates. This was particularly clear in Romania from the 1970s onwards, when Ceauşescu began to demand that the media and culture turn away from foreign models and instead seek inspiration in Romanian culture.[18]

[18] Nicolae Ceauşescu. 1984. *Romania pe Drumul Constructiei Societatii Socialiste Multilateral Dezvoltate. Rapoarte, Cuvintari, Interviuri, Articole. Vol. 26: May 1971–Februarie 1972*. 1972. Bucharest: Ed. Politica, p. 236.

This led to the introduction of ostensibly patriotic television programmes, as well as the establishment of the national festival Song of Praise to Romania (*Cîntarea României*), an annual event comprising folk dance, folk music, and patriotic songs that was first launched in 1976 and was broadcast live until 1989.[19] In Poland, too, political elites frequently demanded that television serve the goal of nation-building. For instance, a 1969 article summarizing the conclusions of a party meeting listed 'the formation of patriotism' among the main functions of television, alongside 'combatting foreign ideologies and foreign influences and attitudes' and 'battling unwanted occurrences in the economic, social and cultural life of the nation'.[20]

In East Germany, Yugoslavia, and the Soviet Union – none of which constitute nation-states in the classic sense of the term – the relationship between television and nation-building was more complex. But even in these instances, television was expected to cement a sense of shared belonging. East Germany provides a case in point: the role of serving the whole German nation was reflected in the original name, German Television Broadcasting (Deutsche Fernsehfunk).[21] After the construction of the Berlin Wall in 1961, the focus shifted towards promoting the legitimacy of the new East German state and cementing a negative image of the Federal Republic among GDR citizens.[22] In this regard, GDR television contributed to the construction of a distinct East German nation,[23] but the idea of GDR television as *German* television did not disappear: broadcasters still sought to convince viewers that their television spoke for the entire German nation.

In Yugoslavia and the Soviet Union – both multi-ethnic, multinational and multi-lingual states– television promoted both federal unity *and* national particularity. Yugoslav documents regularly emphasized the role of broadcasting in strengthening a common, pan-Yugoslav identity, while at the same time acknowledging and promoting the identities of the country's constituent nations and nationalities.[24] The organizational logic

[19] Petrescu (2007).
[20] 'Radio i TV w Służbie Partii i Narodu,' in *Radio i Telewizja*, Issue 21, 1969.
[21] Dittmar (2007), p. 215. [22] Hesse (1988).
[23] Palmowski (2009), pp. 81–89, 120–131.
[24] For instance, a 1969 document discussing the involvement of television in cultural policy stated that television was expected to contribute to closer relationships between Yugoslav nations and nationalities, as well as to counteract nationalist interpretations of history and fears about one's nation being under threat. See AJ, f. 507, k. 49, d. A-CK SKJ, VIII, II/4-a-69(1–4), 'Kulturna politika i televizija,' 1969, p. 4.

reflected this vision of 'unity in diversity': Yugoslav television operated as a federal institution comprising distinct republican and provincial broadcasters, each catering to its own republican or provincial audience but also engaging in programme exchange and co-production. In the Soviet Union, a similar arrangement was in place: television channels likewise broadcast on a central, republican, and municipal basis, thereby allowing and promoting an interlocking web of identities.[25] Differences should be noted, too. While Yugoslavia never established a separate pan-Yugoslav channel – except for the introduction of the short-lived channel Yutel in 1990, at the brink of the country's collapse – the Soviet Union had a more centralised system, with Central Television, broadcast from Moscow, functioning as an obligatory channel for regional broadcasters. Soviet television therefore had an unmistakable centralising function in which the voice and image of Moscow were taken to represent the nation, just as the Russian Republic was often synonymous with the whole of the Soviet Union.[26] By comparison, TV Belgrade in Yugoslavia never had such a privileged status vis-à-vis other republican and provincial broadcasters.

In sum, the public mission of television in the state socialist world resembled the mission of public broadcasting in the West: it served as a vehicle of public education, information, and entertainment for all and fostered a sense of shared belonging to the nation. However, there are a number of crucial differences. In contrast to their Western counterparts, state socialist elites expected all television content, regardless of genre, to further the communist agenda. If a production ventured too far from this agenda, the authorities were quick to remind television professionals of their priorities. As one Soviet official made clear in 1968 (at a point when Soviet tensions with the outside world were at their sharpest), the most important thing for Soviet television, and the aspect that differentiated it most clearly from capitalist television, was its involvement in propaganda: 'In comparing the television programmes of the Soviet Union and capitalist countries one should never forget that the creators of Soviet programmes must above all recognize their subordination ... to the Soviet Union's propaganda tasks, to socialist construction, to providing the most thorough coverage of the life of the country, and to educating the culture of the people.'[27] In Poland, a party resolution adopted in 1969, no doubt

[25] On this point see Chakars (2015), p. 158. [26] Roth-Ey (2011).

[27] A. Bogomolov, 'O televizionnoi programme, zritele i gazete,' *Sovetskoe radio i televidenie*, 8 (1968), 33–36, p. 33.

influenced by the repercussions of the Soviet invasion of Czechoslovakia the previous year, was similarly unequivocal and stated that 'the press, radio and television should serve the Party and the nation in the creation of a socialist form of public life in Poland'.[28] Other countries in the region were no exception.[29]

To conclude, state socialist television did indeed offer a *public* service, pursuing many of the goals associated with the public broadcasting institutions of Western Europe. Considerable resources were poured into the production of educational programmes aimed at diverse social groups, documentaries on a wide variety of topics, and cultural programmes that covered a range of forms from theatre and cinema to opera and jazz. Yet efforts to make quality information, education, and entertainment available to all were desirable only in so far as they were connected to the communist cause. In this sense, the public mission of state socialist television was truncated. As we shall see further on in this chapter, the public sphere engendered by state socialist television was similarly circumscribed. While communist authorities were, in principle, rather open to programming designed to foster public deliberation and social critique, television professionals involved in such programming had to tread a fine line between politically desirable participation on the one hand and overly explicit criticism of party rule on the other.

PUBLIC MISSION AND ENTERTAINMENT: BETWEEN PUBLIC NEEDS AND AUDIENCE DESIRES

Although all television cultures examined in detail in this book were underpinned by similar conceptions of television's public mission, the different functions of the medium were not seen as equally worthy of public investment. The provision of entertainment, in particular, was often contested. Should entertainment have been acknowledged as a legitimate function of television or was it a necessary evil to be tolerated in order to attract audiences to other, more worthwhile, types of output? To be sure, no self-respecting television professional or member of the state socialist elite would be prepared to bow to viewers' preferences by

[28] 'Radio i TV w Służbie Partii i Narodu,' *Radio i Telewizja*, Issue 21, 1969.

[29] For an example from East Germany see 'Über die Programmtätigkeit des Fernsehens in der Deutschen Demokratischen Republik,' October 1955 BA DR 8–3, republished in Hoff (2002), p. 15; and for Romania, Nicolae Ceauşescu. 1984. *Romania pe Drumul Constructiei Societatii Socialiste Multilateral Dezvoltate. Rapoarte, Cuvintari, Interviuri, Articole. Vol. 26: May 1971–Februarie 1972*. 1972. Bucharest: Ed. Politica, p. 247.

embracing entertainment unreservedly. Such an approach would come too close to the commercial logic where, so the argument went, editorial and creative choices were led by audience desires, thus maintaining a status quo where the working class lacked education and cultural sophistication. Instead, state socialist television needed to address the real needs of the public by helping the population rise to higher levels of knowledge and refinement. As a result, all television cultures in the region were marked by a disjunction between the perceived public good and actual audience desires. While audiences by and large saw television as a source of entertainment, both politicians and producers tended to emphasize the importance of educational, informational, and cultural programming. This created what Anikó Imre aptly calls a 'schizophrenic situation, where TV as a public educational ideal and TV as it actually functioned in the living rooms were segregated'.[30]

Evidence of such a schizophrenic situation can be found across the region. In the Soviet Union, public pronouncements and official documents largely neglected entertainment programming, often mentioning it in a negative light. 'There is such a thing as too much entertainment', argued a 1967 article. 'The misuse of TV is dangerous, for both viewers and television itself. [After hours of watching] viewers can no longer make sense of what they're seeing and hearing.'[31] Likewise, TV critic L. Futlik bemoaned the 'selfish' attitudes prevailing among audiences and complained that 'the most powerful weapon of political propaganda most often becomes merely a means of entertainment'.[32] These views contrasted sharply with the realities on the ground. As a survey conducted in the late 1960s revealed, audience members from all walks of life agreed that the role of television in acquainting the population with 'the most important news of international life' was key, yet also emphasized that television 'brings joy and enjoyment' and allows audiences 'to fill free time when there is nothing to do'.[33]

It is tempting to suggest that Soviet political elites were particularly reluctant to acknowledge the legitimacy of public investment in entertainment – after all, the Soviet Union was the flag bearer of state socialism and had to ensure that its media reflected the correct priorities. Our sources do support this argument up to a point. In Yugoslavia, for instance, elites were more open to accepting the value of entertainment

[30] Imre (2016), p. 34. [31] Evans (2016), p. 66.

[32] L. Futlik. 1965. 'Bez grima,' *Iskusstvo kino*, 7: 90–95, p. 92

[33] L. Kogan. 1969. 'My i sovremennoe TV,' *Sovetskoe radio i televidenie*, 1: 22–25, p. 24.

on television from early on – an attitude to popular culture which had a long history. As early as 1954, no less a figure than Edvard Kardelj, a leading member of the Yugoslav League of Communists and the main theorist of Yugoslav socialism, argued that sweeping attacks on detective novels, jazz, and comics were harmful and that the solution lay not in the rejection of popular entertainment forms as such, but in the infusion of 'new content', rooted in Yugoslav ideology.[34] Nevertheless, entertainment never ceased to be seen as potentially problematic. Yugoslav politicians often complained about the low quality, 'emptiness', and 'banality' of television entertainment and warned that popular magazines and radio and television programmes promoted 'a foreign way of life, thinking and understanding of social values'.[35] Like their counterparts elsewhere in Eastern Europe, Yugoslav elites were reluctant to embrace audience demand for entertainment wholesale. At a meeting held in 1964 by the Ideological Committee, Stipe Šuvar, a leading politician and sociologist, insisted that radio and television programmes should not be based on what the audiences wanted, because audiences were not sufficiently educated and were easily satisfied with programming that was of a 'low level' and espoused 'bourgeois' values.[36] Similar views were reiterated again and again in later years.[37] Even though Yugoslav politicians were more tolerant of entertainment from early on, they were prepared to endorse it only in so far as it remained attuned to communist values.

Nonetheless, it would be misleading to suggest that the pervasive paternalism of state socialist television cultures meant that audience

[34] Gabrič (1995), p. 203ff. See also HDA, f. 1228, k. 932, 'Aktuelni problemi zabavno-revijalne štampe,' 1962.

[35] AJ, f. 142, k. S-437, 'Informacija o aktuelnim pitanjima u oblasti informisanja i ostvarivanju uloga i zadataka Socijalističkog saveza,' 1969, pp. 9–10. For similar arguments see also HDA, f. 1220, d. 834, 'Stenografski zapisnik sa zajedničkog sastanka Ideološke komisije Centralnog komiteta Saveza komunista Hrvatske in Ideološke komisije Glavnog odbora Socijalističkog saveza, održanog 25. maja 1964. godine,' pp. 28 and 51; and AJ, f. 142, k. S-437, 'Orientacijoni program rada Saveta SSRNJ za štampu, radio i televiziju za 1980. godinu,' 16 November 1979, p. 2.

[36] HDA, f. 1220, d. 834, 'Stenografski zapisnik sa zajedničkog sastanka Ideološke komisije Centralnog komiteta Saveza komunista Hrvatske in Ideološke komisije Glavnog odbora Socijalističkog saveza, održanog 25. maja 1964. godine,' p. 23.

[37] For instance, in his 1984 study of television and culture, sociologist Mate Bošnjaković argued that television should avoid dividing culture into 'serious' and 'less serious' and instead offer a genuinely mass form of culture that eschewed simplification and ensured that the masses could satisfy a variety of cultural needs with programmes of high quality. See Bošnjaković (1984), p. 14.

preferences were disregarded altogether. By the late 1960s, broadcasters across Eastern Europe were collecting audience data on a regular basis, drawing on a variety of methods from audience surveys and panel interviews to the analysis of audience letters. Even in the Soviet Union, where the pressure for conformity was stronger, the constant demand for entertainment programming evident from audience research did not fall on deaf ears. During the late 1960s, this evidence prompted sociologists and younger television professionals to argue in favour of entertainment. In an article published in 1969, sociologist L. Kogan went as far as to claim that the central function of television should be 'hedonistic'. When turning on a TV set, he insisted, a person wants to rest and relax: 'It is unlikely that many of us, settling down comfortably in front of the set, are thinking: 'Now I'm going to widen my knowledge'.'[38] On this basis Kogan argued that if television were to fulfil its educational function, it needed to entertain viewers.

In the early 1970s, after the Soviet Gostelradio was entrusted to the arch conservative Sergei Lapin, its audience research division was closed,[39] suggesting that the new management found limited value in empirical research into audience preferences. Nonetheless, the meticulous tracking of audience letters continued, and both the political elites and the broadcast management became more accepting of the need for programming that was entertaining and capable of attracting a large audience. In a speech in 1975, Enver Mamedov, the deputy head of Gosteleradio, argued that Soviet television had become less 'snobbish' and more appealing to a mass audience, and even Leonid Brezhnev reportedly acknowledged that 'the Soviet person has the right to relax in front of the television after a day's work'.[40] Of course, this concession to entertainment and mass taste had its limits. As Mamedov explained to colleagues in the mid-1970s: 'Our programmes in the area of culture are, of course, addressed to the widest possible audience. At the same time, we are not attempting to appeal to just any level of qualification or to lower our demands, but rather we are striving to raise this level, and to widen the spiritual riches of the individual.'[41] In a state socialist country – and perhaps

[38] L. Kogan. 1969. 'My i sovremennoe TV,' *Sovetskoe radio i televidenie*, 1: 22–25, p. 24.
[39] Roth-Ey (2011), pp. 206, 279. [40] Roth-Ey, 2011, pp. 206, 279.
[41] TsAOPIM, f.2930, op.2, d.851, ll, 'Stenogramma sobraniia aktiva partiinoi organizatsii Gosudarstvennogo komitete SM SSSR po televideniiu i radioveshchaniiu: O dal'neishem uluchshenii ideino-politiheskoi raboty partiinykh organizatsii Goskomiteta SM SSSR po televideniiu i radioveshchaniiu, usilenii bor'ba s proiavleniami burzhuaznoi ideologii i morali,' 8 April 1975, pp. 20–21.

in the Soviet Union, in particular – there was simply no room for programming based solely on audience preferences or for entertainment for its own sake. Even when seeking to produce programming with a mass appeal, television professionals could never forget that ultimately their task was to educate and to elevate, rather than merely satisfy existing desires.

Much as in the Soviet Union, attitudes to entertainment in East Germany softened markedly during the last two decades of state socialist rule. As two leading historians of East German television have argued, professionals found that 'out-of-date programme formats' allowed viewers to switch channels to West German television. The only way to avoid a mass exodus of viewers was for television to 'become more modern and, above all, more entertaining'.[42] This was one of the impulses behind Honecker's famous 1971 speech in which he urged TV professionals to 'take into account the need for good entertainment ... and to meet the expectations of every part of the working population, whose working day begins very early and who therefore by the early evening want better quality TV programmes'.[43]

Elsewhere in the region, trends over time are less clear than in the Soviet Union and East Germany, but evidence abounds of elite acceptance of entertainment and audience preferences. In a 1960 document on the tasks of Polish television, a high-ranking party official and head of the Polish radio and television committee listed the provision of 'decent entertainment' among the most important tasks of television.[44] Similar arguments can be found in internal reports prepared by the Polish audience research unit. For instance, a study based on the analysis of audience letters received by Polish television in 1970 highlighted the importance of entertainment and presented it – much as Brezhnev reportedly did in the Soviet Union – as a just reward for the citizens' labour: 'Apart from providing information television fulfils the noble role of providing millions of people entertainment and providing conditions for mental rest and relaxation after work.'[45] Romanian Party officials and television professionals shared similar views. At a meeting held in 1970, a member of the Party Committee for Propaganda and Agitation urged his colleagues to take

[42] Steinmetz and Viehoff (2008), p. 286. [43] Quoted in Gumbert (2006), p. 164, note 51.

[44] Włodzimierz Sokorski. 1960. 'Najbliższe zadania,' *Radio i Telewizja*, Issue 38 (787), 18 September 1960, p. 1.

[45] TNS OBOP, Stanisław Szczygielski, *Rola Telewizji w Środowisku Żołnierzy Służby Zasadniczej*, Wydawnictwa Radia i Telewizji: Warszawa, 1969, p. 40.

audience views seriously, to retain shows that viewers found attractive, and even to schedule them strategically to attract audiences to other content.[46] A number of Romanian television professionals and members of the party and cultural elites agreed, arguing for the necessity of entertainment in contemporary life.[47]

To what extent were these elite views reflected in the genre composition of the state socialist broadcast output? Did the share of entertainment grow in line with shifts in elite opinion? Were some countries more open to entertainment than others? To ascertain this, we conducted an analysis of TV schedules during a sample week in early October, at five-year intervals, starting in 1960 and finishing in 1990. We grouped all programmes into five categories, broadly corresponding to their main functions:

- information (which comprised news and current affairs programmes);
- education and documentary (which also included children's programming with educational aims);
- culture (which covered live transmissions and recordings of theatre, opera, classical music concerts and competitions, poetry, and cultural magazines);
- entertainment, fiction, and sports (which also comprised any children's programming of this kind);
- other (which primarily covered advertising and programme announcements).[48]

As evident from this cross-country comparison (Figure 5.2), the only clear outlier with regard to genre composition was East Germany, where the average proportion of entertainment was markedly higher than elsewhere, averaging more than 50 per cent, while the proportions of cultural and educational content were notably smaller than in the rest of the region.

This result suggests that cross-country differences in elite attitudes to entertainment had a limited impact on programme output, at least as far as the quantitative balance of genres is concerned. The proportion of entertainment in Yugoslavia, for instance, was only marginally higher than in the Soviet Union, despite more accommodating elite attitudes towards the genre from early on. Yet, these results are surprising only if we limit ourselves solely to domestic political factors and only if we

[46] ANR, f. CC PCR-SPA, d. 18/1970, p. 43. [47] Ibid. pp. 14–16 and 23.
[48] For further details see the Methodological Appendix.

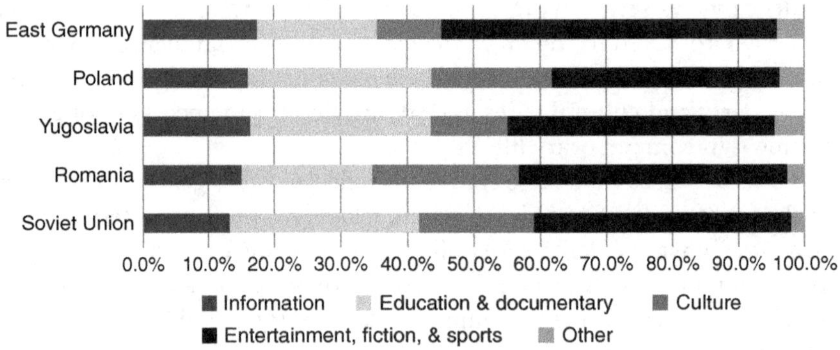

FIGURE 5.2 Programme structures in five state socialist countries, 1960–1990.
Note: Data based on the analysis of TV schedules for a sample week, at five-year intervals, from 1960 to 1990. For further details see the Methodological Appendix.

assume that state socialist elites had an unlimited ability to shape the nature of the broadcast output. As soon as we take into account cross-border influences, the picture changes. This was first and foremost the case in East Germany, where the proximity and accessibility of West German television forced East German broadcasters to measure their success not simply in the propaganda value of their messages but in the number of viewers watching.[49] The connection between West German television and entertainment can be glimpsed most clearly by the second programme reform of 1982–1983, which was drafted in response to the beginning of commercial television in West Germany. This reform went further than the 1972 reform in increasing the amount of films and series, raising the level of imports, reducing current affairs programming, and increasing the variety of programming.[50] Faced with the extent of competition from beyond the Iron Curtain, East German television had little choice but to step up its provision of entertainment and rethink its scheduling practices. As a result, TV professionals began to place East Germany's most popular programmes in opposition to popular West German programmes or those which contained politically unfriendly messages.[51] A good example of this

[49] Cf. Steinmetz and Viehoff (2008), p. 292. [50] Hickethier (1998), pp. 205–206.

[51] Ultimately, however, these policies were only moderately successful. Research suggests that between the Honecker-influenced programme reform of 1972 and the fall of East Germany in 1989, viewing figures for domestic TV at prime time were never higher than 40 per cent. DRA 61/18/24/4. Viewer reports 1980–1990; SAPMO-BArch, DY 30 / vorl. SED 25946 (1979): Information über wichtige Ergebnisse der Fernsheharbeit im I. Quartal 1980; SAPMO-Barch DY 30 / vorl. SED 30112 (1983): Bericht der 28. Programmwoche vom 04.07. bis 10.07.1983.

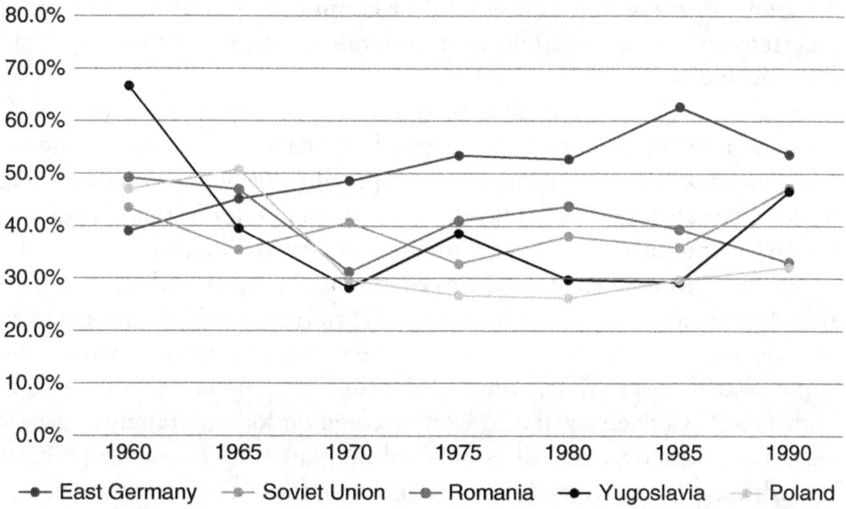

FIGURE 5.3 Trends in the proportion of entertainment in five state socialist countries, 1960–1990.
Note: Data based on the analysis of TV schedules for a sample week, at five-year intervals, from 1960 to 1990. For further details see the Methodological Appendix.

practice is the variety show *A Kettle of Colour* (*Ein Kessel Buntes*, 1972–1992) which was scheduled to clash with the evening news bulletin on West German channel ARD.

This interpretation receives further support when we investigate changes in the proportion of entertainment programming over time (Figure 5.3). Again, East Germany is the only country where a clear and upward trend is visible, most likely as a result of the growing investment in entertainment programming in response to competition from the West. In the remaining four countries, changes in the proportion of entertainment are more haphazard, and there is little evidence that the softening of elite views on entertainment led over time to a net growth in entertainment programming.

Of course, we should also keep in mind that the data on the overall volume of entertainment only tells part of the story. Above all, quantitative results do not enable us to trace the qualitative transformations in the nature of each category of programming, such as the growing hybridization of genres and the rise of edutainment and politicized entertainment. To put it differently, while the proportion of entertainment may have remained the same, the greater acceptance of entertainment meant that programmes classed as educational or cultural may have become more entertaining, while entertainment programming grew more explicitly didactic and politicized.

Existing studies of individual programmes and our own analysis developed in the chapters that follow suggest that such hybridization was indeed becoming a widespread phenomenon, especially during the latter two decades of state socialist rule. Educational programmes, for instance, regularly used elements of entertainment or fictional storytelling, or adopted the competition format, to make their programmes more appealing and effective. As Imre argues, such 'edutainment' was a recognizable feature of state socialist television programming across the region and became increasingly sophisticated over time, often achieving a popular status among audiences.[52] Conversely, it also became common for entertainment genres such as game shows as well as fictional programming to convey political and educational messages. In the Soviet Union, for instance, quizzes such as *Let's Go, Girls!* (*A nu-ka, devushki!*, 1970–1985) and its male equivalent *Let's Go, Guys!* (*A nu-ka, parni!*, 1971–1973) played a part in outlining normative gender roles in a socialist society, while the programme *Auction* (*Auktsion*, 1969–1970) sought to advertise both consumer products and 'cultured consumption' to viewers.[53] In East Germany, the entertainment programme *It's Fun Together* (*Gemeinsam macht's spaß*), for example, had the intention of advertising to viewers the close cultural ties between socialist nations.[54] As we show in Chapter 9, the dramatic form was also used for educational purposes, including teaching history. These examples suggest that even in cases where the share of entertainment remained broadly stable over time, growing genre-hybridization reflected a broad acceptance of the legitimacy of entertainment. We can therefore argue that state socialist broadcasters by and large became increasingly adept at entertaining their audiences but did so in ways that remained consistent with their vision of television as primarily a tool of the state socialist revolution, education, and cultural elevation.

TELEVISION AS A VEHICLE OF A STATE SOCIALIST PUBLIC SPHERE

Having established the ways in which state socialist television helped provide public access to information, education, and entertainment, it is

[52] Imre (2016), pp. 40–65. [53] Evans (2016), p. 202ff.
[54] Steinmetz and Viehoff (2008), pp. 300–301; Honsberger (2016), pp. 83–96.

now time to turn to the other aspect of television's engagement with the public realm: its potential to contribute to a public sphere. Various authors have noted that the application of the Habermasian notion of the public sphere to the state socialist context is problematic.[55] Habermas himself insisted that the bourgeois public sphere is 'a category typical of an epoch' and belonged to 'the unique developmental history of that civil society originating in the European High Middle Ages'.[56] Following on from this argument, he also insisted that the category of the public sphere '[cannot] be transferred, ideal typically generalised, to any number of historical situations that represent formally similar constellations'.[57] Indeed, the sociopolitical conditions prevalent in state socialist countries failed to meet the basic conditions for the kind of public sphere Habermas identified in eighteenth-century Britain, France, and Germany. Most obviously, the Habermasian public sphere was a *bourgeois* public sphere, premised on the existence of 'a market that, tending to be liberalized, made affairs in the sphere of social reproduction as much as possible a matter of private people left to themselves and so finally completed the privatization of civil society'.[58] As we will see in Chapter 6, it is not so much that state socialist societies were devoid of privacy but rather that privacy always remained subjected to public control and is therefore best conceived as a 'public' privacy. Moreover, the bourgeois public sphere was premised on the freedom of assembly and expression, both of which were restricted during state socialist rule. Publications deemed hostile to the party were often arbitrarily closed down or subjected to strict control and censorship, making it virtually impossible for critics of state socialist rule to participate in mainstream public debate. Finally, for Habermas, the public sphere offers a realm where the public can hold the authorities in check and thereby impose limits on its power. While, as we shall see, state socialist citizens were not completely powerless in face of the party apparatus and could – also with the help of the media – subject the authorities to critical scrutiny, such critique was either expressed in semi-public fora or needed to avoid directly challenging state socialist rule.

Even this brief overview of the conditions that led to the emergence of the bourgeois public sphere makes it clear that these ideas cannot be applied to the state socialist context. Nevertheless, public life under

[55] E.g., Killingsworth (2007); Rittersporn et al. (2003). [56] Habermas (1989), p. xvii.
[57] Ibid. p. xvii. [58] Ibid. p. 74.

communism was not necessarily reduced to the 'representative publicness' that Habermas associated with the European Middle Ages,[59] or to the staged, party-orchestrated 'plebiscitary-acclamatory' public sphere he thought was characteristic of dictatorships in highly industrialized countries.[60] Rather, we argue that the specific political, economic, and cultural constellations that emerged under state socialist rule gave rise to a distinct form of a *semi-public sphere*, which was subjected to party-state intrusion and therefore was either truncated in scope or had to exist largely on the margins of public life, in domains removed from direct public gaze. An important part of this semi-public sphere encompassed dissident and exile activities and relied on a variety of underground publications and outlets published abroad. Yet, to limit ourselves solely to these channels would mean missing a wide range of practices and publications – including many that involved mainstream television – that played a key role in establishing a semi-public realm of debate under communism. As Anke Fiedler and Michael Meyen rightly note in their analysis of public communication in East Germany, an exclusive focus on the forms of communication associated with dissidents can lead us to miss the ways in which even the politically staged public sphere could enable readers to gain insight into the objectives of the rulers and participate in discussions with state socialist decision-makers.[61] More generally, limiting the existence of the semi-public sphere under communism solely to dissident activities also reproduces the unhelpful binary of the party-controlled 'official' sphere and the 'unofficial', 'alternative', or 'counter' public sphere, which glosses over the many ways in which the two spheres intersected, interacted, and indeed depended on each other.

To counter this binary vision, we propose to think of the semi-public sphere under communism as a realm that spanned official and alternative domains and was often stimulated *both* by conscious attempts of dissident circles to create an alternative sphere of communication *and* by the party-endorsed promotion of popular participation and social critique. As a result, this semi-public sphere emerged through a range of different channels. In what follows, we discuss three such channels, all of which at least partially involved television: forms of communication established by dissident and exile circles; mainstream media content that either directly or indirectly elicited public deliberation and expressed social critique; and the practice of writing letters to the mass media. The shared trait of all

[59] Ibid. pp. 5–12. [60] Ibid. p. xviii. [61] Fiedler and Meyen (2015).

these channels was their restricted publicity: if content was exposed to the public gaze, the scope of opinion and critique could not directly challenge party rule. If, on the other hand, debate and critique ventured beyond the politically permissible, they had to remain outside of direct public view.

Because of their overwhelming reliance on print publications, the forms of communication maintained by dissidents and exiles may seem less relevant to our study, but it is worth noting that by the latter half of the 1980s, television also began playing a role in this context. Thanks to the proliferation of home video recorders, it became possible to distribute and view materials unavailable through state television channels, including pornography and Western films and series, as well as more explicitly political content produced by dissidents and exiles.[62] In Czechoslovakia, at least two 'unofficial' video news magazines were circulating in the second half of the 1980s, both mimicking the format of broadcast news. These magazines were distributed using video cassettes, passed on through transnational social networks of dissidents and their friends, diplomats, and tourists, and screened to small audiences in semi-private settings.[63]

While clearly produced with the intention of establishing a separate sphere of communication which would offer an alternative view on both domestic and foreign developments, such dissident and exile outlets were never fully independent from the party-state and tended to use the language and symbols of official politics.[64] It was not uncommon for dissidents to operate in both official and unofficial capacities, or for their status to change over time. Dissidents could be censored and closely monitored and yet also sometimes nurtured and courted by the regime.[65] It is this close entanglement with, and mutual reliance on, official and unofficial communication channels that also enabled former dissidents to merge into the mainstream when the opportunity arose in the late 1980s.

[62] Wasiak (2012). [63] Lovejoy (2013), p. 207.

[64] Oushakine (2001); Rittersporn et al. (2003).

[65] Bathrick (1995), p. 11. The fate of Yugoslav film director Želimir Žilnik, known for his socially engaged and critical work, offers another case in point: after a spell of internationally acclaimed productions in the 1960s, Žilnik came under harsh criticism and felt compelled to emigrate to Germany in the early 1970s, yet returned to Yugoslavia in the late 1970s and directed a range of television films and docudramas for state broadcasters. See Vučetić (2012), pp. 159–162; and Vučetić (2016), pp. 275–282.

The second channel of the semi-public sphere in the state socialist context comprised content published in mainstream outlets, including television programmes prompted by policies aimed at encouraging public debate. Attempts to use television as a means of popular participation and social critique became particularly prominent during the 1960s. Yugoslavia stands out for its concerted attempt to turn the country's media into a genuine forum in which different opinions would be confronted and critical views raised. This goal was mentioned in official documents and elite debates during the 1960s. For instance, a programmatic 1965 document insisted that Yugoslav media were expected to function not only as means of the top-down transmission of information but as a 'political forum' designed to give voice to public opinion and help solve the pressing tasks of Yugoslav society. The 'current stage of development', argued the document, required the working people of Yugoslavia 'to use the mass media to express their views regarding their own and social life and further development', as well as engage in the 'struggle of opinions' and constructive criticism aimed at improving current conditions.[66] Other party documents from the same period echo these views, calling on the media to become 'a forum for the popular masses' and encourage a confrontation of opinions and popular engagement,[67] as well as to ensure the greater visibility of workers' views on screen.[68]

Views such as these encouraged television professionals to experiment with programmes designed to elicit participation and critique. In 1965, TV Belgrade launched *Current Debates* (*Aktuelni Razgovori*, 1965–1969), a talk show series addressing pressing social problems – including economic reform, living standards, unemployment, and social inequalities – and involving contributors ranging from factory workers to some of the highest representatives of the Yugoslav economy and politics.[69] As explained in the yearbook of Yugoslav Radio-Television, the programme was meant to provide an opportunity for 'workers, students, agricultural workers, and citizens of all professions' to ask questions and discuss matters of social and economic reforms under way in the country with the highest political

[66] AJ, f. 142, k. 207, 'Teze o mestu, ulozi i zadacima štampe, radija i televizije u našem društvu,' 1965.

[67] AJ, f. 142, k. 207, 'Razširjena skupina za masovna komunikacijska sredstva,' 1965.

[68] AJ, f. 142, k. 207, 'Komisiji sveznog odbora SSRNJ za politički i idejno-vaspitni rad,' 1965.

[69] RTS-CIJMPA, Report 371, 'Pet godina "Aktuelnih razgovora",' p. 1.

representatives.[70] Entertainment genres gained a polemical edge, too. For instance, the comic TV serial *Sleep Peacefully* (*Spavajte mirno*, TV Belgrade, 1968) tackled issues of unemployment, income disparities, social solidarity, and corruption, all introduced through the experiences of a central character tellingly named Lucky Menace (Srečko Napast), who had recently lost his job and was caught stealing caviar at a local supermarket.[71] During the trial that followed Lucky defended himself by pointing to the disjunctions between the political ideals and reality of life in Yugoslavia: how could he be jobless and hungry in a country that ostensibly served the working people; how could delicacies such as caviar be enjoyed by the elite yet be inaccessible to him?

While Yugoslavia's attempts to use television as a means of critique were particularly advanced, it was not the only country to enlist television as a means of public engagement. In Poland, for example, a 1969 party resolution stated that the media would be expected to 'provide a forum for the expression of opinions and social critique',[72] a view backed a year later by the Communist Party's first secretary, Władysław Gomułka.[73] In a similar vein, the GDR Party Congress in 1963 called for a form of 'channelled' criticism through which socially important topics could be broached, so long as solutions were offered.[74] The programme *Prism* (*Prisma*, 1963–1990), which was inspired by West German current affairs programmes *Panorama* and *Report*, similarly allowed for limited discussion of social problems.[75] Likewise, at a meeting of Romanian party elites and television professionals in 1970, several participants highlighted the value of social critique on television and expressed positive opinions about the show *Searchlight* (*Reflektor*, 1967–1977), which aimed to expose the problems encountered daily by Romanian citizens, focusing on a range of issues from the failings of state infrastructure to the inability of local authorities to supply basic goods to citizens.[76]

[70] *Godišnjak Jugoslovenske radiotelevizije 1966*. Belgrade: Jugoslovenska radiotelevizije, 1967, p. 168.

[71] Mihelj (2013).

[72] 'Radio i TV w Służbie Partii i Narodu,' in *RTV Radio i Telewizja*, Issue 21, 1969.

[73] Quoted in TNS OBOP, Stanisław Proc. 1970. *Notatka – Informacja o Rozwoju Audytorium i Widowni Radia i Telewizji*, Warszawa: Ośrodek Badania Opinii Publicznej, pp. 2–3.

[74] Holzweißig (2002), p. 114.

[75] See Merkel (2000).

[76] ANR, f. CC PCR-SPA, d. 18/1970, p. 32.

Programmes inviting audience participation and the voicing of critical opinions on television also helped to promote the practice of letter writing. Programmes such as *Prism, Searchlight*, and *Current Debates* contributed to the perception of television as an important public force, which was capable of acting in the interests of citizens, rather than bureaucrats. State socialist broadcasters were inundated by audience letters and telephone calls expressing criticism of various aspects of life under communism or asking for advice on a range of personal and public matters. In Yugoslavia, the producers of *Current Debates* processed a total of 11,770 letters and more than 20,000 telephone calls posing questions for the program, and they devised themes and questions for guests in part based on input from audiences.[77] The serial *Sleep Peacefully* likewise prompted thousands of letters and phone calls, many of which were rather candid in tone and congratulated the serial's creators for daring to voice what they believed everyone felt.[78] In Poland, too, a survey conducted in 1971 revealed that as many as 47.8 per cent of Polish audiences believed that TV and radio would be able to act on their behalf to resolve complaints.[79] While many letters sent to Polish radio and television referred to personal matters, some also addressed issues of public concern, including living conditions, workplace conditions, unjustified punishments in the workplace, unjustified discharges from work, salaries, work instability, the treatment of citizens by public service sector, and pensions.[80]

The extent of audience complaints and requests for advice shows once more that state socialist broadcasting institutions functioned as mediators between the state and its citizens. The exchange of letters sustained a semi-public sphere, which was inclusive and participatory and was used by audiences to air their opinions and criticisms. Yet this public sphere existed outside the public view – or rather, it was visible only to the select few: broadcast professionals themselves and the representatives of public institutions contacted on behalf of audiences. In this context it is important to note that the aforementioned survey in Poland

77 RTS-CIJMPA, Report 371, 'Pet godina "Aktuelnih razgovora",' p. 1.

78 RTS-CIJMPA, Report 354: 'Analiza pisma gledalaca upućenih serijskoj emisiji "Spavaje mirno" + pisma gledalaca upućenih serijskoj emisiji "Spavaje mirno" - izvodi,' 1969, Part II.

79 TNS OBOP, Andrzej Duma. *Rola Polskiego Radia i Telewizji jako Instytucji Skargi Wniosków. Wynik Ankiety pt. Porady i Interwencje*. Warszawa: Wydawnictwa Radia i Telewizji, 1974, p. 32.

80 Ibid. p. 13.

revealed that audiences felt radio and television were more appropriate addressees for complaints than were newspapers, work unions, courts, militia, and the government.[81] As the author of the report concluded, these results suggested a lack of trust in local authorities and public institutions more generally.[82] Television and radio, in this sense, functioned as substitutes for institutions of democratic governance, yet did so in a way that was safely removed from direct public gaze.[83] Perhaps this was the only way in which an ostensibly state-controlled institution could simultaneously also function as a mediator between the state and its citizens.

Where such outbursts of social critique occurred in the public view, as was the case with polemical and satirical programmes, sanctions were more harshly imposed. The producers of such programmes came under harsh criticism or worse if they overstepped the boundaries of the politically permissible. In East Germany, Gerhard Scheumann, the idealistic creator of *Prisma*, found that his attempts to publicise issues of public importance came face to face with the recalcitrance of the SED elite; he was forced to resign within two years of the programme's launch. Upon resignation, he left a twelve-page 'testament', which lamented the fact that the programme frequently failed to realize its possibility of acting as an instrument of public opinion. Scheumann wrote of frequent cases where individuals attempted to deal with 'certain problems of socialist development', only to find that the authorities gave the 'comradely advice' that, in the absence of change, it would better not to 'stir things up'. The tragedy for Scheumann was that, in following this 'comradely advice', burning social issues never became the object of public discussion, which turned 'a publicly known problem into a taboo' and therefore limited its possibility for resolution.[84] In Romania, too, party authorities feared the criticisms

[81] Ibid. pp. 26–27. [82] Ibid. p. 5.

[83] Broadcast institutions were neither alone nor the first to perform such a mediating role. The print media, ranging from daily newspapers to specialist journals, had long nurtured the tradition of letter writing, and major titles typically possessed a department dedicated to logging, processing, and investigating readers' letters. The practice of letter writing also extended beyond the media and included addressees ranging from party leaders to state and party agencies. This ability to keep officials in check was considered to be an important part of socialist democracy and contributed to what Stephen White (1983) has called the press's 'ombudsman role'. See Fitzpatrick (1996); Kozlov (2013), pp. 16–17; Merkel (2000); White (1983).

[84] Gerhard Scheumann. 1965. 'Prisma-Testament' (August 1965), reproduced in Riedel (1994), p. 136. On the programme see also Hickethier (1998), pp. 286–287; Holzweißig (2002), pp. 114–115; Steinmetz and Viehoff (2008), pp. 260–261.

aired in *Searchlight*, and by 1977 the programme was defanged. Yugoslav television producers were also not immune to censorship and other forms of pressure; the writer-director of the *Sleeping Peacefully* series, Radivoje-Lola Đukić, was pushed into premature retirement in 1970.[85] As these examples testify, the media's quest for social dynamism, in the form of criticism and debate, albeit instigated by the state socialist authorities themselves, ultimately came into conflict with the party's desire to maintain a positive public image.

Even so, it is important to keep in mind that programmes expressing critical views on the current state of affairs in the state socialist bloc rarely disappeared fully from public view. Instead, the language of criticism became more innocuous or more reliant on Aesopian modes of communication offering multiple possible interpretations. As Stephen Lovell shows, even an ostensibly mainstream, party-supported television programme such as the Soviet serial *Seventeen Moments of Spring* (1973) could support Aesopian readings. Despite being produced with the support of state agencies and marked by an unmistakably anti-Western tone, the serial could also be read as a subtle commentary on the Soviet elites of the Brezhnev era.[86] Likewise, the comic sketches traditionally broadcast during Romanian New Year's Eve programmes regularly included jokes intended as comments on the dire state of the country (see Chapter 10). A measure of public criticism thus persisted in public view throughout, but was either presented in a form that made it intelligible only to the initiated few, or was aired during exceptional moments when the usual restrictions on public discourse were temporarily relaxed.

The fact that openly critical television programmes proliferated during the 1960s, and again during the late 1980s, is not a surprise. After all, these were periods that coincided with a relaxation of party controls. Yet we should be wary of assuming that such timing means that the party was hostile to public deliberation. On the contrary: the impetus for public engagement and critique often came from the party itself and was rooted in the notion of the state socialist newspaper as a 'collective organizer'. In his original formulation, Lenin linked this organizational function to a vision of society in which newspapers would be tied to a network of local party agents, which would 'form the skeleton of [an organization] that is sufficiently large to embrace the whole country'.[87] If the state socialist

[85] Mihelj (2013), p. 259. [86] Lovell (2013), pp. 303–321.
[87] Vladimir Ilyich Lenin (1961 [1902]), 'What Is to Be Done?,' in V. I. Lenin (1961) *Collected Works*, Vol. 5. Moscow: Progress Publishers, pp. 502–503.

media were to succeed in acting as collective organizers, it was not enough for them to engage in acts of 'representative publicness' that displayed the power of the party before the population; they also had to ensure that their output allowed audiences to participate in the construction of the communist project – including by means of critique.

State socialist societies thus stood in an ambiguous relationship with public deliberation. On the one hand, the transformative, participatory ideals of the state socialist project meant that public engagement was encouraged; on the other hand, such engagement could also result in deliberation that undermined the legitimacy of party rule. Because of this inherent ambiguity, deliberation could never be fully public or pushed entirely into the private realm. Instead, its participants had to learn to negotiate the fine line between the politically acceptable and unacceptable and to choose appropriate forms of expression – more or less public, more or less explicit – depending on how challenging or damning their opinion was. If they failed to make the right choice, or if the political terrain shifted suddenly, they risked being pushed altogether out of the public realm and into the restricted semi-publicity of dissident and exile outlets.

CONCLUSIONS

State socialist television performed a range of ostensibly public functions. Its mission centred on goals familiar from institutions of public broadcasting in the liberal democracies of Western Europe and beyond: to provide audiences with access to information, education, and entertainment, as well as to foster a sense of national belonging. And much like their public broadcasting counterparts in the West, television professionals in state socialist countries were often guided by paternalistic assumptions and traditional cultural hierarchies: they privileged classical concerts and ballet over popular music and TV sitcoms, and were reluctant to take audience preferences as the key guide of editorial decisions. State socialist television also helped generated something akin to a public sphere, fostered not only through underground communication channels established by dissident and exile circles or through use of Aesopian language understood only by the initiated few, but also by mainstream programming explicitly designed to encourage public debate and social critique.

At the same time, state socialist television's public remit was clearly restricted. Efforts to make quality informational, cultural, educational, and entertainment content available to all were desirable only as long as they steered clear of explicit criticism of the state socialist ruling classes and the ideals of communism. In moments of heightened international conflict or domestic instability – for instance, the Soviet invasion of Prague in 1968, or the emergence of the Solidarity movement in Poland – television broadcasters were sternly reminded of where their loyalties should lie. Likewise, the scope of public deliberation was inevitably limited. The peculiar nature of state socialist rule meant that deliberation and criticism had to remain restricted in scope or only partially public, with participants forced to toe a fine line of the politically permissible or to use semi-public outlets to communicate their views. As a result, the public sphere in the state socialist world had a distinctly semi-public, truncated character.

Apart from highlighting these shared traits of state socialist television cultures, we have also noted the contested nature of television's public mission, especially with regard to entertainment. We showed that television cultures across the region were marked by a characteristic disjunction between elite views and audience preferences with regard to entertainment, but we also noted slight differences between countries and the gradual softening of elite attitudes to entertainment over time. Interestingly, our analysis of the share of entertainment programming has revealed that East Germany was the only country where the share of entertainment was notably higher than elsewhere in the region, as well as the only country where a clear upward trend in the share of entertainment was evident over time, a fact connected to its exposure to West German TV signals. This suggests that the articulation of television's public mission was not dependent solely on differences in the extent of party-state control but could also be shaped by the transnational orientation of the broadcast system, specifically by its exposure to Western television signals.

With regard to the public sphere and its relative openness, here too, significant differences and shifts over time could be observed. As one would expect given its somewhat lower level of party-state control, Yugoslavia stood out for its concerted attempt to turn the country's media into a forum in which different opinions would be confronted and critical views raised. Yet changes over time were much more marked than differences across countries: by and large, openly critical television programmes proliferated in all countries during the (late) 1960s and then again during the late 1980s. As seen in Chapter 3, these periods also coincided with a relaxation of party control over cultural and media production, which confirms that the scope of television's support for public deliberation in state socialist Eastern Europe was largely dependent on the extent of party-state control over the medium. That said, it is important to acknowledge that the initial impetus for the opening up of the televised public sphere came from the party itself, which sought to use the media to enact the participatory ideal of the communist project. It was therefore not that the party as such was hostile to public engagement and critique, but rather that the deliberation it sought to encourage often ended up spilling over the boundaries of the politically permissible.

The contestations surrounding entertainment and the party's ambiguous attitudes to public deliberation bring to the fore the role of television as a social centre and anchor of normality during a period when socialist orthodoxy was becoming increasingly unorthodox. The gradual, if cautious, acceptance of entertainment as a legitimate part of the communist project embodied a departure from the more orthodox emphasis on education, information, and cultural sophistication, yet at the same time the forms of entertainment endorsed on television never veered too far away from paternalist concerns, ensuring that a sense of adherence to orthodoxy and normality was maintained. Likewise, in a context where party support for different forms of public deliberation had the potential to spiral out of control, televised deliberation helped delineate the limits of public critique, marking the point where forms of public engagement crossed from being seen as consistent with communist ideals to being perceived as threats to the communist project.

6

Privacy

In the previous chapter, we saw how television helped shape the public realm under communist rule. In this chapter, we shift the focus towards the other side of the 'grand dichotomy' and explore television's relationship to the private sphere. In line with the analytical framework introduced in Chapter 2, we consider two dimensions of television's engagement with privacy: in the first part of the chapter, we focus on its *domestication*, namely the gradual adoption of television as a domestic medium, viewed primarily in the context of one's home. We examine how television as a material object gradually entered domestic life to become an essential part of the modern home and how it was integrated into family life. In the second part we shift attention to the patterns of *privatization* prevalent in television programming. We shine the spotlight on a range of fictional serial programmes that dealt with personal relationships or were set within the domestic living spaces of ordinary citizens.

In examining these issues, we ask whether and to what extent the processes of the domestication and privatization of state socialist television resembled those common in the West at the time. This is a pertinent question, because the private possessed an uncomfortable place within the communist vision of society. The early decades of communist rule were characterized by a radically public orientation, which demanded the sacrifice of domestic comfort for the construction of a better tomorrow.[1] This public orientation was pushed further by the work of state security services, which had the power to open private life to state scrutiny.[2] As a result, several authors have emphasized the dominance of public over

[1] E.g. Wolle (2013. [2] See Hornsby (2013); Miller (1999); Verdery (2014).

private spheres under state socialism, highlighting the extent to which the private was virtually eliminated.[3] Equally, however, scholars focusing on the last decades of communist rule – the period of late socialism – have detected a loosening of attitudes towards privacy, arguing that the conditions of late socialism fostered a more accepting relationship to the private sphere. This resulted in a complex intertwining of private and public lives during the period.[4] While official discourse pointed to the superiority of public values, party policies – often consciously – promoted a clawing back of private space from the public, allowing for the emergence of what Günter Gaus, writing about East Germany, famously called a 'niche society' of petit-bourgeois comfort.[5] It often seems, then, that late socialist societies were pulling in two conflicting directions: while public values continued to be lauded over private ones, citizens were also offered a modicum of privacy in exchange for political quiescence.

To this end, some scholars have suggested that the traditional bipartite division of private and public is redundant when talking about state socialism and needs to be augmented by concepts that acknowledge the hybrid space between the two. A particularly useful conceptual solution, one directly relevant to the analysis in this chapter, was proposed by Katerina Gerasimova, who distinguished between two modes of the social under communist rule: public privacy and private publicity.[6] The notion of public privacy describes instances where the party allowed and acknowledged certain aspects of private life while retaining a measure of control over them. A good example is provided by collective apartments, where personal life was open to the scrutiny of others and spaces were designed to enforce mutual dependency between individuals and families. Private publicity, by contrast, refers to forms of public activity enacted within private spaces, such as debates about matters of public concern in family homes or the use (and abuse) of public facilities and goods for personal gain. As we shall see, this notion of public privacy offers a valuable conceptual framework for capturing the peculiarities of television's interaction with private life during communist rule, especially with regard to representations of privacy on screen.

[3] E.g. Kharkhordin (1999); Figes (2007). [4] Betts (2010); Field (2007); Harris (2013).

[5] Gaus (1983). See also Fulbrook (2005).

[6] Gerasimova (2002). Another conceptualization designed to overcome the bipartite distinction between the private and the public, centred on the notion of the 'social sphere', was proposed by Garcelon (1997).

To investigate the domestication and privatization of television in state socialist countries, we draw on a range of sources. The integration of television into domestic life is examined primarily through life history interviews, most of which included memories – often very detailed ones – of interviewees' first encounters with the television receiver, recollections of the position of the television receiver in the home, and the social and spatial organization of viewing practices that emerged around it. Interview materials are complemented with a range of other sources, including the representations of television in domestic space appearing in interior decoration booklets, the popular press, and television fiction. Together, these sources enable us to reconstruct the ways in which television was domesticated by viewers themselves – an aspect of television culture that often remains neglected, especially in historical research – while also situating audience practices and perceptions in the broader context of popular and professional discourses on television circulating at the time. To investigate representations of privacy on screen we focus on serial television fiction, a genre that is often singled out as being particularly closely intertwined with the domestic context of television viewing and prone to plots that focus on personal relationships. Using a combination of quantitative and qualitative methods, we seek to establish the relative prominence of serial fiction focused on privacy and identify key traits of private life as represented in the dramas.

While discussing television's engagement with the private realm, we also examine its involvement with gender relations. How did the domestication and privatization of television in state socialist countries interact with gendered practices and assumptions? Were they marked by gendered patterns similar to those prevalent in the West at the time, and did they reproduce the traditional divisions between a feminine private sphere and a masculine public sphere? Or did they follow distinct patterns of their own, grounded in the specificities of state socialist gender policies?

TELEVISION AS A DOMESTIC OBJECT

In examining our materials on domestic television culture, we were struck by the similarities – not just between the five countries in our analysis, but also with patterns in Western liberal democracies. Just as in the United States during the 1940s,[7] or in Italy, Belgium, or the United Kingdom

[7] McCarthy (2001).

during the 1950s,[8] early experiences of television in Eastern Europe typically involved collective viewing in public settings, such as department stores, exhibitions, or community halls, or else in semi-public settings, such as the homes of neighbours and family members lucky enough to possess their own television set. In the Soviet Union the novelty of television was so strong that some owners of TV sets, aware of the novelty value of their new possession, indulged in the entrepreneurial practice of charging their neighbours to watch television – much to the chagrin of communist authorities.[9]

Recollections of encountering television for the first time while visiting neighbours or relatives were particularly common among our interviewees. A Polish viewer born in 1949, for instance, remembered watching television at his friend's home and later in his neighbours' flat, where the TV receiver was located in a separate room designed for collective viewing with guests:

> When I was in primary school, I had a friend called Witek who lived not far from school and his family had a TV set. So when there was something for us to watch … we would go to his place. … There were four or five of us. I can't remember whether his mother was home or not. And we would sit around the table and watch it and then we would discuss it. … Later on, in my building, the neighbours had a TV. They had a big flat and had a separate room in which only a TV set, a sofa and some chairs were put so it was like a cinema. People from the neighbourhood would go there. (Pol-02-1949-male)

The quasi-theatrical, semi-public experience of collective TV viewing in the homes of friends and neighbours was recalled by several other interviewees, including a Romanian woman born in 1944 who remembered watching television at her friend's apartment, where people from the same bloc of flats 'would gather in the hallway … and the chairs were arranged as in the cinema, so that as many as possible could sit' (Rom-19-1944-female). A handful of interviewees also remembered being at the receiving end of such collective viewing, spoke of the sensation provoked by their family's acquisition of the TV set, and recalled the experience of having extended family, neighbours, and friends crammed into a small room to watch the evening news bulletin or live transmissions of a music concert or sports competition (e.g. Pol-14-1959-female, YuCro-05-1957-female). In most cases, such experiences were recalled

[8] Hanot (2003), pp. 36–37; Örnebring (2007); O'Sullivan (1991), p. 164; Penati (2013), pp. 75–114.

[9] Chakars (2015), p. 151.

as exceptional – almost festive – in stark contrast to the more routinized experiences of viewing that came to prevail once television receivers became more widely available.

Some of the interviewees also remembered watching television for the first time in public spaces. A viewer who grew up in Yugoslavia spoke of seeing the TV for the first time at the Zagreb International Fair in 1956 and recalled following the experimental transmissions of TV Zagreb later that year on one of the main streets in Zagreb (Yu-Cro-19-1941-male). Community halls, associated with the local workers' collective, village community, or school or party organizations, were also common locations for early TV viewing. A Croatian viewer recalled watching a football match on television for the first time in the late 1950s in a communal room in his father's factory workplace (Yu-Co-20-1941-female), while a Ukrainian interviewee described watching TV in the 'red corner'[10] in the local community hall (USSR-Ukr-14-1947-male). The practice does not appear to have been an isolated incident: a (male) Leningrad worker wrote in 1960 of his factory hostel's red corner 'with a TV, books, magazines, and nice girls using it'.[11] The positioning of the television alongside other items of culture also illustrates our argument about television as a means of cultural enlightenment (see Chapter 5).

The practice of collective, state- or party-funded acquisition of the TV set and its positioning in communal spaces appears to have been reasonably widespread across state socialist Eastern Europe and arose as a logical extension of collective radio listening in workers' clubs and village reading rooms.[12] In contrast, oral history research conducted in Italy showed that public TV viewing mostly occurred in local bars[13] and was therefore dependent on private initiative and commercial motivations. While both practices gave rise to similar experiences of collective viewing, and were typically associated with sports and entertainment programming, their political and economic underpinnings reflect differences in the wider political and economic context.

[10] 'Red corners' were commonly found in Soviet communal buildings. They were originally adorned with religious icons and later filled with communist-related reading materials and posters.

[11] Kelly (2014), pp. 65–66.

[12] On such collective listening in the Soviet Union during the 1920s and the 1930s see Lovell (2015), pp. 51–61.

[13] Penati (2013), pp. 75–114.

By and large, however, our oral testimonies suggest that the practice of public viewing was short-lived and quickly gave way to viewing in domestic settings. Initially, possessing a television receiver was clearly a marker of social distinction, much as elsewhere in the world.[14] One Polish interviewee recalled how 'people used to show off if they owned one. It was very special to have a TV set' (Pol-25-1949-male), while another insisted that in the early years, television 'increased everyone's social status, just like a car' (Pol-22-1944-male). However, our research also suggests that in television's early years, earnings alone were not sufficient to be able to purchase a TV set: to do so required a high level of social capital – being on good terms with a local party official, for example – especially if one wished to acquire a more high-tech set not available in regular shops. As evident from viewer testimonies, television's early adopters (or those who acquired colour TVs before others) tended to be not just wealthier but also better educated and better connected. A Romanian viewer recalled that the first TV set he ever encountered was owned by a colleague of his grandfather, who was a university professor. His daughter studied at the Joint Institute for Nuclear Research in the Soviet Union and was able to send her parents a television set (Rom-01-1945-Male). Contemporary audience research likewise indicates that in the early stages, television ownership and viewing were more widespread not only among those who had higher earnings but also among those who were better educated, held white collar rather than blue collar occupations, and lived in urban environments.[15] The social distinctions that early TV ownership symbolised were therefore embedded in the particular forms of social stratification characteristic of state socialist economies.[16]

Apart from being a marker of social status, the acquisition of a private TV set also signalled one's personal participation in the process of becoming modern. As Tim O'Sullivan has observed with regard to early television in the United Kingdom, acquiring a set was 'a visible sign of joining, or at least not being left out of, "the new" '.[17] Several of our older interviewees, too, remembered the arrival of the first TV set as a symbol of

[14] Leal (1990); Penati (2013), pp. 87–89; O'Sullivan (1991), p. 166; Mäkikalli (2016), p. 2.

[15] See, for instance, the results of an audience study conducted on a nationally representative sample in the Yugoslav republic of Serbia in 1968, RTS-CIJMPA, Report 263, Igor Leandrov, 'Sondaža auditorija radija i televizije 1968,' *Rezultati istrazivanja programa*, Issue 1, 30 April 1968, pp. 3–4.

[16] On the specificities of social stratification and class structure in communist countries see e.g. Parkin (1969); Szelényi (1999).

[17] O'Sullivan (1991), p.166.

modernization. In the words of a Polish viewer born in 1925, television was 'something that was present elsewhere in the world and we only just got it so it felt as if we had joined the modern world. So not only Germany or France had TV but we did too' (Pol-16-1925-female). Other interviewees proudly recalled their family being among the first to acquire modern domestic appliances – not only the TV set but also a refrigerator, a washing machine, or a telephone line – and thereby acting as the local vanguard of progress (e.g. Pol-13-1951-male, Yu-Cro-05-1957-female).

Notions of modernity were also incorporated into elements of design. In much the same ways as with the design of TV sets produced in the United Kingdom,[18] appliances produced in East European factories varied in the materials and design used, with different styles embodying different visions of modernity. The earliest sets, such as the Polish Wisła, produced in the late 1950s by the Warsaw Television Works, had an ornate wooden casing that linked the modern home with nature. In contrast, sets produced from the late 1960s were characterized by simple shapes and a lack of ornaments, with some, such as the portable Iskra TV-31 Minirama produced in Yugoslavia, embodying distinctly futuristic visions of modern life, symbolised by slick shapes, bright colours, and curved plastic edges. Portable TV sets such as the Minirama or a similar appliance advertised in Poland in the late 1960s also associated modernity with mobility and leisure, in a manner reminiscent of the imagery surrounding early portable sets produced in the United Kingdom.[19]

As the diffusion of TV receivers progressed, and the TV set shifted from a luxury item into an everyday necessity, the aura of distinction and progress associated with it gradually faded and became limited only to the latest technological advances, such as colour TV receivers in the late-1960s and the early-1970s or video recorders in the 1980s. The social composition of viewers changed accordingly. As revealed by a large-scale comparative study conducted in 1966 in three urban centres where television ownership was fairly widespread – Ljubljana, Warsaw, and Budapest – the average earnings of TV owners were no higher than those of non-owners. Instead, the two groups differed markedly in marital status and family situation: those owning a TV were typically married, had children, and lived in larger households.[20] Slowly but surely, homes

[18] Chambers (2011). [19] *Radio i Telewizja*, Issue 28, 7 July 1968, cover page.
[20] Stupan et al. (1967), pp. 110–119.

across the region thus became unthinkable without television. The TV set became a regular feature of popular and professional publications offering advice on the design and furnishing of modern homes. This transition is nicely illustrated by the contrast between two Soviet interior design publications: an illustrated collection of articles published in 1954 and a book issued in 1966. While the former contains no mention or image of television, the latter includes several illustrations of modern dwellings featuring TV receivers.[21]

Interior design publications as well as oral testimonies and family photos from the era also clearly show that television had assumed a central space in the modern home and was positioned in a way that made it visible to all members of the household. As a Romanian viewer born in 1973 recalled:

> Yes, I remember the TV had a central role in the house, as it was positioned in the hallway, where we all gathered to watch what was on. And anyway, since it was placed in the hallway, as a middle way between the kitchen and the balcony, we automatically saw what was going on. (Rom-05-1973-female)

Also very common was the position of television in the vicinity of the dining table, allowing family members to watch television while having a meal – a practice mentioned by several interviewees and visually depicted in a range of popular TV serials from the era. For instance, in the eleventh episode of the Polish comic serial *War on the Home Front* (*Wojna domowa*, TVP, 1965), we see the main characters, the members of the Jankowski family, having a meal while watching television and arguing over whether teenage son Pavel may be allowed to watch a feature film that is due to start after the evening cartoon. Scenes depicting very similar furniture arrangements, often featuring characters dining or conversing while watching TV, also appear in a range of other serials set in domestic environments, including the Romanian *Tanta and Costel* (*Tanta si Costel*, TVR, 1965–1970) and the Yugoslav *Theatre in the House* (*Pozorište u kući*, TVB, 1972–1984) and *Headfirst into Strawberries* (*Grlom u jagode*, TVB, 1975).

While the centrality of television in the home environments and routines of socialist families closely resembles the spatial and social arrangements of television in Western homes, it is also worth noting subtle

21 S.S. Alekseev. 1954. *Inter'er zhilogo doma. Sbornik statei.* Moscow: Gosudarstvennoe izdatel'stvo literatury po stroitel'stvu i arkhitekture; B. M. Merzhanov and K. F. Sorokin. 1966. *Eto nuzhno novoselam*. Moscow: Ekonomika.

differences. What often transpires from viewer testimonials and family photos from the region is the small size, multifunctionality and limited privacy of domestic spaces into which the TV was incorporated. Due to the phenomenon of communal apartments and endemic housing shortages into the 1960s and beyond, it was not uncommon for families – especially younger ones – to share their household with members of the extended family or strangers or to live in small rented accommodations. In such settings, the TV was typically positioned in multifunctional spaces: a kitchen that doubled up as a living and dining room, or a living room that was transformed into a bedroom overnight – the so-called 'combined room' as it was referred to in the Yugoslav context.[22] A Polish interviewee born in 1973, for instance, recalled living in her grandmother's house, where members of her own family shared a single room with a TV set in a corner, while her aunt and uncle stayed in another room (Pol-4–1973-female). Likewise, a Croatian viewer born in 1975 remembered residing with her family in a small rented apartment where the TV was placed in the kitchen that simultaneously served as a dining and living room (Yu-Cro-03–1975-female). An arrangement of this kind is still found in some apartments in the region, such as the one inhabited by two of our interviewees from Serbia (Figure 6.1).

Such spatial arrangements became less common as housing construction advanced. Several of our interviewees described larger apartments with a separate living room where the TV receiver would be placed, typically integrated into a combination shelving system such as the one that features in the Soviet serial *Day After Day* (*Den' za dnem*, 1971–72) or in the Polish series *The Forty-Year-Old Man* (*Czterdziestolatek*, TVP, 1974–1977) as well as in private family photos (Figure 6.2).[23] The placement of TV in the living room was also preferred in professional interior design booklets and similar publications[24] and featured in furniture and interior design exhibitions.[25] Nonetheless, on the whole, the arrangements described in oral testimonies from Eastern Europe differ markedly from those common in

[22] Erdei (2015).

[23] For examples of such amateur photos from Poland see NAC, 40-2-51-1 (1980), 40-4-292-7 (1971), 40-R-53-9 (1974–1980), 40-D-44-16 (1980), 40-9-325-3 (1974), 40-2-285-2 (1981). Closely similar domestic arrangements appear also in Hungarian amateur photographs from the same period, see Fortepan.

[24] See, for instance, Boris Fomin, 1978. 'Televizor v vashem dome,' *Govorit i pokazyvaet Moskva*, 15 November 1978; Lech Pijanowski. 1968. *Telewizja Na Co dzień*. Warsaw: Wydawnictwo Związkowe CRZZ, p. 10.

[25] See photos of Polish furniture exhibitions, NAC 40-3-85-4 (1970) and 40-4-377-7 (1978).

FIGURE 6.1 Interviewees from Serbia in front of the TV set in their kitchen. *Source*: Aleksandra Milovanović, private collection.

FIGURE 6.2 Hungarian family watching television, c. 1981. *Source*: Fortepan 60523 / Gárdos György

viewer recollections in countries such as the United Kingdom or Belgium, where families typically deliberated over which of the many rooms was more suitable for the TV set and hence clearly had more space at their disposal.[26] Yet again, we therefore find that the domestic cultures of television in the state socialist world, while in many ways similar to their counterparts in the West, also exhibited distinctive characteristics, which were a direct consequence of the specific economic and political environment in which they were embedded.

As television became part of everyday domestic routines, it simultaneously became enmeshed in the structures of family life and, in particular, the distinct gender politics of life during state socialism. The gendering of viewing practices in the state socialist world displays both similarities and differences to those that existed in the West. The gendered nature of control over programme choice, the amount of viewing and television-related conversation, as well as the technical competence required to manipulate the TV – all familiar from research conducted in the West[27] – can all be discerned from our viewer testimonies.[28] A Polish interviewee vividly remembered the keen interest her father took in the technical aspects of the TV set:

> My dad really looked after the house; we didn't have much money but he could do a lot of DIY so he was constantly expanding and developing our TV. When we lived in Piaseczno there was a kinescope factory nearby so whenever he could get a larger kinescope he did and he would enlarge our TV. So we always had a bigger TV then any of our friends or family members. My dad was already trying to have something like a modern home cinema system. (Pol-14-1959-female)

TV programmes featuring television similarly displayed these gendered patterns of technical competence and control over viewing choices. In the first episode of the Yugoslav series *Headfirst into Strawberries* (1975), for instance, we see the father installing the TV set, while in the Polish serial *War on the Home Front* (1965), the father has the final say in determining whether or not his son can be allowed to watch a film that is due to start on TV.

Despite these similarities between capitalist and socialist worlds, divergent gender patterns in terms of employment contributed to markedly different viewing routines. Because of the higher rates of women's employment in state socialist countries (see Chapter 3) and the persistent burden

[26] Hanot (2003), p. 37; O'Sullivan (1991), p. 167.
[27] E.g. Morley (1986); Parks (2000); Penati (2013), pp. 156–163.
[28] On this gendered aspect of media technology see Golubev and Smolyak (2013), 517–541.

of domestic labour, women in this part of the world had considerably less time to watch television compared to men, as well as compared to women in the West. Of course, in both state socialist and capitalist economies, women in waged labour spent considerably less time watching television than did housewives or employed men. However, since the proportion of such women in state socialist countries was larger, the practice of women's daytime viewing, common in the West, was comparatively rarer.[29] Statistics from the Soviet Union are particularly striking: in 1967 women spent on average five hours fifty-two minutes per week watching television, while men spent on average exactly ten hours in front of the screen. Men enjoyed over eight hours a week more leisure time than women, a discrepancy accounted for almost entirely by the different levels of domestic labour undertaken by women and men.[30]

The gendered inflections of domestic TV cultures, which existed in both state socialist and capitalist countries, were evidently affected by differences in the gendered structures of labour in the two systems. As we shall see later in this chapter, as well as in Chapter 8, these distinctly state socialist gendered patterns of viewing had their counterparts in the gendered nature of television programmes, including the near absence of soap operas and the relative lack of daytime programmes aimed at housewives. As Imre argues: 'Unlike TV in the United States, which explicitly favoured the housewife in the postwar home who may be receptive to advertising, socialist TV targeted the man or the masculine worker, who plops down on the sofa after a long day at the factory.'[31] We could therefore argue that state socialist TV cultures were less prone to support the traditional spatial alignment between gender relations and the public-private divide than were their Western counterparts and were in some ways less feminized. Even though television became an unmistakably domestic medium, the spaces of television were not women's spaces, but spaces of information, education, and entertainment designed primarily for men. During the day, the state socialist woman was expected to engage in the world of work outside the home, and once she came home, her first duty was to tend to domestic chores. Only when the entire 'double burden' of waged and domestic work was out of the way could she relax in front of the TV set.

[29] Skórzyński (1972), pp. 265–290. [30] GARF, f.R-6903, op.3, d.417, ll. 2–10.
[31] Imre (2016), p. 191.

DEPICTIONS OF PRIVACY ON SCREEN

Serial TV fiction provides an ideal vehicle for discussing the paradoxes of privacy on state socialist television. Having evolved out of the temporal logic of the television schedule and its close ties with domestic routines and family life, serial TV fiction has captured viewers' attention through its ability to establish a sense of intimate connection with a recurring cast of characters, as well as by focusing on personal dramas and plots set in domestic environments not unlike those lived in by the viewers themselves.[32] One of the earliest attempts to tackle these issues in societies under communist rule comes from Paulina Bren, who has claimed that in the aftermath of the Soviet invasion of 1968, Czechoslovak authorities sought to use television – and serial fiction, in particular – as a privileged vehicle for the promotion of a 'quiet life' dedicated to family, work, and the local community. Czech serial fiction offered narratives of everyday domestic life that shunned public concerns, thereby discouraging the kind of public activism that led to the turmoil of 1968.[33] Similarly, research on East Germany has suggested that, across the 1970s and 1980s, broadcasters sought to promote private values through TV drama.[34] Available studies from Poland and Hungary also suggest that the vagaries of domestic life and family and community relationships featured prominently in at least some of the serial dramas produced during state socialism.[35]

This research raises a number of interesting questions: Was serial fiction equally 'privatized' across all state socialist countries? What kind of privacy was depicted on screen, and how did it relate to the public thrust of communist politics? As we show on the pages that follow, the proportion of privatized fiction varied considerably across countries, in ways that can be linked to differences between state socialist television systems outlined in Chapter 3. Furthermore, the depictions of privacy promoted in these serial dramas were in tune with collective values and promoted a distinctly 'public' form of privacy. Rather than luring viewers away from public concerns, serial dramas often used domestic settings and personal relationships as a means of commenting on public issues and promoted forms of private life consistent with the public thrust of the communist project. To demonstrate these points, we first use a

32 See, for instance, Geraghty (1981), pp. 9–26. 33 Bren (2010), pp. 126–127.

34 S Pfau (2002), pp. 299–314; Pfau et al. (2010).

35 For Poland and Hungary, see Imre (2016), pp. 199–222; Ostrowska (2013), pp. 65–80.

quantitative analysis of all serial fiction produced during state socialism to show how widespread the turn to domesticity and personal life was across the region. In the second step, we look more closely at a selection of privatized serial dramas from the five countries, focusing on how the nature of privacy was articulated across three interconnected themes: community, family, and gender.

Extent of Privatization

To investigate cross-country differences in the extent of privatization, we first need to clarify what we mean by privatized fiction. Such a term could encompass any series set in a domestic environment, or it could alternatively include any serial that focuses on personal themes, such as the family and romantic relationships. Both, arguably, could contribute to building a distinct image of privacy, and we have therefore sought to work with both definitions by ascertaining (a) how many shows were set in domestic settings, and (b) how many centred on personal plots. Under domestic settings we have included apartments and houses, holiday houses, peasant dwellings, and collective apartments, while public settings covered any location outside the home, ranging from parks, concert halls, and cafes to schools, workplaces, and courts. Personal plots are understood as narratives focused on the individual and his/her interests – intimate relationships, family themes, and friendships – while public plots were concerned with narratives affecting the broader society, such as fighting internal or external enemies, labour, and student life.

Naturally, this approach raises questions about the capacity of quantitative data to capture the multifaceted reality of televised depictions of privacy. In particular, it may be objected that the very attempt to separate private from public contradicts our earlier observations about the intertwining of private and public within socialist societies. Indeed, both the qualitative analysis presented in the next section and prior research on serial fiction produced during state socialism[36] show that serial dramas often combined private and public, with the personal plot functioning as a means of enhancing political messages rather than fostering a focus on privacy. The design of our study sought to take this into account by identifying the two most prominent plots for each series, which enabled us to distinguish between series focused predominantly on personal plots, those containing mixed personal and public plots, and those focused

[36] Reifova et al. (2013), pp. 91–106.

mostly on public plots. The same procedure was used for settings. That said, the essential point is that the quantitative findings should be read alongside the detailed qualitative discussion in the next section.

Before embarking on a closer examination of intra-regional variations between state socialist TV cultures, it is worth comparing our quantitative results with patterns established in the West. The absence of a comparable data set for North American or Western European countries of course means that opportunities for comparative analysis are limited. Nonetheless, it is worth noting the complete absence in our materials of soap operas, understood here as a serial dramatic form aimed primarily at female audiences, revolving around melodramatic narratives and identifications centred on women, designed to appeal primarily to viewers' emotions, and characterized by an open-ended narrative structure without a clear resolution or end.[37] As we shall see further on in this chapter, serial fiction in state socialist countries, much as in the West, often focused on family life and personal relationships. Yet it never adopted all of the distinguishing characteristics of soap operas – in particular the open-ended narrative structure, the melodramatic plot, and the distinct orientation towards female audiences.

Arguably, one reason for this conspicuous absence can be found in the characteristics of socialist TV viewing cultures. As we have noted, state socialist countries were marked by high levels of women's employment, which meant that women also had less time to watch television, especially during the daytime. Socialist TV dramas therefore had to appeal to a different profile of viewers than did Western soaps – one that typically comprised the whole family and included women who were juggling a full-time career outside the home as well as handling domestic chores. As we show later on, this audience profile was reflected in the characteristic family and gender roles depicted in serial fiction.

Although the absence of soap operas was a region-wide phenomenon, depictions of privacy in Eastern European serial fiction were far from homogeneous. As our quantitative data show, the presence of private plots and domestic settings varied considerably. The results for both plots and settings are similar, with the same hierarchies of private and public observable in both (Table 6.1). If we were to generalise the main

[37] Although the definitions of soap opera circulating in academic discourse are far from uniform, these features tend to be highlighted in a range of classic studies of soap operas. See e.g. Ang (2005 [1982]); Geraghty (1991); Hobson (1982); Spigel (1992). For a critical overview of different definitions of soap operas as a genre see Allen (1989), pp. 44–55.

TABLE 6.1 *Plots and settings of serial fiction*

	Mostly private plots	Private and public plots	Mostly public plots or other	TOTAL	Mostly domestic settings	Domestic and public settings	Mostly public settings or other	TOTAL
USSR	8.3%	14.1%	77.6%	177	12.4%	10.0%	79.0%	186
GDR	22.7%	26.6%	50.7%	232	11.4%	29.8%	58.8%	222
ROM	30.0%	20.0%	50.0%	20	3.6%	64.3%	32.1%	28
POL	19.4%	41.7%	38.9%	138	18.8%	42.2%	40.0%	140
YUG	35.9%	41.2%	22.8%	299	8.3%	56.0%	35.7%	310

Note: Figures based on all serial dramas broadcast between 1961 and 1990. Total numbers for settings and plots vary depending on the availability of data for each serial drama. For further details see the Methodological Appendix.

trends, three main levels of privacy can be observed: Yugoslav and Polish series were most privatised, with 60 per cent or more of shows featuring at least one private plot or domestic setting. At the other end of the spectrum was the Soviet Union, where barely one-fifth of the programmes were situated in the domestic sphere and only marginally more included at least one prominent personal plot. In the middle were East Germany and (less clearly) Romania, with about half of the series containing at least one prominent private plot (though our findings for the latter should be taken with caution, given the low number of domestically produced serial dramas).

These results can be linked to the three types of state socialist television systems proposed in Chapter 3. The market state socialist system, found in Yugoslavia, produced the most privatized serial fiction, while the hard-line state socialist system, embodied most clearly in Soviet broadcasting, gave rise to the least privatized serial dramas. The remaining three television cultures ranked between the two extremes: consistent with the traits of the reformist state television system, Polish serial fiction was similar to its Yugoslav counterpart, while Romanian and East German serial dramas were closer to Soviet fiction. Two systemic dimensions of variation can help account for these differences. The first is the extent of party-state oversight over television, which was most intense in hard-line state socialist television systems, where communist elites had more opportunities to ensure that television programming was aligned with the public thrust of the communist vision of progress. The second dimension is transnational orientation: Yugoslav television was systemically most open to the West and contrasted sharply with Soviet television in this respect. As we show in Chapter 7, this corresponded with greater openness to Western imports on Yugoslav screens. Arguably, television professionals working in countries more exposed to Western programming were more likely to emulate aspects of Western formats, including the focus on private life, and also had to contend with audience expectations that may have been shaped by foreign programmes. This also helps explain why the levels of privatization in East German and Romanian television were considerably higher than in the Soviet Union: despite high levels of party-state control, TV broadcasting in these two countries was systemically considerably more open to the West, which was reflected in greater proportions of programming imported from the West as well as (in the German case) greater exposure to dramas shown on West German television.

Articulations of Public Privacy: Community, Family, and Gender

Quantitative results can only tell us so much: while the fact that a show was set in an apartment rather than a police station is significant, numbers alone cannot tell us about the nature of those spaces, or the events that took place there. For this, we require a closer analysis which focuses on characters and plotlines. This section examines a number of prominent shows which sought to depict private life during socialism. In general, we have selected shows which represent the development of serial fiction in our sample countries across three decades. The analysis focuses on how the ideals of public privacy were articulated across three interconnected themes: community, family, and gender. These are not the only areas that could have been analysed (the question of generation was also of key importance), but they are sufficient to show some of the complexities of televised privacy in socialist culture. In so far as possible, we seek both to highlight the shared traits detected in all of the countries in our sample and to highlight some of the significant cross-country differences and changes over time.

Community

As we have seen in the previous section, many state socialist serial dramas were set within an apartment or domestic space, and they homed in on the intimate lives of their characters. Yet it would be hasty to call these dramas of the private sphere: although focused heavily on the domestic, they were usually dramas of negotiation in which characters sought out the correct relationship between the domestic and the social, the family and the neighbourhood, or the nuclear family and the wider family. As Irina Reifová and colleagues have suggested, this was often achieved by combining personal and public plots and having one mirror the other. A storyline about opposition to a reconstruction project at the city hall might be mirrored by the lead character's wife leaving him because the demolitions would cost her parents their home.[38] A similar intertwining of the private and the public can be found in serial dramas from across the region. In the Soviet case, serials following the lives of extended families in villages and small towns, set against the background of major events from official Soviet history, offer particularly good examples.[39]

[38] Reifová et. al. (2013).

[39] For an analysis of such dramas see Prokhorova and Prokhorov (2017), pp. 158–162.

But even in dramas focused predominantly or exclusively on personal lives, public concerns played a prominent role and typically overshadowed the pursuit of individual interests. As Ilia Utekhin has suggested, because of the widespread visibility of personal lives – particularly within communal apartments, but also in the context of the housing shortages noted in the previous section – something akin to a sphere of the 'quasi-familial' was formed in societies under communist rule, where the boundary between public and private was often blurred.[40] This quasi-familial sphere can be glimpsed in the Soviet drama *Day After Day* (1971–1972). The show depicts life in a Moscow communal apartment in which reside two elderly residents, a cohabiting couple, a young male engineer, and a female nurse. While the show often dwells on the characters' private spaces within the apartment, most of the action takes place in the apartment's communal areas, where characters discuss everything from their love lives to their troubles in the workplace. In one episode, the characters all congregate in the kitchen to sing songs, thus underlining the sense of collectivity; in another, they ally themselves to force an unsuitable boyfriend out of the apartment. Similar formulas can be witnessed in numerous follow-ups of the early to mid-1970s with titles such as *Our Neighbours* (*Nashi sosedi*, 1970-c. 1976); *Various People* (*Raznye liudi*, 1973); and *In One Micro-District* (*V odnom mikroraione*, 1976). What is depicted in such shows is a close-knit collective of mutual concern traversing the private and social spheres. This fits with a Soviet vision of society as a densely packed network of groups both formal and informal – the 'great Soviet family' – that would enact the collectivist ideals of state socialism.[41]

Mary Fulbrook has identified similar collectivist notions in her work on East Germany, which she describes as a 'honeycomb state' of mutually overlapping cells where the boundary between state and society was rendered indistinct.[42] In *Heute bei Krügers* (*Today at the Krügers*, 1961–1963), the country's first serial about everyday life, the focus was on how the collective could help to inculcate communist ideals even amongst the most recalcitrant, prompting scholars Katja Kochanowski, Sascha Trültzsch and Reinnhold Viehoff to conclude that private life was

[40] Utekhin (2001). See also Field (2015).

[41] A similar intertwining of the private and the public can be found in serial dramas following the lives of extended families in villages and small towns, such as *The Eternal Call* (1973–1983) and *Shadows Disappear at Noon* (1971). See Prokhorova and Prokhorov (2017).

[42] Fulbrook (2005).

forced to take a back seat in these early dramas.[43] Across the 1970s, they suggest, television drama responded to a call for a more audience-friendly form of TV drama by dialling down the didacticism, although in hit shows such as *The Beloved Fellow Men* (*Die lieben Mitmenschen*, 1972–1974) and *Pensioners Never Have Time* (*Rentner haben niemals Zeit*, 1978), the private sphere remained a means for discussing public concerns. Though less explicitly ideological in its focus, the popular GDR series *Stories over the Garden Fence* (*Geschichten übern Gartenzaun*, 1981) similarly focused on the unlikely private space of citizens' allotments, emphasizing harmonious relationships between individuals of different social origins and different generations. Characters in such shows did encounter problems: in one episode, the main character Claudia gets so tired of her children arguing with her friend that she cuts short a holiday, while a friend of her daughter's struggles to make contact with her stepson. However, these problems were soon resolved through the ingenuity and essential goodness of the characters. In essence, then, the aim of such programming was to depict an ideal notion of private life. Such a life would not be atomized and individualistic, but characterized by fulfilling and mutually supportive relationships with family, friends, and neighbours. We can therefore argue that both in the Soviet Union and in East Germany, privatized serial fiction often constituted a form of edutainment – that is, a hybrid programme genre that, as argued in the previous chapter, used the appeal of entertainment to convey educational messages aligned with communist ideals.

In the Yugoslav case (and to some extent in Poland, too) a somewhat different dynamic emerges. Many of the most popular serials either focused on the family at the expense of community, revealed community tensions, or depicted a form of community at odds with traditional communist values. The widely popular sitcom, *Theatre in the House* (*Pozorište u kući*, 1972–1984), offers a good example of some of these tendencies. Set in an apartment block in Belgrade, the sitcom follows the daily lives of the Petrović family (Figure 6.3). Although superficially similar to East German and Soviet shows in terms of its urban setting and focus on everyday life, *Theatre in the House* is more focused on the family itself, with the action enclosed almost entirely within the walls of the family apartment.

This is not to say that the series' moral messages ran counter to community values. In one episode of the second series, Petrović family

[43] Kochanowski et al. (2013).

FIGURE 6.3 Members of the Petrović family from the Yugoslav series *Theatre in the House*. *Source*: RTS-PATVB

members pretend to be away for New Year's Eve, while effectively hiding and celebrating on their own in the apartment, and yet are visibly relieved when the neighbours unexpectedly crash their party. This was not an isolated example: several other episodes use a similar plot, with friends or neighbours initially causing disturbance and provoking comical misunderstandings and confusion, and later joining in the celebration of unity and harmony.[44] Also telling is the fact that the Petrović family is frequently in touch with the outside world through modern means of communication – especially the telephone, but also radio and television – which tie the family universe to the wider Yugoslav collective.[45] Nonetheless, the relative absence of the community is telling, as is the fact that the series was often publicly criticised for being too narrow and enclosed and too disengaged from the wider society.[46] A similar family-centred universe emerges in the Polish series *War on the Home Front* (*Wojna Domowa*, 1965–1966), which follows the daily life of the Jankowski family and likewise privileges storylines centred on the family unit over the wider community.

Even in those Yugoslav and Polish dramas that centred more explicitly on the community, the nature of communal life was different from the one encountered in Soviet and German examples. For instance, the widely acclaimed Yugoslav serial *Our Small Town* (*Naše malo misto*, 1971–1972), set in an idyllic small town on the Adriatic coast, depicts a communal way of life that is clearly very harmonious, but removed from the ideals of work and industrial efficiency, and centred instead on the pleasures of leisure, consumption, and interpersonal relationships.[47] The community depicted in the Polish series *The Forty-Year-Old Man* (1974–1977) is at first sight much closer to the communist ideal; it follows the life of a model socialist citizen, construction engineer Stefan Karwowski, as he works on some of the landmark accomplishments of Polish engineering (Figure 6.4). On the other hand, however, the series also offers a satirical take on the Polish success story,[48] showing images of quickly deteriorating household appliances in newly built apartments (Episode 2) and small abuses of position, such as a doctor switching on a siren to avoid traffic congestion (Episode 1).

By the 1980s, such departures from the ideal, harmonious socialist community were becoming more and more daring and increasingly common not only in Yugoslavia and Poland, but also in East Germany. The German serial *High-Rise Tales* (*Hochhausgeschichten*, 1980) suggested

[44] See Daković and Milovanović (2016), p. 140.
[45] For an insightful analysis of this aspect see Erdei (2017), pp. 551–552.
[46] Mihelj and Huxtable (2016b), p. 2252.
[47] Mihelj (2013); Duda (2016).
[48] Majer (2005).

FIGURE 6.4 Stefan Karwowski with his wife, Magda, from the Polish series *The Forty-Year-Old Man*. *Source*: FFN.

that high-rises were not mini-communities, but atomised and individualistic spaces. One episode consists of the characters making room for an ‘apartment club’ in the basement of their building to facilitate communication between increasingly alienated inhabitants.[49]

The Polish comedy *4 Alternative Street* (*Alternatywy 4*), which was produced during the Martial Law period but premiered only in 1986, continued the 1970s trend of satirising the country's housing conditions but went much further in mocking the clichés of the ‘block of flats’ genre. In place of the harmonious collectives of the past, the apartment block housed a ragtag bunch of individuals, including a party *apparatchik*, a petty thief (depicted positively), a dissident university professor, and a factory foreman. As Dorota Ostrowska has argued, ‘the workers [in the show] were not heroic; worse, they were not even conscientious.

[49] Steinmetz and Viehoff (2008), pp. 448–449; Raundalen (2014).

They were corrupt, incompetent, lazy and drunk most of the time.'[50] In this sense, the show pointed to a social system that was in the process of decaying. But at the same time, the random characters, for all their differences, seem to get along fine. Even during a time of collapse, community was the one thing that remained.

If series such as *4 Alternative Street* still retained hope in the healing power of the community, the Yugoslav serial *Grey Home* (*Sivi dom*, 1984–1985) abandoned all pretence of a communal safety net. Set in a youth corrective facility, the serial follows the lives of youths who repeatedly try, and fail, to escape from their misery; surrounded by heartless guards, they have no community to support them and no hope for a happy ending. The serial, which achieved cult status among young audiences in the 1980s, chimed with the widespread sense of crisis that gained momentum in Yugoslavia after the death of the country's President Tito in 1980.[51] Although representing a rather extreme version of the disintegration of socialist communities on the small screen, this series clearly forms part of a wider trend that marked the televised representations of community in the 1980s in the broader region. While most still at least paid lip service to the ideal of the community, a closer look reveals a portrayal of privacy that departed from the harmonious idyll that had characterized previous decades. The only country where such a disintegration of fictional communal life was conspicuously absent was the Soviet Union – yet this was simply because Soviet television, unlike other broadcasters in the region, largely abandoned fictional representations of private life. By the 1980s, Soviet serial dramas focused almost entirely on the individual at work or on action heroes, which meant that the narrative action no longer took place in domestic spaces but on the battlefield, the border post, or in the workplace.

Family and Gender Relations

As shown in the previous section, socialist dramas of the private often centred on the community and showcased a form of private life that privileged the common good over private interests. In this context, one might expect that family life and its everyday complications would be a marginal concern. And yet, family dramas – and, in particular, family sitcoms – were a relatively common sight on television screens across Eastern Europe. In this sense, socialist serial fiction had much in common

[50] Ostrowska (2013), p. 76. [51] Spasovska (2017).

with serial dramas produced in Western Europe and North America, which also regularly dwelled on everyday dramas of family life.[52]

The discourses surrounding family dramas on both sides of the Iron Curtain were also in many ways strikingly similar. As Lynn Spigel notes in her analysis of popular and professional discourses in the United States, television's central characteristics were thought to be its immediacy and its intimacy.[53] Family drama tapped into these characteristics, offering viewers a connection with familiar characters depicted in intimate situations. Despite the differences between Western and communist discourses on privacy, commentators in the state socialist world, too, found it important for serial fiction to feature identifiable characters who would speak to viewers in everyday language. In 1973, Soviet journalist A. Egorov argued that

> the family chronicle . . . summons up the very nature of television communication. In the family's evening get-together in millions of homes comes a spectacle which closely coincides with the life of these very houses. The theatrical enclosure in the TV window is viewed as a continuation of one's own walls, and there is the pleasure of becoming the fifth player in a game of dominoes or, conversely, offering your plate towards the screen so as to sample Auntie Nastia's special borsch.[54]

Much as in the West, the family provided an identifiable locus of identity on state socialist TV screens, mirroring the domestic environment in which viewers were ensconced and thus turning the protagonists of TV shows into 'media friends'.[55]

Yet how did this focus on family life fare in the context of a political system that was radically public in its orientation? As noted earlier, Paulina Bren's analysis of Czechoslovak serial fiction suggests that such TV families existed 'in and of themselves' and seemed to be uninterested in public life.[56] Television's focus on the family therefore appeared to be the harbinger of a dangerous turn towards the private, away from the civic concerns that were so fundamental to traditional communist discourse. However, to see the situation in such stark terms obscures the ideological work performed by TV representations of family life, if not in Czechoslovakia then certainly in other state socialist countries. In early

[52] E.g. Gunter and Svennevig (1987); Haralovich (1988); Spigel (1992); Taylor (1989).
[53] Spigel (1992), pp. 136–142.
[54] A. Egorov. 1973. 'Istorii ne tol'ko semeinye,' *Sovetskoe radio i televidenie* 7 (1973): 27–28.
[55] Bloch (2013). [56] Bren (2010), pp. 126–127.

Soviet family dramas, such as the Estonian serial *What's New in the Koosta Family?* (*Mis Koosta peres uudist?*, 1971) or the long-running Lithuanian sitcom *The Petraitis Family* (*Petraičių šeimoje*, 1964–72), the private sphere provided a means for discussing wider public issues. One episode of *The Petraitis Family* poked fun at rumours circulating in Lithuania that a war was imminent, by having one character who believed the rumours stock up on matches and soap.[57] By having a naïve character believe such rumours, viewers learned to regard such opinions negatively, particularly when corrected by a more trusted member of the Petraitis family. Thus, in this case, viewers' trust in the family at the centre of the show allowed for the transmission of political messages to the public – perhaps more effectively than did traditional, non-fiction mass media.

Many other socialist family dramas included characters that were similarly naïve or otherwise failed to live up to the standards of model state socialist citizens but ultimately realized their mistakes with the help of others. In the aforementioned Polish serial *The Forty-Year-Old Man* (1974–1976), members of engineer Karwowski's family are occasionally lured by fashion and appear somewhat snobbish, but the wider community helps them steer away from these traps.[58] Likewise, housemaid Tina in the Yugoslav series *Theatre in the House* (1972–1984) is rather naïve and easily seduced by material comforts, but it is clear that other members of the family regard her as an outlier, with the teenage son on one occasion referring to her as 'a victim of consumerist psychology' (Episode 1, Season 2). In both cases, then, the family setting is used to communicate messages with public resonance, attuned to a recognizably communist vision of modern society – in this case, a society where consumerism, snobbism, and conspicuous consumption are to be sneered at and guarded against. Yet again we therefore see that state socialist serial fiction, though focused on private life, retained a pronounced didactic tone, aligned with the public mission of state socialist television discussed in the previous chapter.

Family dramas also contributed to promoting desirable forms of socialist family life, showcasing models of personal conduct appropriate for men and women, parents and children, and relatives and neighbours. Depictions of an idealised form of family life, underpinned by established hierarchies of gender, generational, class, and racial relations, were of

[57] A. Egorov. 1973. 'Istorii ne tol'ko semeinye,' *Sovetskoe radio i televidenie* 7 (1973): 27–28.
[58] Ostrowska (2013), p. 76.

course an integral part of serial family dramas elsewhere in the world. Yet, in serial fiction produced in state socialist countries, these model relationships were influenced by ideals rooted in the communist vision of progress. This is particularly evident in depictions of women and gender relations. The presence of women at work was perhaps the most visible difference between the Western and the state socialist serial, reflecting a socialist vision of gender equality in which the equal presence of women at work was not simply a desideratum, but an achievement. In general, programming produced within the socialist context featured women in the context of their workplace. An extreme case is provided by the unnamed 'working woman' in the Polish serial *The Forty-Year-Old Man* (1974–1976), who pops up as a different character and in a different profession every week, exclaiming, 'I'm a working woman and I'm not afraid of any kind of work.'[59] Such female characters evidently stood in stark contrast to the domesticated housewives commonly encountered in early US family dramas.[60]

Yet socialist television did not ignore the various obstacles to women's employment. While the central female characters in socialist TV families were typically professionals with their own careers, the narrative plots regularly reflected popular anxieties about the negative consequences for family and community of women's employment. In Episode 26 of the first season of the Yugoslav show *Theatre in the House* (1972–1984), Olga Petrović, who started the series as a housewife, resolves to find employment. Before her decision becomes public knowledge, she encounters several male neighbours who laud her supposed dedication to the household and family, express envy for her husband for having 'a proper housewife', and generally lament the consequences of women's employment. Despite such comments, Olga persists and later in the show finds permanent employment, and is supported by both her husband and her mother in this endeavour. While such a set-up sends a reasonably clear message about the preferred attitude to women's employment, it also allows more critical voices to air, again using the family setting to send educational messages about preferred conduct.

Several family dramas also reflected an awareness of the double burden carried by women in state socialist countries. In many cases, television programming took this gendered division of labour for granted. For instance, Imre draws attention to the role of Magda Karworski, the wife

[59] Imre (2016), p. 205. [60] E.g. Haralovich (1988); Spigel (1992).

of the *Forty Year-Old Man* (1974–1977) who 'is visibly suffering under the double burden of domestic and paid work'.[61] Likewise in the Romanian comedy *Love is a Great Thing: Tanta and Costel* (*Iubirea e un lucru foarte mare: Tanța și Costel*, 1962), where we see Tanta, Costel's disappointed wife, in the kitchen preparing the New Year's meal. In other cases, there was some awareness of the inequality of these gender roles, and the need for men to take on their fair share. The first episode of the East German series *Today at the Krügers* (*Heute bei Krügers*, 1960–1963) saw Anna Krüger at work in the 'Factory of a Thousand Little Things' and then battling with the housework. The episode followed Anna as she struggled to persuade first her children, then her husband to help her with domestic chores, an endeavour in which she was eventually successful.

It is not a coincidence that this critical take on women's double burden, leading to a successful redistribution of domestic chores among family members, comes from East Germany. Our analysis suggests that the output of East German television displayed a different image of women to the other countries in our sample. This finding is consistent with the country's policies towards women which, while contradictory, did succeed in alleviating some of the burdens placed upon them.[62] In 1979–80, for instance, East Germany's Deutscher Fernsehfunk (DFF) broadcast the serial *Good Morning, Beautiful!* (Guten Morgen, du Schöne! 1979–80) which took the form of a fictionalised monologue on women's lives, based on interviews carried out in East Germany with women of all ages and origins. However, German authorities did not welcome the characters' complaints about the country's stifling atmosphere appearing in *Good Morning, Beautiful!*: some parts were only shown on television after the fall of the wall, while others were shunted into the 'graveyard' slot on the second channel.[63] This suggests that depictions of public privacy on socialist TV screens, while allowing for a measure of contestation, nonetheless had to remain within the bounds of the publicly permissible.

East German series apart, socialist serial dramas were generally reluctant to do more than tip their hat to the issue of gender inequality. Indeed, many series even appeared to suggest that the social equilibrium depended on the maintenance of a more traditional gender balance. In an episode of the Polish serial *War on the Home Front* (1965), father and son try to surprise Zofia on Mother's Day by helping out with the

[61] Imre (2016), p. 205. [62] Harsch (2008); Fulbrook (2005), pp. 141–175.
[63] Steinmetz and Viehoff (2008).

domestic chores. However, the men prove unable to accomplish even the most basic household chores, with the mother increasingly uneasy about giving away control of her household responsibilities. Thus, the message was that men might occasionally help out around the house, but that a more radical change to gender roles could lead to chaos. These conclusions chime to some extent with arguments developed by Bren in relation to Czechoslovak series, where women figured in central roles and became pivotal in maintaining social order and rebuilding the nation as a counterweight to male inadequacy. In her account, the process of normalization entailed both a turn from the public to the private sphere and a concomitant shift from men to women as the privileged actors of late socialism.[64] However, our research suggests that Bren's account cannot be extended in full to all the other state socialist countries. Although some shows in our sample illustrated anxieties over ageing and sexual potency, men possessed stable, and relatively untroubled, roles as workers and as fathers.

A similar range of subtle criticism, limited negotiation, and reaffirmation of traditional values can be detected also in representations of extramarital affairs and sexuality in socialist serial fiction. Extramarital affairs were a frequent plot ingredient in many countries, increasingly so towards the end of communist rule. In the aforementioned Polish serial *Forty-Year-Old Man* (1974–1977), it is often intimated that the husband referred to in the show's title is having an affair, while the wife in the cult Romanian comedy *Tanta and Costel* (*Tanța și Costel*, 1965-1970) suspects her husband of having an affair when he fails to arrive home at the appointed hour. Likewise, the central male character in the Yugoslav series *Our Small Town* (1971–1972), the town's doctor Luigi, is visibly attracted to younger women, and although he never engages in an explicit affair on screen, sexual innuendos are an integral part of the serial's slapstick humour throughout.

Again, East German serial dramas went furthest in challenging the traditional family ideal. *Stories over the Garden Fence* told the story of the divorced nurse Claudia Hoffmann and her four children; the sitcom *But Dad!* (*Aber, Vati!* 1969, 1972) focused on a widowed father's fish-out-of-water struggles to look after his children. Furthermore, GDR dramas were also open to plots that challenged traditional gendered notions of sexuality. For example, the series *The Seven Affairs of Doña Juanita* (Die sieben Affären der Doña Juanita, 1973) placed the romances

[64] Bren (2010), pp. 159–176.

of its sexually confident female 'Don Juan' at its heart. While her many affairs were depicted as a process of learning, her quest was not to find 'Mr. Right', but rather to combine her career with a fulfilling relationship. This once again illustrates the fundamental differences between East Germany and the other countries in our sample.

CONCLUSIONS

As shown in this chapter, television's relationship to privacy in state socialist countries had much in common with its counterparts in the capitalist economies of the West but was also marked by important differences. This applied both to the diffusion of television as a domestic object and part and parcel of daily routines, as well as to the depictions of privacy on screen. Much as in the West, television was initially associated with collective viewing in public and semi-public spaces and functioned as a marker of social status and modernity but then quickly turned into an everyday necessity designed primarily for domestic viewing, assumed a central place in family homes and everyday life, and became associated with characteristic gendered patterns of control, power, and authority. Yet at the same time, our materials suggest that cultures of television in the state socialist world formed part of a type of domesticity that was embedded in distinctly state socialist structures of the economy, politics, and society, marked by different patterns of social stratification and distinction, smaller sizes of private dwellings, housing shortages, and higher levels of women's employment. These gave rise to a TV viewing culture that was unmistakably modern but also inflected by a recognizably communist vision of modernity and progress.

A balance of similarities and differences with the West can be observed in depictions of on-screen privacy, too, although the differences appear more pronounced. Much as with Western television, series set in the domestic sphere were common. However, socialist serial dramas were *not* dramas of the private but instead situated private lives within the wider web of relationships occurring within apartment blocks, allotments, or workplaces which traversed the public-private boundary. Even when focusing squarely on family life, state socialist serial fiction used the private setting to convey messages of public significance and showcase modes of private behaviour and relationship consistent with communist ideals. The distinctly communist vision of modern life also informed depictions of gender relations. Although representations of women and their position within the family were highly traditional, and continued to take for granted a woman's place tending the private sphere, women were also depicted as workers and as key drivers of socialist modernization. This was a key difference from Western serial fiction of the same period, which generally confined women to the domestic sphere.

These shared characteristics of privatized fiction in the state socialist world aside, our analysis also shows that depictions of privacy in serial fiction varied considerably across countries. As the quantitative analysis revealed, Yugoslav and Polish television showed a considerably higher degree of comfort in depicting the private sphere, while Soviet television largely preferred to depict public-oriented plots and settings in its serial fiction. A similar pattern emerged from our qualitative analysis: Yugoslav and Polish television were less inclined to depict community and personal relationships in an idealised manner and more often dramatized the tensions created between official ideals and realities on the ground. In contrast, Soviet serial fiction remained faithful to an idyllic depiction of private life, in which common aspirations took precedence over the pursuit of individual pleasures and interests. Taken together, the quantitative and qualitative layers of analysis suggest that television cultures emerging in the context of hard-line state socialist television systems were less open to narrative plots focused on personal life and domesticity, and even when they engaged with such plots, they were more likely adopt a didactic approach.

That said, the alignment between systemic and cultural features was not perfect – a fact revealed by the considerably more daring depictions of gender relations and sexuality in East German serial dramas. In this sense, we could say that liberalism in one aspect of private life does not always coincide with liberalism in another: while East German serial fiction was consistent with the hard-line nature of its television system, more prone to depict communal life in an idealized manner, and in that sense resembled Soviet dramas, its treatment of women's role in the family, and extramarital affairs and sexuality, was considerably more liberal. The precise reasons for this would require a more detailed examination, but it is feasible to expect that the more liberal depiction of the changing shape of the family and gender roles was linked to the country's more progressive gender policies and higher divorce rates.

7

Transnationalism

So far, we have examined the role of state socialist television in mediating cultural perceptions and routines close to home: its central location in family homes and in everyday routines; its involvement in negotiating the rules of private conduct and communal life; its role in establishing a shared public realm available to all socialist citizens; and its contribution to furthering the political, educational, and cultural goals of communist-led states. Yet the reach of state socialist screens extended well beyond the realms of domestic life and beyond the boundaries of nations and states. The ideological vision and political reality of communism were profoundly transnational, premised on the belief in the transnational camaraderie of the working class. Although the patterns of international alliances among state socialist countries changed considerably over the course of the Cold War, this vision of transnational solidarity among workers remained central to the communist project throughout the period. It served as the basis for close political, economic, and cultural ties among communist-led countries, as well as for their engagement both with the liberal democracies of the West and with the Global South.[1]

As we show in this chapter, state socialist television cultures shared a commitment to transnationalism: television schedules included substantial proportions of imported material, as they did elsewhere in the world, and audiences often thought of the small screen as a means of connecting with the distant corners of the globe. In this sense, the chapter confirms

[1] A selection of recent examples of such research includes Bracke and Mark (2015); David-Fox (2015); Gorsuch and Koenker (2013).

that state socialist television formed an integral part of global networks of television broadcasting, and contributes to the growing literature on transnational television history.[2] Yet, in line with the comparative thrust of our book, our focus here is on situating state socialist TV transnationalism comparatively. Using the analytical framework introduced in Chapter 2, we therefore investigate the relative *openness* of state socialist television cultures to transnational exchanges and ties and the *origins* of these cross-border interactions and links. Did television succeeded in establishing a cross-border television culture that was pan-socialist and attuned to the vision of the transnational solidarity of the working classes? Or did it rather, as a Romanian song from the 1970s suggests, offer a 'magic window' that was oriented primarily to the West and used the appeal of Western actors, artists, and fictional characters to bring colour to an otherwise 'bleak programme'?

When I turn on the TV, / through its magic window / the whole world comes in all of a sudden, / and together with it, I live / a wonderful story / and everything seems so new and strange.

Sometimes I begin a trip on the sea / between agitated waves / and I travel around the world like Magellan. / At other times, I fly towards the sun / and with traveling birds / I live a year in one moment.

Often, I get visits / from great actors from around the world. / One time, I had coffee with Jean Marais, / and Gabin once told me / that with a girl like me, / he would gladly play Maigret again.

In my own house / for the beautiful Davis Cup / tennis players like Năstase and Ţiriac competed.

What wonderful moments / having great significance / have coloured my bleak programme.

During the weekend / I live an adventure with Mannix, / and I've lately started to enjoy / listening to Bernstein. / I am friends with Barney and his beloved wife / and I am also friends with Aschiuta / and those announcers who invite us to / 'watch Programme X'.

When I turn on the TV, / through its magic window / the whole world comes in. Mihaela Mihai: 'Television'[3]

To answer these questions, we first analyse the balance of domestically produced and imported TV materials and the origin of foreign programming across the five countries, drawing on original quantitative data sets produced for this purpose, as well as on a range of archival and other

[2] E.g. Badenoch et al. (2013); Fickers and Johnson (2012); Hilmes (2011).

[3] AMDTR, rebroadcast during the special TV programme celebrating the 57th anniversary of Television Romania, *Why Do We Love Television Romania* (*De ce iubim Televiziunea Română*), 31 December 2013.

sources. Apart from describing how the patterns of cross-border television flows varied across countries and changed over time, we also consider the contextual factors that can explain these variations. In the second part of the chapter, we ask what foreign television programmes meant for state socialist audiences and their perceptions of their country and the world. Could greater openness to foreign content and imports from the West promote cosmopolitanism, specifically a sense of transnational ties with other socialist countries, or did it rather prompt viewers to embrace the lifestyle and values associated with consumer capitalism, as communist elites feared?

TRANSNATIONAL PROGRAMME FLOWS

As noted in Chapter 3, state socialist TV broadcasters eagerly participated in cross-border exchanges of technology, personnel, and programming from early on and established transnational infrastructures to facilitate such exchanges both within the state socialist world and beyond. These included the Intervision programme exchange organized through the Soviet-dominated OIRT, bilateral agreements, and occasional collaborations with the Eurovision programme exchange through the EBU. Yet questions remain: were state socialist countries all equally open to television imports; how did the dependence on foreign programming change over time; and how can we explain these cross-country differences and changes? Did the state socialist transnational exchange infrastructure succeed in countering the pull of programming produced in the capitalist world, giving rise to a distinctly socialist form of TV transnationalism? To answer these questions, this section draws on a range of archival and secondary sources, as well as on two sets of original data covering our five countries: (1) data on all the programmes broadcast on national channels, using a one-week sample at five-year intervals between 1960 and 1990, and (2) data on all fictional TV series broadcast between 1961 and 1990. In line with the analytical framework introduced in Chapter 2, two distinct aspects of transnational flows are examined: the openness to foreign inflows and the origin of imports.

Ours is not the first attempt to map transnational television flows in the Cold War era. Over the course of the 1960s and the 1970s, scholarly concerns over the impact of transnational media flows, associated with discussions about cultural imperialism and Americanization, became intertwined with the Cold War competition over former colonies in the Global South and fed into a succession of debates within the United

Nations and UNESCO, culminating in a drive to create a new, more balanced world information order.[4] To provide empirical evidence of global communication imbalances, UNESCO commissioned several surveys of international communication flows, including two that looked at television broadcasting and covered several state socialist countries.[5] Both surveys suggested wide differences in the levels of imported programming broadcast on state socialist television, highlighting the exceptional status of the Soviet Union as by far the most closed to imports. They also showed the prominence of entertainment programming among imports and a substantial presence of Western imports.[6] However, because of a limited time span and inconsistencies in the selection of countries – only some countries appeared in both surveys – UNESCO data offer limited opportunities for in-depth comparisons and longitudinal analysis. To compensate for this, our own analysis covered a considerably longer period and kept the selection of countries constant.

OPENNESS TO FOREIGN PROGRAMMING

With regard to openness to foreign imports, our results are broadly aligned with those of the UNESCO surveys and confirm the existence of marked intra-regional differences, as well as the prominence of entertainment among imported programming. With regard to both imported programming as a whole, and imported serial drama (Table 7.1), the Soviet Union was by far the most resistant to foreign material. The country in our sample with the next lowest level of imports, East Germany, devoted almost four times as much of its schedule time to foreign programming, and the serial fiction broadcast in the country included twice as much imported material. Poland and Romania were more open to imports on both counts; the only slight discrepancy is found with Yugoslavia, the country most welcoming to imports when looking at programming as a whole, yet more inward-looking when considering only serial fiction, where the proportion of imported material is lower than for all other countries except the Soviet Union. It is also clear that in all the countries, imports were considerably more prominent in the realm of serial fiction than in programming as a whole.

[4] UNESCO (1980). [5] Nordenstreng and Varis (1974); Varis (1984).
[6] Nordenstreng and Varis (1974), p. 25.

TABLE 7.1 *Estimated share of imported programming and serial fiction*

	Share of imported programming in total broadcast content, 1960–1990	**Share of imported programming in total serial fiction broadcast, 1961–1990**
USSR	5.2%	35.9%
GDR	19.8%	71.7%
Poland	22.0%	79.5%
Romania	24.7%	90.6%
Yugoslavia	27.8%	65.3%

Note: Figures for programming based on the analysis of TV schedules for a sample week, at five-year intervals, from 1960 to 1990. Figures for serial fiction based on all serial dramas broadcast between 1961 and 1990. For further details see the Methodological Appendix.

How can we explain these findings? As far as the total volume of imported programming is concerned, the differences between the countries can largely be ascribed to the size of the economy, measured by the country's gross domestic product. The Soviet Union, which was by far the largest economy in the region, was also the least reliant on imports, while the two smallest economies, Yugoslavia and Romania, imported far more of their programming. That economic considerations played an important role in shaping decisions over the volume of imports is confirmed by other sources. As a representative of Yugoslav television explained in 1968, foreign programmes were often both better and cheaper than domestically produced content.[7] The same argument was brought up by a Romanian television professional in an attempt to explain the limited volume of domestic drama production: 'Rather than make a production that cost 5,000 Lei, it was better to buy a series that cost 200' (Rom-13-1932-Male).

Yet, when looking at comparative data on serial fiction, the link with economic wealth is less straightforward: Yugoslavia produced considerably more serial drama than its relatively small economy would suggest. This can be explained by its greater investment in serial fiction, as well as by elite concerns over the growing appeal of imported serial drama. Virtually from the beginning, serial drama was a staple of Yugoslav domestic TV production, with the first series, *The Service Station*

[7] 'Uvozna zabava jeftinija' *TV Novosti*, 27 January–2 February, 1968, p. 5.

(*Servisna stanica*, 1959), broadcast live from the studio of TV Belgrade merely a year after the launch of regular broadcasting.[8] As the popular press of the era attests, serial fiction was considered one of the greatest achievements of Yugoslav broadcasting and, as one article put it, Yugoslav television was virtually unthinkable without it.[9] Contemporary audience research confirmed the popularity of domestic serial production compared to imports of the same genre,[10] and domestic entertainment, including serial fiction, was explicitly identified among political and cultural elites as an effective means of rivalling the potentially detrimental effects of imported programming.[11]

The importance of considering factors beyond economic performance comes to the fore even more clearly when we look at changes over time. Although all the countries saw their gross domestic product decline substantially from the second half of the 1970s onwards,[12] this did not necessarily have the effect of increasing their reliance on imported programming. On the contrary, all countries saw the proportion of foreign content decline between 1975 and 1980 (Figure 7.1). A marked increase in imports came only towards the late 1980s and was linked with political changes at the time and the gradual opening to the West.

Furthermore, when countries did register a spike in imports – as was the case in 1970 for Romania and in 1975 for Yugoslavia and East Germany – this was likely due to factors other than fluctuations in the national economies. In Romania and Yugoslavia, the sharp rise in imports followed the introduction of a second channel – in 1969 in Romania and in 1971 in Yugoslavia – which increased the total volume of broadcast hours and created a level of demand that could not be satisfied by domestic production alone. In East Germany, on the other hand, the launch of a second channel in 1969 did not have an immediate effect; the marked increase in foreign programming is noted only in 1975 and is arguably due to policy changes introduced in the early 1970s.[13] In Poland and the Soviet Union, likewise, the introduction of

[8] Novaković (1984). [9] 'Svemoćni V.D. Raka,' *TV Novosti*, 5 July 1974, pp. 18–19.

[10] AHRTV, Radio-televizija Zagreb. 1982. *Narodna revolucija u igranim programima Televizije Zagreb: Rezultati istraživanja javnog mnijenja in pregled sadržaja*. Zagreb: Radio-televizija Zagreb, Centar za studij programa.

[11] AJ, f. 142, k. S-437, 'Informacija o aktuelnim pitanjima u oblasti informisanja i ostvarivanju uloge i zadataka Socijalističkog saveza,' 1979, pp. 9–10.

[12] Berendt (2009), p. 34. [13] Dittmar (2005).

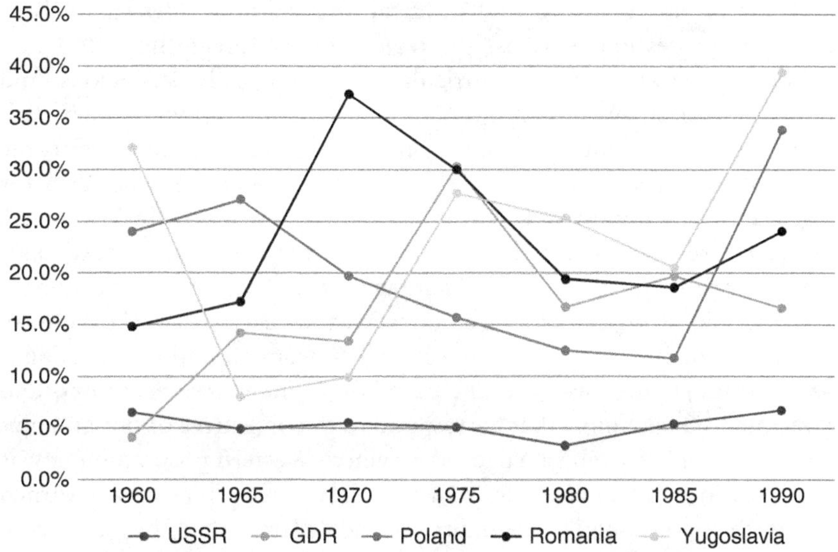

FIGURE 7.1 Trends in the share of imported programming in total broadcast content, 1960–1990.
Note: See notes for Table 7.1.

additional channels had little effect on the proportion of imports, suggesting that other causes were at play in these countries.[14]

Several factors may have contributed to these patterns, which are difficult to confirm or disprove them solely based on the data we have. Nonetheless, we can offer some tentative suggestions. On the one hand, it is plausible that the decline in imported content in times of economic hardship was fuelled by elite concerns over the cultural and political impact of imported programming, which led to a greater investment in domestic production. Following this logic, countries in the region may have decided to give priority to domestic production over imports even when economic considerations may have suggested otherwise. Such an argument is plausible, and our data on the volume of domestic serial drama clearly show that the 1970s were marked by sharp increases in the absolute volume of domestic serial production.[15]

[14] Trends in the proportion of imported serial fiction are less uniform, but here, too, our data confirm that economic decline did not necessarily make television cultures more open to foreign products.

[15] In Poland, Romania, the Soviet Union, and Yugoslavia, the number of serial dramas produced during the 1970s was more than double the number produced during the 1960s. In East Germany, the number rose by 10 per cent in the same period.

There is also evidence that political and cultural elites, as well as television professionals across the region, found foreign imports – and Western programming, in particular – ideologically suspicious and resisted it even when the economic need for imports increased. As explained in an internal industry report issued in Poland in 1971, the introduction of a second channel in 1970 had increased the need for imported programming, yet at the same time, differences in ideological messages presented an obstacle, as imports from the West, in particular, could carry with them 'a hidden agenda of cultural expansion'.[16] Likewise, in Romania, Ceauşescu insisted in 1971 that the country 'must end the importation of decadent films from abroad that introduce a retrograde, bourgeois view' and called on Romanian screenwriters and directors to 'make films that correspond to the objectives of our communist education'.[17] Even in Yugoslavia, where Western programming was available in abundance, political and cultural elites repeatedly warned about the 'consumerist mentality' allegedly promoted by such programmes and called for more attention to be paid to the ideological orientation of imported materials.[18]

Economic obstacles were at work, too, at least when it came to purchasing programming from beyond the state socialist world. This was due to a lack of foreign currency that resulted from the combined effects of economic decline and the failure of state socialist countries to export their own programmes beyond the Iron Curtain. Some Western broadcasters allowed their state socialist counterparts to buy programming on credit, which led over time to huge debts.[19] The Polish example demonstrates the consequences this had for the balance of domestic and foreign programming: by the end of the 1970s, the lack of hard currency meant that Polish television was unable to purchase foreign content and, because of a lack of colour film, it was able neither to produce new shows suitable for programme exchange nor to make export copies of old shows. The only

[16] Sergiusz Mikulicz. 1971. 'Współpraca z Zagranicą.' in *Z Anteny PR i Ekranu TV*, Warszawa: Wydawnictwa Radia i Telewizji, p. 118.

[17] Nicolae Ceauşescu. 1984. *Romania pe Drumul Constructiei Societatii Socialiste Multilateral Dezvoltate. Rapoarte, Cuvintari, Interviuri, Articole. Vol. 26: May 1971–Februarie 1972*. 1972. Bucharest: Ed. Politica, p. 236.

[18] E.g. AJ, f. 142, k. S-437, 'Informacija o aktuelnim pitanjima u oblasti informisanja i ostvarivanju uloge i zadataka Socijalističkog saveza,' 1979, pp. 9–10; HAD, f. 1228, d. 5601, 'Smernice za programsku politiku jugoslovenskih TV stanica za 1981. godinu,' 1980, p 7.

[19] Heinrich-Franke and Immel (2013).

foreign programmes that could be broadcast were those bought on credit and imported from Intervision.[20]

Our longitudinal data also confirm the unique position of the Soviet Union and offer further evidence of its status as a core country. Of our five countries, Soviet television was by far the most resistant to imports, and its reluctance to broadcast foreign programmes continued regardless of changes in the political and economic environment. The share of imported material in all Soviet programming remained consistently low throughout the sample period (Figure 7.1). In this case, neither an adverse economic climate nor the introduction of new channels was reason enough for the core state socialist country to drop its guard when it came to foreign television.

Taken together, these results echo the findings of prior comparative work on television imports, which likewise singles out economic wealth as a key determinant[21] but also acknowledges that in some cases, smaller economies produce a higher percentage of domestic entertainment than their relative economic wealth would suggest.[22] This means that the patterns of state socialist imports were in part shaped by the same causal factors identified in the Western world and in the post-socialist context. That said, our analysis also indicates that the size of the economy interacts with other contextual factors, some of which are characteristic of the state socialist world (ideological considerations and obstacles to foreign payments) and others which are more universal in reach (the country's core-periphery position and the introduction of a second channel). It is therefore likely that the volume of imports globally is determined by differing constellations of factors, which vary depending on the nature of political rule.

ORIGIN OF IMPORTS

Significant variation between state socialist television cultures can also be seen in the origin of imports. While Romania and Yugoslavia relied overwhelmingly on imports from Western Europe, North America, and Australia, East Germany and the Soviet Union imported most of their foreign programming from the state socialist world (Table 7.2). As also

[20] Jerzy Peltz. 1982. 'Dla Telewizji czyli Dla Widza,' *Antena*, issue 1 (1982), p.3; Danuta Kwiatkowska. 1981. 'Kilka Pytań do Jacka Fuksiewicz, szefa Naczelnej Redakcji Programów Filmowych,' *Antena*, Issue 37 (1981).

[21] Dupagne and Waterman (1998); Štětka (2012b). [22] Picard (2011), p. 52.

TABLE 7.2 *Origin of imported programming and serial fiction*

	Origin of imported programming, 1960–1990		Origin of imported serial fiction, 1961–1990	
	From Western countries	From state socialist countries	From Western countries	From state socialist countries
USSR	23.7%	74.3%	29.2%	70.1%
GDR	43.6%	55.6%	41.0%	58.3%
Poland	65.5%	31.8%	65.0%	33.5%
Romania	83.1%	16.2%	66.7%	32.0%
Yugoslavia	88.6%	9.2%	83.0%	16.1%

Note: Figures for programming based on the analysis of TV schedules for a sample week, at five-year intervals, from 1960 to 1990. Figures for serial fiction based on all serial dramas broadcast between 1961 and 1990. For further details see the Methodological Appendix.

evident from the data, the presence of imports from the Global South was negligible across the region, a result that is out of tune with the international ambitions of several countries, most notably the Soviet Union, but also Yugoslavia, to intensify their ties with the former Western colonies in Asia, South America, and Africa. In Yugoslavia, for instance, editorial policies reflected the country's commitment to the Non-Aligned Movement and called for more imported programming from non-aligned countries,[23] yet our analysis suggests that these demands had little effect on the patterns of foreign TV flows.

These figures suggest that the attempt to centre transnational programme flows on the state socialist world was only moderately successful: only two out of five countries relied primarily on state socialist imports. While we should be wary of generalising this result to the state socialist world as a whole – not least because of the peculiar positions of Romania and Yugoslavia, to which we return later – this result is nonetheless indicative of the limited appeal of state socialist television vis-à-vis its Western rival. Existing research also shows that while state socialist countries imported a substantial proportion of their programming from the West, broadcasters in the capitalist world were far more reluctant to accept state socialist

[23] HDA, f. 1228, d. 5601, 'Smernice za programsku politiku jugoslovenskih TV stanica za 1981. godinu,' 1980, p 5.

imports.[24] Crucially, however, these results suggest that state socialist television cultures were more transnational – and indeed more global – than their Western counterparts: while state socialist television schedules included a substantial volume of content originating from both sides of the Iron Curtain, television screens in the West were oriented almost exclusively to other Western countries. As a result, state socialist television cultures were considerably more likely to function as global cultural fora, offering audiences a chance to engage with programming providing competing versions of modernity and progress – an issue we return to in the second part of this chapter.

Let us now look more closely at the factors that help explain these patterns, starting with the most obvious: the transnational orientations of state television systems and specifically their institutional and technological ties with Western broadcasters. This factor clearly helps explain the marked reliance on capitalist imports in Yugoslavia and Romania. As a member of the EBU rather than the OIRT, Yugoslav television could import Western European programming more easily and cheaply than could other state socialist countries. Both Romania and Yugoslavia also opted for the PAL standard of colour broadcasting, which was more commonly used in Western Europe and facilitated the transmission of Western imports. Finally, compared to the rest of the region, both countries enjoyed closer relationships with Western countries, and especially with the United States, and used these relationships to assert their independence from the Soviet Union. In Romania, the period of opening to the United States in the late 1960s and the early 1970s thus coincided with a wave of American television fiction, ranging from the children's drama series *Daktari* and the detective series *Kojak* and *Mannix* to the science fiction series *Lost in Space*.[25] This was also a period when several major media events were covered live on Romanian television with the help of US satellite links, including the Apollo space missions and Ceauşescu's visit to the United States in 1970.[26] American imports were a familiar sight on Yugoslav screens, too. Over the course of the 1960s and the 1970s, Yugoslav viewers

[24] Dawson (1989), pp. 66–68; Eugster (1983), p. 282; Heinrich-Franke and Immel (2013).

[25] Bondebjerg et al. (2008), p. 177; Štětka (2012a), p. 110.

[26] NARA, RG 59 General Records of the Department of State, 1763–2002, Central Foreign Policy Files, 1966–1969, Box 453, Telegram from the US Embassy Bucharest to US Department of State, 'Ceauşescu visit – TV satellite transmissions,' 11 November 1970.

could follow the series *Bonanza*, the medical drama *Dr Kildare*, and the soap opera *Peyton Place*, among many others.[27]

However, differences in foreign policies and institutional and technological ties are insufficient to explain the peculiarity of Polish imports: although Polish television was firmly integrated into state socialist infrastructures and geographically insulated from cross-border television signals from the West, it nonetheless imported the majority of its programming from beyond the Iron Curtain. To explain this, it is useful to consider domestic factors, in particular the fact that imported entertainment of any provenance or type was simply a means of appeasing and distracting the domestic population. If we are to believe the US foreign diplomat working for the US consulate in the Polish city of Poznan in 1967, Polish television sought to use 'a dose of bourgeois Western escapist television fare' to prevent the population from attending religious services. Commenting on the television schedule planned for 25 May, the feast of Corpus Christi, he argued that American and British entertainment programmes were explicitly used 'to appeal particularly to younger viewers with the obvious purpose of keeping them at home rather than participating in, or even observing, the traditional religious celebrations and processions'.[28]

Elsewhere in the region, too, similar pragmatic domestic considerations were at play. In Romania, Western television was being used as means of boosting audience numbers for domestic television and appeasing the local population – an aim expressly noted in Romanian secret police archives.[29] Likewise, in Yugoslavia, there is reason to believe that the prominence of imports from the West, while often remarked upon negatively among the communist elites, ultimately also helped distract the population from political and economic problems in the country and thereby served to maintain the stability of communist rule, at least in the short run.[30] These examples confirm that the transnational orientation of broadcast infrastructure, and the foreign policy orientation in which it was rooted, while clearly decisive, likely operated alongside domestic policy concerns, as well as considerations of audience preferences.

[27] Mihelj (2013).
[28] NARA, RG 59 General Records of the Department of State, 1763–2002, Central Foreign Policy Files, 1966–1969, Box 409, Airgram from the American Consulate Poznan to the Department of State, 'The Schedules and Religious Observances,' 26 May 1967.
[29] Bondebjerg et al. (2008), p. 177.
[30] Vučetić (2012), pp. 383–394.

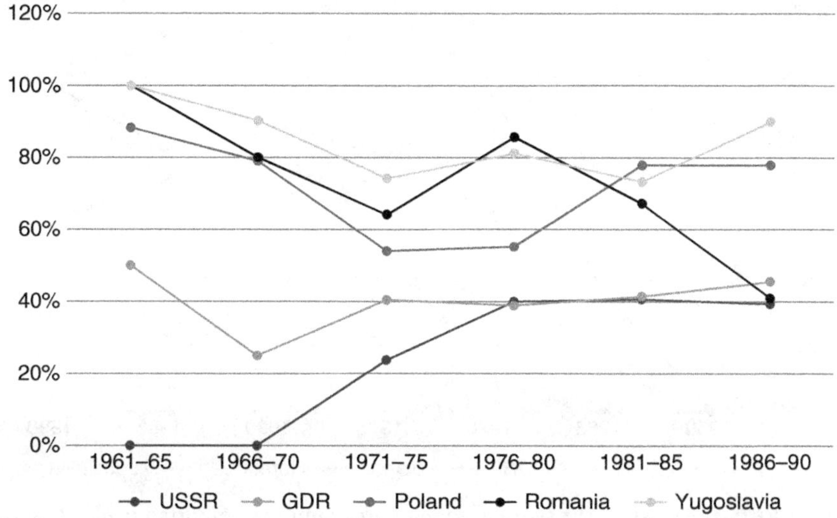

FIGURE 7.2 Trends in the share of foreign serial fiction imported from Western countries, 1961–1990. *Note*: Percentages refer to the share of serial fiction imported from Western countries, relative to all foreign serial fiction broadcast. Figures based on all serial dramas broadcast between 1961 and 1990. For further details see the Methodological Appendix.

The analysis of longitudinal trends brings us to a similar conclusion: foreign policies and the transnational orientation of television systems are crucial, but not sufficient to explain ebbs and flows in the provenance of television imports. This is particularly clear when looking at serial fiction, where it is difficult to see much correspondence between changes in foreign policy and the proportion of Western imports (Figure 7.2). For instance, the 1960s – a decade marked by an intensification of both political and cultural exchanges between the blocs[31] – brought a decline in the levels of Western fiction in most countries. Likewise, the gradual opening to the West in the late 1980s did not bring a notable increase in Western content – the only exception being Yugoslavia, where levels of Western imports jumped from 73.3 per cent in the first half of the 1980s to a whopping 90 per cent in the second half of the decade.

The situation is different when we look at programming as a whole, where correspondence with foreign policy shifts is clearer (Figure 7.3).

[31] E.g. Gorsuch and Koenker (2013).

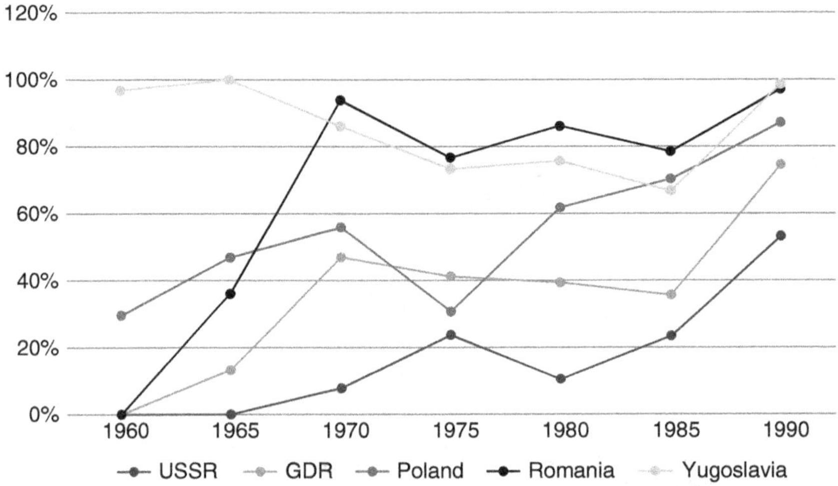

FIGURE 7.3 Trends in the share of foreign programming imported from Western countries, 1960–1990. *Note*: Percentages refer to the share of broadcast hours imported from Western countries, relative to the total volume of broadcast hours. Figures based on the analysis of TV schedules for a sample week, at five-year intervals, from 1960 to 1990. For further details see the Methodological Appendix.

The levels of Western imports rose over the course of the 1960s, consistent with the intensification of both political and cultural exchanges between the blocs during this decade. (Yugoslav television remained very open to programming from the capitalist world throughout the decade, in line with its longer tradition of openness to the West, established before the 1960s.) Between 1970 and 1985, fluctuations in the level of Western imports were limited, with most countries registering a mild decline – possibly due to economic decline and the difficulties in acquiring materials from the West, discussed earlier in this chapter. By 1990 many state socialist regimes had collapsed or were in the process of doing so, causing the proportion of imports from the West to skyrocket. Even in the Soviet Union, the materials produced in the capitalist world now constituted over half of imported programming – a clear indication that the country had lost its ability to influence transnational flows in the region and had turned into a periphery dependent on imports from the West.

These results indicate that decisions over fictional imports were less dependent on foreign policy shifts than were decisions concerning other types of foreign programming. Two related explanations can be offered. One is the fact that fictional content, and entertainment more generally, was considered politically more neutral than were information genres. This is particularly true of entertainment content centred on personal relationships and everyday life. As a Romanian television professional involved in programme imports explained, the teams involved in the process often chose to opt for 'love stories' rather than programmes with explicit political messages (Rom-13-1932-Male). The second possible explanation lies in the popular appeal of serial fiction and other types of entertainment, which turned them into effective means of attracting audiences. These arguments are supported by the fact that sports programming constituted by far the largest proportion of East-West programme exchanges organized through the cooperation between Eurovision and Intervision.[32] In sum, our investigation of the origins of television imports shows that in the state socialist world, decisions over where to import materials from were certainly guided by foreign policy orientations and dependent on the transnational orientation of television systems, but were also informed by domestic policy concerns and, in the case of entertainment programming, considerations of audience demand.

EXPERIENCING TRANSNATIONAL TELEVISION

Having mapped the transnational flows of TV programming in the state socialist world, it is now time to ask what these cross-border flows meant for audiences. Did transnational television contribute to a sense of belonging to the world – especially given that socialist citizens' ability to travel abroad (except for Yugoslavs) were limited? What attracted audiences to foreign programming? Did Western programming incite a desire for a different way of life – a way of life associated with a different vision of modernity linked with economic competition, the pursuit of material comfort, and political and cultural freedom?

The last of these questions often features in both popular and scholarly debates on Cold War media and culture. When Vaino Väljas, President of the Estonian SSR until the country's independence, was asked why the country had seceded from the Union, he blamed Finnish television.[33] Likewise, a *Washington Post* article published almost three decades after the fall of the Berlin Wall argued that *Dallas* (1978–1991) had helped

[32] Eugster (1983), p. 108. [33] Petrone (2008).

win the Cold War by exposing state socialist citizens to the wealthy lifestyle of the Ewings family and inciting a desire for attaining a similar level of comfort and luxury in their home countries.[34] In some scholarly works, too, cross-border television is adduced as a factor in the downfall of Eastern European state socialist regimes in 1989, as well as inciting resistance to communist rule in China.[35] As seen in the previous section, similar assumptions about the impact of Western television were common during the Cold War, too, and were shared by political elites and scholars both east and west of the Iron Curtain.

Yet there is little empirical evidence to suggest that viewing Western television in state socialist Eastern Europe was correlated with a critical attitude to the ruling ideology – hardly a surprising result for anyone familiar with existing research on the cross-cultural reception of Western programmes and the impact of transnational communication flows more generally.[36] In fact, research on East Germany – the only state socialist country in Eastern Europe where the question of foreign television reception was examined in a more extensive manner – has suggested that foreign TV viewing was negatively correlated with dissatisfaction with the ruling order and may even have strengthened it.[37] Rather than taking the opinions of West German news as gospel, many GDR citizens used Western news as a point of comparison which allowed them to 'check or identify gaps' in the Eastern version of events, or else they saw both sides as 'coloured' by ideological biases.[38] There is also evidence to suggest that viewers were alienated by the politicized tone of West German television, whose determination to depict life in East Germany as full of hardships failed to reflect viewers' everyday experiences.[39] Finally, it is also possible to speculate, by analogy with some of the findings of research on audiences of international radio broadcasting in Eastern Europe, that substantial segments of state socialist audiences were attracted to Western television primarily because of its entertainment value and not because of its political messages.[40]

In what follows, we examine viewers' experiences of transnational television by drawing on materials from the five countries included in

[34] Gillespie and Welch (2008). [35] E.g. Lull (1991); Schiller (1992).

[36] The classic study on the topic is Liebes and Katz (1990). For a comprehensive overview and reassessment of debates on the influence of cross-border media flows see Norris and Inglehart (2009).

[37] Meyen (2001); Kern and Hainmueller (2009). [38] Meyen (2003a), pp. 63–64.

[39] Gumbert (2006), p. 159. [40] Bashkirova (2010).

our study, which also allows us to reflect on cross-country similarities and differences in viewer responses to foreign content. Of course, the qualitative nature of materials we build on in this chapter – consisting primarily of oral history interviews – means that we are not offering a representative analysis of state socialist viewing cultures, but merely suggesting likely trends. With these qualifications in mind, we can advance three conclusions that emerge from our analysis. First, television programming and the televised coverage of international events constituted a memorable aspect of past television viewing and contributed to a sense of cosmopolitan belonging among state socialist audiences. Second, our findings suggest that state socialist viewers largely turned to international television content to satisfy their need for entertainment. Third, foreign programming and other aspects of TV transnationalism did not always promote unambiguous admiration for different ways of life and views on the world.

Before proceeding we should note that the state socialist experience of transnational television cannot be reduced solely to encounters with imported programming broadcast through domestic television channels. In many countries in the region, viewers also encountered transnational television by tuning in to cross-border television signals – especially in East Germany, but also in parts of Yugoslavia, Romania, and Soviet Estonia. We should also keep in mind that over the course of the 1980s, the gradual penetration of satellite television and the proliferation of home video recording multiplied opportunities for the transnational circulation of television programming, even in parts of the region that were hitherto geographically removed from the reach of foreign signals.[41] In addition, domestically produced content, such as news and travel programmes, also frequently offered images of the world beyond the nation. Moreover, events broadcast from one's own country – such as international music festivals and sporting competitions – could also feature as part of the transnational imaginary.

FOREIGN TELEVISION AS A WINDOW ON THE WORLD

Our oral history testimonies confirm the centrality of international content to the state socialist viewing experience and its importance in enhancing the perception of television as 'a window on the world'. International content was evidently memorable: international media

[41] Szekfü (1989); Wasiak (2012).

events frequently featured as part of our interviewees' earliest memories, and imported programmes were regularly mentioned as favourites; interviewees also often mentioned adapting their daily schedules to ensure they were at home to watch their favourite foreign programmes.

International sports competitions, in particular, were recalled by many of our interviewees as some of the most memorable of the entire state socialist period. This included events such as East Germany's victory over West Germany in the 1974 World Cup, the Soviet Union's controversial basketball triumph over the United States at the 1972 Olympics, and Romanian gymnast Nadia Comaneci's perfect 10 performance at the Montreal Olympics in 1976. Such events frequently appeared as part of interviewees' earliest encounters with television. This was the case, for instance, with a Polish interviewee born in 1947 who recalled watching the Olympic Games in Rome in 1960 together with his father at a neighbours' house (Pol-10-1947-male). International sports competitions also occasionally functioned as an impetus for viewers to search across the border for the best coverage if events were not covered on domestic television. In Romania, Ceauşescu's refusal to pay for the rights to the 1982 World Cup in Spain led viewers living in the vicinity of the border to tune into Bulgarian and Yugoslav coverage; some citizens were even said to have taken unapproved leave from work to travel to regions with better reception.[42] One of our Romanian interviewees recalled the lengths he went to in order to watch games that were not broadcast on domestic television: 'I used to go into the mountains with friends, carrying those antennas that resembled a washing bowl. One of us carried a TV set, we connected it to a car battery and charged it, and that's how we watched the game' (Rom-07-1967-male).

Sports competitions were not the only occasions that prompted audiences to undertake extreme measures of this kind. Some Estonian viewers were reportedly so overwhelmed by the possibility of seeing the French pornographic film *Emmanuelle* on Finnish television that those in the south of the country who did not enjoy good reception of Finnish TV signals travelled north to watch the film (USSR-Est-24-1947-female, USSR-Est-26-1969-male).[43] Also common were viewer recollections of how their families adapted their daily routines to ensure they would be home in time to watch their favourite foreign serial. For instance, a Polish

[42] Mustata (2013b); Sorescu-Marinković (2012).

[43] For mentions of similar practices see also Lepp and Pantti (2013).

interviewee remembered planning his family weekend routines around the TV schedule, so that the children could watch an imported US serial (Pol-10-1947-male).

Another aspect of transnational television featuring prominently in several testimonies was the broadcasting of music festivals. One of our Romanian interviewees, for instance, fondly remembered watching the international classical music festival named after George Enescu, together with his grandfather and other families who gathered at a family friend's house (Rom-01-1945-male). The international song festival Sopot, organized by Polish television since 1964, also known as the Intervision Song Contest,[44] likewise received several mentions, especially among our Polish interviewees, one of whom referred to the festival as 'a window on the world' (Pol-24-1950-female). As one might expect, several Yugoslav viewers mentioned watching the Eurovision Song Contest: as the only state socialist member of the EBU, Yugoslavia was an eager participant of the annual song contest, which served as a further confirmation of the country's peculiar position in the Cold War contest.[45] Yet, some of the fondest and most vivid memories of our Croatian and Serbian interviewees were reserved for the Italian music festival San Remo. As one enthusiastic viewer explained, the live broadcast of San Remo was a true 'window on the world' for local inhabitants and had a profound impact on him as a 'citizen of an enclosed, poor country where the consequences of the war were still keenly felt' (Yu-Cro-07-1954-male).

Foreign language acquisition was another way in which foreign television content contributed to state socialist cosmopolitanism. This was particularly common in regions exposed to foreign television signals in different languages but was also widespread in state socialist countries that did not dub imported programming. In parts of Romania close to Yugoslav borders, for instance, inhabitants learned the Serbian language primarily through intensive exposure to television during the 1980s, without any formal instruction.[46] In coastal parts of Yugoslavia within reach of Italian television signals, television likewise had the effect of acting as a means of language instruction. As a Croatian interviewee who grew up in the region explained, she and her sister both learned Italian from television and at that time even used to respond to telephone calls in Italian (Yu-Cro-06-1967-female).

[44] Pajala (2013). [45] Vuletić (2007). [46] Sorescu-Marinković (2010).

The only exception to the trends outlined so far was mainland Russia. In contrast to interviewees from other parts of the region, Soviet viewers who grew up in Russia rarely mentioned foreign television, except in relation to the 1980s. International sports and music competitions also rarely featured among recollections, and when they did, they were not perceived as a connection to the outside world. These results resonate with the low proportion of imported content on Soviet television and the inaccessibility of cross-border signals in mainland Russia. They also demonstrate that the Soviet viewing culture – except in regions bordering the West – was as much an outlier as the Soviet programming culture: both were overwhelmingly self-sufficient and closed to foreign influences.

Thus in some respects – and with the exception of the Soviet Union – state socialist television enabled the populations of communist-led countries to become citizens of the world, despite restrictions on their ability to travel. It is tempting to suggest that the transnational connections established by television acted as an antidote to national belonging in contexts that were often deeply nationalistic: communist elites across the region often resorted to nationalism to buttress their fledgling legitimacy and to counter popular fears about Sovietization.[47] Yet as existing research shows, national belonging and cosmopolitanism are not mutually incompatible.[48]

Our materials, too, offer some evidence for the double-edged effects of cross-border television flows, particularly in the case of international sports. For example, one of our German interviewees (who could not by any stretch of the imagination be described as a GDR patriot) nevertheless suggested that he was very pleased by the GDR's 1–0 victory over West Germany at the 1974 World Cup (which took place in West Germany) because he resented West Germany's 'snooty' (*hochnasig*) attitude towards the East (GDR-10-1944-male). The potential of sports coverage to unite the nation was not lost on communist authorities, who used it strategically to attract domestic audiences to domestic television and boost popular support for the party. For example, Rüdiger argues that GDR authorities were eager to use the coverage of the 1972 Olympics in Munich to further the political interests of the party – particularly in

[47] E.g. Mevius (2010); Suny (1993); Verdery (1995).

[48] E.g. Beck and Levy (2013). In relation to media use see Norris and Inglehart (2009), pp. 184–198.

competition with West German broadcasters ARD and ZDF.[49] However, the patriotism induced by sporting events also presented problems for state socialist regimes: as Robert Edelman has suggested, the televising of foreign football could expose Soviet fans to expressions of anti-Soviet sentiments, for instance amongst Czechoslovakian fans after the invasion of 1968.[50] Examples such as this suggest that transnational television flows could cut both ways: fostering imaginary ties with places and people beyond one's home county, while also reinforcing national pride.

FOREIGN ENTERTAINMENT AND THE LURE OF THE WESTERN WAY OF LIFE

The prominence of entertainment emerged as another important trend in our analysis of viewer encounters with foreign television – especially young viewers, who tended to reel off a bewilderingly long list of foreign television shows. The following excerpt, taken from an interview with a viewer who grew up in Soviet Estonia, is typical in this respect:

> Um ... I remember from the seventies I remember ... well I think I started watching when I went to the first grade and that was in 1978 so my first memories are *Sapphire and Steel, Charlie's Angels*, then uh *Battleship* [sic] *Galactica*. Then later on there was the *Knightrider* ... Oh yes, there was *McGyver*, there was *Dempsey and Makepeace, Lassie, Little House on the Prairie, Moonlighting*, then there was *Dallas, Dynasty, Miss Marple, Miami Vice*, and there were some others which were kind of not serials but kind of shows like the *Muppet Show, Bill Cosby Show, Married with Children, Alf*. (USSR-Est-25-1971-female)

This is not say that foreign informational and educational programmes were entirely absent from oral testimonies. Several interviewees also remembered watching international news coverage or mentioned foreign political events they learned about through television. A Serbian interviewee, for instance, remembered watching the coverage of a United Nations session and the historical meeting of the US and Russian presidents (Yu-Srb-01-1969-male), while a Ukrainian interviewee recalled following *Vremia* without fail because he was interested in international news (USSR-Ukr-10-1955-male). Viewers within reach of cross-border signals from abroad also remembered watching foreign news, particularly so in East Germany, where – judging from our interviewees – most viewers watched West German news bulletins such as ARD's *Tageschau* and

[49] Steinmetz and Viehoff (2008), pp. 351–352. [50] Edelman (2013).

ZDF's *heute*, often in combination with their East German counterpart, DDR-F's *Aktuelle Kamera*. Yet, with the exception of East Germany, mentions of informational and educational content pale in comparison to the breadth of recollections of foreign entertainment. This may be in part due to the greater volume of entertainment among imports, but also resonates with audience preferences for entertainment genres, discussed in Chapter 5. Linguistic obstacles may also have contributed: watching foreign news or educational programmes – if followed via cross-border signals – required a greater level of linguistic skill than watching a fictional programme. This becomes evident in the testimony of a Romanian viewer, who remembered seeing the first images of the Romanian revolution in 1989 on Bulgarian television but argued that he otherwise preferred to watch films, as they were easier to understand than news (Rom-22-1975-male). Given the linguistic competencies required to understand foreign news, it is not surprising that watching foreign news was most frequently mentioned among German viewers, who had access to foreign news in their native language.

As these examples indicate, much of the foreign content recalled by our interviewees not only belonged to the category of entertainment but also came from the Western world. This was particularly evident in Soviet Estonia, East Germany, and Yugoslavia – that is, parts of the region where viewers were exposed to television signals from the West or had access to a notable volume of Western imports via domestic television. By and large, Western imports in these countries were considerably more memorable than was state socialist programming. While, as we have seen, interviewees often recalled a long list of films and serial fiction imported from the West, often naming individual actors or characters, such a level of detail was more unusual in memories of state socialist imports.

Is it feasible to argue that greater exposure to Western content also led to greater appreciation of the Western way of life and, as local political and cultural elites feared, of 'consumerist' and 'bourgeois' values? Naturally, the answers to these questions differed depending on the programme, the country, and the viewer. Moreover, memories of watching Western television in the state socialist era were often intertwined with comments about the perceived 'Westernization' of domestic television in the post-Cold War era or otherwise inflected by retrospective interpretation. Nonetheless, two broad points can be derived from our materials. First, a notable number of viewers across the countries where such content was common suggested that Western television had an aura of superior quality. Second, the appeal of Western programming lay principally in seeing a different, somewhat exotic way of life and did not necessarily translate into an unqualified approval of the Western way of life.

The status of Western television as a marker of quality emerged particularly clearly in testimonies that described domestic shows that were purportedly inspired by Western programmes or otherwise perceived as Westernized. A Yugoslav viewer, for instance, spoke of the San Remo music festival as 'the bright sparkle of the West' which served as a model for all festivals in Yugoslav Croatia, while a Polish viewer fondly recalled watching the Polish crime drama *07 Come In* (*07 zgłoś się*, 1976–1987) and ascribed much of its attraction to its 'Western feel', associated with luxury and modernity:

> They had amazing cars, that seemed super. Ladies wearing furs. There was a Western vibe to this show, I remember, that's what I thought. I remember this one episode, there were some guys on a plane, that plane seemed so modern to me and then their cars. Now when I watch it I think to myself, 'oh my god, what is this', but back then ... (Pol-02-1973-female)

This association with wealth and luxury was a common perception of life in the West. It was often invoked by Croatian and Serbian viewers, many of whom – unlike viewers from other countries – remembered the excitement of watching Western serial fiction on Yugoslav television and commented on it in detail. With regard to *Dynasty*, in particular, material comforts and luxury were key points of attraction and were regularly contrasted with the lower material standards and greater uniformity at home. A viewer from Serbia, for instance, recalled being surprised at the size of the Carrington residence and wondering what the use was of such a large house (Yu-Srb-06-1969-male), while an interviewee from Croatia explained:

> We all watched *Dynasty* regularly. First, because this was a view of something worldly, of some kind of luxury, of something that went beyond the confines of the setup we lived in, in which it was desirable for everyone to be the same, for everything to be uniform ... that we all had the same tracksuits, that we all ate approximately the same food, that there wasn't anything that was outside of some kind of middle class. *Dynasty* was the opposite of all this; there was luxury, kitsch, prestige, even too much kitsch, but it didn't bother us because it was the opposite of what we lived with then. (Yu-Cro-01-1975-female)

Yet, at least judging from our Yugoslav interviewees, the appeal of seeing a wealthier, more luxurious lifestyle did not necessarily go hand in hand with unqualified admiration. For several viewers, *Dynasty* may have been appealing because of the material wealth and luxury it showed, but its main message lay in the universality of human nature and relationships, which transcended differences in material standing. As one viewer put it, *Dynasty* depicted 'the fantasy of life among the upper class' while at the same time showing 'that among them, too, the same shit goes on as among us' (Yu-Cro-19-1936-male). Although we should acknowledge that such responses may well be coloured by a dose of retrospective interpretation arising from a dissatisfaction with life in post-socialism, they also raise doubts about the ability of Western television imagery to incite an unqualified longing for life in the West.

Other aspects of Western programming that provoked reservations about life in the West among our Yugoslav as well as our East German interviewees included the presence of violence and moral licence (e.g. GDR-07-1954-female, GDR-23-1932-male, Yu-Srb-17-1930-female, Yu-Cro-13-1972-female), which were occasionally interpreted as signs of the greater security and moral superiority of state socialist life (though, again, these judgements may be retrospective ones). A Croatian viewer, for instance, remembered being attracted as well as disgusted by the immorality of relationships depicted in *Dynasty* (Yu-Cro-13-1972-female). A German viewer, on the other hand, recalled watching Western crime dramas but argued that they were so full of 'violence, death, and murder' that he could not watch them anymore (GDR-23-1932-male). Depictions of gender roles could prove controversial, too. Although several Croatian and Serbian interviewees claimed that cult Western imports such as *Peyton Place* prompted Yugoslav women, and occasionally men, to adopt a different clothing style or hairstyle, some of these changes could also encounter resistance. As one female interviewee explained, women in her immediate working environment were expected to wear skirts at the time, and if they did wear trousers to keep warm in winter, they had to change into a skirt upon arrival to the workplace (Yu-Srb-09-1940-female). Her testimony echoed with the recollections of a male viewer who argued that the way of life depicted in *Peyton Place*, including the views on gender relationships, were simply unacceptable in Yugoslavia at the time and were in fact still unacceptable to him personally as well (Yu-Srb-08-1930-male).

Such ambiguous readings of Western programmes were not limited only to entertainment: in East Germany, where viewers often watched

West German informational programmes, differing reactions were present, too. In this respect, our analysis confirms the results of prior research on East German viewing habits, which suggested that the widespread practice of watching West German news did not always translate into the outright acceptance of its messages.[51] Although the majority of our interviewees recalled watching Western news because it was more reliable, some aspects of West German news may have been perceived as too different. For instance, one GDR viewer who watched West German Bundestag debates saw the cut and thrust of parliamentary debate as inappropriate and alien:

> I found it terrible when political programmes were broadcast directly from West Germany in which the parties abused each other. I found that so impossible. How can you rule together when you abuse each other like that? That didn't happen here. (GDR-16-1930-female)

In sum, the audience reactions outlined here shed doubt on the ability of Western programming to inspire wholehearted support for the Western way of life – at least as far as Yugoslavia and East Germany are concerned. Rather, it appears that such programming invited disparate readings and incited conversations about different modes of human conduct and ways of living a modern life, ranging from fashion choices and attitudes to material wealth, moral standards, and political life. While many viewers were attracted by aspects of life in the West as depicted on the screen – the greater material comfort, daring fashion choices, more liberal attitudes to sexuality, or different political views – it was equally common for our Yugoslav and East German interviewees to weigh the attractions of the West against the qualities of life in the state socialist world. These results suggest that the transnational flows of television programming, originating from different parts of the world, transformed television cultures in these two countries into symbolic battlefields in which competing visions of modern life vied for dominance.

At first sight, one may be surprised by the fact that the evidence for such ambiguous consequences of foreign content is clearest for the two countries where audiences were most exposed to Western programming – Yugoslavia and East Germany. If elite anxieties over Western television were correct, then one would expect the opposite to be true. Our results, however, lead to a different conclusion: ample access to Western television seemed to accompany greater scepticism about the benefits of life in

[51] E.g. Gumbert (2006); Meyen (2003a).

capitalist economies. This interpretation is also broadly in line with the 'firewall theory' of the influence of transnational media flows, proposed by Norris and Inglehart. Drawing on the result of an extensive investigation of links between news consumption and economic values, they concluded that the impact of cosmopolitan communications is dependent on the type of society: in more parochial and poorer societies, and in countries with heavier restrictions on the media, exposure to foreign programming is correlated with greater support for values associated with consumer capitalism; in more cosmopolitan societies and wealthier economies, it is correlated with lower support for such values.[52] Our own investigation suggests that a similar argument can be extended to the impact of foreign entertainment and to the context of state socialism: in countries that were wealthier (East Germany), had a more liberal approach to the media (Yugoslavia), and were more open to the Western world (both East Germany and Yugoslavia), exposure to Western television content could have the effect of 'inoculating' viewers against capitalist values.

CONCLUSIONS

The analysis presented in this chapter reveals several shared elements of state socialist television transnationalism. State socialist television cultures formed an integral part of a wider global network, both from the point of view of programme exchanges and from the perspective of audience experiences. Indeed, television cultures in the state socialist world were in some ways more internationalized than were their counterparts in the Western world: while state socialist audiences could gain access to a notable volume of capitalist imports, viewers in the capitalist world had fewer opportunities to interact with programmes produced on the other side of the Iron Curtain. Yet seen from such a global vantage point, state socialist television emerges as a periphery, rather than the centre that it aspired to be. Western broadcasters were never particularly taken by the programming offered by their state socialist counterparts, while state socialist broadcasters often found capitalist shows to be an effective and affordable means of attracting viewers. Indeed, in three of our five countries, levels of Western imports exceeded those from the state socialist world.

[52] Norris and Inglehart (2009), pp. 199–219.

Apart from revealing the shared traits of state socialist television transnationalism, our results also highlight profound differences between countries. The five television cultures varied considerably in their openness to imports, with the Soviet Union standing apart as the most resistant to foreign materials. In that sense, it is comparable to its Cold War rival, the United States. A similar pattern of diversity emerges with regard to the origin of imports. The Soviet Union again stands out for its overwhelming reliance on state socialist programming, while Yugoslavia, which was most open to Western content, stood at the opposite end of the spectrum.

Our cross-country comparison and longitudinal analysis have also enabled us to reflect on the causal forces that gave rise to such patterns of imports and exports. Predictably, television cultures that evolved in the largest economies (East Germany and especially the Soviet Union) were considerably less reliant on imported materials than those that emerged in smaller economies (Yugoslavia and Romania). Furthermore, television systems that were more integrated into the organizational and technological infrastructures of Western broadcasting (Yugoslavia and Romania) gave rise to television cultures that were considerably more reliant on Western imports than those that were organizationally and technologically tied primarily to other state socialist countries (East Germany). Soviet television culture, which aspired to act as a core and model for other television cultures in the state socialist world and beyond, was by far the most resistant to foreign inflows and especially to imports from the West. Yet not all variation can be explained by reference to the size of the economy, the relative core-periphery position, and the transnational orientations of television systems. In addition, our analysis has also identified a range of intervening factors that need to be considered when explaining the transnational dynamics of state socialist television.

The cross-country differences revealed in our analysis of programme flows are to an extent reflected in differences between viewing cultures. For viewers who grew up in Soviet Russia and Ukraine, foreign programming and international media events constituted a far less prominent part of the viewing experience. In contrast, for interviewees who came from other parts of the region, the transnational aspects of television featured prominently in their recollections. Recollections of Western imports likewise differed, with memories of Western programmes being much more vivid and detailed among Yugoslav, German, and Estonian viewers – and hence in parts of the region where viewers were exposed to the greatest volume of Western television.

Despite the memorability of Western programmes, it is difficult to argue that such content inspired unqualified admiration for life in the West. Certainly, Western programming allowed state socialist citizens a glimpse of a world that was different from their own, and for that reason it may have played a destabilising role in state socialist polities. Nevertheless, our evidence suggests that audience fascination with Western programming did not necessarily translate into a wholehearted embrace of the Western lifestyle. In Yugoslavia and East Germany – the two countries where audiences were most exposed to Western content – watching Western programmes could have the exact opposite effect, prompting doubts about the superiority of life in a capitalist economy. Due to the restricted scope of testimonies about watching Western television in the remaining three countries, we could not establish whether or not such ambiguous reactions to Western content were common elsewhere. As we have argued, it is quite possible that reactions to Western broadcasts varied with social context, inspiring support for capitalist values in countries where living standards were lower and where exposure to different values and ways of life was more limited, while encouraging doubts about the capitalist alternative among wealthier and less restrictive societies.

PART III

THE TIMES OF STATE SOCIALIST TELEVISION

8

Everyday Time

'*Time* always put you in a different reality and allowed you to feel the time of real life, and of the whole planet, and of your country, a country which was moving towards communism' (USSR-Ukr-11-1952-male). So argued one of our interviewees, a Ukrainian pensioner born in 1952 who had worked as an engineer during the Soviet period. This quotation, which connects the main Soviet daily news broadcast with entry into a different temporal reality, brings to the fore many of the themes explored in the third part of this book. To start with, it reminds us that the communist vision of modernity was markedly future-oriented and teleological, premised on the notion of an ongoing revolution designed to bring communist-led societies from the transitional state of socialism to the conditions of fully fledged communism, in which class distinctions, private ownership, money, and the state would be absent. As noted in Chapter 4, a temporal orientation towards the future is shared by all varieties of modernity.[1] Yet the communist conception brought this future-orientation to an extreme: the teleological character of the communist understanding of progress, coupled with the heavy involvement of the party-state in directing social development, meant that talk of the future was omnipresent to an extent unseen in other political systems.[2]

In this chapter we ask how this pronounced orientation to the future played out in the context of everyday television programming and

[1] See also Koselleck (2004).

[2] For a selection of studies examining the different forms and uses of images of the future and utopian ideals in communist-led societies see Balina and Dobrenko (2011); Buck-Morss (2002); Stites (1988).

viewing. As argued in Chapter 2, thanks to its ability to establish a 'live' connection with the passage of time, broadcasting is oriented primarily to the present. At the same time, we have pointed out that this present-centeredness does not eliminate all possibilities for engagement with the past and the future. Rather, the past and the future become incorporated into the live unfolding of television's present. The quotation from our Ukranian interview offers a glimpse of how this could be achieved in the context of daily news: from the point of view of this spectator, the Soviet news bulletin *Time* succeeded in engendering a sense of connection with the future, tying developments in the here and now to the onwards march of progress. Many television professionals aspired to the ideal of a live connection between the news of the day and the dynamism of revolutionary progress. As the producer of *Time* argued, the show needed to be 'as dynamic, as interesting, and as saturated as time itself'.[3] There was, then, a promise of the extraordinary embedded in the very ordinariness of television: by virtue of its live connection with the present, everyday television had the potential to lift viewers from the banality of daily life into the dynamism of revolutionary time.

Yet as we show in this chapter, such a successful link between the present and the future, inspiring a sense of audience participation in revolutionary progress, was difficult to achieve on a day-to-day basis. Communist officials kept complaining about the lack of speed and movement in television programming, and they feared that television's repetitive viewing rhythms produced something inimical to socialist temporality: passivity instead of participation. We should be wary of accepting the stereotype of passive viewers at face value – there is in fact plenty of evidence that audiences in communist countries were actively critical of television's offerings – yet, as we shall see, the evidence is scarce of viewers experiencing everyday television as a means of connecting to revolutionary changes in society. The sense of participation in a different temporal reality through the TV screen, so vividly remembered by our Ukrainian interviewee, was an exception to the rule.

Nonetheless, it would be wrong to think that television professionals failed altogether in their attempts to use everyday television programming to involve viewers in changes (encompassing social, economic, and personal transformations) directed towards a revolutionary

[3] Quoted in Evans (2016), p. 116.

communist future. To understand this, we need to examine the basic structures of everyday programming and viewing practices and reflect on the principles on which they were based. As we shall see, television producers in the state socialist world soon realized that television's embeddedness in everyday routines offered a useful instrument for inculcating new habits, thereby creating the society of the future. To be sure, viewers did not necessarily see their viewing routines as specifically socialist, nor did they necessarily agree with television's messages. Yet the very fact that they engaged in these viewing routines aligned their lives with the vision of a society steadily moving towards a communist future. Such, then, is the key paradox confronted in this chapter: while television was successful in instilling everyday routines underpinned by the communist vision of the future, these routines rarely fed into a sense of live participation in revolutionary progress.

To demonstrate this paradox, we draw on a range of sources. In the first two sections we outline how TV elites in Eastern Europe sought to reorganize schedules in order to capture viewers' attention and inculcate daily routines aligned with the communist agenda for the future. For this purpose, we rely both on archival sources drawn from broadcasting institutions and on the analysis of TV schedules, seeking to bring to light not only the aims and expectations of TV professionals but also to elucidate how these aims and expectations became articulated in actual scheduling patterns. The last section draws on oral history interviews to investigate how and whether these scheduling techniques shaped viewers' everyday practices. In doing so, we seek to reconstruct audiences' lived experience of daily television viewing and the extent to which it instilled a sense of participation in revolutionary progress.

Throughout the chapter, we also comment on cross-country differences and reflect on how the patterns of temporal organization found in state socialist television cultures resembled or departed from those seen in the West. Apart from paying attention to temporal orientation as such, these comparative reflections also consider other aspects of temporal organization, linked to two further dimensions of comparison: gendering and secularization. As we shall show, these are two aspects in which the temporal logic of everyday television in state socialist countries differed from patterns found in the West.

FINDING TIME FOR TELEVISION

As television viewing became more widespread, broadcasters in Eastern Europe began to realize the power of the new medium to intervene in viewers' everyday routines and to use those interventions to promote particular messages. As an internal document discussing programme policies for TV Belgrade stated in 1967, 'Drawing on the habits of viewers and their rhythms of life, television ... can impose certain contents, and by manipulating time it can guarantee a relatively high level of audience.'[4] Yet while it was clear that television was fast becoming a favourite pastime among millions of viewers, it was equally evident from viewers' letters and other sources that the maximization of television's potential required a more rational and purposeful use of screen time. In 1956, several East German viewers complained about the late start time of broadcasting, which meant that 'one seldom gets to bed before 23.00'.[5] Similar concerns were raised by Yugoslav viewers in 1965, with one pointing out that 'most workers go to work early in the morning and therefore cannot follow late night programmes'.[6] Also common were complaints about the irregularity of the broadcast schedule and the unreliable nature of published schedules. Complaints such as these prompted intense debates about the most effective ways of organizing daily and weekly schedules, often coloured by a keen awareness of television's public mission, as discussed in Chapter 5. How long should a TV programme last, when should it begin and end, and how should it be organized to maximize the ability of television to deliver on its promise of information, education, and entertainment for all, and thereby give rise to the society of the future? How could schedulers ensure that viewers remained alert to the achievements of the regime and the challenges of building a communist future?

The timing of debates about scheduling differed from country to country, depending on the timing of television development (see Chapter 3). In East Germany, which was one of the earliest adopters of television technology in the region, such debates were common from the early 1950s. In 1954, two years before the start of regular broadcasts, the country's main listings journal, *Broadcast News*, solicited viewers' opinions on the start and end times for broadcasting. Viewers' opinions

[4] RTS-CIJMPA, Report 161, 'Programska politika TV Beograd u 1967. godine,' 1966, p. 6.
[5] SAPMO-BArch DR 8/444, 'Analysis of Viewer Post,' December 1956 (11 January 1957).
[6] 'Television's Opening Hours,' *TV Novosti*, 27 February–3 March 1965, p. 2.

reflected their different labour routines, with the majority opting for a 7 PM start to enable day-shift workers to watch the entire evening schedule.[7] Yet, such timing did not satisfy everyone: a letter from Saupersdorf, a small town in Saxony, complained that most of the workers in the region were miners who needed to wake up at 3:30 AM for their morning shift and therefore went to bed early and slept through the best programmes in the evening.[8]

In Yugoslavia complaints about the timing of programming were still common almost a decade later, consistent with the later introduction of television in the country.[9] In the Soviet Union, too, the most intense discussions about scheduling occurred during the 1960s. Between 1966 and 1969, the professional journal *Soviet Radio and Television* printed a series of articles under the heading 'Scheduling: The Question of Questions', which aired professionals' opinions on best practice and the aims of scheduling. In Romania, where the pace of TV diffusion was the slowest of the five countries examined here, complaints about the basics of scheduling persisted into the early 1970s. In 1970, Nicolae Breban, a member of the Central Committee in Romania, complained that programmes were broadcast haphazardly and sometimes changed without warning. He argued: 'Let's create a certain tradition when everybody can say that, for instance, on Tuesdays at 19:45 one can turn the TV on. Without such predetermined slots we can't achieve anything.'[10]

As the examples cited so far attest, the earliest dilemmas about scheduling revolved primarily about start and end times, reflecting the viewers' desire to watch as much of the broadcast schedule as possible. This was probably because there was so little to watch: in its first month of regular broadcasting in January 1956, DFF aired only two to three hours of programming a day. In the remaining four countries in our sample, too, the volume of broadcast hours was initially very limited: in October 1960, the total volume of programming over the course of a week ranged from less than fifteen hours in Romania to barely more than thirty-four hours in Yugoslavia (Chapter 3, Figure 3.3). But as broadcast hours increased, the debate shifted to questions of precise daily and weekly patterns of programming, largely with the intention of ensuring that the right kinds of

[7] SAPMO-BArch, 1954 DR 8/444 [8] Ibid.
[9] E.g. 'Television's Opening Hours,' *TV Novosti*, 27 February–3 March 1965, p. 2.
[10] ANR, CC PCR-SPA 18/1970, p. 33.

programming reached their designated audiences on the right day and at the right time.

At this point, the idea of creating thematic 'blocks' of programming became increasingly widespread within the state socialist world. These blocks were typically aligned with different public goals – information, cultural refinement, education, or entertainment – and were designed for specific audiences who were expected to be in front of the screen at different points in the day. In Poland, for example, the viewing day was divided into an educational block spanning the morning and early afternoon, with a mix of content designed for either school-age children or adults on shift work, an afternoon block aimed at children, young adults, and families, and then an evening block comprising the daily news broadcast and an entertainment programme aimed at adults.[11] The evening block of adult programming was divided from the afternoon, family-friendly block with the broadcast of the children's programme *Goodnight* (*Dobranoč*, 1962–, also called *Wieczorynka* or *Dobranočka*) at around 7 PM, which marked the boundary between children's and adults' time. Similar practices could be observed elsewhere in the region, where a daily evening slot of children's programming was introduced, such as the *Little Sandman* (*Sandmännchen*, 1959 to date) in East Germany and *Goodnight, Children!* (*Spokoinoi nochi, malyshi!* 1964–) in the Soviet Union. These programmes were scheduled immediately before the evening news bulletin and likewise signalled the time when TV viewing became the domain of adults.

A related practice adopted in several countries involved weekly scheduling patterns – not only the more immediately observable distinction between longer weekend schedules and shorter workday schedules but also the practice of broadcasting particular genres on set days in the week. Such patterns could be seen in most of the countries in our sample. In Yugoslavia, editors sought to establish a particular identity for each day of the week, so that each evening would predictably bring either a new episode of a foreign TV series, or a feature film, or a documentary, or the next instalment of a domestically produced sitcom.[12] In a similar manner, Polish television associated each day with a distinct genre: during the 1970s, Monday was reserved for TV theatre, Thursday for action or crime dramas, Friday for comedies or light-themed films, Saturday for

[11] Szostak (2013), pp. 163–64.

[12] RTS-CIJMPA, Report 161, 'Programska politika TV Beograd u 1967. godini,' 1966, pp. 16–24.

adventure fiction, and Sunday for comedies, musical films, or variety programmes.[13] As documents from the era attest, these weekly patterns formed a deeply entrenched part of viewer routines, and TV producers were keen to keep changes to a minimum. In an article published in the Polish TV magazine in 1978, the programme director of TV Poland promised viewers that their routines of watching specific programmes on particular days and at particular times would remain intact despite the substantial expansion of programming.[14]

In contrast, Soviet television seemed reluctant to adopt such an elaborated weekly pattern; it was normal practice for serial fiction to be broadcast on consecutive days rather than in weekly instalments. Quite why such differences appeared is difficult to establish with precision, but it is tempting to speculate that Soviet TV professionals, in accordance with their more rigid views on entertainment programming discussed in Chapter 5, were perhaps somewhat reluctant to turn such programming into a regular 'fix' audiences could expect every evening, week after week.

While schedulers worked with their own beliefs and prejudices when compiling schedules, they also considered viewers' preferences. In doing so, they were caught between two competing imperatives. To base schedules completely on audience demand would make television incapable of serving the transformative agenda of the revolution. Yet at the same time, audience views had to be taken into account in order for programmes to achieve their transformative goals. Maximizing audiences, and thus maximizing the impact of programming, meant finding out about audiences' routines and preferences. As a result, TV professionals started relying on increasingly sophisticated quantitative and qualitative sociological methods designed to inform the most effective scheduling practices. Particularly common was the use of audience surveys revealing the proportions of TV owners available to watch television at different times in the day and on different days in the week. For instance, a side-by-side analysis of results for surveys using similar methodologies, conducted in 1965 in East Germany and in 1968 in Poland and Yugoslavia, shows a broadly similar temporal distribution of viewing: the proportions of available viewers were highest between 7:30 and 9:30 PM.[15]

[13] Pokorna-Ignatowicz (2003), p. 63.

[14] Włodzimierz Grzelak. 1978. 'Telewizja 78,' *RTV Radio i Telewizja*, Issue 2, 1978, p. 4.

[15] Based on survey results retrieved from SAPMO BArch. Schriftgut Zuschauerforschung, H 074-00-02-0014, 'Auswertung der Umfrage im Stadt- und Landkreis Rostock,'

In many ways, the practices of scheduling investigated so far are similar to those followed elsewhere in the world at the time. Establishing a predictably organized television schedule, synchronised with viewers' daily lives and instilling viewer routines designed to maximize audience figures, were shared goals of broadcast scheduling everywhere, regardless of the type of television system. But while commercial broadcasters sought to maximize audience numbers to ensure that viewers were exposed to the specific advertisements targeted at them, in the state socialist context, scheduling was designed to ensure that viewers found their way to programmes that were deemed worthy from the perspective of the public mission of socialist television as discussed in Chapter 5: first and foremost, information and current affairs programming, followed by educational and cultural programmes. By encouraging the consumption of such programmes, television sought to help build a New Socialist Person – a working citizen who was expected to be educated, informed, culturally sophisticated, politically engaged, and devoted to the building of the communist future.[16] In this sense, the temporal arrangements of everyday television in state socialist countries were informed by a markedly future-oriented and teleological vision, more so than those found in the liberal democracies of the West.

This orientation to the communist future was also evident in the dilemmas surrounding the organization of prime-time schedules. A common practice across the region was the strategic scheduling of entertainment in ways that were designed to attract viewers to important informational, current affairs, or educational programmes. The director of scheduling for Soviet Central Television, A. Bogomolov, argued that the 'alpha and omega of drawing up a schedule' was to place films, concerts, or plays before political programming to ensure the highest possible audience.[17] Indeed, as Christine Evans has shown, the more Soviet schedulers analysed the preferences of TV viewers, the more they realized the importance of placing entertainment, rather than propaganda, in the prime-time schedule.[18]

March 1965, pp.12–13; TNS OBOP, 'Program Ramowy Telewizji w Świetle Sposobów Odbioru, Opinii i Postulatów Telewidzów,' 1968, pp. 108–109; and RTS-CIJMPA, Report 263, 'Praćenje TV programa,' 1968.

16 Cheng (2009); Duda (2015).

17 A. Bogomolov. 1966. 'O televizionnoi programme, zritele i gazete,' *Sovetskoe radio i televidenie* 8, pp. 33, 36.

18 Evans (2016).

Similar proposals about the strategic use of popular genres were aired elsewhere in Eastern Europe. At a meeting of party officials and television professionals held in Romania 1970, a member of the Party Committee for Propaganda and Agitation urged his colleagues to take audience views seriously, keep shows that viewers find attractive, and schedule them strategically to attract audiences to other content.[19] In East Germany, tactical scheduling took on a particular urgency in light of competition from West German channels. Schedulers sought to ensure that their news programmes would be broadcast before West German bulletins and that East German current affairs and political programmes such as *Prisma* would be broadcast in prime time in a slot when there would be no films on East Germany's second channel and no entertainment programming on 'enemy television'.[20] Thus, in the East German context, scheduling played a key role in the cultural Cold War in steering viewers towards the regime's messages and its future-oriented vision.

SCHEDULING EVERYDAY TELEVISION

Having discussed the general dilemmas and practices of scheduling in Eastern Europe, we can now move on to the schedules themselves and consider how the aims of TV professionals were articulated in practice. To this end, we have analysed samples of schedules gathered in all five countries for a sample week in October at five-year intervals, starting in 1960 and ending in 1990. On the pages that follow, we will zoom in on a selection of scheduling patterns where the specificities of everyday television temporalities in state socialist Eastern Europe become most clearly apparent: block scheduling and prime-time scheduling.

To start with, block scheduling was evident across the region and became well established between the mid-1960s and the mid-1970s. The key blocks of programming were distributed over the course of the day in broadly similar ways, with educational and children's programmes scheduled during the day, and the bulk of informational, cultural, and entertainment content for adults appearing during prime time in the evening. Another shared trait was the desire to cater for either

19 ANR, CC PCR-SPA, 18/1970, p. 43.

20 SAPMO BArch, DY 30 / vorl. SED 14358/1, 'On the Development of the Schedule for Channel 1 and 2 of DDR-F, 1975–76,' 29 April 1974.

Yugoslavia

TV Belgrade 1 (Serbia)
9:10 Educational programme (TV Zagreb)
10:00 Cube, Cube, Cubelett: How to Grow Strong (Children's programme)
10:30 Animated film
(Break)
15:30 Animated film – repeat
15:35 Cube, Cube, Cubelett – repeat
16:15 Daily News 1
116:35 Daily News in Hungarian language
17:00 Daily News in Albanian language
17:30 Little World: Holidays at Velebit (Children's programme, TV Zagreb)
18:00 Through Vojvodina
18:15 Legends and Ballads
18:35 Scientific Studio
19:15 Children's cartoon
19:30 Daily News
220:00 Yankee (Film, Sweden)
21:35 Books and Ideas (Culture magazine, TV Zagreb)
22:05 Daily News
322:20 Live sports event
22:35 The Globe (TV Sarajevo)

TV Skopje 1 (Macedonia)
10:30 German language(break)
16:30 German language
17:00 Chronicle in Albanian language
17:20 News
17:30 Discoveries (Documentary)
18:00 TV programme overview
18:35 From Studio to Studio (No detail)
19:20 Children's cartoon
19:30 TV News
20:00 Feature film
21:30 TV News 2

USSR

Channel 1
9.00 News
9.10 Morning Gymnastics
9.30 Youth Creativity
9.55 Information programme
10.30 Youth on Screen
11.10 The Good Woman Schröder (Film, GDR)
(Break)
13.50 Everyday Life on Great Construction Projects (Documentary Film)
14.50 Concert of Song and Dance by Moscow Pioneers
15.35 Children's Film: Treasure Island (USSR, 1971)
17.00 Science Today
17.30 Poetry: Margarita Aliger
18.00 News
18.15 There's Sun in Every Drawing (Children's programme)
18.30 Great Feat (Documentary on post-WWII reconstruction)
19.00 Musical Evenings for Youth (Classical Music)
21.00 News
21.30 You Can Do It! (Quiz)
22.15 Poetry: Vera Schneider (GDR)
22.35 Sportlotto followed by News

FIGURE 8.1 Sample weekday schedules from Yugoslavia and the Soviet Union. Due to the absence of a pan-Yugoslav TV channel, schedules for the first channels from two Yugoslav republics are included: Serbia and Macedonia. *Sources: TV Novosti* and *Govorit i pokazyvaet Moskva.*

shift workers or schoolchildren who attended school in shifts: in the Soviet Union, it was common for the first channel to repeat highlights of the previous night's main prime-time programming, while in Yugoslavia, blocks of educational and children's programmes would frequently appear in the morning and then again in the afternoon. These traits are clearly observable in a sample of typical weekday schedules from the 1970s (Figure 8.1).

Apart from cross-country similarities, slight differences between countries are also worth noting. First, because of the presence of a designated educational channel in the Soviet Union, other Soviet channels lacked extended blocks of daytime educational programming. As evident from schedules of the two Yugoslav channels both feature daytime educational programmes, while the daytime schedule of the Soviet first channel is filled with children's and youth programmes and repeats of cultural and entertainment broadcasts from the previous evening, aimed at workers on night shifts – in this case, the East German film *The Good Woman Schröder*.

Another interesting difference appears between Yugoslav and Soviet schedules, on the one hand, and schedules from the remaining countries, on the other. In both Yugoslavia and the Soviet Union, schedules included designated blocks of programming which were filled with broadcasts produced elsewhere in the federation. This difference can be linked to the disparate ethnocultural structures of the countries and their broadcasting systems, namely the fact that both Yugoslavia and the Soviet Union were organized as multinational, federal states and that their broadcasting systems reflected these federal arrangements. For instance, in the Yugoslav schedules reproduced here, TV Belgrade's schedule includes programmes from TV Zagreb and TV Sarajevo. The Soviet example included here features no programmes from other TV studios – in line with the more centralised broadcasting system compared to its Yugoslav counterpart – but the schedule for Channel 2 for the same day included programmes from Yalta and Tbilisi. We can therefore argue that in both countries, broadcasters sought to weave markers of ethnocultural diversity into the very fabric of everyday television and thereby remind viewers in each republic of the shared, pan-Yugoslav or pan-Soviet march towards the communist future.[21]

Arguably, the practices of thematic block scheduling outlined so far were rooted in the notion of television as a vehicle of public goods, as discussed in Chapter 5, and aligned with the future-oriented vision of communist modernity. The structure of everyday temporality inherent in the logic of block-scheduling outlined so far sent a clear message about how the daily life of socialist citizens should be organized in order to achieve the personal transformation required by the communist agenda

[21] The same was true of broadcasts on regional television channels, which highlighted the common histories and interests of local people and the Soviet people as a whole as a way of engendering identity and national belonging. See Chakars (2015), p. 158.

and thereby give rise to a society capable of ushering in the communist future. Daytime was for work or at the very least for education and the attainment of new skills and knowledge that would enable viewers to fully participate in the country's onward march towards communism, while evenings were dedicated to cultural refinement, political engagement, and relaxation.

Yet, while such a temporal logic was indeed in line with the communist vision, we should also point out that the schedule patterns resulting from this logic were not far removed from those familiar in public broadcasting in Western Europe and elsewhere. As shown in Chapter 5, the overall distribution of television genres in state socialist countries and on public broadcasting television in Western Europe or Australia were very similar, marked by a rather high proportion of educational and cultural content – in contrast to commercial television, where programming was dominated by entertainment (Chapter 5, Figure 5.1). While a detailed schedule analysis would be needed to ascertain this fully, on the basis of these proportions alone it is feasible to argue that daytime schedules on public broadcasting channels were as marked by the prominence of educational programming as their counterparts in the state socialist world.

A similar argument can be developed with regard to the second prominent scheduling pattern, namely the strategic use of entertainment during prime time. In both the Yugoslav and the Soviet examples listed earlier, evening schedules consisted of a mix of programmes aimed at creating a discerning, informed viewer – daily news bulletins and current affairs programming, as well as cultural programmes dedicated to poetry, classical music, literature, and similarly high-minded content – and entertainment or fictional broadcasts such as feature films, sports programmes, or serial fiction. The two groups of programmes alternated with remarkable regularity. Although such a strategy was designed to attract audiences to programmes that extolled the virtues of communism or contributed to viewers' cultural sophistication, the resulting temporal structure was again broadly similar to the one found in TV schedules elsewhere in the world, in the sense that it was marked by high proportions of entertainment and fiction. It is also worth noting that more explicitly propagandistic content, such as the *Leninist University of Millions* (*Leninskii universitet millionov*, 1974–1985), was pushed to the margins of prime time or remained outside of the evening slot altogether. This suggests that reaching and retaining a mass audience took precedence over delivering the most desirable messages or was at the very least seen as equally important.

The exception to this rule came on festive occasions, or in moments of crisis, such as during Martial Law in Poland or during the period of TV austerity in Romania in the 1980s. On such occasions, explicit political and propagandistic content became more pronounced and regularly featured in the prime time. A typical weekday schedule for Romanian TV in the late 1980s, for instance on 27 January 1988, included only two hours of broadcasts, the vast majority of which were clearly propagandistic in tone: it opened with the news bulletin at 8 PM, which was followed first by a selection of extracts from Ceauşescu's speeches at 8:20 PM, then at 8:40 PM by a programme promoting the achievements of communism in Romania, entitled 'We Are Living Through Great Times and Experiencing Great Achievements', then by a film produced by the Army at 8:55 PM, closing with another news programme at 9:50 PM. The link between everyday TV temporality and the onward march of the revolution is abundantly clear: the intention of such schedules was to link the daily realities of Romanian citizens to the extraordinary temporality of Ceauşescu's revolutionary agenda and persuade them that the dawn of the communist future was within reach.

However, such ideologically saturated schedules were the exception rather than the rule. Everyday television in Eastern Europe was largely devoid of explicitly propagandistic programming and was similar to daily patterns of television elsewhere in the world, despite being guided by a different, more future-oriented, vision. Only two distinctive patterns emerge from our schedule analysis: one is linked to the specifically gendered nature of state socialist television cultures and the other to their secularized character.

The first distinctive trait is evident in the relative lack of daytime programming designed for housewives, which is a direct consequence of the characteristic double burden shouldered by women in state socialist countries, noted earlier in the book – namely, the fact that women were much more likely to be employed while also carrying the responsibility for domestic work. This meant that they had less time to watch television and were typically not at home during the day. This is not to say that broadcasts for women did not exist: such programmes could be found across Eastern Europe and some of them were scheduled during mornings and early afternoons (with others broadcast at the weekend). Yet, the content of such broadcasts signalled that the sphere of woman's work did not end at the doorstep but extended into the sphere of waged work outside the domestic sphere. In line with this, such programmes commonly focused on topics such as family, childcare, cooking, and fashion, thereby signalling women's inherent connection with the private sphere and caretaking roles, but they also addressed women as workers. For instance, Romanian programmes such as the *Programme for Women* (*Emisiune pentru femei*) in the 1960s or the *Family Almanach* (*Almanahul familiei*) in the 1980s covered issues such as clothing and fashion, restaurant dining, cosmetic treatments, food for newborn babies, the home pharmacy, and culinary recipes, as well as challenges faced by working women and mothers.[22] The Soviet programme called *For You, Ladies!* (*Dlia vas, zhenshchiny!*), broadcast on Central Television in the late 1960s and the 1960s, covered a similar mixture of themes. An episode broadcast in 1959 included a report on children in school and issues of pedagogy, a cookery item entitled 'Useful! Tasty! Cheap!', and an interview with Valentina Gaganova, a decorated Hero of Socialist Labour.[23]

The same logic extended to entertainment genres: the Soviet game show *Let's Go Girls* (*A nu-ka devushki*, 1970–1985) featured young working class competitors from 'essentially female' professions, such as bakers and candy makers, who competed in skills relevant to their own professions as well as in housekeeping and consumer skills.[24] Despite adopting an entertainment format, the show associated womanhood not only with the sphere of domesticity but also with the sphere of work, thereby reproducing and naturalizing the women's double burden on screen. In this way, the state socialist approach to gender was inscribed into both the content and the temporal logic of women's programming.

Another distinctive element of everyday TV temporalities in the state socialist world was linked to their secular character and becomes evident when we examine weekend schedules. In contrast to Sunday schedules in the West, which often featured live transmissions of religious ceremonies or dedicated religious programmes such as the BBC's *Songs of Praise* or RAI's weekly broadcasting of the Sunday service, Sunday programming in Eastern Europe included no reference to religious services. This secular character of everyday television was a direct result of official communist policies, which remained hostile towards religion throughout the state

[22] Imre (2016), p. 192.
[23] GARF, f. R-6903, op. 26, d. 173, ll. 149–177, 'Efirnaia papka: *Dlia vas, zhenshchiny No. 6*,' 27 July 1959.
[24] Evans (2016), pp. 208–215.

socialist period and saw religious beliefs and practices as atavistic remnants of the past that had no place in the building of the communist future. In line with this, Sunday TV schedules were resolutely secular, marked by a high proportion of entertainment programming interspersed with cultural and informational content.

Also telling is the fact that Sunday schedules typically featured extended blocks of attractive programming aimed at two groups thought to be especially susceptible to religion's charms: peasants and children. Broadcasts for peasants and countryside dwellers sought to attract viewers by incorporating popular elements, including folk dances and song.[25] Such material was not overly ideological in character, suggesting that the aim was to capture the attention of viewers and prevent them from attending church, rather than feeding them a particular message. A similar argument applies to Sunday programming aimed at children. In the Soviet Union, popular children's programmes were always broadcast in the morning slot when Orthodox believers would attend services. Examples of this were the popular children's programme *Alarm Clock* (*Budil'nik*, 1965–1998) and the military magazine programme *I Serve the Soviet Union* (*Sluzhu Sovetskomu Soiuzu*, 1967–1991). Elsewhere in the region, television would attempt to broadcast more attractive fare during religious holidays, with a high proportion of fiction, cartoons, and other entertaining content. It is feasible to argue that such popular broadcasts for countryside dwellers and children served as an attractive alternative to the Sunday mass, turning television into a vehicle of secularization.

In sum, daily and weekly scheduling practices in Eastern Europe resulted in temporal patterns that were broadly attuned to the communist vision of progress but were also in many ways similar to patterns familiar from public broadcasting TV channels in the West. Schedules were aligned with the rhythms of the working day and week, educational and children's programming were scheduled predominantly during the day, and a mixture of key informational and entertainment programming for adults appeared in the evenings. The only distinctive traits were the lack of daytime programming aimed exclusively at housewives on working days and the absence of religious programming on weekends – traits aligned with the higher rates of women's employment in state socialist countries and the secular character of communist politics. As such, we might conclude that socialist programmers produced a TV schedule

[25] Evans (2016), p. 77.

that was specifically socialist in its intentions and form and had the potential to encourage temporal routines aligned with the communist agenda, such as dedicating daytime (regardless of one's gender) to waged labour and education, and evenings and weekends to political information, cultural refinement, and relaxation (but not to religious rituals). Yet, it remains to be seen whether such scheduling practices had the desired effects on audiences. Were their daily and weekly viewing routines attuned to the aims of the communist revolution? Did they recognize the importance of watching the most culturally sophisticated and ideologically saturated programmes? It is to these questions that we turn in the next section.

LIVING WITH EVERYDAY TELEVISION

As we have seen, television professionals across Eastern Europe believed in the transformative power of television and worked hard at creating a schedule designed to align daily routines with communist ideals. In contrast, sociologists and TV critics often embraced a more pessimistic attitude to the new medium and its effects. Much as in Western Europe, North America, and elsewhere, elite discourses about television were haunted by the spectre of the zombified viewer who watched television passively and indiscriminately. Such a viewer would be unable to use television for the high-minded goals of education, cultural refinement, and political engagement. This image of an inert, undiscerning viewer is nicely captured in this bit of doggerel, published in the Soviet Union in 1966:

> In his slippers and pyjamas
> He watches everything on TV
> Treating every programme
> As serious as can be
> Sundays he even watches
> The programmes for the kids
> What, miss the quizzes, *KVN*,
> *Youth on Screen*? God forbid!
> An evening watching an epic
> About a cook preparing a meal
> Then a meeting with a veteran
> And a worker tempering steel ...[26]

[26] A. Bogomolov. 1966. 'Rebus ili sistema?' *Sovetskoe radio i televidenie* 5, p. 8.

Printed in the professional publication *Soviet Radio and Television* (*Sovetskoe radio i televidenie*), these verses were intended as an introduction to a discussion of survey results which showed that many viewers watched television 'from end to end'. The article's author wondered about the psychological effects of watching so much television: 'Isn't that too much for one person? In such a case even a good programme can seem dull and uninteresting. Most importantly, this useless, contemplative sitting creates a laziness of the mind or, if you like, a social passivity.'[27] All the efforts of TV producers were, it seemed, in vain: even the most intricate and well-meaning scheduling efforts had little hope of success in the face of such an unsophisticated, lazy, and unresponsive audience.

A closer look at viewer recollections and historical audience research from across Eastern Europe reveals this picture to be misleading. The practices of everyday TV viewing emerging from these sources reveal a set of patterns that overturn the stereotype of the passive, undiscerning viewer. Moreover, they challenge the idea that TV schedulers were successful in their efforts to use television as a means of inculcating belief in the revolution and the imminent arrival of a communist utopia. Instead, the reality seems to be somewhere in between: TV professionals were largely successful in aligning the everyday rhythms of TV viewing to communist ideals, but this temporal alignment did not necessarily result in a heightened sense of participation in the revolution.

Viewer testimonies reveal a wealth of viewing practices that are part of a modern experience of television shared worldwide. Television was fitted into the rhythms of the working day and week and closely intertwined with the rituals of domestic life, from family meals to bedtime routines. The vast majority of viewers recalled watching television in the late afternoon and especially during the evenings, after coming home from work or school, after or during family meals, and before going to bed. This meant that television contributed to a standardization of everyday temporalities by aligning the rhythms of domestic life with a shared, standardized system of time reckoning and by stimulating the adoption of similar routines across millions of homes. In this sense, everyday television temporalities in Eastern Europe formed part of a global system of ordering daily life that was rooted in the requirements of modern industrial societies, with its origins in eighteenth-century Western Europe.[28] If the

27 Ibid. p. 8. 28 Glennie and Thrift (2009); Zerubavel (1982).

effective functioning of industrial production and modern transport required adherence to a shared system of clock and calendar time in the public realm, television and radio broadcasting helped weave this standardized system of time reckoning into the fabric of domestic lives.

One such daily ritual, reported by virtually all interviewees who grew up with television, was the bedtime routine, which involved watching programmes that marked the end of children's viewing time and the beginning of adult's time. In the following extract, one of our interviewees, a forty-two-year-old woman from Poland, remembers her daily routine as a child, including watching the already mentioned children's broadcast *Good Night* (*Dobranoč*, 1962–) before going to bed:

> My mom always told me to go to bed after *Good Night*. The opening credits of *Good Night* there was I think a little hedgehog walking and after the cartoon the porcupine would go to bed . . . So my mom seeing the little hedgehog yawning she would always say, 'Okay, *Good Night*, evening prayer, wee wee and bed.' She would always say that. But occasionally I was allowed to stay up a little longer . . . When I was younger they would always send me to bed after *Good Night*, but after a while when I was a bit older I was allowed to watch a film after *Daily*, and it was like 'wow, I watched the film after *Daily*!'. It was something big. (Pol-02-1973-female)

The routine described in this extract was typical across the state socialist world. From *Good Night, Children!* in the Soviet Union to *Our Sandman* in East Germany, children across Eastern Europe understood the boundary between children's and adults' time to be marked by the evening cartoon and the beginning of the evening news bulletin. For one Croatian viewer, the association between the evening news and going to bed was so strong that she jokingly recalled becoming sleepy when meeting a famous TV news anchor from her childhood as an adult (YuCro-13-1972-female). Given that the borderlines between the two TV temporalities – children's and adults' – were so clearly delineated, it is no surprise that our Polish interviewee understood the opportunity to view the post-news film as marking something akin to a rite of passage – of having crossed over into adult time.

For adults, by contrast, the typical daily TV routine revolved around the evening news broadcast, usually scheduled to start between 7 and 9 PM, typically followed by a TV series or a feature film. For many interviewees, missing the daily news bulletin was simply unheard of.

As one of our Croatian interviewees recalled, 'not watching *The Daily* was not an option; this was an obligatory programme, there was no chance of me changing the channel and so on. And if we had guests at the time, we nevertheless all watched *The Daily*' (Yu-Cro-01-1975-female). As we shall see, the privileged status of the evening bulletin did not necessarily mean that everyone watched it to keep abreast of the latest political developments or that they believed what was reported. Some viewers claimed to have been most interested in the weather forecast, while others said they watched news merely as a prelude to their favourite series or TV game show, suggesting that the strategic scheduling of entertainment programming during prime time did have the desired effect of boosting the viewership for information programming. A Polish viewer, for instance, noted that his family watched the daily bulletin but 'only because there usually was a film on right after that' (Pol-07-1963-male), while another remembered watching a short current affairs programme on Fridays because it was scheduled between sports news and a film, so he 'had to sit and wait for the film and listen to this gibberish for fifteen minutes' (Pol-01-1974-male). While such testimonies suggest that the motivations for watching news and current affair programming varied, they also confirm that the daily bulletin constituted a central part of the daily routine for the majority of viewers across the region.

Another way that television was imprinted onto viewers' routines was through repetition in weekly schedules. Most prominent in interviewees' reminiscences was the difference between weekdays and the weekend. On weekends schedulers sought to create content that could be enjoyed by the whole family, such as *The Sunday Album* (*Album Dumnical*) in Romania, or *A Kettle of Colour* (*Ein Kessel Buntes*) in East Germany, which ensured higher audiences. Sunday mornings were often reserved for blocks of children's programming, such as *Telemorning* (*Teleranek*) on TV Poland, which regularly featured in recollections of childhood viewing. As we saw in the previous section, television schedulers also realized that repetitive scheduling allowed viewers to plan their routines more easily. Over time, these associations became second nature to viewers, and even at a distance of more than a quarter of a decade, some viewers were able to recall them with great precision, as was the case with one of our Romanian interviewees: 'On Tuesdays I remember they used to show a play, on Wednesdays they showed a film at *Tele-Cinema* (*Telecinemateca*), on Saturdays *Tele-encyclopaedia* (*Telenciclopedia*), and on Sundays we had the

Sunday Album (Album Duminical)' (Rom-19-1967-male). Similar responses could be found amongst several viewers from Poland and Yugoslavia.

If these temporal arrangements were analogous to those found beyond the state socialist world, our analysis also revealed three patterns that were specific to the state socialist context. The first involves the scarcity of women's daytime viewing and corresponds to the relative absence of daytime programming aimed at housewives noted earlier in the chapter. By and large, female interviewees, as well as other interviewees remembering the TV viewing habits of women (especially mothers) in their life, hardly ever mentioned them watching television during mornings or early afternoons. The only exceptions were women who were on maternity leave or the rare women who opted out of waged labour and hence departed from the prevailing pattern. The latter was the case with the mother of one respondent from Russia, who stayed at home with the children and hence had time to watch television during the daytime (USSR-Rus-09-1962-female).

By and large, however, such examples were an exception. For the majority of women in the region, watching television during the daytime was simply out of question; even when they were at home, the pressure of household chores meant that their viewing time was very limited. In this sense, television viewing was, as in Western Europe or North America[29] in direct competition with the demands of domestic work. This transpires in many female testimonies, as for instance in the interview with a Romanian viewer born in 1932, who explained that she could only watch television in the evenings, as daytime was taken up either by her job or by shopping and household chores; this was the case even on weekends, when she had to catch up with the housework she did not manage to do during the week (Rom-17-1932-female). Thus, despite the formal commitment of socialist regimes to gender equality, the persistence of traditional gender roles across the region meant that there was a clear imbalance in terms of television viewing routines.

The second characteristically state socialist viewing pattern emerging from our data involves the competition between secular and religious temporalities. As shown in the previous section, broadcasters sought to ensure that the attention of viewers, especially children and countryside dwellers, was diverted away from religious services on a Sunday. This is reflected in the testimonies of some of our interviewees, especially those

[29] E.g. Spigel (1992).

from Poland, where religiosity and attendance at religious ceremonies remained relatively high throughout communist rule. As one Polish interviewee recalled, 'when some church holidays were approaching, you knew that there would be some more interesting shows on' (Pol-17-1948-female). This created a situation when the religious temporal order, typically enforced through parental authority, and the secular temporality, embodied in the television schedule, would clash with one another. In some cases, religion prevailed: two Polish interviewees recalled that they were unable to watch the Sunday children's programme *Teleranek* at 9PM because they had to attend Mass at the same time, and one remembered how she planned to 'talk to the priest and ask him to change the time of the Mass' so that she could watch the programme (Pol-06-1973-female, see also e.g. Pol-05-1971-female). In other cases, religious habits were adapted to accommodate the TV schedule. In Yugoslavia, one interviewee recounted how she and her siblings asked for permission to attend an early church service so that they could be back home in time for their favourite children's series:

> Something I remember most vividly from 1967 were the serial programmes that were broadcast on Sunday mornings at 10 AM, usually of foreign production. ... But we were going to church, and we went to church every Sunday. And mum said: 'You have to go to church,' so that she could have a bit of peace and quiet and cook lunch ... But the Mass was starting at 10 ... and we were always late. And then we agreed with mum that we no longer want to attend the big Mass and instead went to the Mass early in the morning at 8 to this small church so that we were ready for the serial films for children. (Yu-Cro-05-1957-female)

On occasion, even figures within the church were forced to bend to television's will. Suto Andras, who was responsible for Hungarian-language programming in Romania, took great pleasure in the fact that priests had to shorten their Sunday sermons to take into account the fact that viewers tended to rush home to watch his 12:30 broadcasts.[30] As these examples suggests, the secular character of television did not erase religious observance altogether, but it certainly challenged the hegemony of religious temporality and hence indirectly contributed to secularization.

The third pattern visible from our data and possibly characteristic of the state socialist context is the relative prominence of selective viewing.

[30] ANR, CC PCR-SPA, 18/70 (1970).

As suggested by our oral testimonies as well as historical audience research from the region, TV viewers in state socialist countries were rather discerning in their choices, contrary to elite anxieties, and rarely watched television from 'crust to crust' as the Russian phrase puts it – except in the early years of the medium, when television was a novelty and broadcast hours were very limited. According to a survey conducted on sample of 1,180 viewers in the Soviet republic of Estonia in 1967, only 10 per cent of viewers reported watching television non-stop, while the rest turned on the set to watch a preselected programme. Of the latter, the majority (61.7 per cent) then continued watching at least for a short while to see what happened next, while a minority (24.2 per cent) viewed only the programme they had pre-selected.[31]

Oral testimonies likewise confirm that once television became a regular part of daily life, watching became a purposeful activity. Several interviewees reported switching the receiver on in the evening with the intention of watching the evening news and associated indiscriminate, non-stop viewing with the period of dramatic changes in the late 1980s and the early 1990s, or more generally, with the post-socialist period. The following excerpt from an interview with a Croatian viewer born in 1973 offers a case in point:

> In contrast to today the volume of programming then was evidently restricted. [My parents] watched above all the *Daily News* and they watched certain films.... At that point, one would not watch television as today, meaning that one would not watch it the whole day ... Usually it would be switched on purposefully, when a particular programme was scheduled. (YuCr002-1973-male)

We should of course be careful not to take such testimonies and survey results at face value and treat them as evidence of the kind of discerning viewing envisaged by TV professionals. It may well be that audiences resorted to selective viewing to avoid watching ideologically oriented material or emphasized such practices in order to demonstrate their sophisticated, discerning attitudes to the medium in front of the interviewer, thereby reacting to elite discourses that mocked undiscerning television viewing. In some cases, there may have even been other, more practical considerations at work – at least in the Soviet context, where television sets had a nasty habit of blowing up. An article published in

[31] Rut Karemiae. 1967. '...kak tiazhelye pushki v boiu!,' *Sovetskoe radio i televidenie* 7 (1967), p. 32.

1987 suggested that nearly 20,000 sets caught fire a year;[32] *Izvestiia* suggested that between 1982 and 1987, more than 900 people died as a result of such fires.[33] Many of the Russian and Ukrainian interviewees mentioned this danger, and in Poland, where Soviet television sets were often exported, viewers mentioned similar problems. This clearly affected viewing practices, with many viewers asserting that it was not possible to leave a television switched on the whole time.

Taken together, our analysis demonstrates that the temporal patterns inscribed into daily and weekly schedules left a clear imprint on daily routines and also gave rise to patterns that can be deemed distinctly state socialist. Yet, while the daily structures of TV programmes may have stimulated the adoption of temporal routines aligned with the communist vision, it is less clear whether they managed to instil a sense of participation in revolutionary movements towards the communist future. In a handful of cases, as with the Ukrainian viewer quoted in the introduction, who felt that the daily news bulletin had the capacity to lift him onto a different temporal plane, television evidently did have such an effect. A Russian female viewer, born in 1967, likewise recalled enjoying the Soviet news bulletin *Time* and spoke enthusiastically about watching it every day and thinking proudly of the progress made by her country:

> Yes! Yes! We watched it, they showed things about agriculture, about the country, in every news programme. ... We thought that we were living in such a good country, when there won't be any more wars. ... Very interesting, it was, very. It was constructed in a very interesting way, that programme, *Vremia*. The programme, I remember, lasted 30 minutes! And it was possible to watch with pleasure – as an adult and as a child. (USSR-Rus-05-1967-female)

Some of the interviewees who grew up in Yugoslavia were also inclined to speak proudly about achievements reported in the news at the time, even if sometimes with an awareness that such behaviour may seem positively odd from the contemporary vantage point. For instance, a male viewer born in 1957 insisted that at the time, 'one had something to show' on TV: 'Then we were a country that was, already from the 1960s, producing airplanes on its own, producing tanks on its own, had two nuclear reactors ... and could supply everything that was needed in this

[32] Boris Fomin. 1987. 'Mozhet li zagoret'sia televizor?,' *Govorit i pokazyvaet Moskva*, 7 October 1987.

[33] Oberg (1989), p. 270.

country' (YuSrb-18-1957-male). In a similar way, a female viewer born in 1960 recalled her fascination with reports on the foreign travels of President Tito and spoke of the pride she felt at the time when seeing her country and the leader doing so well and obtaining international recognition (YuSrb-04-1960-female).

In contrast to such rare recollections of enjoying the news and sharing in the sense of pride and progress promoted by the broadcasts, a notable minority of interviewees was rather vocal in criticising news programmes from the era. Such participants claimed that either they or members of their family were openly suspicious of the news broadcasts aired at the time. For instance, one participant from Romania recalled disliking the news presenters because he 'had the feeling that they do everything in order to block us from seeing beyond the limits imposed by the system' (Rom-10-1967-male), while a viewer from Poland remembered watching the daily bulletin with his father who 'used to comment on it a lot, telling me which news was lies or propaganda' (Pol-10-1947-male). Likewise, a Serbian interviewee insisted that she and her family watched the daily bulletin only so they could criticise it (YuSrb-02-1946-female). Although we should take such emphatic testimonies with a grain of salt, and acknowledge they are inevitably coloured by retrospective evaluation, the level of detail provided suggests that they are rooted at least in part in actual past experiences. It is important to note, however, that even in cases where interviewees recalled being critical of the news they would rarely ignore it altogether. For instance, as one Polish interviewee explained, '*Daily* was the voice of authorities so we used to listen to know what they were planning to do with us' (Pol-09-1956-female). The daily dose of news therefore represented a stable point of reference in the daily routine even for those who had profound misgivings about the ideological messages engrained in the broadcasts.

A similar argument can be developed with regard to the remainder of the interviewees, who were neither explicitly positive nor negative about news programmes of the era, but instead mentioned them only as a regular part of their routine: something one watched seemingly regardless of the actual content. As noted earlier, oral testimonies suggest that viewers watched the news for a variety of reasons – some out of interest in the content but many simply out of habit or because it was followed by an interesting film or entertainment show. News programmes therefore only exceptionally offered a route to a different temporal reality. In some cases, they were perceived as exactly the opposite – as exceptionally monotonous and boring broadcasts, completely disconnected from one's daily concerns, let alone from revolutionary change. One Russian interviewee, for instance, recalled finding the Soviet news programme *Time* so boring that he 'wanted it to finish, because it was very dreary ... You had the feeling that how much farmers sowed, how much grain they yielded, it had no ... I felt that it didn't have any connection to my life' (USSR-6, 1960, female).

Nonetheless, we could argue that despite all the boredom, frustration, or even anger they may have provoked, news broadcasts functioned as an important axis of orientation in daily life. On the one hand, they provided a stable point in the daily routine, deeply entrenched in the rituals of domestic life. On the other hand, they also offered insight into the official and hence somehow 'normal' depiction of the life and times and delineated the sphere of what was publicly desirable and acceptable. Even for those who doubted the veracity of the reports, mocked the pompous rhetoric of revolutionary progress, or simply felt it had no impact on their daily lives, the revolutionary temporality embedded in TV news formed a part of reality they could not afford to ignore.

CONCLUSION

In this chapter we have examined whether everyday television in Eastern Europe was geared to a distinct sense of time, grounded in the teleological, future-oriented temporality of the communist project. We showed that television professionals used the medium to mould audiences' viewing practices through scheduling, thereby encouraging the kinds of behaviour deemed conducive to a communist future. We suggested that despite these distinct motivations, scheduling practices in state socialist countries shared many characteristics with those familiar in Western countries, including block scheduling, weekly repetition, and the predominance of entertainment during prime time. At the same time, we also identified some specifically state socialist aspects of scheduling, such as its secular nature and the relative lack of daytime programming aimed at housewives.

We then examined how the everyday temporalities of television were experienced and appropriated by viewers themselves and asked whether and to what extent TV professionals succeeded in aligning the daily rhythms of audience life with the communist vision of progress. Again, we noted several similarities with the West and argued that television in the state socialist world, much as elsewhere, contributed to the universal, global standardisation of time-reckoning and the organization of daily life. Specificities were noted too, broadly aligned with those seen in schedules: the secular nature of Sunday schedules displaced the hegemony of religious time among viewers, and oral testimonies also revealed a lack of daytime viewing among women. Perhaps the most interesting finding is that television was perceived not as an instrument of distraction and an aimless pastime, as communist elites feared, but as a purposeful activity directed at specific programmes.

Overall, this chapter has suggested that broadcasters in state socialist countries succeeded in creating a mass medium that was viewed by almost all members of society, that shaped their daily routines in desired ways, and that created viewing rituals which, irrespective of one's ideological viewpoint, constituted a shared locus of sociality. To some extent, broadcasters also managed to imbue those routines with preferred content: the positioning of the news in the schedules after the children had gone to bed, and in conjunction with attractive entertainment programming to follow, was a canny decision that ensured that the party's voice would be heard by the maximum possible audience. Yet on the whole, as we have seen, aligning daily routines with communist goals did not necessarily lead to a sense of participation in a shared movement towards the communist future. Television in state socialist countries was thus a generator of new routines but not necessarily of new loyalties; it tied viewers to a shared rhythm of everyday life which was in some ways distinct to state socialism, without inspiring a corresponding sense of participation in the construction of a communist future.

9

History

We have now seen how a distinctly communist sense of the passage of time, future oriented and teleological, became embedded in everyday television schedules and viewing practices. In this chapter, we investigate how this pronounced future-orientation played out in a different aspect of television's temporality, namely its engagement with the past. As noted in Chapter 2, classic theories conceptualize television as a medium of the present, closely intertwined with the rhythms of daily life and with the 'speeding up' of time characteristic of late modernity. Some commentators go so far as to see television as irredeemably locked in the present, identifying it as one of the key causes of cultural amnesia or associating it with the 'collapse of memory' in contemporary societies.[1] From this perspective, television's only claim to historical time comes through its liveness – that is, through its ability to offer a live, visually and aurally palpable connection with history as it unfolds. In this sense, the sights and sounds televised live during major events such as royal weddings or terrorist attacks function as 'electronic monuments' that offer participants an enduring point of reference for their personal recollections of historical events.[2] By analogy, the first accounts of major events provided by television news, along with their retellings across other news genres, can be seen as the first drafts of history.

Yet as a wealth of recent research has shown, television's engagement with history does not end with the erection of electronic monuments and the writing of history's first drafts. Over the course of the second half of the twentieth century, television became a key means of learning about the

[1] E.g. Hoskins (2004); Huyssens (1995). [2] See Dayan and Katz (1992), pp. 211–213.

past and contributed to shaping historical awareness and collective memory through a variety of genres.[3] Despite its pronounced future orientation, the state socialist world was no exception. Indeed, the materials we examine in this chapter suggest that state socialist television was inherently bound up with the past, perhaps even more so than its counterpart in the West. Historical events and narratives, especially those linked to the foundational myths of the communist revolution, were among the central themes of television programming across several genres from documentaries to film and serial fiction. Many of the most popular TV programmes from the state socialist era, such as the Soviet spy thriller *Seventeen Moments of Spring* (*Semnadtsat' mgnovenii vesny*, 1973), the Polish war serial *Four Tankmen and a Dog* (*Czterej pancerni i pies*, TVP, 1966–1970) or the Romanian *The Freckled Boy* (*Pistruiatul*, TVR, 1973), revolved around historical events and received wide acclaim among both elite and general audiences at the time. Not only that: television was often singled out as a particularly effective means of shaping historical awareness and was explicitly tasked by the authorities with history education.

In this chapter, we ask how and why television became an important instrument of public history education. We first consider the factors inherent to the state socialist setting, such as the distinct teleological, future-oriented temporality discussed in the previous chapter. In line with this temporality, the revolutionary advances of today had to be presented as an integral and inevitable part of a longer historical trajectory, initiated by the communist takeover and oriented towards fulfilment in the communist future. As our analysis of official documents and cultural commentaries shows, television came to be seen as an important instrument of ensuring this continuity. In the second part of the chapter we examine how the commitment to the historical continuity of the revolution became articulated on screen, particularly serial fiction. Using a combination of methods, we identify the shared elements of historical narratives, as well as some of the key points of variation across countries, and consider the factors that can explain this variation.

Yet, it is also important to keep in mind that the 'history boom' on East European screens coincided with a parallel turn to history in Western

[3] For a selection of the literature examining different forms and aspects of televised history across a range of countries see Bell and Gray (2010); Gray and Bell (2013); Dillon (2010); Edgerton and Rollins (2001); Hérnandez Corchete (2008); Kansteiner (2006); Keilbach (2010); Kleinecke-Bates (2014).

Europe and the United States, as evident in the proliferation of programmes such as the *The Forsythe Saga* (BBC, 1967) and *Upstairs, Downstairs* (ITV, 1971–1975) in the United Kingdom, or *Roots* (ABC, 1977) and *Holocaust* (NBC, 1978) in the United States. As a result, the prominence of televised history in the state socialist world cannot be seen exclusively through the lens of communist politics but also needs to be interpreted as an integral part of a global shift in what François Hartog calls 'regimes of historicity', namely the ways in which societies relate to the past, present, and future.[4] Building on Hartog's work, we argue that the transnational 'TV history boom' formed part of a transition from the modern regime of historicity, which dates from the French Revolution and privileges the future, towards a contemporary regime, in which a loss of belief in the future coincided with an acute sense of the disappearance of the past. This new 'regime', which emerged during the late twentieth century, tends to refract the past through the prism of the present, giving rise to new practices of historicisation. As we show in this chapter, this transition was driven in part by the coming of age of the first post-World War II generation but was also enabled by the rise of new forms of expression and popular culture tied to the medium of television.

TELEVISION AS A HISTORY TEACHER: PROJECTING THE CONTINUITY OF THE COMMUNIST REVOLUTION

To someone familiar with the cultural anxieties surrounding televised history in the Western context,[5] the tone of cultural commentaries and official documents on the topic from state socialist countries may come as a surprise. Political elites and television professionals were generally positive about the medium's capacity to disseminate historical knowledge and saw it as not only able to offer deep insight into historical events and situations, but also able to engender a sense of personal involvement with historical developments. In the Soviet Union, critics wrote with admiration and at length about the depictions of history on the small screen, including those appearing in popular genres and in serial fiction. In a review published in 1969, film critic V. Tuliakova discussed the spy serial *The Adjutant of His Excellency* (*Ad'iutant ego prevoskhoditel'stva*, Mosf'ilm, 1969), set during the Russian Civil War, and commended it for its depiction of heroism and sacrifice, which 'immerses us in a great and

[4] Hartog (2015). [5] Visible, for instance, in McArthur (1976).

optimistic world, which is internal, hidden from understanding, and in our heroes' ideas about life'.[6] By depicting historical events and heroic acts in this manner, she argued that the series pushed viewers not only to marvel at the historical achievements of predecessors but to look at themselves and their own actions, inspiring similar heroism in the present: 'The film forces us not only to look at the country's past, but at our own; it educates us [*vospityvaet*] with the desire to live life asking ourselves: today am I worthy of being called a Person?'[7]

Such views were not limited to the Soviet context. One Polish commentator, for instance, singled out serial fiction as a particularly effective means of public history education, capable of offering a detailed portrayal of the social atmosphere of the period and combining it with a strongly patriotic account, as well as drawing lessons from history that apply to the present.[8] Another Polish observer argued that historical themes on television could enlighten viewers, and enable them 'to place [themselves] in the continual history of the distant and near yesterday up until today'.[9] In Yugoslavia, too, historical programmes were praised for their 'contribution to the invigoration and appreciation of revolutionary events and traditions'.[10] It is worth noting, however, that no other country quite matches the Soviet Union in the extent and depth of reflection on televised history – a trait that, as we shall see later, also has its counterpart in the considerably greater prominence of historical serial fiction on Soviet screens.

Given these positive attitudes it is no surprise that television was often explicitly tasked with shaping historical awareness among the public. With the communist horizon seeming ever more distant, national leaderships looked to history to provide a solid national foundation. In the Soviet Union, several resolutions called on television to help commemorate the country's past achievements, a role which was emphasized in the run-up to major historical anniversaries. For instance, a resolution issued in 1975, dedicated to the seventieth anniversary of the mass political

6 V. Tuliakova. 1970. 'A esli eto ne detektiv?' *Sovetskoe radio i televidenie* 6 (1970): 13–15, p. 14.

7 Ibid. p. 13. See also I. Katsev. 1970. 'Podpolnyi front,' *Sovetskoe radio i televidenie* 3 (1970): 39–40.

8 Ewa Banaszkiewicz. 1979. 'Histora – temat Filmowy,' *Radio i Telewizja* 17(1979): 1.

9 Zbigniew Wasilewski. 1972. 'Telewizja Współczesnością Stoi,' *Radio i Telewizja* 48 (1972).

10 AHRTV, Radio-televizija Zagreb. 1982. *Narodna revolucija u igranim programima televizije Zagreb: Rezultati istraživanja javnog mnijenja i pregled sadržaja*. Zagreb: Radio-televizija Zagreb, p. 1.

unrest that spread across the country in 1905, demanded that television contribute to the 'uncovering of the full glory of the historical achievements of our Party, the liveliness of its revolutionary traditions, and the foresightedness of its Leninist policies'.[11] Likewise, a 1980 Yugoslav editorial policy document stated that television should use celebrations of important jubilees of the country's revolutionary past and cultural heritage to 'contribute to the strengthening of the awareness of our workers' movement and of the continuity of the revolution, to the affirmation of the Marxist approach to the national question, to the critical questioning of cultural and other traditions, and to the education of young generations in the spirit of the most progressive examples from our history'.[12] In this way, television was expected to keep the revolutionary past alive and tie it to ongoing revolutionary processes, using historical achievements to drum up support for the communist project in the here and now.

The magnitude of party-state interest in historical programming is also evident from the extensive state support received by many television productions and from the amount of political interest and scrutiny such projects attracted among the highest party echelons. Several Yugoslav TV serials involved close collaboration with the Yugoslav People's Army, which lent both soldiers and military equipment to help reproduce scenes of historical battles. For instance, the shooting of the serial *Bonfires of Kapela* (*Kapelski kresovi*, TV Zagreb, 1975), which follows the rise of the resistance movement in the coastal regions of Croatia during World War II, involved several thousand army soldiers, equipped with weapons, who acted as extras for mass battle scenes.[13] In the Soviet Union, the production of the cult serial *Seventeen Moments of Spring* (1973), likewise set during World War II, relied on input from KGB officials, some of whom were listed in credits under false names.[14] In some cases, however, the mutually supportive relationship between producers and the party-state disintegrated. The production of the Romanian serial *Lights and Shadows* (*Lumini Si Umbre*, Baftea Studio and TVR, 1981–1982), which followed the lives of several families in

[11] 'TsK KPSS prinial postanovlenie 'O 70-letii revoliutsii 1905–1907 godov v Rossii,' *Kommunist* 2 (1975): 3–6.

[12] HDA, f. 1228, d. 5601, 'Smernice za programsku politiku jugoslovenskih TV stanica za 1981. Godinu,' pp. 7–8.

[13] 'Kapelski kresovi', *List RTZ*, No. 35, 10 November 1975, p. 7; 'Svim oružjima,' *Studio*, No. 608, 29 November–5 December 1975, pp. 7–9.

[14] Lovell (2013), p. 309.

a Romanian village between 1944 and 1947, was interrupted three times by Nicolae and Elena Ceauşescu, who recognized themselves in some of the fictional characters and objected to the way they were depicted.[15]

One of the key motivations for investment in historical TV programmes stemmed from concerns over the trans-generational transmission of revolutionary values. Born in the post-war years, children and young adults coming of age during the late 1960s and early 1970s were often viewed with anxiety: would the post-war generations, who had never experienced the cruelty of war and the privation of post-war reconstruction, be able to appreciate the sacrifices of their parents and grandparents and carry the torch of revolutionary progress into the future? The rise of youth cultures and student protests that spread across major urban centres both east and west of the Iron Curtain[16] lent further credence to such anxieties and underscored the perceived need for history programming targeted specifically at children and youth.[17]

Archival documents and critical reviews of historical programming abound with comments about the potential of television to educate young audiences. The Soviet documentary *Little Earth* (*Malaia zemlia*, 1979), based on Leonid Brezhnev's ghostwritten memoir, was seen by one observer as an excellent instrument for the 'military-patriotic education of Soviet youth ... who have never heard the screech of a falling bomb, have never seen collapsed houses, sinister ruins, the roar of fire'.[18] A decade earlier, *Drawing Fire*, set during World War II, was recommended for a state prize partly for its educational potential among youth audiences.[19] Historical television programmes, along with films, also became an integral part of formal history teaching in several countries. In parts of

[15] Eugenia Mihalcea. 2004. 'Censurat de trei ori,' *jurnalul.ro*, 23 Feb 2004. http://jurnalul.ro/special-jurnalul/cenzurat-de-trei-ori-72550.html.

[16] See Gorsuch and Koenker (2013).

[17] As research from the era attests, these anxieties were not merely the domain of the elites. According to a public opinion survey conducted in 1965, 60% of respondents agreed that there was a social necessity to transfer the memory of World War II to younger generations; by 1973 this number grew to 63%. TNS OBOP, *Zmiany Opinii Dotyczących Tradycji II Wojny Światowej*, August 1973 Ośrodek Badania Opinii Publicznej i Studiów Programowych.

[18] A. Mares'ev. 1979. 'Malaia zemlia. Podvig,' *Sovetskoe radio i televidenie* 7 (1979): 10.

[19] GARF, f. R6903, op. 28, d. 21, ll.106–109, 'Pis'mo N. Mesiatseva v komissiiu po gosudarstvennym premiiam RSFSR v oblasti literatury, iskusstva i ispolnitel'skogo masterstva pri Sovete ministrov RSFSR,' 25 April 1965.

Yugoslavia, the enormous popularity of the *Bonfires of Kapela* among young audiences was used as evidence of television's ability to influence young viewers and their attitudes to history and led history teachers to adopt the serial as an aid in their lessons.[20] In Romania, too, both film and television serials were used for the purpose of history teaching, and over the course of the early 1970s several 'class experiments' were conducted to ascertain the efficacy of education using audiovisual means.[21]

This embrace of television as a means of history education begs the question of what exactly, in the eyes of professionals and commentators, made the medium so suitable for the role. Although the arguments varied from country to country and from programme to programme, television's ability to engage audiences on a personal, intimate level was a shared trait. Part of television's appeal inhered in its audiovisual nature and thus its ability to make the experiences of wartime heroes more palpable for post-war generations.[22] Beyond the power of the moving image, commentators also mentioned the distinct qualities of television as a medium, especially the domestic viewing context and the characteristically intimate mode of address, but also the serial form of narration. In a review of the Soviet police procedural *The Meeting Place Cannot Be Changed* (*Mesto vstrechi izmenit' nel'zia*, Odessa Film, 1979), set in the post-World War II period, the reviewer focused on the specific intimacy of television and how this serial fostered identification with the characters, arguing that 'this ability to directly move people, to actively penetrate into their everyday existence is something that is essential to television'. As a result of this intimate connection, television helps viewers 'empathise more directly [with the characters], they connect more strongly with them – they take them for real people, as dear acquaintances, existing somewhere in front of them; separated from them only by the glass wall of the screen'.[23] Similar

[20] 'Klinci za klice.' *Studio*, No. 621, 1976, pp. 2–5.

[21] Virginia Cretu. 1980. *Educatia elevilor prin film si pentru film*. Bucharest: Editura Didactica si Pedagogica, p. 140.

[22] A former Soviet soldier, decorated as Hero of the Soviet Union, thus spoke of television as a means that will offer young audiences 'the possibility of seeing the pages of our memoirs'. A. Mares'ev. 1979. 'Malaia zemlia. Podvig,' *Sovetskoe radio i televidenie* 7 (1979): 10. Visual aspects were also emphasized in an article about the Soviet documentary series *Our Biography* (1976–1977), which told the history of the Soviet Union from 1917 to 1977 and allegedly aimed 'to give bright, magnetic images of the representatives of all generations of Soviet people'. See 'Eto nasha s toboi biografiia,' *Sovetskoe radio i televidenie* 1 (1979): 8–9, p. 8.

[23] V. Mikhalkovich. 1980. 'Mech i vesy,' *Sovetskoe radio i televidenie* 2 (1980): 27–31, p. 29.

qualities were highlighted also in a review of *Drawing Fire* (1965), where television's domestic viewing context was thought to generate an intimate connection between viewers and television personalities. The television hero was thought to 'achiev[e] proximity with the viewer in a way that neither the theatrical nor the film hero has managed', making it possible for the viewer 'to look at the hero more thoroughly'.[24] As a result, it was felt that viewers would build para-social relationships with characters, whom they would treat as close family members or old friends.

As this reference to the hero suggests, a part of television's personalized appeal included its ability to depict ideal forms of character development and produce easy-to-understand plot lines. These elements were frequently mentioned in reviews of Yugoslav war serials aimed at youth and children. Critics highlighted the ability of these programmes to portray historical characters and events in a manner appealing to young audiences, either because of simple narratives with a lot of emphasis on action or because of characters that were in many ways similar to viewers and hence facilitated identification. The critical reception of the serial *Outcasts* (*Otpisani*, TVB, 1974), which focuses on a group of young resistance fighters in the Yugoslav capital of Belgrade in the early 1940s, offers a case in point (Figure 9.1). One review of the series noted that the key protagonists were presented as regular people with both strengths and weaknesses, thus making them more appealing to young audiences who could identify with the heroes and imagine themselves as resistance fighters.[25] Another review likewise commended the contemporary feel of the key protagonists, in particular their use of contemporary jargon and the fact that 'they behave as the young people today imagine heroes to behave'.[26] Similar arguments were raised in relation to the previously mentioned serial the *Bonfires of Kapela* (1975). According to one commentator, the key reason for its success lay in the use of 'a human approach which foregrounds ideals close to the contemporary youth'.[27]

What transpires from all the materials surveyed so far is an underlying concern with the continuity of the revolution – that is, with the ability of socialist societies to continue their pursuit of the communist goals defined

[24] A. Donatov. 1965. 'Kak byt' chelovekom,' *Iskusstvo kino* 5 (1965): 133.
[25] 'Petorica za specijalne zadatke.' *TV Novosti*, 6 December 1974, p. 5.
[26] 'Otpisani.' *TV Novosti*, 3 January 1975, p. 3.
[27] 'Klinci za klice.' *Studio*, No. 621, 1976, pp. 2–5, p. 5.

FIGURE 9.1 Scene from the Yugoslav serial *The Outcasts* (1974). *Source*: RTS-PATVB.

during the revolutionary takeover. This concern goes a long way towards explaining the markedly positive attitudes to televised history among political and cultural elites in Eastern Europe. As pointed out in the previous chapter, the communist project was reliant on a markedly future-oriented and teleological understanding of progress. This was premised on the belief in an ongoing revolution, through which communist parties would lead societies from the transitional state of socialism into fully-fledged communism. The need to establish and maintain the collective adherence to this belief underpins many of the key issues we have surveyed so far surrounding televised history, from a concern with the passing of revolutionary traditions onto new generations to the emphasis on appealing to viewers on an individual level and instigating their personal engagement with revolutionary traditions.[28] In this sense, the strong investment in televised history in state

[28] This peculiar presentism of the past was captured particularly well in a review of *Eternal Call* (*Vechnyi zov*, 1973–1983), a Soviet serial that followed the fortunes of the Savelovs, a working class family from a small Russian village, from 1905 until 1961. The reviewer used the serial as a springboard for a broader reflection on Soviet art and its relationship with history, emphasizing its ability to highlight continuities between the past and the present: 'Soviet art searches for internal moral connections between life today and life yesterday, traces back the most diverse and most unexpected linkages of events; it couples

socialist countries can be seen as a direct consequence of the communist understanding of society and progress.

Nonetheless, we should avoid the temptation to explain the fascination with television history solely with reference to the particularities of communist modernity. Building on Hartog's discussion of the global shift in regimes of historicity, we can argue that communist concerns with the continuity of the revolution were just an extreme form of a broader, transnationally shared anxiety linked to the global retreat of the modern regime of historicity. On both sides of the Cold War divide, the 1970s were a time when the future-oriented mode of engaging with the passage of time – a mode shared by all the varieties of modernity examined in Chapter 4 – was in terminal decline. Rising in its stead was a present-centered regime of historicity, in which the reassuring vision of a better future for all was increasingly replaced by a perception of the future as a threat, or at least, a source of anxiety. In this sense, communist anxieties surrounding the ability of youths to appreciate past sacrifices were but one expression of a more broadly shared sense of uncertainty surrounding the future. Indeed, a similar generational conflict was a feature of public discourse and cultural politics during the 1960s and the 1970s in the West, too, and there is enough evidence to suggest that it shaped historical TV programming at the time. In West Germany, for instance, the different representations of history broadcast on television reflected generational divisions in the country, with the first post-war generation adopting a markedly different stance on the Nazi past than their predecessors.[29]

Viewed from this perspective, the privileged status of television as a means of history education can likewise be interpreted as an integral part of the transition from the future-oriented to the present-centered regime of historicity. Hartog himself noted the role of the modern media, including television, among the drivers of presentism, arguing that they play an important role in conveying the present, at the moment of its occurrence, 'as already history, already past', thereby anticipating 'how it will be regarded when it is completely past'.[30] Our analysis confirms the centrality of television to the presentist regime of historicity

historical occurrences, which somehow lead from our today to distant days of the past – to people, perhaps, who are forgotten, but existed in a living reality and have preserved living traces which are thus inevitably reflected in later human fates.' N. Tolchenova. 1976. 'Oruzhiem pravdy i sovetsi,' *Sovetskoe radio i televidenie* 10 (1976): 30–32, p. 30.

[29] Kansteiner (2006); Gassert and Steinweis (2006).

[30] Hartog (2015), p. 114.

but offers a more elaborated examination of why the medium was so well suited to this role. As we have seen, the aspects that made television so effective a means of history education in the eyes of state socialist elites included some of the key traits of television culture: privacy, intimacy, domesticity, and the medium's characteristic narrative structures, which are ultimately rooted in its bond with the present.

These traits are universal in scope and can also be found in Western historical programming produced at the time. As Glen Creeber argues in his analysis of *Roots* (ABC, 1977) and *Holocaust* (NBC, 1978), both miniseries relied on the intimacy and repetitiveness of the serial form to capture the attention of the audience and foster identification with the characters over a long span of time. Seriality also enabled the development of a complex narrative arc, comprising multiple plotlines and characters spanning both private and public life, which could capture the complexity of history while also enabling viewers to contemplate the subject from the individual, personal perspective of the historical subjects.[31] As we shall see further on, historical fiction produced in state socialist countries shared many of these characteristics. Arguably, these transnational similarities confirm the role played by television in establishing a link between the past and the present and thereby in contributing to the rise of a presentist regime of historicity on both sides of the Iron Curtain.[32]

REVOLUTIONARY HISTORY ON THE SMALL SCREEN: AN OVERVIEW

Having considered elite views, it is now time to turn to the television programmes themselves. How common was historical programming at the time, and to what extent did it succeed in promoting a distinctly communist vision of the past? What were the shared straits of televised history in the region, and how did representations of the past differ across countries? Finally, did televised history in the socialist world reflect the waning appeal of the modern regime of historicity?

[31] Creeber (2004), pp. 23–36.

[32] In this context, it is also worth noting that televised depictions of history produced east and west of the Iron Curtain circulated transnationally. As our research shows, television in Eastern Europe imported several historical dramas produced in the West, including *The Forsythe Saga* (BBC, 1967) and *Roots* (ABC, 1977). Although such foreign programmes were selected for their congruence with the communist vision of the past, it is likely that they served as a point of reference for domestic production.

Given the range and volume of historical content produced and broadcast across the five countries examined here it is impossible to provide an exhaustive investigation of all its aspects. Instead, the pages that follow offer a snapshot based on the analysis of historical serial fiction. There are two main reasons for focusing on historical serials. First, the genre embodies many of the traits believed to be key to the personalized appeal of televised history, including seriality and the combination of public and personal plots. Second, as historical audience research shows, historical serial dramas were frequently among the most widely watched broadcasts at the time. In the Yugoslav republic of Croatia, 95 per cent of the population saw at least one episode of the *Bonfires of Kapela* and 60 per cent watched the whole serial when it first aired.[33] In Poland, opinion polls showed similar trends, with a survey conducted in the late 1980s revealing that historical serials were liked by 70 per cent of the viewers and were preferred to historical films (66 per cent) and historical books (44 per cent).[34] In Germany, serials such as *Paths over Land* (*Wege übers Land*, 1968) received 54 per cent of viewers, while *Archive of Death* (*Archiv des Todes*, 1980) received a 44 per cent share of the audience, which is high when one takes into account the rival charms of West German television.[35] This is not to say that all historical serial fiction was equally successful. In East Germany, for instance, the more earnest biopics, such as those on *Martin Luther* (1983) and wartime communist leader *Ernst Thälmann* (1986) were far more coldly received, receiving viewer shares of only 9.5 and 21 per cent, respectively.[36] This suggests that it was not history as such that provided a recipe for success, but the packaging of narratives in an attractive form, often following the conventions of action films combined with romance.

To obtain a general overview of historical serial fiction we first examined all the serial dramas produced and broadcast across the five countries between 1961 and 1990, noting how many of the serials were set in the past and on which historical periods they focused. As the results of our quantitative analysis show, historical dramas constituted a sizeable

[33] AHRTV, Radio-televizija Zagreb. 1982. *Narodna revolucija u igranim programima televizije Zagreb: Rezultati istraživanja javnog mnijenja i pregled sadržaja.* Zagreb: Radio-televizija Zagreb, p. 15.

[34] TNS OBOP, Centrum badania Opinii Społecznej, *Przeszłość jako przedmiot zainteresowań i dyskusji*, Warsaw, July 1988.

[35] Meyen (2003b), p. 116; Steinmetz and Viehoff (2008), p. 62.

[36] Steinmetz and Viehoff (2008), p. 62.

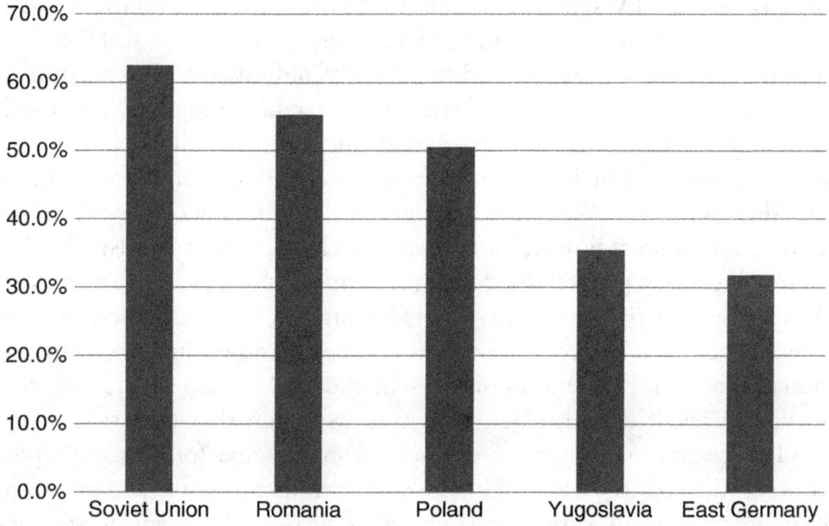

FIGURE 9.2 Share of historical drama in domestically produced serial fiction.
Note: Figures based on all serial dramas broadcast between 1961 and 1990. For further details see the Methodological Appendix.

proportion of domestic serial fiction across all five countries (Figure 9.2). Even in Yugoslavia and East Germany, where the majority of serial production focused on contemporary events and themes, the absolute number of historical serials was nonetheless impressive: East German television broadcast a total of seventy-one such serials, while Yugoslav audiences could watch no fewer than 137. These results confirm that fictional engagement with the past was high on the agenda of television producers in all countries and reflects the considerable elite investment in televised history. However, the prominence of historical narration on state socialist screens can also be interpreted as a sign that the communist vision of progress was unable to provide a guide for interpreting the present and for steering it closer to communist ideals. Instead of providing audiences with compelling narratives of contemporary life, guided by a commitment to the ongoing revolution, television turned to the revolutionary past, in the hope that the magic of televisual narration might inspire revolutionary acts in the future.

While the engagement with historical themes was present across the five countries of our sample, there were also clear variations between countries. These variations can be accounted for by the relative core-periphery position of the country and its broadcasting system, the impact of cross-border TV signals and imported programming, and the particularities of national histories and official narratives of the past. Historical dramas were most prominent in the Soviet Union, where they accounted for over 60 per cent of all serial fiction produced in the country. This result is in line with the considerable extent and depth of elite reflection on televised history which, as argued in the previous section, exceeded that of other countries. We could also argue that the Soviet Union, as the leading communist power, had a particularly high stake in ensuring that its revolutionary past retained a lasting impact on its present and future. As a result, its serial fiction was steeped in history, inviting audiences to re-experience the achievements of their forebears and ensure the continuation of these achievements in the present and the future. Seen in a different way, this result can also be interpreted as a sign that the crisis of the modern regime of historicity reached its most acute form in the Soviet context: the country where the stakes of demonstrating the success of the ongoing revolution were highest was also the one which was most prone to turn for inspiration to the past.

At the other end of the spectrum we find East Germany, where historical fiction constituted less than a third of total serial production (31.8 per cent), closely followed by Yugoslavia (35.2 per cent). In case of Germany, the country's Nazi past and post-1945 partitioning made the production of simple, pride-boosting historical narratives rather difficult. In Yugoslavia, the reasons are less immediately apparent but were likely linked, at least in part, to the country's unorthodox communist policies and its somewhat more liberal television system. We should also acknowledge the possible impact of Western fiction in both countries, even though the direction of this impact seems to have varied with context. On the one hand, it may be possible that the popularity of Western dramas focused on contemporary life prompted TV producers to adopt a similar approach in their own work – an interpretation that helps explain the clear downward trend evident from our data in the proportion of historical serials on GDR screens from the early 1970s onwards. On the other hand, Yugoslav sources from the same period suggest that Western fiction may have had the opposite effect and acted as a motivation for greater investment in the domestic production of historical serials.[37] Again, this interpretation is

[37] See, for instance, 'Klinci za klice.' *Studio*, 621 (1976): 2–5, p. 5; and AHRTV, Radio-televizija Zagreb. 1982. *Narodna revolucija u igranim programima televizije Zagreb: Rezultati istraživanja javnog mnijenja i pregled sadržaja*. Zagreb: Radio-televizija Zagreb.

supported by longitudinal trends in our data: the proportion of historical serial fiction in the country rose from less than 20 per cent in the 1960s to 40 per cent and more, during the 1970s, and stayed at this level until the mid-1980s.

Of course, the sheer volume of historical drama says little about the actual nature of historical representations and the extent to which they promoted a distinctly communist perception of the past. To begin addressing this issue, we shall first look at the main events and periods foregrounded in the serials. As evident from our data, a sizeable proportion of historical serial fiction focused on events and periods linked to the foundational moments of communist rule: the immediate pre-communist period, the revolution up to 1941 in the Soviet case, and World War II period in others (Table 9.1). It is particularly telling that World War I received scant attention and was explicitly thematised as a central event in only three out of a total of 472 historical serial dramas. This result may in part be due to the difficulty of turning the events of World War I into an appealing narrative, but it also testifies to the influence of the communist narrative on televised history in the region. For virtually all countries in the region, World War I represented a key turning point, which brought substantial changes to state borders and international status. Yet in the narratives promulgated by historical fiction, these events were completely overshadowed by the communist takeover.

As one might expect, the focus on the foundational moments of communist rule was most prominent in the Soviet Union: dramas dedicated to these events accounted for almost two-thirds of all historical serial fiction (65.8 per cent), with almost half of that focused on the 1917 Bolshevik Revolution and the events up to 1941. This result again reflects the leading position of the country in the state socialist world and its investment in televising revolutionary history, and is aligned with official Soviet historiography.[38] In Yugoslavia, the proportion of dramas dedicated to key revolutionary events was also high, totalling over half of all historical serials (50.8 per cent), with a particularly high share of World War II dramas (41.2 per cent). This is consistent with the central role of the war in the historical narrative promoted in the country. The narrative of the People's Liberation Struggle, as it was commonly referred to, functioned as a veritable myth of origin, which linked the joint national liberation struggle of the Southern Slavs to the international struggle of the working

[38] Similar patterns have been observed also in Soviet cinema. See Youngblood (2007); Levitsky (2012).

TABLE 9.1 *Key events and periods represented in historical serial fiction*

	USSR		Yugoslavia		Poland		Romania		GDR	
	N	%	n	%	N	%	n	%	N	%
Early modern period & 19th century	16	*10.3*	29	*21.5*	35	*37.2*	9	*56.6*	13	*18.3*
Pre-communist period	28	*18.1*	13	*9.6*	15	*15.6*	0	*0*	15	*21.1*
Revolution to 1941 (USSR only)	51	*32.9*	n/a	*n/a*	n/a	*n/a*	n/a	*n/a*	n/a	*n/a*
World War I	0	*0.0*	2	*1.4*	0	*0.0*	1	*6.6*	0	*0.0*
World War II	23	*14.8*	56	*41.2*	23	*24.4*	6	*37.5*	10	*14.1*
Post-World War II	20	*12.9*	17	*12.5*	15	*15.6*	0	*0*	13	*18.3*
Historical progression	17	*11.0*	20	*14.7*	6	*6.4*	0	*0*	19	*26.8*
All historical serial fiction	155	*100*	136	*100*	94	*100*	16	*100*	71	*100*

Note: Figures based on all serial dramas broadcast between 1961 and 1990. For further details see the Methodological Appendix.

class and the establishment of communist rule in the country.[39] In contrast, East German historical serials were least likely to deal with the rise of communism and World War II. Instead, the largest proportion of historical serial fiction dealt with historical developments over a longer span of time (for instance, encompassing both World War II and pre-war years, or stretching into the post-war years). This can be seen as a direct consequence of the aforementioned problematic status of Nazi rule in the communist narrative of history, which ruled out the possibility of constructing uplifting stories about the war. Instead, these more extended narratives offered the opportunity to place Nazism contextually within a broader trajectory that connected its wartime defeat to Soviet liberation and a prosperous socialist society.

In Poland and Romania, a significant proportion of serials (24.4 and 37.5 per cent respectively) were set during World War II (although we should note the limited volume of serial fiction in Romania overall). Much as in Yugoslavia, this was in line with official narratives of the past in the two countries, which likewise made wartime events central to the legitimacy of communist rule.[40] Yet what is striking in both countries is the high proportion of historical serial dramas dedicated to the early modern era and the events of the nineteenth century – periods far removed from the rise of communism. Arguably, it is not a coincidence that this pattern emerges in the two countries that acquired independent statehood before the twentieth century and which hence incorporated the arrival of communist rule into a longer narrative of national history. In contrast, Soviet, Yugoslav, and East German serials rarely ventured that far into the past, which is consistent with the different history of statehood in the three countries and the greater importance accorded to twentieth-century events.

In Romania, the emphasis on national history was particularly pronounced, especially after Ceauşescu's rise to power in 1965, when official narratives of the past become markedly nationalist, minimized the role of Soviet influence, and focused instead on the contributions of Romanian forces.[41] This new, nationalist narrative was soon reflected in major film productions, many of which turned to events and personalities from earlier periods of Romanian national history.[42] Our analysis shows

[39] Perica (2002), pp. 95–98. [40] Bucur (2009), p. 147.

[41] See Bucur (2006), pp. 171–193 and 183–184.

[42] Examples include *The Forest of the Hanged* (*Padurea Spanzuriatilor*, 1965) and *The Dacians* (*Dacii*, 1967). See Alexandru (2009).

a similar pattern in serial TV fiction. For instance, the thirteen-part drama series *The Musatini Family* (*Musatinii*, 1971) was based on events following the death of Steven the Great (1457–1504), one of the most prominent heroes of Romanian national history, while the widely watched adventure serial *All Sails Up!* (*Toate pînzele sus!*, 1976–1978) was set during the nineteenth century and followed the maritime adventures of a Romanian-French crew on board a ship that ventures to Latin America.

In Poland, too, the early modern era played an important role in national history, and characters and tales from this period were already familiar to audiences. Several television serials set in this period, including the serials *Chłopi* (*Peasants*, 1972) and *The Adventures of Mister Michael* (*Przygody Pana Michała*, 1969), were based on Polish novels which formed part of the literary canon and were widely read at the time, hence offering a convenient basis for appealing television productions that also satisfied the requirements of the traditional cultural hierarchies.[43] Also part of the same category was *Janosik* (TVP, 1973), a popular adventure serial about a famous Carpathian robber – a Polish equivalent of Robin Hood – who lived at the turn of the seventeenth and eighteenth centuries.

Of course, the focus on pre-communist history does not mean that these serials abandoned the communist narrative altogether. As Imre notes in her analysis of *Janosik* and the Hungarian serial of the same genre, *The Captain of the Tenkes* (*A Tenkes kapitánya*, Hungarian Television, 1964), historical adventure serials typically revolved around plotlines that pitted innocent peasant characters against the wealthy and exploitative elites, thereby replicating the revolutionary narrative in a different historical setting. Their reliance on folk mythology, mediated through esteemed literary forms, was likewise fully in line with communist cultural values and policies.[44] Yet at the same time, these serials also offered a means of bending the shared, transnational narrative of the communist revolution to the sensibilities of local nationalisms, thereby capitalizing on the dual legitimacy of both transnational and national narratives.

[43] The serial *Chłopi* (*Peasants*, 1972) was based on Władysław Reymont's novel of same title, while *The Adventures of Mister Michael* (*Przygody Pana Michała*, 1969) was based loosely on Henryk Sienkiewicz's *Trilogy* (*Trylogia*, 1875–1877) and Eliza Orzeszkowa's *On the Niemen* (*Nad Niemnem*, 1888).

[44] Imre (2016), pp. 134–135.

Taken together, our quantitative analysis thus reveals the decisive influence of national history and official narratives of the past and, especially, of the role of communist rule in the trajectory of state- and nation-building. Even though the greatest proportions of dramas across all the five countries were dedicated to events and periods deemed central to the communist narrative of the past, more detailed patterns can only be interpreted in light of specific national narratives of national history.

SCREENING WORLD WAR II: TALES OF HEROISM, TALES OF SACRIFICE

World War II looms large in the history of state socialism. For the Soviet Union, it was a trial by fire, surviving which formed a bedrock of legitimacy. For the other four countries in our sample, the relationship of the war to state socialism was more conflictual. Out of the ashes of the war came the realities of violent conflict, occupation, and new historical myths that attempted either to come to terms with the past or to hide uneasy truths. For this reason, World War II serves as a useful case study for uncovering the different ways that socialist broadcasters came to terms with the past. As we have seen, the war served as a key historical setting in a sizeable proportion of serial fiction in all countries and offers a useful basis for a closer examination of historical narratives across the five countries, and further reflection on both similarities and cross-country differences. On the pages that follow, we pay particular attention to five serials, produced between 1965 and 1975, which embody key representational tropes and achieved high viewer ratings or significant attention: *Four Tankmen and a Dog* (*Czeterej pancierni i pies*, TVP, 1966–1970) from Poland, the *Freckled Boy* (*Pistruiatul*, TVR, 1973) from Romania, the *Bonfires of Kapela* (*Kapelski kresovi*, TVZ, 1975) from Yugoslavia, *Drawing Fire* (*Vyzyvaem ogon' na sebia*, Mosfilm, 1965) from the Soviet Union, and *Every Man Dies Alone* (*Jeder stirbt für sich allein*, DEFA, 1970) from East Germany. Where relevant, we also situate these five dramas in the broader context of historical serial fiction produced in the five countries.

These five serials have a number of things in common. Each features a heroic plot involving personal transformation and sacrifice: each storyline centres on one or more main protagonists who start as ordinary individuals caught in the maelstrom of history but gradually transform into heroes who are fully dedicated to fighting the enemy, prepared to sacrifice their personal safety for the collective cause. In the Soviet,

Yugoslav, and German examples, the climax of the narrative coincides with the death of the hero, hence dramatizing the ultimate sacrifice for the communist cause.

In *Drawing Fire*, the storyline follows Ania Morozova, who returns home to find her town bombed and her relatives killed, and then joins the partisans, who are seeking to retake control over a nearby airfield occupied by German forces. Through the serial, Ania grows increasingly skilled and knowledgeable and learns from past mistakes. In the closing shootout, the Germans are finally defeated, but partisan forces suffer heavy losses in the process, including Ania. A similar character development occurs in the *Bonfires of Kapela*, where the plot follows the formation of an anti-fascist resistance unit in the coastal region of Yugoslavia, which is occupied by Italian forces. One of the key protagonists is Zlatko Mateić, nicknamed the Hawk, a high school pupil who, frustrated by the fascist occupation, decides to leave his hometown and, together with his school friends, joins the partisans. Over the course of the serial, the Hawk becomes a leading figure of his unit and engages in several successful operations against the enemy but, in the penultimate episode, dies under enemy fire. *Every Man Dies Alone* focuses on an ordinary, working class couple, Otto and Elise Hempel, who are initially completely uninterested in politics but later become politicized and initiate a postcard campaign, trying to incite a mass rebellion against the Nazis. This leads them to being arrested, sentenced to death, and executed.

While the traits of character transformation and heroism are also present in the Romanian and Polish serials, this final sacrifice is not so prominent. In *Four Tankmen*, the key protagonist and one of the four tankmen, Janek Kos, a Polish teenager, initially tries to join the war font primarily to find his father, who has been missing for four years and has presumably also joined the resistance movement. Much like Zlatko and Ania, Janek grows into a hero over the course of the episodes, effortlessly defeating the enemy in a range of situations. In contrast to the Soviet and Yugoslav heroes, however, Janek survives the war unscathed, and in the final episode, he and his fellow tankmen return home and marry their sweethearts. In *The Freckled Boy*, the key protagonist, a thirteen-year-old boy named Mihai, likewise survives until the end of the series, but his close friend, the fugitive Andrei, who turns out to be a communist hero, dies in the final episode while trying to stop the Germans from advancing into his town. While the motive of heroic sacrifice is clearly present, the fact that the story is largely narrated from the perspective of the teenage boy relativizes the positive status of sacrifice and draws attention to the suffering caused by it, thereby also suggesting a limit to the heroic narrative. Although his friend's death prompts young Mihai to grab a gun and shoot at the Germans himself, he is ultimately unable to overcome his sadness: in the closing shots, we see him in the crowd, distraught, and unable to join the collective euphoria that engulfs his town upon the arrival of the liberating army.

Another trait shared by the five serials is the combination of a public plot centred on fighting a common enemy and personal plots involving either romantic relations or ties between family members and friends. As noted in Chapter 6, such dual plot patterns were a widespread characteristic of serial fiction across Eastern Europe and formed one of the means by which state socialist television helped constitute a distinctly socialist form of public privacy. The same argument applies also to the five historical dramas examined here. Personal plots are particularly pronounced in *The Freckled Boy* and *Every Man Dies Alone*, both of which take place largely away from the battlefield. In the Romanian series, the narrative revolves primarily around the bond between the young boy Mihai and the communist fugitive Andrei, and various family members and friends, including Mihai's father, his history teacher, and his dog. In the German series, personal plotlines also function as a key narrative axis: the Hempels start their postcard campaign after losing their son and witnessing the violent death of their Jewish neighbour at the hands of the Nazis.

In the remaining three serials, much of the action occurs on the battlefield, yet personal narratives also play an important role. In *Four Tankmen*, the storyline focuses on the interaction between the tankmen and their dog, Czarik, and although the war provides an essential backdrop, friendship and comradery are in the foreground (Figure 9.3). A strong emphasis on friendship and loyalty is evident also in *Drawing Fire*, where Ania's collaboration with fellow resistance fighters is essential to the success of the military operation. The personal is also foregrounded in the dramatic finale to the serial, where we see a small child running towards Ania: it is her own son, Kolia, who was presumed dead. Finally, in *The Bonfires*, frequent battle scenes are interspersed with storylines of comradery among the partisans and their friendly relationships with locals, as well as with a romantic plot involving Zlatko and his high school sweetheart. However, all the serials firmly subordinate the personal to the collective: friendship and loyalty form the basis for pursuing shared goals,

FIGURE 9.3 Tankmen Olgierd and Gustlik with their dog Szarik, from the Polish serial *Four Tankmen and a Dog*. Source: FFN.

and personal losses, however painful, are overshadowed by the greater good of collective action. In this sense, historical serial dramas fit the broader pattern identified in Chapter 6: personal plots function as hooks for messages of public significance and serve to showcase modes of heroic private behaviour consistent with communist ideals, thereby adding another layer to the televised forms of public privacy.

It is worth reflecting how this prominence of heroic narratives and the subordination of the personal to the public fits with the transition in the regimes of historicity discussed earlier. Although we should acknowledge that our analysis here is based on a very small sample of serials, these results seem to suggest that state socialist historical dramas not only departed from the modern, future-oriented regime of historicity but in fact adopted elements of the pre-modern, didactic mode of engaging with the past that Hartog suggests dominated historical writing from antiquity to the eighteenth century.[45] Instead of searching for the unique and unrepeatable and looking to the future as a source of intelligibility, state

[45] Hartog (2015), pp. 28–32.

socialist television turned to the past to showcase exemplary models for future imitation. As we have seen, this gesture was rooted in the conviction that a televisual rendering of the past would help bring the revolutionary past to bear on the present and the future and inspire a renewed commitment to revolutionary goals. Yet the presence of this ostensibly pre-modern regime should be read not so much as a sign of historical 'backwardness' but as an attempt to shore up a fragile sense of historical continuity at a time when there existed intense debate about the disappearance of the past. Indeed, the two regimes of historicity often intertwined. For instance, the final season of *Eternal Call* (*Vechnyi zov*, 1983), a Soviet serial that followed the fortunes of a working class family from 1905 to 1961, features a storyline about disappearance of Semyon Fyodorov, reported missing in action during World War II. The final episode of the serial, set in 1961 and entitled 'Immortality', begins with Semyon's mother receiving a letter with news of Semyon's death from a former Norwegian partisan. The episode shows Semyon's mother and brother travelling to Norway, where they learn of Semyon's heroic escape from a POW camp and his assistance to Norwegian partisans. The episode ends with his family tearfully laying a wreath at a memorial. Here, then, a didactic narrative of wartime heroism was tied up with the ritualised forms of mnemonic practice characteristic of the contemporary, presentist form of historicity.

Apart from these shared characteristics, significant cross-country differences should be highlighted. *Every Man Dies Alone* stands out for the absence of triumphal, patriotic messages – a trait shared by other historical serials produced in Germany. Because of the pervasiveness of Nazism and the subsequent partitioning of Germany, an unproblematic, pride-inducing patriotic narrative about World War II was simply impossible. To convey a more uplifting message, television producers had either to move beyond World War II or to adopt a transnational angle that emphasized the contribution of the German resistance to Nazism to the victory of communism internationally. As a result, a significant proportion of GDR historical fiction covers a broader historical sweep that includes the war in a wider perspective and thereby enables the narrative to conclude on a more positive note. A good example is provided by the serial *Merciless Front* (*Front ohne Gnade*, 1984), set between 1934 and 1949, which follows the struggles against fascism from the Spanish Civil War through World War II to the founding of East Germany. Alternatively, the pre-1945 period is simply blocked out altogether, as if history began with the defeat of the Nazis and the establishment of East Germany – a solution adopted, among others, in *Beginning of All Love* (*Aller Liebe Anfang*, 1980), which tells the story of a former soldier trying to restart his life after being discharged from the front. A notable proportion of East German serials also emphasized international connections in resisting the Nazis, thus linking East Germany to a more optimistic narrative of the transnational resistance movement. For instance, in the aforementioned *Archive of Death* (1980), the storyline follows a group of German resistance and Polish fighters as they try to uncover the Nazis' plans for a deadly advance. Ultimately, however, the easiest route was to abandon historical themes altogether – an option which, as we have seen, became increasingly common in GDR serial fiction from the 1970s onwards.

The war serials produced across the five countries also differed in their treatment of the war as a transnational event. As we have just discussed, East German historical serials frequently revolved around transnational links of the German resistance movement, thereby presenting World War II as a battle that required its participants to rise above their national allegiances and bond with likeminded forces from other nations. Similar instances of international collaboration were foregrounded also in Polish and Soviet serials, including the two examined more closely here. The crew in *Four Tankmen and a Dog* comprises two Polish and two Soviet soldiers, and the transnational aspects of the struggle are emphasized at several points in the serial. During the first episode, Janek meets a Georgian man, Grigori, who also wants to join the war effort and enthusiastically exclaims: 'My war, your war. One war.' Later in the same episode, Grigori appears again, this time already as part of the joint Polish–Soviet tank crew, which symbolizes the joint, transnational fight against the fascist enemy. The Soviet serial *Drawing Fire* likewise involves a transnational alliance: here, the Russian resistance fighter Ania collaborates with both Polish and Czech partisans, and the successful recapture of the airfield is dependent on their joint efforts. While this episode had its roots in historical events, there is little doubt that the emphasis on international collaboration was intentional and actively encouraged by the authorities. The creators of *Drawing Fire* were awarded a silver pin as 'Brothers in Arms' by the Polish Ministry of Defense and a gold pin for honoured members of the Society of Polish–Soviet Friendship,[46] and the serial was commended for its internationalist message in a letter of justification sent to the State

[46] 'Fil'm stal sobytiem,' *Tsentral'noe televidenie*, 29 August 1966, pp. 2–3.

Prize Committee.[47] In many cases, the push to present the war through an international lens was so strong that the narratives lost any grounding in historical reality. This was particularly clear in *Four Tankmen*, where the narrative of Soviet–Polish friendship served to erase the history of Soviet raids and mass murders of Polish soldiers during the war.[48]

However, the realities of the wartime past were in some cases too difficult to ignore, subverting the producers' emphasis on international solidarity. The popular GDR serial *Paths over Land* (1968), which took in a historical sweep from 1939 until the 1960s, offers a case in point. It featured as its heroine Gertrud Kalluweit, a farm worker who takes over a Nazi-expropriated farm in occupied Poland. Horrified by Nazi brutality, she adopts a Jewish girl and prevents her husband from turning in a group of Polish partisans hiding in their basement. When the serial was broadcast in Poland in 1969, it provoked an angry reaction among viewers. After a preview screening in Warsaw, two viewers who had been interned in Auschwitz questioned whether Germans had ever helped Poles during the war, poured scorn on the adoption storyline, and claimed never to have met or even heard of German communists or resistance activities during the war.[49] Thus, the film shows how TV producers' attempts to rewrite the past came up against the power of vernacular historical memory.

In contrast to the Soviet, East German, and Polish examples, Yugoslav and Romanian serials were largely devoid of such transnational plots. While the wider international context of the struggle was not ignored entirely, it functioned as a largely inconsequential backdrop to what was, in essence, a national struggle for liberation. In the last episode of *The Freckled Boy*, communist resistance forces occupy the local police headquarters, and Andrei delivers a public speech that gives all the credit for the liberation to Romanian communist forces. Although the narrative evidently refers to the events in August 1943, the speech makes no reference either to King Michal I, who led the coup against Romania's fascist government at the time, or to the Red Army, which also played an instrumental role in the events. This narrative was fully in line with the

47 GARF, f. R6903, op. 28, d. 21, ll. 106–109, 'Pis'mo N. Mesiatseva v komissiiu po gosudarstvennym premiiam RSFSR v oblasti literatury, iskusstva i ispolnitel'skogo masterstva pri Sovete ministrov RSFSR, 25 April 1965.

48 Kotański (2004), p. 48.

49 SAPMO-BArch, DY 30/IV A 2/9.02/69, Helmut Sakowski to W. Lamberz (6.2.69); W. Lamberz to Erich Honecker (17.2.69), no pagination.

nationalist account of the war that was promoted by Ceauşescu's regime after his rise to power in 1965 and which replaced the previous, pro-Soviet version of the narrative.[50]

In the *Bonfires of Kapela*, the plot is likewise overwhelmingly focused on the national angle, with the war emerging almost exclusively as a national struggle between Yugoslav partisans on the one hand and Mussolini's Italy and domestic traitors on the other hand, with little if any support from either the Soviets or other Allies. The same is true for the vast majority of Yugoslav war serials; even in cases where Allied forces are in the foreground, as in *Major Arterton's Mission* (1986), which tells the story of the British secret service operation on Yugoslav soil, international allies appear as suspicious observers rather than loyal friends. From this perspective, Yugoslav war dramas, much like Romanian ones, were steeped in national historical narratives and did little to promote a sense of a shared, pan-socialist revolutionary history. As in Romania, this tendency was aligned with official narratives of the past, which emphasized the country's independence from both the Soviet Union and Western allies.

In sum, the fictional narratives of World War II produced by broadcasters in Eastern Europe were clearly aligned with the communist historical narrative and promoted the value of heroic sacrifice for the common good and a better future of all. At the same time, this pan-communist narrative was adapted to local conditions: East German narratives were less heroic than those from other countries, and while several Soviet, Polish, and East German serial dramas included prominent transnational plots, Yugoslav and Romanian serials largely presented World War II as a national struggle. As with the cross-country differences revealed by quantitative analysis earlier, these variations can be linked primarily to the specificities of national histories but also to the relative core-periphery positions of each country. The absence of triumphalist messages in East German World War II dramas was evidently rooted in the country's Nazi history, while the lack of transnational plots in Romanian and Yugoslav serials reflects the two countries' relative independence from the Soviet Union.

CONCLUSIONS

The materials presented in this chapter confirm that state socialist television cultures were heavily involved in shaping the past. This commitment

[50] Boia (2001), p. 77; Bucur (2006), pp. 171–193, 183–184.

to history stemmed in large part from the communist understanding of progress, and, in accordance with its teleological nature, the memory of past revolutionary achievements was used as guidance for the future. As we have shown, television was believed to provide a particularly apposite instrument of establishing the continuity between the past, the present, and the future: rather than scorning the medium for its amnesiac qualities, critics believed that its characteristic intimacy and domesticity, as well as its seriality and ability to intertwine public plots with personal narratives, provided effective means of eliciting audience engagement with the past. Our cross-country comparison of historical television fiction also confirms the importance of the local context in shaping television's encounter with history. Historical dramas were clearly underpinned by a shared communist narrative of history, which gave primacy to events and periods associated with the communist takeover and emphasized the importance of individual sacrifice for the common good.

Nonetheless, we have argued that it would be misleading to interpret the prominence of historical narratives solely in light of the communist vision of history and progress. Indeed, televised history was far from absent from Western screens at the time, and Western historical dramas shared many of the characteristic features found in state socialist serial fiction. We have therefore suggested that the 'history boom' seen on state socialist screens was in fact transnational in scope and can be interpreted as an expression of a global loss of faith in the future or, to put it in another way, a decline in the modern, future-oriented regime of historicity. Concerns about the ability of state socialist societies to continue their pursuit of communist goals, which motivated the turn to televised history, thus formed part of globally shared anxieties surrounding the future and constituted an integral corollary of presentism as the new dominant mode of engaging with the past. Due to its intimate bond with the present, television emerged as a particularly effective means of expressing the presentist relationship with the past.

Yet despite the palpable enthusiasm surrounding televised history among state socialist officials and critics, we have argued that its prominence can be seen as a sign of weakness, suggesting that the communist vision failed to provide compelling narratives of the revolutionary present and future. Not only that: as our qualitative analysis suggests, state socialist broadcasters responded to the uncertainties surrounding the future by reverting to a pre-modern mode of historicity, offering their audiences heroic tales and exemplary models to emulate in the present.

As we have seen, state socialist commentators were rather optimistic about the potential of televised history to inspire a renewed commitment to communist goals. Yet, viewed from the perspective of the regimes of historicity, such optimism was misguided: once consigned to the past, the historical achievements of the revolution were bound to be outdated and could not inspire genuine rapture about the past. While the magic of television could help new generations empathize with the achievements of their forebears and perhaps even prompt imitation in the present, it was incapable of pushing the revolution further and ushering in a new wave of revolutionary innovation. Instead, the televised revolution arguably acted as a conduit of stability, adding to the comforting sense of normality at a point when the reassuring vision of a better future was disappearing from sight.

10

Extraordinary Time

On major public holidays, such as Labour Day or the anniversary of the end of World War II, state socialist broadcasters abandoned their usual working routines and aired special programmes to create a sense of extraordinary occasion, commemorate past revolutionary achievements, and celebrate the ongoing movement towards the communist future. Such media holidays typically involved a disruption of established programming, scheduling, and viewing habits, designed to encourage reflection on the past, the present, and the future. As such, they arguably offered a particularly effective means of lifting viewers above the banality of the everyday, catapulting them into the vibrant movement of revolutionary time, oriented towards the future.

In the first part of this chapter, we examine a range of such media holidays from the five countries, paying particular attention to occasions linked to the festive calendar, including major state socialist holidays such as Labour Day and New Year's celebrations. We first outline key characteristics of the festive media schedules across the five countries. This is followed by a comparative analysis of two major types of media holidays that appear across all countries: those linked to a distinctly communist vision of modern progress and society (communist holidays) and those without a marked communist identity (non-communist holidays). We consider the different strategies used by broadcasters to engender a sense of extraordinary occasion, as well as the extent to which they succeed in inspiring a sense of festivity among audiences.

In the second part of the chapter we shift attention to a different category of television's involvement with extraordinary time: media disruptions. We focus on some of the most dramatic events from the state socialist era: the deaths of major communist leaders such as Yugoslavia's Josip Broz Tito in 1980 and the Soviet Union's Leonid Brezhnev in 1982, the proclamation of Martial Law in Poland in 1982, the ousting of Ceauşescu in Romania, and the fall of the Berlin Wall in 1989. Unlike the TV festivities examined in the first part of the chapter, these disruptive occasions were at odds with the teleological temporality of the communist project, raised anxiety over the ability of communist-led societies to master the future, or even threatened to stop revolutionary progress in its tracks. Yet as we shall see, the five examples of media disruptions differed in many respects, including the extent to which they were pre-planned and expected, the extent to which they were consensual or conflictual, and the extent to which they were followed by fundamental changes to the existing social and media order. Some brought only limited change and eventually evolved into reaffirmations of the status quo, while others fostered a much more profound transformation that involved the collapse of communist rule. As such, these examples offer a basis for reflecting on the involvement of television cultures in the gradual disintegration of the communist order.

MEDIA HOLIDAYS

The category of media holidays includes a broad range of festive media occasions from major national holidays and New Year's Eve celebrations to key sports or cultural events such as the Olympics, as well as major achievements such as Yuri Gagarin's journey into outer space in 1961.[1] On the pages that follow, we shall focus on a selection of such festive occasions, all linked to the established festive calendar in selected countries. Such a focus enables us to include a range of events, which differ in scale, extent of state and party involvement, and success among audiences. At the same time, they offer a framework for meaningful comparisons, both across countries and across different types of media holidays. The occasions we chose were also all well remembered by the majority of our interviewees, which enabled us to draw on our oral history materials, alongside archival sources, to assess the extent to which these media holidays resonated among audiences.

Before we turn to the analysis of specific holidays, let us first summarize the key characteristics of the state socialist festive calendar (Table 10.1). As one might expect, most public holidays in the region

[1] For an analysis of Yuri Gagarin's landing as a media event see Lundgren (2012; 2015).

TABLE 10.1 *Major public holidays in state socialist countries*

Date	Holiday	GDR[a]	Poland	Romania	USSR	Yugoslavia[b]
1 January	New Year's Day	▲	▲	▲▲	▲	▲▲
8 March	Women's Day				▲	
Varies	Good Friday	▲				
1 May	Labour Day/ Day of Worker Solidarity	▲	▲	▲	▲	▲▲
2 May	Youth Day			▲		
9 May	Victory Day				▲	
Varies	Whit Monday	▲				
4 July	Day of Fighters					▲
22 July	National Day of the Rebirth of Poland		▲			
23 August	Day of Liberation from Fascist Occupation			▲		
7 October	Day of the Republic	▲				
7–8 November	Great October Socialist Revolution				▲▲	
29 November	Day of the Republic					▲▲
5 December	Constitution Day				▲	
25 December	Christmas Day	▲	▲			
26 December	St. Stephen's Day	▲	▲			
30 December	Day of the Republic			▲▲		

Legend: ▲ – one-day holiday, ▲▲ – two-day holiday

Note: The listing only includes holidays on which most people were off work. Each country also celebrated several other days, but typically in a less extensive manner.

[a] Until 1967, Victory Day was celebrated on May 8 in East Germany but was then eliminated in connection with the reduction of the working week to five days. Several traditional religious holidays were also eliminated during the reform: Easter Monday, Ascension Day, Corpus Christi, Reformation Day, and the Day of Repentance.

[b] The full Yugoslav calendar also contained holidays which were observed in only some of the republics and are not listed here.

either commemorated key historical events from communist history or celebrated particular social groups and identities deemed central to the communist vision of the world and its future. Examples of the former include the October Revolution Anniversary in the Soviet Union, and the Day of the Republic in East Germany, which commemorated the establishment of the German Democratic Republic on 7 October 1949. Among the latter we find 1 May, designed to celebrate the comradery of the working classes, and 8 March, dedicated to women and aimed at showcasing the appreciation of women and their achievements in state socialist countries. Through such festive occasions, communist party-states sought to institute distinct senses of temporality and belonging, rooted in the foundational moments of communist rule in the region and tied to the onward march of revolutionary progress, led by the working classes. The relative uniformity of festive calendars across the five countries also suggests that state socialist countries lived in a shared temporal universe and moved through time in a synchronised, transnational rhythm.

Apart from these communist holidays, festive calendars from the state socialist era also included a handful of holidays that had little communist significance: New Year's Day, celebrated across the region, and religious holidays such as Christmas and St. Stephen's Day, celebrated in Poland and East Germany. While the prominence of New Year's Day can be linked to a distinctly communist, secular temporality, the presence of religious holidays may come as a surprise. Yet it also serves as a reminder both of the internal diversity of the state socialist world and of partial similarities with countries elsewhere in the world.

Communist authorities officially regarded religion as a dangerous superstition that threatened the new scientific order. Nonetheless, as noted in Chapter 3, countries differed significantly in their treatment of religion, and these differences were reflected in the amount of recognition afforded to religious ceremonies and festivities. Yugoslavia, Romania, and the Soviet Union adopted more stringent policies and erased religious holidays from their festive calendars altogether. In this context, New Year's Day festivities effectively provided a replacement for Christmas, and many traditions associated with the latter were stripped of their religious connotations and transferred to the former; the Christmas tree was thus replaced with the 'New Year Tree', and Father Christmas was substituted with 'Grandfather Frost'.[2]

[2] Cucu-Oancea (2005); Dushechkina (2003); Gradišnik (2015).

By contrast, in Poland and in East Germany, hostility towards religion was less fierce. In Poland, the sheer size of the Catholic congregation (and, from 1978, the presence of a Polish pope), its role in the anti-Nazi resistance, and its contribution to national integration all made it less vulnerable than in other countries.[3] In East Germany, despite frequent shifts in the party line, religion was seen as an integral part of national identity, and religious figures such as Martin Luther and Thomas Müntzer were celebrated as national heroes and even precursors to communism.[4] As a consequence, some of the traditional religious holidays – above all Christmas, but also Good Friday and Whit Monday in the case of East Germany – were officially recognized in the festive calendar. As we show later in the chapter, these cross-country differences also had their counterpart in the different treatment of religious holidays on screen, with media holidays in Poland and East Germany less secularized than in other state socialist countries. This also means that Polish and East German television cultures were, in this respect, somewhat closer to television cultures in Western Europe and North America at the time, where the small screen regularly participated in the celebration of religious holidays – a tradition that continues into the present.[5]

Apart from differences in the extent of secularization, state socialist television holidays appeared similar across the region. Due to this, the analysis that follows foregrounds intra-country rather than cross-country comparison and examines similarities and differences between communist and non-communist holidays. As we shall see, the two categories of holidays were produced in somewhat different ways, using different strategies of disrupting routine TV temporality, and encountered different kinds of receptions among audiences.

Producing Communist Media Holidays

Media holidays linked to communist festive occasions were much more commonly associated with live broadcasts than were those associated with non-communist holidays. The most prominent of these was the Labour Day parade broadcast, which was initially organized in all of our five countries and constituted a central part of the broadcast schedule,

[3] Ramet (1984), p. 9. [4] See Roy (2000); Fleischauer (2010).

[5] Despite the recognition that broadcasting forms an important part of religious celebrations in Western Europe and North America, in-depth scholarly studies remain scarce. For rare book-length treatments see Johnston (2015); Werts (2006).

FIGURE 10.1 Labour Day parade followed by TV cameras in Budapest, Hungary, 1974. *Source*: Fortepan / Angyalföldi Helytörténeti Gyűjtemény.

typically starting in the morning and lasting for several hours.[6] The Labour Day parade offers a textbook example of a media event as defined by Dayan and Katz: the parade was organized outside the media and covered live, followed by all channels, planned months in advance, accompanied by solemn commentary, addressed at large audiences, and included performances that unmistakably celebrated unity rather than division. The event typically featured groups of workers from different professions, thereby seeking to enact the concerted movement of all segments of society towards a shared, communist future (Figure 10.1). The broadcast commentary included the mention of major achievements in the recent past and plans for the future. In some countries, several parades took place in parallel in different cities and towns, and the live broadcast switched from one location to the other in a bid to enact the joint march of workers from all parts of the country. In many cases, coverage of the parade also included reports from other countries, thereby extending the sense of unity beyond the borders of state and nation. In East Germany, for instance, the marathon five-hour broadcast of the parade in 1975 covered

[6] In Yugoslavia, the military parade, originally organized for May Day, was moved in 1965 to 9 May (Victory Day) and for financial reasons took place only every five years.

events in Berlin, Halle, Neubrandenburg, and Frankfurt-am-Oder and also contained link-ups with the parades in Moscow, Warsaw, Prague, Budapest, Bucharest, and Sofia.

Similar media events were associated with some of the other festive occasions. In the Soviet Union, the schedule on 7 November, the anniversary of the October Revolution, included a live broadcast of a parade, while in Yugoslavia, the festivities on 25 May, designated as Youth Day, culminated in the live coverage of a mass rally. By and large, however, live broadcasts constituted a relatively minor proportion of festive schedules, and several major media holidays were devoid of them. Far more ubiquitous were two other strategies: the broadcasting of dedicated festive programmes recorded in advance and a high proportion of cultural, entertainment, and children's programming. As with the live broadcasts, these programmes regularly included references to past revolutionary achievements and visions of the future.

Let us illustrate this by looking at sample festive schedules from Yugoslavia and Romania (Figure 10.2). Both schedules are from the Day of the Republic, a major holiday that commemorated a key moment in the country's communist history: the abdication of King Michael and the communist takeover on 30 December 1947 in Romania, and the establishment of a federal Yugoslavia with a temporary communist-led Yugoslav government on 29 November 1943. In both countries, the schedule reveals a day filled with festive programming tailor-made for the occasion: children's programmes dedicated to the country, festive concerts, dance programmes, documentary films and literary broadcasts celebrating the anniversary, and even a festive sports tournament. In addition, the festive atmosphere was generated through special editions of routine programmes and through documentary and fictional broadcasts dedicated to events and personalities associated with the holiday.

Several programmes used the festive occasion to connect the present moment with revolutionary events from the past or with projections of future developments. In Romania, the schedule featured a programme tellingly entitled *Daring for the Future*, while the Yugoslav schedule included a broadcast with a similarly revealing title, *How Our Homeland Grows*; both were aimed at the segment of society most obviously linked with the future, namely children. References to past events abounded, too. Yugoslav television marked the occasion by broadcasting the first episode of *The Bonfires of Kapela* (*Kapelski kresovi*, TV Zagreb, 1975), a new serial that followed the formation of a partisan unit

Romania **Sunday, 30 December 1979** **Day of the Republic**	**Yugoslavia** **Saturday 29 November 1975** **Day of the Republic**
TV Romania 1	**TV Belgrade 1**
9:00 *Thoughts on the Day of the Country* (Children's programme: Pioneers celebrate the Day of the Republic) 9:35 *Dick Turpin* (Children's programme) 10:00 *Village Life* (Patriotic songs and poems) 11:45 ADAS (Unknown) 11:50 *Ode to My Country* (Romanian music) 12:30 *For the Country* (Festive programme including current affairs, music and poetry dedicated to the Day of the Republic) 13:00 *Telex* (News) 13:05 *Sunday Album* (Variety) 14:00 *Woody* (Cartoon) 14:20 *Songs of the Wood* (Current affairs) 14:40 *Moscow Circus* (Entertainment) 15:00 *Telesport* (Sports magazine) 16:30 *Paul Gauguin* (Documentary) 17:25 *Daring for the Future* (Festive children's programme: international contest for pioneers dedicated to the Day of the Republic) 18:35 *The Year of the Great Forum: Year XXXV of our Freedom* (Documentary) 19:00 News 19:20 *Glory to You, Our Beloved Republic* (Literature, music and dance dedicated to the Anniversary of the Republic) 20:20 *Ecaterina Teodoroiu* (Film, d. Dinu Cocea, 1978) 21:45 News 22:00 Closedown	9:30 News 9:40 Wind orchestra concert 10:10 *The Sun is Watching Over You* (Festive children's cultural programme) 10:40 *How Does my Homeland Grow?* (Festive children's programme, TV Skopje) 11:10 *Victory* (Reportage, TV Sarajevo) 12:10 *Warning* (No detail, TV Zagreb) 13:00 *Knowledge – Property* (Programme for farmers, with elements of entertainment, education and information) 15:00 Volleyball 16:40 News 17:00 Handball (Tournament dedicated to the Day of the Republic) 18:15 *Children are Singing* (Festive children's concert) 19:15 Cartoon 19:20 *A Screen for Every Home* (No detail) 19:30 News 20:00 *Bonfires of Kapela* (TV serial) 21:20 *Word by Word* (Festive entertainment, including a talk show and piano music) 22:20 News 22:40 Partisan songs

FIGURE 10.2 Sample festive schedules, Romania and Yugoslavia. *Sources: Tele Radio* (Romania) and *TV Novosti* (Yugoslavia).

in Axis-occupied Yugoslavia, while the Romanian schedule included a film about the Romanian national hero Ecaterina Teodoroiu and a documentary detailing the achievements of the country in the past year, referred to as 'year 35 of our freedom'.

Also notable is the high proportion of cultural, entertainment, and children's broadcasts, which exceeded the volume of such content on regular weekdays. In both Romania and Yugoslavia, several children's programmes were scheduled both in the morning and in the afternoon, while afternoons and evenings featured a range of entertainment, sports, and fictional content. Finally, it is also worth noting the strategic scheduling of popular genres either directly before or after news bulletins or festive programmes with a more explicit ideological message. In Yugoslavia, the first episode of *The Bonfires* was broadcast directly after the main evening news bulletin, while in Romania the film about Ecaterina Teodoriou was sandwiched between one of the key festive programmes, entitled *Glory to You, Our Beloved Republic*, and the late-night news. Similar examples could be found in other countries. For instance, on Labour Day in 1975, Soviet broadcasters split the immensely popular variety show *Little Blue Flame* (*Goluboi ogonek*, 1962–1985) into two parts, which allowed them to schedule the most ideologically saturated programme, a reportage on the Labour Day parades across the world, between them. Such strategic scheduling demonstrates that TV producers recognized that viewers could not be won over by noble sentiments alone but also needed diversion.

Producing Non-Communist Media Holidays

Most of the strategies identified in communist media holidays – dedicated festive broadcasts, a higher proportion of cultural and entertainment programmes and content for children, and extended broadcast hours – can be found also in non-communist media festivities such as the New Year's Day and religious holidays. There were, however, also some telling differences. First, explicit references to the revolutionary past and future were far less common. These were occasions designed to celebrate the generic secular passage of time or the passage of religious time, not the movement towards the communist future. Second, the emphasis on entertainment was even greater than during communist media holidays. While festive programming associated with communist celebrations did, as we have seen, include a notable share of entertainment, such programmes were often used strategically to attract audiences to more ideologically saturated programmes or possessed their own ideological agenda (as, for instance, in fictional programmes dedicated to the communist revolution). In contrast, non-communist TV festivities were unambiguously and unashamedly centred on entertainment for its own sake. In the Soviet Union, for instance, the main highlight of the New Year's Eve programming was the aforementioned *Little Blue Flame*. The show was broadcast on all festive occasions but reached its most elaborate iteration on New Year's Eve in a broadcast lasting several hours and featuring comedy, celebrities, chat, and cabaret. Listings magazines likewise had no doubt that entertainment was the key function of television on such occasions: a characteristic New Year's Eve programme announcement published in 1972 in Yugoslavia promised viewers a day full of humour and light-hearted music.[7]

The same applies to religious media holidays in East Germany and Poland: although the schedules featured some programmes with religious themes, entertainment content was at the forefront. There were no live broadcasts of religious ceremonies, and religious content was typically present in a light-hearted and cultural form, without much concern for religious ideas as such. In Poland, for example, the Christmas Eve schedule in 1975 included a variety talk show programme called *Christmas Eve in Wanda Warska's Cellar* [*Wieczór Wigilijny w Piwnicy Wandy Warskiej*], in which individuals gathered around a table, discussing old Christmas traditions and signing traditional carols, while on Christmas Day, the main channel broadcast a special variety show with carol singing. A similar format was adopted by the East German variety and chat show *Between Breakfast and Roast Goose* (*Zwischen Frühstück und Gansebraten*, 1957–1991), broadcast on Christmas morning more or less throughout East German TV's existence. Although the presence of such programmes meant that German and Polish media holidays were less thoroughly secular than were their counterparts in other state socialist countries, they also shared the emphasis on light-hearted entertainment characteristic of non-communist media holidays everywhere in the region. It is feasible to argue that TV festivities accompanying Christmas in the West, despite a notable entertainment component and broadly secular character,[8] had a more pronounced religious or spiritual dimension, including at the very least broadcasts of religious ceremonies or sermons.

Another shared characteristic of Christmas and New Year's Eve schedules was the relative lack of ideologically saturated programming. If such content appeared, it was typically very limited in duration and featured outside of prime time. In East Germany, this absence was particularly pronounced, which was in part due to the country's proximity to West Germany. As a result, the battle for viewership became a fight for political loyalty, especially so on days such as Christmas, when the vast majority of the population would dedicate a significant portion of their time to

[7] E.g. N. Milenković. 1972. 'Mjuzikl začinjen humorom,' *TV Novosti*, 29 December 1972, pp. 12–13.

[8] On the secular character of Christmas in British popular media see Brabazon (2008).

television. Festive television thus played an integral part in turning Christmas into a Cold War battlefield.[9] As director Walter Heynowski put it in 1961: 'The Christmas period holds a great significance for the German soul. Whoever gives the best presents wins the greatest sympathy. So we will attempt to arrange a "good spread" of presents [*eine "schöne Bescherung"*]. It follows that this year we must create a fun and entertaining festival schedule so as to have something with which to oppose the psychological stirrings of our opponent.'[10] As our analysis demonstrates, East German broadcasters fought this battle by virtually voiding the schedule of ideological content.

On the New Year's Eve, TV programmes were not only less ideologically saturated, but also often included content with a satirical take on the realities of life under communist rule. This was true even of those countries where the media were otherwise tightly controlled. In Romania, the variety show *Revelion*, which typically lasted from 9 or 10 PM to 5 or even 6 AM, was an eagerly awaited part of the 31 December schedule, featuring dance and musical numbers, as well as satirical sketches poking fun at the absurdities of Romanian life. For example, one sketch by well-known comic actor Toma Caragiu made subtle references to the ban on Christmas and the state-enforced use of the 'winter tree' instead of the Christmas tree and then went on to discuss both the shortage of suitable 'winter trees' on the market as well as the lack of space in which to display the tree at home, thus making light both of the country's shortage of material goods and of Romanian citizens' less-than-spacious living conditions.

In the Soviet Union, similar material was occasionally broadcast as part of the *Little Blue Flame*, but satire also appeared in some other programmes. On New Year's Day 1976, Soviet Central Television broadcast the premiere of the made-for-TV romantic comedy *Irony of Fate* (*Ironiia sud'by*, dir. El'dar Riazanov, 1975). The plot follows the Muscovite Zhenia who, having passed out drunk the night before, wakes up the next day in Leningrad due to a mix-up. However, because of the uniformity of Soviet architecture and street naming, he does not realize he is in a different city. When he tries his key in the door of his apartment on Constructors' Street in Leningrad, the door opens, and Zhenia, still in a drunken stupor, gets into bed, again without noticing that this is neither his apartment nor his own bed. When the apartment owner, Nadia, returns home, her fiancé leaves, suspecting her of having an affair, and

[9] Perry (2001). [10] Quoted in Dittmar (2010), pp. 198–199.

slowly but surely Nadia and Zhenia begin a romance. Today, the film is considered a classic and is still watched by huge audiences when it is repeated during the New Year's holiday.

In other words, New Year's was a time when television in the state socialist world appeared to be less ideologically controlled and detached itself from the distinctly communist sense of time promoted during communist holidays. Instead, television viewers were invited to partake in the collective celebration of the here and now, encouraged to laugh at themselves and at the society they were part of, with all its idiosyncrasies and problems. We should of course beware of interpreting these instances of mild satire as evidence of the subversive role of television festivities. Rather than having a lasting disruptive effect on established hierarchies of power, such satirical elements – much like satirical print publications, such as the magazine *Crocodile* (*Krokodil*, 1922–1991) in the USSR or *Owlglass* (*Eulenspiegel*, 1954–) in East Germany – functioned as safety valves which allowed the public to let off steam without presenting a fundamental challenge to communist rule. It is also not a coincidence that such satirical content was associated with a festive occasion and hence with a time when the usual routines of life and work, as well as TV programming and scheduling, were disrupted. In this sense, the media festivities accompanying New Year's celebrations resembled what Arnold van Gennep would call a rite of passage[11]: after an initial separation from the world of the year that is ending, television entered into a liminal stage during which the established rules and restrictions were temporarily lifted, thus allowing broadcasters to put aside their usual commitment to public education, enlightenment, and propaganda and focus instead on fun and games, while also laughing at the frustrations of everyday life under communist rule. Yet this liminal stage had to come to an end, and was unavoidably followed, as soon as the holidays were over, by a resurrection of order and a return to the usual routines and temporal organization.

Experiencing Media Holidays

So far, we have investigated the different strategies used by TV professionals to create a protracted sense of festivity across whole days. But were these strategies successful in generating a sense of occasion among audiences, and did they manage to instil a sense of participating in a movement

[11] van Gennep (2010).

towards the communist future? Again, a stark difference emerges between communist and non-communist media holidays. With regard to the former, the picture that emerges from both oral history interviews and historical audience surveys seems to be one of indifference, if not negativity. The reception of Labour Day festivities in East Germany is characteristic in this respect: neither viewing shares nor satisfaction ratings were especially high. In 1975, for instance, the main highlight of the broadcast day – the live broadcast of the parade – was watched by a maximum of 9.5 per cent of viewers, most of whom were not particularly impressed by its quality. Although viewership predictably increased during prime time, satisfaction ratings did not: the programme that achieved one of the highest viewing figures – the play *The Dove* (*Die Lachtaube*, 1975), celebrating the life and work of Helmut Baierl, a writer and vice president of the Academy of Arts – was assessed as bad by viewers, who gave it an average rating of 4.32, with 1 being the best mark and 5 the worst. In its characteristic understatement, GDR researchers described viewers' opinions as 'mixed'.[12]

While viewers' negative assessments are telling, the low viewership figures may be somewhat misleading. For large sections of the audience, public holidays involved obligatory attendance at outdoor celebrations, which precluded joining such events via television. Viewing figures from East Germany seem to confirm that: while the share of viewers among young people was close to zero, figures among viewers more than sixty-five years of age were significantly higher.[13] Some of our interviewees from across the five countries likewise reported attending the events *in situ* rather than watching them on TV. In other words, at least some of the Labour Day parades and similar mass festivities were bound to be unsuccessful as media events, because they were highly successful events in real life, at least as far as mass participation was concerned.

Participation in outdoor events certainly provides part of the explanation for the relatively limited number of our interviewees who recalled watching television during communist media holidays. Yet our interviews also suggest that in many cases, the programming provided on such festive occasions was easily forgettable. Of those who recalled participation in communist festivities via television, most had little to say about them and

[12] DRA, Sofortresonanz Ergebnisse, Schriftgut Zuschauerforschung, 15 May 1975, H081-03-02-0055, 18.PW-1975.

[13] Ibid.

either spoke of them with indifference or on occasion expressed negative views. One Romanian man, for instance, remembered the pageantry around Labour Day and Romania's Day of the Republic with a heightened sense of frustration:

> I was watching at times, but I was generally so fed up with these festivities ... because usually they would get us out and gather all of us in the square for the May Day and the August 23rd parades. I had to come from the factory and organize people to participate in the parade. We would then go to the centre of the town and ... oh, all that orchestrated masquerade! But we had to do it, we didn't have any other option, because if you missed it you were subsequently being punished, they would ask for you at the Party headquarters.
>
> Q: But when you got home from the parade, did you usually watch the festivities broadcast on television?
>
> A: No, no, I wasn't watching the parades ... only in passing, just because the TV was on. (Rom-39–1945-male)

Yet not all recollections of communist media holidays were negative or indifferent. Across all five countries, at least one or two interviewees recalled enjoying such occasions. One Polish interviewee, for example, claimed that he 'loved watching the military parade on the Red Square on the anniversary of the October Revolution or on the first of May' and 'was always impressed with the lines of soldiers marching' (Pol-03-1949-male). Positive comments were especially common among Yugoslav interviewees. One female interviewee, for instance, spoke of 'adoring' the live broadcasts of the mass rally on Youth Day and described it as a 'great spectacle' (YuSrb-03-1973-female), while another remembered watching such events with her friend who shared her fascination with 'socialist pathos' and even cried while watching the live transmission (YuSrb-04-1960-female). Because of the relatively low number of interviewees, any conclusions about cross-country differences should of course remain speculative. Nonetheless, the relative prominence of positive testimonies among former Yugoslav viewers may suggest that communist media holidays in Yugoslavia were somewhat more successful in engendering a shared sense of festivity than their counterparts elsewhere in the region.

There is of course a question mark over what these fond recollections of communist media holidays mean. In most cases, what attracted viewers to such occasions was not – or at least not only – the ideological message but also their aesthetic qualities, their impressive scale and organizational complexity, or simply their entertainment value. While such experiences suggest a level of positivity towards the political regime that managed to organize such events, it is difficult to argue that such enjoyment demonstrates a sense of commitment to the communist cause. The following excerpt from an interview with a Serbian viewer, who recalls television programming during Yugoslavia's Day of the Republic, is typical in this respect:

> Yes, we were watching [television] because on holidays they usually had a richer programme and there were films during the day . . . Usually they were broadcasting good war films for these holidays, and I could watch those a hundred thousand times. . . . There would be films from the morning onwards, which didn't happen on working days. So I loved these holidays, there were always some good domestic films and sometimes a foreign one. And for the evenings they were also saving us special episodes of some series, so that they also had some kind of holiday and it was a kind of special episode. (YuSrb-02-1946-male)

From the perspective of audiences, then, media holidays associated with communist festivities were not particularly successful or at the very least held an ambiguous relationship with the communist vision of progress and society. When they succeeded, they did so largely because they offered viewers good entertainment, or because they provided access to events that were aesthetically pleasing or impressive in their scale and complexity. Whether or not such programmes carried distinct messages about communism, or sought to engender a sense of continued participation in the revolutionary project, seemed to be of secondary importance.

The picture emerging from archival sources and viewer testimonies associated with religious holidays and New Year's festivities is markedly different: in contrast to communist media holidays, these occasions attracted high ratings, represented a key highlight of the year, and were eagerly awaited and keenly followed. Viewer research conducted in 1975 in East Germany, for instance, shows that viewership figures were high across the festive period but especially for variety programmes like *Between Breakfast and Roast Goose* and *Night of the Notables* (*Nacht der Prominenten*, 1972–1987) on Christmas Day and the music programme *Tempo '76*, which was broadcast on New Year's Eve.[14] In Yugoslavia, a survey of 800 Serbian viewers conducted in 1976 revealed that 82 per cent of those asked watched television on New Year's Eve, and 89.1 per cent watched it at some point during the New Year's holidays; as

[14] DRA, Sehbeteiligung und Bewertung der Sendungen der 52. Woche, 6 January 1976, DRA H081-03-02-0555, 52.PW-1975. Researchers did not ask whether viewers watched shows from the West, too.

in East Germany, the majority of viewers were attracted to television primarily as a source of entertainment.[15]

Oral history testimonies from across the region likewise confirm that these media holidays were occasions where the majority of viewers watched television and often did so extensively and with pleasure. The proportion of interviewees who remembered such festive programming was much higher, negative opinions were limited, and instances of enthusiastic recollections considerably more common. Judging from the testimonies, viewers typically looked forward to the programming on offer during such holidays, especially entertainment broadcasts and films. As one of our Polish interviewees explained: 'That was something you would wait for because the programmes were much more interesting. Foreign films were on. We also couldn't wait for the New Year's Eve because the programmes were on all night: about 3–4 films were shown' (Pol-14–1959-female).

The sense of comforting repetitiveness and familiarity associated with non-communist media holidays is also worthy of note. Many testimonies suggested that these festive occasions were unthinkable without television. For one Russian viewer, for instance, the *Little Blue Flame* was so deeply entrenched as part of the festive routine that the New Year was simply unthinkable without it: 'people would probably have decided New Year hadn't come!' (Rus-09–1962-female). Likewise, a Polish viewer recalled specific TV presenters associated with the New Year's Eve broadcast – 'Suzin, Loska and Edytka' – and described them as 'an essential ingredient' (Pol-02–1973-female). This familiarity and repetitiveness associated with television formed an integral part of the wider ritual of New Year's and Christmas celebrations, associated with family gatherings, socialising with friends, or certain types of food. In this sense, non-communist television festivities functioned as one of the cornerstones of sociality and belonging and fostered a sense of shared movement through time.

In sum, media holidays in the state socialist world were at their most successful when they were least communist, that is, when they were not associated with any distinct communist messages and were delivered with a hearty serving of good entertainment or spectacle. That said, these festive occasions were rather successful in their integrative, unifying intentions: while they may not have inspired a shared commitment to

[15] RTS-CIJMPA, Report 780, 'Gledaoci o novogodišnjem programu Televizije Beograd,' 1976.

communist values, they nonetheless instilled a sense of common movement through time, provided shared experiences and reference points, and hence constituted an important basis of common sociality. As such, they also contributed to a sense of stability and normality, reassuring viewers that while things were perhaps not as they should be, life was at least proceeding in a familiar, predictable, and hence in some ways comforting manner.

MEDIA DISRUPTIONS

In contrast to media holidays, the media occasions we refer to as media disruptions entailed a very different, far more unsettling departure from routine. Part of this disturbance had to do with their unplanned character: even though some of the occasions we analyse –the deaths of Tito in 1980 and Brezhnev in 1982, but also the announcement of Martial Law in Poland in 1981 – were at least in part expected, and hence the media spectacles that attended them were pre-planned, their impact could not be pinned down in advance, and they were thus fraught with uncertainty. Tied to this was the length of the disturbance: media disruptions usually lasted longer than media holidays, and often it was unclear when and how they would end. The so-called 'Romanian revolution' first erupted onto TV screens during the live transmission of Ceauşescu's speech on 21 December 1989, when the crowd that gathered in front of the Presidential Palace began to shout and scream, which led to the broadcast being cut short. The turmoil ended on 27 December, when the filmed execution of Ceauşescu and his wife was shown on television, but a sense of unease and doubt over the future lingered for much longer. The introduction of Martial Law in Poland on 13 December 1981 inaugurated a state of emergency that lasted more than a year, led to a drastic reduction in broadcast hours, and coloured the kinds of programmes that were shown on state television throughout the period. In this sense, the disruptive occasions analysed here share the temporal nature of what Tamar Liebes, in her analysis of the live coverage of natural catastrophes and terror attacks, called 'disaster marathons'.[16] Rather than being contained within a relatively short, temporally delimited window, they lasted for days, weeks, and sometimes even years.

In addition to being unexpected and temporally extended, all the events discussed in this section represented a challenge to the existing order,

[16] Liebes (1998).

either in the form of the straining or collapse of communist rule or in the form of the deaths of its leading protagonists. As such, they brought a sense of insecurity and anxiety and introduced a mode of extraordinary temporality that was very different from the one engendered by media holidays. While the departure from established routines brought by TV holidays served to remind viewers of the deeper meaning of the communist order and sought to inspire a renewed commitment to status quo, TV disruptions not only abandoned existing routines but also questioned the narrative of revolutionary progress underpinning these routines: Would the onward march towards the communist future resume and continue unabated, or was it time for a change to social organization or even for an abandonment of communism altogether?

As we shall show, the five cases of media disruptions differed considerably in the extent to which they were pre-planned and expected, the extent to which they were consensual or conflictual, and the extent to which they were followed by fundamental changes to the existing order. Some of them ended up bringing only limited change and eventually evolved into reaffirmations of the status quo, while others were part of a more profound transformation that involved the collapse of communist rule and fundamental shifts in the media. Table 10.2 summarizes the characteristics of the five cases and lists them roughly in order depending on the level of pre-planning and the extent of the change with which they were involved.

Before proceeding a brief note about the logic of comparison employed is in order. Each of the five cases is taken from one of the five countries, but because the events in question are markedly different, differences in their media treatment are largely due to the characteristics of the events rather than to the nature of the television cultures and systems. However, if we situate these media disruptions in the longer trajectory of political and media changes that took place in each of the countries, it becomes possible to build a cross-country comparison of the involvement of television cultures in the downfall of communist rule.

Tito's and Brezhnev's Deaths: Pre-planned, Expected, and Consensual Disruptions

Responses to the deaths of Brezhnev and Tito were largely pre-planned and to some extent expected by all the parties involved – the communist authorities, the media, and the audiences – and as a result also consensual. Both leaders had been ill for a while and, in the case of Tito, it was clear

TABLE 10.2 *Five cases of media disruptions: an overview*

Event	Type	Extent of pre-planning	Consensus or conflict?	Extent of social change	Extent of media change
USSR *10–15 Nov 1982* Death of Leonid Brezhnev	Death of a major leader	Largely pre-planned and expected by authorities, the media, and audiences	Consensual	New leader in power; existing political order retained	Return to the existing media order, followed by gradual changes
Yugoslavia *0–08 May 1980* Death of Josip Broz Tito	Death of a major leader	Largely pre-planned and expected by authorities, the media, and audiences	Consensual	New leader in power & change in the form of government; existing political order retained	Return to the existing media order, followed by gradual changes
Poland *13 Dec 1981–1922 Jul 1983*, Introduction of Martial Law	Civil war/ Suppressed revolution	Pre-planned by the authorities, unexpected by audiences and the media	Conflictual	Suppression of opposition; existing political order retained	Return to the existing media order
East Germany *09 Nov–01 Dec 1989* Fall of Berlin Wall	Revolution	Only partly pre-planned by the authorities and the media, unexpected by the audiences	Largely consensual	Fall of communist rule; new political order instituted	Gradual introduction of a new media order
Romania 21–27 Dec 1989, Overthrow of Ceauşescu	Revolution	Unplanned and unexpected among all parties	Conflictual	Fall of communist rule; new political order instituted	Sudden introduction of a new media order

that the illness was terminal. Yugoslav media professionals had been preparing for the inevitable for several months, serving their audiences regular updates on Tito's health and producing dedicated programming. Two Croatian interviewees, both of whom were children at the time, recalled sending get well soon cards to Tito while he was in hospital (YuCro-06–1967-female, YuCro-03–1973-female), while a Serbian viewer, whose friend's uncle worked as a cameraman at the time, spoke of the technical preparations for Tito's death and funeral months before it happened (YuSrb-10–1965-male).

In the weeks before his death, Brezhnev's health was better than Tito's, and he even attended a parade on the 65th anniversary of the Russian Revolution. However, Brezhnev, too, had been ill for some time, and his declining health played out on screen. Historians have even argued that the image of the ailing leader on screen became a symbol of the regime's decrepitude.[17] Broadcasters were therefore prepared for the death of the country's leader: in fact, they had a ready-made formula at their disposal, tried and tested after Stalin's death in 1953, as well as after the death of Mikhail Suslov, a chief party ideologist, in January 1982. On both occasions, Soviet airwaves were filled with solemn music that replaced the existing schedule. The same formula was applied following Brezhnev's death, making this otherwise unsettling event somehow predictable and known.

In both countries, the death of the leader stopped all scheduled programming in mid-flow. In the Soviet Union, a previously announced pop concert and ice hockey game were replaced with documentaries on Lenin and the Great Patriotic War and a concert of Tchaikovsky's *Symphonie Pathétique*. News readers appeared in formal dress on the daily news programme *Vremia* at 9 PM, and the news of Brezhnev's death was finally read out by famed newsreader Igor' Kirillov at 11 PM.[18] In Yugoslavia, solemn music started playing on radio stations, television screens suddenly went black, and after a while, a news reader appeared on screen and read the formal announcement, several hours after the actual death had occurred.[19]

The initial disruption was followed by several days of extraordinary programming, much of it produced in advance and aimed at directing the process of collective mourning. The Soviet TV schedule for Saturday, 13 November, three days after Brezhnev's death, is indicative

[17] Dönninghaus and Savin (2014). [18] Dobbs (1996), pp. 85–86.
[19] Bringa (2004), p. 166.

Soviet Union	
Saturday 13 November	
Central Television 1	
8.00	*Time*, followed by symphonic music
10.00	*The Image of the Communist in Soviet Representative Art* (Documentary)
10.30	Beethoven: *Kreuzer Sonata*
11.00	News
11.10	Tchaikovsky: *String Quartet No.2*
12.00	A. Tolstoi, *The Russian Character* (Literary reading)
12.25	Instrumental music by Bach and Chopin
14.00	News
14.10	Sibelius: String Quartet
14.30	P.V.S. (Film for Children)
15.40	Babdzhanin: String Trio
16.00	News
16.10	Shostakovich: *Symphony No.5*, Third Movement
16.30	B. Lavrenev, *The Break-Up* (d. P. Bogoliubov, Iu. Muzykant, 1952)
19.00	News
19.10	Piano Music
19.30	R. Rozhdestvennskii, "210 Steps" (Literary reading)
20.25	Violin and Cello ensemble from the Bol'shoi Theatre
21.00	*Time*, followed by symphonies by Beethoven, news, then closedown.

FIGURE 10.3 Sample media disruption schedule: Brezhnev's death, Soviet Union. *Source: Govorit i pokazyvaet Moskva.*

of the strategies adopted in this process (Figure 10.3). Aside from news broadcasts, a couple of literary readings, a film for children, and another for adults, the whole schedule was devoted to classical music. In this way, television completely abandoned its established routine and in doing so indicated to viewers both the extraordinary nature of the event and the necessary attitude to it.

The disturbance on screen was closely intertwined with disruptions in everyday life. A football match between two major Yugoslav teams, scheduled to start shortly before the official announcement of death, was interrupted in its forty-first minute, and as the announcement was read over the loudspeakers, the crowd's cheering was first replaced by silence and then by collective singing of a popular tune pledging allegiance to Tito. An extensive TV report from the game was planned for later that evening, and the TV crew present at the stadium kept their cameras rolling throughout, recording images of footballers, some of whom had collapsed on their knees crying.[20] These images, joined by several other depictions of mourning across the country, were later shown in the news bulletin and in the years that followed, became part of the iconic imagery associated with the event.

Several of our interviewees recalled similar instances where television played an integral role in the wider shock. Viewers often recounted the day in minute detail, remembered which programmes were interrupted or cancelled, and recalled the name of the announcer delivering the news. The sense of shock associated with the occasion was in part due to the fact that both leaders had long been in power: Brezhnev had ruled the country for eighteen years, and Tito had ruled for well over thirty. Their appearances in the media had become a part of daily life, and viewers had grown used to seeing and hearing from their leader in particular ways – forms which may have seemed ossified and dull but were also routine and comforting. The death of the leader not only brought an interruption to daily routines but also put into question the established social and political order. This sense of fundamental disruption was apparent also in several oral testimonies, as for instance in the following excerpt from an interview with a Ukrainian man:

> To be honest the main event, the one that made the biggest impression for me was the death of Brezhnev. It was in '82, I think, and when they showed ... or rather reported – it was a report on television and not on the radio ... well, I saw it [on television] at least ... And it made a very big impression on me. And not just me ... there were tears in my eyes. To be honest I don't know how to explain it. Because it wasn't just me, it was like ... losing such a person, whom we'd believed in ... or seemed to at least! And with his departure, well, it seemed like it was the end of an era, an epoch. (USSRUkr-13–1950-male)

Among viewers who grew up in Yugoslavia, too, the vast majority recalled the event as a shock and a genuinely sad and anxious occasion; several viewers also remembered themselves or their parents crying in front of the television set and described the sense of anxiety that accompanied the occasion. As one viewer recalled:

> We knew that President Tito was seriously ill, and every day there were updates. Everyone began to talk about what would happen, will we fall apart, will there be war, and this and that. In any case, these updates that were coming ... 'he is feeling better, let him live', and to us I think this was a kind of confirmation that as long as he is alive, even if only with one leg, everything will be all right. And then one

[20] Brkljačić (2003), p. 99.

Sunday, I think it was a Sunday, somebody said that the screen went black, and that Lilić will now talk, and he said: 'President Tito died.' And we were awfully shocked. (YuCro-05–1957-female)

As we shall see, some of the other disruptive events investigated here did not provoke such a pronounced sense of anxiety and shock, even though they represented far more fundamental challenges to the existing order. Surprisingly perhaps, the two events that effectively brought least change to existing political and media arrangements were among those that, at the time, caused the greatest disturbance. It is important to add, however, that this disturbance was carefully managed by the authorities and the media, with citizens being encouraged to channel their mourning and anxiety into the final act – the ceremonial funeral, broadcast live. In Yugoslavia, the funeral was a major media event which attracted dignitaries from across the world, and prior to the funeral, Tito's body was ceremonially taken on its last journey by train from Ljubljana, the capital of the northernmost republic, where he died, through Croatia and Bosnia to Belgrade in Serbia, thereby symbolically uniting the multinational country for one last time. Both the ceremonial transport of the body and the funeral were described by several of our interviewees, who recalled the sense of sadness but also awe and pride at the magnitude of the event and the worldwide attention and coverage it received. The prominence of the funeral in viewers' memories arguably testifies to extent to which the authorities, in conjunction with broadcasters and other media professionals, succeeded in directing the initial shock and anxiety and channelled it into a collective experience that reinstituted order and celebrated unity over disunity.

Yet, this reaffirmation of the existing order was not to last. The sudden disappearance of key figures of the communist order arguably created an opening for change, and over the years that followed, both countries underwent a series of gradual changes to the established media and political order. In Yugoslavia, the 1980s were a decade marked by an increasingly open discussion of topics previously considered taboo. While such issues were initially raised in fictional genres and in low-circulation publications aimed at cultural elites, they gradually moved to the mainstream media, thus slowly expanding the scope of public debate and moving Yugoslav media culture further and further away from the state socialist template.[21] In the Soviet Union, too, changes were gradual rather

[21] On the role of fiction, literary, and cultural journals in the process of opening taboos in Yugoslavia see Wachtel (1998), pp. 219–226.

than sudden. For instance, while the news bulletin *Time* continued to follow established templates of reporting, other shows appeared that provided a qualitatively different take on Soviet reality. Current affairs shows such as *12th Floor* (*12-i etazh*, 1985–1987), *Perestroika Searchlight* (*Prozhektor perestroiki*, 1987–1989), *Before and after Midnight* (*Do i posle polunochi*, 1987–1991), and *Viewpoint* (*Vzgliad*, 1987–1994) began to uncover social problems that had rarely, if at all, been discussed in mainstream media outlets prior to that.[22] At about the same time, domestic TV fiction adopted a more socially engaged and critical tone, and Soviet television also started broadcasting parliamentary debates and congresses.[23] As in Yugoslavia, these changes were gradually transforming Soviet television culture long before the actual demise of communist rule.

Martial Law: A Pre-planned, Unexpected, and Conflictual Disruption

In contrast to the deaths of Brezhnev and Tito, the announcement of martial law in Poland came as a shock for viewers and media professionals alike. On the morning of December 13, General Wojciech Jaruzelski appeared, first on radio and then on television, dressed in a military uniform in front of a Polish flag, and told viewers that the country 'finds itself on the brink of an abyss'. He announced the imminent threat from the opposition movement, led by the Solidarity [*Solidarnocz*] Trade Union, and implicated them with 'mob justice', 'terror', the corruption of youth, and crime.[24] In a bid to crush the opposition, Jaruzelski declared a state of emergency. All programming for the rest of the day was replaced with reruns of Jaruzelski's statement, and regular broadcasting did not resume for several days. During this time, most of the leading Solidarity activists were arrested, and the combined forces of the army, police, and anti-terrorist units proceeded to blockade the striking factories and in several cases opened fire on the protesters.[25] When regular television broadcasting resumed, it was severely reduced in scope: broadcasting hours were cut short, and the second channel was closed.

The abrupt announcement came after a long period of unrest that had started in the summer of 1980 with a wave of strikes in the country's shipyards and factories, organized by Solidarity. Regular media could not

[22] Mickiewicz (1997), pp. 65–82. [23] Ibid. pp. 83–97.
[24] Kemp-Welch (2008), p. 327. [25] Paczkowski and Byrne (2007), pp. 33–34.

report on the strikes, but news of developments nevertheless spread through a range of unofficial channels. Moreover, several mainstream journalists, along with the Polish Journalists Association, became closely involved with the events, acted as information brokers between the protesters and the authorities, and fought for greater freedoms in reporting.[26] In that sense, both the Polish public and the country's media professionals were aware of the gravity of the situation. Yet few were prepared for the draconian measures of martial law, and the extent to which the Jaruzelski regime treated the media and the population with outright hostility: the announcement of martial law was followed by the internment of several journalists, and the Polish Journalists Association was explicitly attacked for 'threatening the interest of the security of the state'.[27] In this context, the media disruption initiated with Jaruzelski's statement could not be the sort of collaborative effort between the authorities and the media seen on the occasions of Tito's and Brezhnev's deaths. Instead, martial law was a conflict-ridden disturbance, which involved a one-sided imposition of order enacted by the communist authorities, with most of the media and the public left in the dark.

Among our interviewees, the event stood out as a defining moment of the state socialist era, and one that instantly changed the course of everyday life. The following excerpt, from a woman who was fifty-three at the time, offers a case in point:

> We turned the TV on and Jaruzelski was doing his speech. He was wearing a military uniform. He announced martial law. It got dark and people lit candles in the windows. We found out that we could not leave the country and the telephone lines were not working. It was very sad. The Poles had to shoot other Poles so that was a bad thing. (Pol-20–1928-female)

As in Yugoslavia and the Soviet Union, viewers' recollections of the day were often strikingly detailed, and several interviewees remembered the disruption of their TV viewing routine as an integral part of the wider shock. This was particularly common among viewers who were children at the time and those whose children were of school age. This was not a coincidence; the announcement came on a Sunday morning, a day and time that were, as seen in Chapter 8, traditionally associated with the popular children's programme *Teleranek* (*Telemorning*). A number of interviewees specifically mentioned their expectation of watching *Teleranek*, only to be confronted with Jaruzelski's statement. One

[26] Curry (1990), pp. 212–236. [27] Quoted in ibid. p. 236.

recalled being rather upset 'because it was one of the few days when mum said I didn't have to go to church and I was hoping to watch *Teleranek* but it wasn't on' (Pol-06–1973-female), while another argued that the absence of *Teleranek* became 'symbolic of that day' (Pol-24–1950-female).

We should also note that the cessation of martial law, although inaugurating a return to old routines, was not associated with a sense of renewed commitment to the communist order such as the one embodied in the funerals of Brezhnev and especially Tito. Nor was the event followed by a gradual reform and opening up of the public space; in contrast to Yugoslavia and also (somewhat later) the Soviet Union, where the years following the two leaders' deaths brought a slow relaxation of media controls, Polish media remained far more resistant to reform until much later. In this sense, the media disruption associated with martial law hardened the existing media and political orders.

The Fall of the Berlin Wall: A Largely Consensual but Unexpected Disruption

In East Germany, too, the established political and media orders remained unperturbed long after *perestroika* started sweeping through the Soviet Union. Yet, over the course of 1989, changes slowly began taking place that significantly shifted the ossified forms of the past. On television, this was shown by the appearance of the western-oriented youth programme *Elf 99* [*Eleven 99*, 1989–1991] in September but also by the changed character of news reporting. In the autumn of 1989, East German news began reporting on major demonstrations; by the end of October, the editor of *Aktuelle Kamera*, the main GDR news broadcast, appeared on screen to promise viewers that the programme would distance itself from the SED.[28] In other words, by November 1989, East German television had already begun to change the cast of characters and the scripts it was using to report on the world.

This process of change was hastened by the opening of borders in neighbouring Hungary and Czechoslovakia, which placed pressure on East German authorities to allow free travel across its borders, too. After a hastily convened Politburo meeting, a decision was taken to allow those in possession of a passport and a visa to exit the country

[28] Großmann (2015), pp. 235–236.

from 10 November. Given that at the time less than a quarter of the East German population had passports, such a decision meant that the process of emigration would be gradual and protracted, which would give officials sufficient time to prepare for the events.[29] However, at a press conference to explain the decision, broadcast live on GDR television, SED spokesman Günter Schabowski, who had not been given full information, declared in response to a journalist's question that the policy take effect immediately.[30] Within three minutes of the end of the conference, the news was rebroadcast on that evening's West German bulletins, which were widely watched in East Germany, under the headline 'GDR Opens Borders'. Within hours, crowds had gathered at the Berlin Wall, demanding to be let through, which eventually they were, leading to scenes of celebration and joy. Three and a half hours stood between Schabowski's announcement and the fall of the Wall. As historian Hans-Hermann Hertle memorably concluded: 'A media fiction gripped the masses and therefore became reality.'[31]

Yet, we should be careful not to overestimate the nature and impact of the fall of the Berlin Wall at the time, both as a real-life occurrence and as a media event. As Julia Sonnevend persuasively shows in her analysis of the Berlin Wall as a 'global media icon', the actual event was far from the magical moment we remember today; rather, the actual press conference was an 'awkward and boring occurrence' that was only gradually turned into an iconic, spectacular media event.[32] This is confirmed by our oral testimonies. While all our East German interviewees recalled the fall of the Wall, none of them spoke of the event as a shock or major disturbance. Rather, the realization of the importance of the event and its connection with the media mostly came *after* 9 November. Some interviewees did not find out about the news until much later; one residential school pupil, who was not able to watch television at school, only found out what was happening the next day on his way home for the weekend, because of the sheer numbers of individuals making their way to Berlin (GDR-15-1972-male). Another viewer likewise only heard about the news on 10 November, having slept through the drama (GDR-07-1954-female).

[29] Sonnevend (2016), pp. 58–59.

[30] On the recording of the conference you can faintly hear Gerhard Beil, the minister of Foreign Trade, correcting Schabowski '[that decision] must be taken by the Council of Ministers', but the fatal step had been taken.

[31] Hertle (2009), p. 187. [32] Sonnevend (2016), pp. 60–83.

Other scholarly sources suggest something similar: although this was a revolution publicized through the media, more often than not people found out about it the next day, either via television or radio or through conversations with relatives and friends.[33] Even among the relatively few who actually watched the Schabowski press conference, at least some were distracted enough not to realize the import of his words:

> I . . . well, I lived in the Centre then, so in the Centre directly by the wall, and I have to say that when Schabowski gave us the news about . . . when he gave the press conference, um, I have to say I didn't realize at all, because I was busy making dinner with the television on. At that time we followed Eastern news more, and I didn't realize at all. It was only afterwards that I thought about the meaning of the words and then quite quickly I heard an amazing movement happening in front of our window. (GDR-02-1956-female)

Ironically, then, the fall of the Wall was virtually ignored by those whose lives would soon end up being most affected by the changes that followed. This was in large part because the event came without any build-up and also without any sense of a historic, monumental shift that would change the future course of the country. To put it differently, this was not a staged, pre-planned media disruption of the kind seen after the deaths of Tito and Brezhnev, or during the Martial Law in Poland; nor was it a sudden, dramatic revolution, broadcast live on TV, as was the case with the events in Romania in December 1989. Furthermore, as we have seen, the fall of the Wall came on the heels of a gradual process of change that had already started transforming the established media order in the country and hence did not bring a sudden shift in the dramaturgy of television. In this sense, then, the actual fall of the Wall was the *least* unsettling of all the media disruptions examined in this chapter, and yet it was precisely this event that eventually evolved into a global media icon of the fall of communism.

The Romanian Revolution: An Unexpected, Unplanned and Conflictual Disruption

The Romanian revolution in December 1989 was different in many respects to the disruptive events we have previously discussed. The developments were unexpected and unplanned to a far greater extent than the other four disruptive events: neither the communist authorities, nor the

[33] See Großmann (2015), p. 255; Vaizey (2014), p. 83.

media, nor the audiences had the faintest idea of how the events would unfold. Furthermore, Romanian television was, at the time, still tightly wedded to the regime imposed by Ceauşescu earlier in the decade: a typical weekday schedule was limited to two hours, and the programming was thoroughly impregnated with ideological messages. Despite developments elsewhere in the region, there was no sign that the established political and media order was willing to give in; in contrast to the GDR, television in Romania showed no sign of change up to the very end. Finally, television played a central role in revolutionary events: if the fall of the Wall initially occurred largely outside of the media gaze, and without live coverage, the Romanian revolution was broadcast live almost from start to finish.

The social tensions in the country started mounting rapidly from mid-December 1989, when public unrest broke out in the city of Timişoara, and was then violently suppressed by combined police and army forces. The events received no coverage in mainstream media, but were reported by Western radio channels that had enjoyed wide audiences across Romania. On 21 December, Ceauşescu sought to use his presidential speech, delivered in front of a large crowd in the centre of Bucharest and broadcast live on television, to denounce the protesters in Timişoara and re-establish his authority.[34] While the programme began as normal, within minutes the crowd began to shout and scream. As planned in a case of commotion, the camera panned to the sky, but sound continued to broadcast, and microphones picked up the confusion of those on the balcony. The broadcast then cut out for three minutes 'for technical reasons', before returning to the balcony a few minutes later.[35] The leader's aura was fatally punctured; he fled Bucharest the next day. The state broadcaster had been taken over by civilians, and started broadcasting the live coverage of the revolution, alternating between broadcasts from the streets of Bucharest and discussions with key revolutionary actors in Studio 4 at Radio-television, which was subsequently renamed as 'Free Romanian Television'.[36] In the evening, an announcement was aired that confirmed the revolutionary takeover of TVR, the defection of the Army, and the flight of the Ceauşescus.[37]

34 Berry (2004), pp. 22–23.

35 Harun Farocki and Andrei Ujică's documentary, *Videograms of a Revolution* (1992) shows how events unfolded on screen.

36 Mustata (2006), pp. 126–127; see also Maierean (2006), p. 27.

37 Mustata (2012), p. 89.

As the authority over Romanian television suddenly shifted from the Ceauşescu regime to the civilians involved in the revolution, the Romanian broadcaster also underwent a rapid transformation in its modes of representation. To start with, the protests and shouts of the crowd broadcast live on 21 December represented a shocking deviation from the choreographed and ceremonial forms in which Ceauşescu was usually displayed in Romanian state media.[38] This was followed, from 22 December, by the sudden explosion in the volume of broadcasting: after a long period of austerity, Romanian television suddenly and violently entered an era of plenty, in which viewers were kept up-to-date with the 'live Romanian revolution' virtually non-stop. In addition, as Dana Mustata and Andreea Maierean point out, television also opened its doors to a host of new actors, adopted a completely different narrative of good and evil, started using autobiographical testimonies and first-person narratives, and directly engaged with viewers, calling upon them to participate in the unfolding events.[39]

Interestingly, our Romanian interviewees had very little to say about this 'TV revolution'. When specifically asked about the changes in television at the time, some of them mentioned the sudden expansion and diversification of programming and the switch to non-stop viewing, but their recollections lacked both the sense of shock and the level of detail seen in testimonies of other media disruptions examined so far. One participant, for instance, spoke of the 'frenzy of liberty' and described how the Romanian broadcaster 'tried to show everything it couldn't show before' (Rom-02-1973-female), while another referred to the 'explosion of information' and said she 'devoured the written and the audio-visual press' at the time (Rom-04-1940-female), but these changes were described rather matter-of-factly, without any mention of a sense of shock or anxiety typically found in Yugoslav and Soviet recollections of Tito's Brezhnev's deaths. Paradoxically, the most unexpected, violent and turbulent of the five media disruptions appears to be the least memorable and dramatic. The precise reasons for this merit further investigation, but at least two tentative explanations can be offered. First, the Romanian 'TV revolution' was so completely unplanned that the viewers' attitudes at the time were left diffuse at the time, without a clear public narrative to

[38] This footage is expertly marshalled in the 2010 documentary *The Autobiography of Nicolae Ceauşescu* (d. Andrei Ujică, 2010), which is entirely constructed from media footage of the Romanian leader from takeover to execution.

[39] Mustata (2006), pp. 128–130; Maierean (2006).

cling to. It is also possible to speculate that the event's disruptive qualities were subsequently dialled down, and are no longer seen as 'revolutionary' because the changes that followed were not as extensive and thorough as the label 'revolution' suggests. The nature of oral testimonies we collected confirms this: most interviewees, when asked about changes after 1989, emphasised continuities, the slow pace of change, or even deterioration of standards, especially with regards to the quality of television programming.

Taken together, the five media disruptions demonstrate the diverse ways in which television could be involved in managing the uncertain and the unexpected. The five cases also remind us that disruption, unexpectedness, conflict and change do not always go hand-in-hand: while it is tempting to think that media disruptions are inclined to be unexpected, unplanned, conflict-ridden and transformative, our examples demonstrate that this is not always the case. Some of the mediated disturbances we examined were at least partly pre-planned, expected, consensual and unifying, yet also shocking and disruptive; others were largely unexpected and conflictual, but at the same time resulted in little or no long-term change. Most notably perhaps, the event that many today associate most closely with the end of communism – namely the fall of the Berlin Wall – was experienced as a major media disruption only by a select few.

CONCLUSIONS

The analysis of the extraordinary temporalities of state socialist television cultures has revealed a number of shared traits across the region, as well as pointing to elements of cross-country variation. As we have shown, the festive TV schedules were broadly similar across the five countries, and rooted in a recognisably communist vision of the passage of time. Most of the TV holidays were intended to function as periodic reminders of communist values and ideals, and used the sense of festivity to encourage viewers to join in the celebration of revolutionary history and progress. At the same time, some of the TV festivities – most notably the Christmas and New Year's celebrations – bore little relation to communist temporality. The presence of religious holidays in two of the five countries also constituted a key cross-country difference, suggesting that state socialist TV cultures differed in the extent of to which they were secularised – a fact that also allows us to situate them vis-à-vis their Western counterparts.

Drawing on the analysis of historical audience research and oral history testimonies, we argued that state socialist media holidays were only partially successful in their intentions. In fact, we suggested that these TV festivities were at their most effective when they were least clearly connected to specifically communist ideals – when they celebrated religious holidays or the secular passage of time, or when they came packed with popular entertainment. Yet at the same time, we also pointed out that we should not underestimate the importance of media holidays to the longevity of communist rule: even if such disruptions to routine did not engender a sense of participation in the communist revolution, they succeeded in fostering a sense of common movement through time, functioned as a basis of shared experiences and references, and contributed to a common sociality. In this sense, they also played their role in the reproduction of the existing social order, even though the adherence to this order did not necessarily entail an active commitment to communist values.

With regard to TV disruptions, we examined the different ways in which television became involved in managing challenges to the established order. In some cases, such disturbances ended in the reaffirmation of the status quo, and were followed by a return to existing routines. In other cases, the challenge to the old was too great to resist, and the disruption had to be followed by more fundamental changes, which ultimately entailed the unravelling of the communist order as such. Considered within the broader context of developments over the course of the 1980s, the five cases of media disruptions provide a useful starting point for a cross-country comparison of the role of television cultures in the fall of communist rule. As our analysis suggests, the critical factor was the timing of the disruption. In Yugoslavia and the Soviet Union, which experienced a major challenge to communist rule early in the 1980s, and where this challenge was managed in a consensual manner, the exit from the communist order was slow and gradual. In Romania, on the other hand, the established order persisted virtually until the end, and when the disruption occurred, the change was rapid and dramatic. The extent to which television played an autonomous role in the developments differed accordingly. In the Soviet and Yugoslav cases, television had little autonomy in directing the events. In the Polish case, the live broadcasting of Jaruzelski's words had the function of a speech act, and effectively instituted martial law. In the GDR and especially in Romania, television autonomously and actively changed the way the events took place: if Schabowski's mistake hadn't been broadcast live, the wall would have fallen differently, and if Ceauşescu's speech had not been televised, and the TV station had not been taken over, the Romanian exit from communism would have been significantly different.

These different examples of media disruptions also remind us of the extent to which state socialist television cultures started changing and became gradually more like their Western cousins long before the end of communist rule was in sight. In Yugoslavia this is perhaps clearest – not only was Yugoslav television most open to Western imports and least tightly controlled; it also started undergoing a gradual process of change soon after the death of President Tito. In the Soviet Union, too, the period of perestroika brought significant changes years before the country abandoned communism, and even in the GDR, shifts in the language of television could be noticed months before the fall of the Berlin Wall. In this sense, the exit from communism was much less dramatic and sudden than it may appear retrospectively, and certainly less so than the established iconography of the fall of the Berlin Wall suggests. The only major exception was Romania, where the televised revolution in December 1989 brought not only a sudden demise of Ceauşescu but also a rapid and dramatic shift in the dramaturgy of television. But Romania was, of course, an exception long before that, ever since the drastic reduction in broadcast hours and imposition of total control by Ceauşescu in the early 1980s. For the rest of the region, the end of communist rule came after a more prolonged period of gradual change. This is not to say that the fall of communism was long expected – on the contrary, as Alexai Yurchak cogently argued several years ago,[40] the political edifice seemed set to last forever, yet when the final moments came, its collapse seemed completely unsurprising.

[40] Yurchak (2006).

11

Conclusions

In writing this book, we have set ourselves two major tasks. The first was to develop a comparative analysis of state socialist television cultures, with the aim of investigating the medium's relationship with the communist project. More specifically, we wanted to ascertain whether communist authorities managed to use the medium to further their revolutionary aims, or if television set in motion a revolution of its own, contributing to developments detrimental to the communist agenda. Our second task was to use the case of state socialist television as a testing ground for a novel form of comparative media research, which focuses on media cultures and is anchored in the notion of entangled modernities. Rather than investigating the media from the perspective of their systemic characteristics, such as media market structures or the role of the state, this approach examines how the media become involved in shaping cultural ideals and narratives and in structuring everyday practices and routines. The analysis of media systems retains an important role in our analysis, as one of the key factors that help explain why media cultures are as they are. However, it is only by focusing on media cultures that we can get a fuller insight into the societal consequences of mediated communication and understand how the media relate, not only to different political systems, but also to competing visions of modern society and to different cultural and social environments.

In the first part of the book, we developed an analytical framework for comparing media cultures, with a focus on television and the Cold War era. We identified seven dimensions of variation between television cultures globally: publicness, privacy, gendering, transnationalism, temporal orientation, extraordinary temporality, and secularization. We suggested that television cultures are to an important extent determined by the characteristics of broadcasting systems – their transnational orientation, their relative core-periphery positions, the extent of state control, and the timing of infrastructural developments – but are also shaped by a host of contextual factors external to the media, from gender relations and ethnocultural composition to the position of religion and the nature of national historical narratives. To prepare the ground for the empirical analysis in Parts Two and Three, we also outlined the historical trajectories of television in Eastern Europe and developed a tripartite typology of state socialist television systems: market state socialist, reformist state socialist, and hard-line state socialist. Drawing on the notion of entangled modernities, we argued that the varieties of modern media cultures and media systems evident in Cold War TV can be thought of as articulations of different notions of modern society, grounded in different versions of structural or functional differentiation and designed to promote disparate visions of progress. These different notions and structures of modernity, and hence the media systems and cultures anchored in them, did not exist in isolation, but became entangled and influenced one another, often giving rise to hybrid forms that incorporated elements inspired by different visions of modernity. In the remainder of the book, we applied the proposed framework to the analysis of state socialist television cultures in five countries, drawing on a range of sources and methods.

In this chapter, we take stock of the arguments and analysis developed over the course of the book and reflect on their significance, from the perspective of the role of the media under communist rule and from the perspective of comparative media research more generally. We start by considering the question of the communist 'television revolution'. We lay out the key characteristics of state socialist television cultures and consider whether these amount to a distinct form of modern television culture, rooted in communist modernity and geared to advance the communist revolutionary agenda. We then move on to examine developments in Eastern Europe after 1989 and consider some of the continuities and discontinuities between the socialist and post-socialist television cultures in the region. Finally, we reflect on the relevance of our comparative framework for understanding media cultures beyond television and for investigating media landscapes beyond Eastern Europe. We emphasize the importance of cultural and comparative analysis for advancing the understanding of mediated communication in non-democratic settings, we discuss the applicability of our findings to the surviving communist-led states, such as China, and we consider the applicability of the analytical tools developed in the book to communication and media developments globally.

THE TELEVISION REVOLUTION

As our analysis has shown, the attempt to mobilize television as an instrument of the communist revolution was in many ways successful. The genre structures and scheduling patterns of the five television cultures were designed to give rise to an informed, educated and 'cultured' working class capable of driving revolutionary progress; they therefore privileged information, educational, and 'high' cultural content over entertainment. In line with the emphasis on mass participation, state socialist television also created spaces for public engagement and contestation, while at the same reminding audiences of the limits of social critique under party rule. Televised depictions of privacy were intertwined with the communist agenda, too: in accordance with the public thrust and communal orientation of the communist project, they promoted a mode of private conduct that valued the common good over private interests. Furthermore, scheduling practices found across Eastern Europe succeeded in aligning the temporal routines of state socialist viewers with a teleological notion of movement towards the communist revolution, punctuated by periodic commemorations of revolutionary history. Markers of religious temporality, by contrast, were almost completely absent. The communist understanding of gender relations left its imprint on television cultures as well: the widespread absence of daytime programming aimed at housewives on workdays was connected to the high proportions of women in the workforce and the vision of a society in which both men and women were expected to engage in waged labour outside of the home. Finally, televised representations of revolutionary history served as constant reminders of past achievements and sought to inspire similar revolutionary acts in the present and future.

That said, our analysis also revealed several instances where the link between televised output and communist ideals was less evident. In our examination of TV transnationalism, for instance, only two of the five countries in our sample sourced the majority of their imported programming from other socialist countries, while the remaining three relied primarily on Western content. The abundance of history on state socialist screens, particularly pronounced in the Soviet Union, can also be interpreted as a sign of weakness: it suggests that the communist vision failed to provide compelling narratives of the present and future. Of course, we could argue that the Soviet Union, as the leading communist power, had a particularly high stake in ensuring that its revolutionary past retained a lasting impact. Yet seen in a different way, the preponderance of history can be seen as a symptom of crisis: the country that sought to be at the forefront of revolutionary progress was also the one that was most prone to turn for inspiration to the past. Significant cross-country variation, as well as change over time, emerged on other dimensions we have examined, from representations of privacy to media holidays. Soviet television stood out as the one most closely aligned with communist agendas, while Yugoslavia frequently featured at the opposite end of the spectrum. These differences, too, indicate limits to the ability of communist authorities to mobilize television for revolutionary purposes.

While our analysis has shown the many ways in which state socialist television was distinct, it is also important to note important similarities to television cultures elsewhere in the world. As shown in Chapter 5, the public mission of socialist television shared the paternalist, didactic ethos of Western public broadcasting, which likewise privileged education and information over entertainment. It is therefore not a surprise that programme structures, as well as the everyday scheduling patterns of state socialist television, largely resembled those found in the context of Western public broadcasting at the time. Beyond public service television, too, similarities can be found. Thanks to the universal qualities of television as a medium – such as its bond with the present and its propensity for domesticity and intimate modes of address – state socialist television cultures shared many qualities with other TV cultures globally, including those arising in the context of commercial broadcasting. As in capitalist contexts, television became an indispensable ingredient of modern domestic life in terms of its patterns of domestic viewing, its entanglement in the gendered division of labour, its intertwining in everyday temporal routines, and its centrality as an anchor of shared rituals.

Even when socialist broadcasters succeeded in producing output that was faithful to communist principles and distinct from its Western equivalent, this did not necessarily achieve the desired effects among audiences. For instance, the analysis of media holidays showed that these extraordinary occasions were most successful with audiences when they were least communist: when they served their viewers an abundant dose of entertainment or celebrated the secular passage of time, rather than commemorating events from communist history. Another important finding emerging from our analysis is the mismatch between audience practices and beliefs: while viewing practices were broadly in sync with communist ideals, with the majority of viewers tuning in for daily news and major media holidays, this did not necessarily translate into mass adherence to the ruling party's goals, at least not in their entirety. In some cases, this disconnect between practice and belief was inscribed into the nature of programming itself. The case of communism's battle with organized religion illustrates this: programming placed in the Sunday-morning slot was generally designed for entertainment purposes (cartoons for children or magazine programming aimed at countryside dwellers), rather than directly seeking to counter religious belief and promote communist views on religion. These findings suggest that state socialist broadcasters succeeded in capturing viewers' attention and instituting shared practices but were less successful in inculcating communist beliefs.

State socialist television, then, had an ambiguous relationship with the communist project. Many aspects of state socialist TV programming were clearly aligned with the communist agenda and designed to give rise to a new society, capable of ushering in the communist future. State socialist audiences, too, adopted several practices that were connected to the communist cause: they followed daily news programmes designed to bring them up to speed with the latest revolutionary achievements and participated in mediated festivities aimed at celebrating the communist past, present, and future. Yet as we have seen, these viewing habits and rituals were not necessarily accompanied by an active commitment to the communist cause. While some of our interviewees reported enjoying such broadcasts and sharing in the sense of pride and progress they promoted, others were critical of their ideological intentions, and the majority recalled watching out of habit, irrespective of content. Even so, the very act of participation in shared viewing routines and rituals, regardless of one's ideological convictions, was important in and of itself. Through these rituals and routines, ideologically saturated programmes became part of the texture of everyday life that was taken for granted, they provided shared experiences and reference points, and they constituted an important basis of common sociality. Because of its habitual and ritualistic nature, television also contributed to a sense of stability and normality, reassuring viewers that while things were not as they should be, life was nevertheless proceeding in a predictable, and hence in some ways comforting, manner.

Rather than acting as a vehicle of revolutionary change, then, television came to serve as an anchor of communist normality, projecting a reassuring sense of stability at a point when the vision of a communist future was becoming ever more distant. It served to delineate the boundaries of the publicly permissible, provided the basis for shared social rituals and common routines, and continually reminded viewers of the past achievements, communal values, and utopian ideals of the communist project. While it served as an anchor of normality, it is worth noting that television was not a medium of stagnation. Despite its repetitiveness, often ossified and formulaic language, and recycling of familiar narratives and tropes, state socialist television was not static. As a new medium, it offered considerable change and novelty: it transformed the configuration of domestic spaces, instituted new daily routines, brought sights and sounds from near and far, and enabled viewers to participate in a range of events they could not have experienced otherwise. With time, TV broadcasters had also become rather adept at using the novelty of television to promote traditional communist values in new ways: they packaged revolutionary ideals in new forms, adapted personal plots and domestic environments to promote public goals, used the liveness of television to produce impressive festive programming, and employed entertainment strategically to further the communist agenda or to attract the attention of viewers to more ideologically saturated programming. In sum, as an anchor of normality, television offered a balance of continuity and change, novelty and reassurance, in ways that made it palatable both to communist authorities and to audiences. As a result, we could argue that the small screen contributed to the longevity of state socialism, especially during the 1970s and the 1980s when the medium became a ubiquitous feature of daily life across the state socialist world.

Yet paradoxically, the very same features that made state socialist television such an important pillar of communist rule undermined the medium's ability to sustain the ideology's legitimacy at the end of the 1980s. As we have seen, state socialist television professionals became rather adept at inculcating communist ideals into a wide range of genres and succeeded in attracting large audiences. However, the disjunction between practice and belief meant that television was unable to engender a deeper belief in communist ideals. As the political infrastructure underpinning the state socialist television culture started to fall apart, the established routines and rituals that sustained the presence of communist ideals in people's daily lives were disrupted. Without them, the belief in the communist vision lost its bearings, too – not because people were unambiguously critical of it but rather because they had long ceased to take literally the messages promoted through television.

CONTINUITY AND CHANGE IN POST-SOCIALIST TELEVISION CULTURES

Since the fall of communist rule, media landscapes in Eastern Europe have undergone a dramatic transformation. Much of the existing literature charting this transformation is limited to systemic features: ownership structures, media regulation, and other aspects of the politics–media dynamics. This body of work has examined key systemic changes that have affected the media in the region since 1989, including the growth of private ownership and commercial media, the transformation of former state broadcasters into public service institutions, and the introduction of new regulations aimed at guaranteeing media independence. Although several authors have noted similarities with the Mediterranean or Polarized Pluralist media-politics model as identified by Hallin and Mancini, the existing research also revealed considerable intraregional differences, as well as distinctive traits that can be attributed to the unique historical experiences of the region.[1] While a consensus on the preferred classification has yet to emerge, it is clear that post-socialist media systems cannot be fitted into a single, internally homogeneous post-socialist model or treated simply as local versions of models found in the West.

One aspect of post-socialist media in Eastern Europe that is often attributed to the lingering effects of communist rule is political control over the media. This has often been linked to systemic media legacies, including media regulation that offers insufficient protection against political and commercial pressures on the media, and low levels of journalistic professionalization.[2] Also common have been the mentions of legacies external to the media, such as the behaviour of political elites, who were socialized during communist rule and continue to treat the media as a handmaiden of politics, as well as attitudinal legacies among the wider population, which does not value media independence.[3] On the whole, however, the discussion of these legacies is still poorly developed. This is largely due to the scarcity of detailed analysis of historical state socialist media systems, both single-country based and comparative, which could provide a benchmark for assessing the extent of continuity and

[1] For recent contributions to this debate see Dobek Ostrowska (2015); Mancini (2015).
[2] E.g. Milton 1997. [3] E.g. Lašas (2015).

discontinuity with the present. In this book, we have proposed a typology of state socialist television systems which should provide a useful starting point for such an endeavour. We should note, however, that our effort here was based solely on existing sources, and hence further analysis is needed to flesh out the differences and similarities in full and to add further dimensions of comparison missing in our typology. Among others, detailed studies of media producers – including, but not only, journalists – are needed to better understand the professional ideologies and practices from the era and the extent to which these differed from their counterparts elsewhere in the world at the time, as well as from their post-socialist successors.[4]

Changes and continuities in the realm of post-socialist media cultures – and television cultures, in particular – have received less systematic attention and fewer comparative treatments than systemic changes, although here, too, the body of work has been growing rapidly. By and large, the key dilemma facing researchers interested in post-socialist television cultures is the same as the one arising in the study of television systems and has to do with finding the best ways of conceptualizing the balance of continuity and change. On the one hand, there is little doubt that television cultures in the region share common features, many of which can be linked to the communist era; on the other hand, post-socialist television cultures also vary considerably from country to country, so much so that one may wonder whether and to what extent the epithet 'post-socialist' is still useful as an analytical category. To compound the problem, changes over time have been notable. In Russia, for instance, television has changed considerably over the course of the 1990s and 2000s. After a period of growing independence initiated by Gorbachev in the mid-1980s, since the 1996 presidential elections, television has increasingly been a tool in the service of the ruling elite. Especially after the arrival of Putin in 2000, television has increasingly been brought under state control – a process accompanied by a return of televised displays of military power and mediated celebrations of national history.[5] Indeed, these and many other continuities with the Soviet era have led Christina Evans to argue that television under Putin in fact 'represents the culmination of a long Soviet – now Russian – era of television', which began in the late 1950s.[6]

[4] For an important recent study of journalistic culture in post-Soviet Russia, informed by a novel understanding of both the Soviet period and the post-Soviet transformation, see Roudakova (2017).

[5] Evans (2016), pp. 250–253; Hutchings and Rulyova (2009).

[6] Evans (2016), p. 2.

Given the marked intra-regional differences and pronounced changes over time, as well as the limited scope of existing comparative research in this area, the brief discussion we offer here cannot do justice to the diversity of post-socialist television cultures. What we offer instead is a tentative sketch of some of the tendencies gleaned from the available literature, and a reflection on how the analytical framework developed in this book can be applied to advance work in this area. Above all, we contend that the best way forward, at least for the time being, lies not in the development of models and typologies but rather in the comparative examination of post-socialist television cultures along the individual dimensions of variation identified in this book. In line with this, the pages that follow offer a discussion of some of the trends and patterns seen in post-socialist television with regards to publicness, privatization, and transnationalism.

Unlike changes in the other dimensions we consider in this book, shifts in television's publicness after 1989 have received considerable scholarly attention so far, including some comparative analyses. Still, the existing literature focuses largely on political communication and hence privileges journalism and news genres rather than entertainment, cultural and educational content. As far as the medium's role in supporting public deliberation is concerned, this research shows that, by and large, TV professionals in both public service and commercial broadcasting have enjoyed more freedom since 1989, although notable differences existed depending on the type of exit from communism: due to the Yugoslav wars, broadcasters in many Yugoslav successor states continued to face considerable political pressures well into the 1990s and beyond.[7] Yet even in countries that have experienced a less disruptive transition to democratic rule, investigative reporting remained marginal, and in some cases – notably in Romania and Hungary – commercial broadcasters chose to adopt an apolitical stance and hence largely avoided engaging in contentious political issues altogether.[8] Recent overviews also suggest that the scope for public deliberation in the region has started shrinking again in the past decade: although not specifically limited to television, data on press freedom gathered by the Freedom House indicate that, after a period of notable liberalization during the 1990s, the state of media independence started worsening again in most countries from 2007 onwards.[9] It remains to be seen, however, how these shifting boundaries

[7] See OSI/EUMAP (2005a, 2008). [8] OSI/EUMAP (2005b), pp. 76–77.

[9] Cf. Bajomi-Lázár (2014), pp. 8, 240–241.

of public deliberation affect television specifically, including genres beyond news. We should also question to what extent the notion of media freedom offers an adequate conceptual basis for understanding the changing shape of public deliberation since 1989, not least because of its embeddedness in traditions of political and economic liberalism. Natalia Roudakova's recent study of post-Soviet journalism in Russia, for instance, suggests that the transformation is better understood in terms of progressive deprofessionalization, and conceptualised using an ethics-based vocabulary, including the notion of truth-telling.[10]

Television's public mission likewise changed considerably after 1989. This was not only because the medium ceased to serve as the mouthpiece of the party-state, but also because television was no longer unequivocally perceived as an institution charged with the provision of public goods. To put it differently, the notion of public service was so inextricably bound with party-state control that both political elites and media professionals failed to disentangle them from one another. This had two important consequences for post-socialist television cultures. In the commercial sector, severing the link with the state also meant relieving television of its public responsibility. Newly established commercial broadcasters in many parts of the region thus remained exempt from public service obligations or were subject to minimal restrictions such as broadcasting state announcements in emergency situations. According to an overview of legislation in fifteen post-socialist countries, published in 2003, public service obligations were imposed on commercial television in Albania, Croatia, the Czech Republic, Estonia, Hungary, Romania, Serbia, and Slovenia but not in Bosnia and Herzegovina, Bulgaria, Latvia, Lithuania, Macedonia, Poland, and Slovakia.[11] In the realm of public broadcasting, the emphasis on a public mission remained, but so did a measure of political control, and the two were often conflated.[12] To make matters worse, public service broadcasters in most post-socialist countries failed to stand up to commercial competition and saw their audience shares decline rapidly over the years.[13] It is also telling that, faced with commercial rivals, public broadcasters often reacted by mimicking the solutions adopted by their competitors rather than by rethinking their public mission.

[10] Roudakova (2017). [11] OSI/EUMAP (2005b), pp. 175–176.
[12] Ibid. pp. 54–65. See also Jakubowicz (2004); Voltmer (2013), pp. 153–160.
[13] OSI/EUMAP (2005b), p. 171.

It is therefore not a surprise that, as a result, entertainment programming started commanding a much more dominant position in the region. Comparative cross-country data on the genre composition of broadcast output is lacking, but a longitudinal study conducted in Croatia, covering both public and commercial broadcasting, provides a useful point of orientation: nationally, entertainment and fictional content grew from 45 per cent in 1979 to 80 per cent in 2009, while informational, educational, and cultural continent declined from 53 to 20 per cent over the same period. Public broadcasting was not exempt from this change: although the decline in the proportion of informational, educational, and cultural content was less dramatic than in the commercial sector, the share nonetheless dropped to 36 per cent in 2009.[14] Importantly, the study also shows that the genre composition of broadcast output started changing rather noticeably well before the end of communist rule: a steady decline in the proportion of information starts already during the 1980s, a finding aligned with our own data for Yugoslavia. These results show a clear shift away from the state socialist model of public mission but also confirm that important changes in this area started taking effect well before 1989. These continuities suggest that, seen from a global vantage point, the decline of public service television in Eastern Europe should be interpreted as an integral part of a transnational decline of public broadcasting that started in the late 1970s . Contrary to common wisdom, the problems experienced in the sector are not due to insufficient embeddedness of the notion of public service; rather, they signal the uprooting of television from its long-established mission of serving the common good, initiated under communist rule.

Another aspect where longitudinal comparisons are likely to generate interesting results concerns television's involvement with the private sphere. Serial fiction offers a particularly good basis for longitudinal comparisons on this dimension: dramas centred on family life, love, marital affairs, and friendship have remained a staple across the region to this day, and much as during the state socialist period, they often draw sizeable audiences. Also significant is the fact that several east European broadcasters produced remakes of popular family dramas from the socialist era: Polish Television produced a new season of *The Forty-Year Old* in 1993, Croatian Radiotelevision and Radio Television of Serbia each produced their own remake of the *Theatre in the House* in 2007, while Czech television launched a sequel of the *Hospital at the End of Town*

[14] Peruško and Čuvalo (2014).

(Nemocnice na kraji mêsta, 1977–1981) in 2003. These remakes of course reflected the changed social environment in which they were produced; for instance, the Czech sequel to the *Hospital at the End of Town* revolved in part around the (failed) privatization of the hospital.[15] However, other serial dramas produced after 1989 departed from the socialist script in more fundamental ways, both with regards to their genre conventions and the nature of the characters. Several broadcasters in the region, both public and commercial, have started producing considerably longer serial dramas and have adopted conventions familiar from soap operas, such as an open-ended narrative structure and melodramatic plots. Some of the most successful productions in this category include Polish family sagas *Clan* (Klan, TVP, 1997–) and *L for Love* (M jak miłość, TVP, 2000–), and the Estonian series *Good Luck 13* (Õnne 13, ETV, 1993–), which has been running for over two decades, as well as Czech soap operas *Street* (Ulice, Nova TV, 2005–) and *Surgery in the Pink Garden* (Ordinace v Růžové zahradě, Nova TV, 2005–). Long-running sitcoms have had successes in the region, too, continuing the tradition of comedy series from the socialist-era but also emulating the formulas of popular Western sitcoms such as *Friends* (NBC, 1994–2004) or *Married with Children* (Fox, 1987–1997). Examples include the Croatian *Villains and Princesses* (Bitange i princeze, HTV, 2005–2010) and the Hungarian series *Those Men!* (Pasik!, 2000–2003).

Apart from adopting different dramatic conventions, post-socialist serial fiction also often presents a rather different image of private life from the one seen in state socialist productions. Although protagonists of working class origin have not disappeared, the socio-economic backgrounds of key fictional characters are now more diverse and often include the nouveau riches of the post-socialist era or descendants of nobility and wealthy families from the pre-revolutionary years. The Polish and Czech productions of serial fiction offer several good examples: instead of working class protagonists such as the engineer Stefan Karwowski in the Polish socialist-era serial *Forty-Year-Old* (1974) or the shop assistant Anna Holubová in the Czechoslovak *Woman Behind the Counter* (1977), Polish post-socialist family sagas including *Clan* and *L for Love* and the Czech serial *Hotel Herbich* (2005) focus on the lives of traditional families originating from the landed classes and aristocracy before World War II.[16] Representations of living standards, attitudes to consumption, and the role of the community also appear to have shifted. While the members of

[15] Čulík (2013). [16] Čulík (2013); Kisielewska (2013).

state socialist TV families were often shown shopping or enjoying consumer goods, they lived in reasonably modest accommodations and largely scorned consumerist values. In contrast, post-socialist family dramas are more prone to accept what Alicja Kisielewska refers to as a 'middle-class mythology' and see the consumerist lifestyle and wealth as integral parts of success.[17] Finally, at least as far as the Polish case is concerned, the post-socialist TV family functions largely as a universe to itself – unlike its socialist predecessor, which was tightly integrated into the local community and the wider society.[18] While existing research is too limited to establish whether these patterns can be generalised to the dramatic production in the region as a whole, they do indicate that post-socialist television cultures are more privatized than their socialist equivalents and that the ideal forms of family and community life represented in them are more prone to celebrate individual success and privilege the well-being of one's immediate family and friends over the wider collective. Indeed, we could argue that this turn to the private and the individual represented the necessary flipside of the diminishing role of television as an instrument of the common good.

Another development that testifies to the growing privatization of post-socialist television cultures is the proliferation of reality TV, a genre often built around public displays of privacy. The wave of reality TV programmes engulfed post-socialist television in the early 2000s, when television schedules across the region began to feature local adaptations of global formats such as *Big Brother*, originally broadcast in the Netherlands in 1999, *The Osbornes*, which premiered on MTV in 2002, and *Idols*, first released on various channels in 2001. Typically broadcast on commercial channels, reality programmes have invariably provoked public consternation and led to debates that reflected the shifting notions of the public-private boundary in the post-socialist context.[19] Arguably, the love-hate relationship with reality programming in post-socialist Eastern Europe stemmed largely from the fact that these shows displayed aspects of privacy that were hitherto hidden from public view or do not fit the polished, respectable image of public privacy constructed during socialism: nudity and sexuality, practices and views unworthy of the high standards of cultured behaviour promoted by state socialist television, and racial and sexual minorities. Together with Imre we could

[17] Kisielewska (2013), p. 99. [18] Ibid. p. 92.

[19] For a sample of literature on reality TV in Eastern Europe see Bardan (2013); Imre (2011); Volčič and Erjavec (2015).

therefore argue that the moral outrage against reality television was triggered by the fact that these shows embodied several 'converging kinds of illegitimacy' at work in post-socialist television.[20] That said, it is also worth noting that both the relative success of reality formats, the nature of local adaptations, and the precise reasons for the public outcry against reality TV varied considerably from country to country, making this genre particularly well suited for a comparative examination of televised privacy in the post-socialist context.

We should of course be wary of exaggerating the trend towards privatization and individualization in post-socialist fiction and entertainment. Much of the qualitative research from the region emphasizes the presence of nationalism, and hence the national community and its interests, as a key backdrop of post-socialist television cultures, even in genres that superficially seem most vested in the celebration of individual success, such as reality shows. This is not apparent only in recently established nation-states in the Baltics or southeastern Europe, but also in countries with longer nation-state traditions, such as Romania, Hungary, or Russia.[21] While the balance of communal values and individual interests on post-socialist television has certainly shifted in favour of the latter, individual behaviour is still observed through a collective lens. However, the nature of the collective has shifted: the emphasis on the community of 'comrades', rooted in different nations but also tied together through the transnational solidarity of the working classes, gave way to national communities defined in ethnocultural terms.[22]

The salience of the national can be gleaned also from research on transnational television flows in the region, yet another dimension where Eastern European television cultures have changed in important ways but also where notable continuities remain. As Václav Štětka shows in his comparative analysis of cross-border programme flows and their reception in Eastern Europe, the inflow of audiovisual imports increased considerably after 1989, and the composition of imports shifted as well, with the vast majority now coming from the West.[23] His analysis also shows that several countries in the region – most notably Russia, but also Poland, the Czech Republic, and Estonia – have been successful in stemming the tide of foreign programming over time and replacing imports with domestically produced programmes equally, if not more, popular

[20] Imre (2016), p. 112.
[21] E.g. Bardan (2013); Hutchings and Tolz (2015); Imre (2011); Volčič and Erjavec (2015).
[22] Mihelj (2011), pp. 86–89. [23] Štětka (2012b).

with audiences. The transnational orientation of post-socialist television cultures is not uniform either: although Western content dominated in most of the region, Russia retained its foothold in some of the former Soviet republics: Ukraine and Belarus were both largely dependent on Russian imports in 2006. Another interesting recent development that has affected transnational television flows in Eastern Europe is the success of Turkish serial dramas.[24] Although part of a global phenomenon, Turkish serial fiction arguably has distinct resonance in this part of Europe due to the region's historical involvement with the Ottoman Empire. Nonetheless, despite significant changes in the transnational television flows in Eastern Europe, continuities are worth noting, too. The relative openness to Western imports remains a key point of differentiation between television cultures in the region, and Russia has remained considerably more self-sufficient in terms of its broadcast content and ability to compete with Western television exports, albeit to a more limited degree than during the Soviet period. In this sense, the patterns of transnational broadcasting in post-socialist Eastern Europe seem to bear the marks of several overlapping 'imperial legacies' constituted over centuries, from those associated with the Ottoman Empire to those linked with Russia and the Western powers.

Let us conclude this brief and vey partial overview by noting another obvious legacy of the state socialist era, namely the television programmes themselves. Much of the programming of that period – especially serial fiction – continues to be rebroadcast on both public and commercial channels across the region, sometimes on channels dedicated to that purpose. Many of the most popular serials from the era, from the Polish *Four Tankmen and a Dog* (1966–1970) and the Romanian *The Freckled Boy* (1974) to the Yugoslav *Theatre in the House* (1974–1984) and the Soviet *Seventeen Moments of Spring* (1973) have been reissued on DVD. Yet in some cases, the continued popularity of socialist-era programming has attracted considerable controversy. In Poland, *Four Tankmen* began to be widely criticised after 1990 and was accused of distorting history by omitting information about the Soviet occupation of Poland and instead promoting an ideologically charged notion of Soviet–Polish friendship during World War II.[25] In the Czech Republic, the rebroadcasting of *The Thirty Cases of Major Zeman* (Třicet případů majora Zemana, 1974–1979) likewise prompted wide-ranging debate, with several right-wing organizations accusing the broadcaster of unlawful public

[24] Yesil (2015). [25] Szostak and Mihelj (2017), p. 329.

promotion of an oppressive regime.[26] These controversies suggest that the state socialist television heritage had become an integral part of the wider process of coming to terms with the communist past. However, it is worth noting that attitudes to socialist-era programming differ considerably across generations. As a recent study of vernacular memories of *Four Tankmen* conducted in Poland in 2014 shows, viewers of all generations appreciate the entertainment value of the series, yet those born between 1940 and 1959 also mention the propagandistic intentions and historical inaccuracies of the series, while those born in 1960 or later largely treat these controversies as insignificant or fail to mention them altogether.[27] This suggests that state socialist television programming may become less controversial with time and gradually turn into an accepted part of cultural heritage.

TOWARDS GLOBAL COMPARISONS

The relevance of the comparative framework developed in this book goes beyond its application to the historical experiences of state socialism and its legacies in post-socialist Eastern Europe. It also provides important lessons for understanding the nature of mediated communication in the surviving communist-led countries, and in non-democratic contexts more generally, as well as offering a template for global comparisons of media cultures beyond television.

State Socialist Television Today: The Success of the Market State Socialist Model

How do our conclusions about historical state socialist television fare when juxtaposed with television in the communist-led countries that still survive? While a comprehensive answer to this question would require further research, the existing literature suggests that several of our conclusions do indeed apply rather well to the twenty-first-century context. Of the three types of television systems we have proposed – the hard-line, the reformed, and the market state socialist television system – the latter appears dominant today, with television systems in China, Cuba, and Vietnam all exhibiting several features similar to those found historically in Yugoslavia. Similarities at the level of television cultures are notable, too.

[26] Pehe (2014). [27] Szostak and Mihelj (2017).

In the Chinese case, the fit is clearest. Television was introduced to the country only in the late 1950s, and it took a long time for the medium to become sufficiently widespread to make a decisive difference to everyday life: it was only in the 1980s that television became the main source of entertainment and news.[28] As a consequence of the economic reforms initiated in 1979, the extent of party-state oversight has decreased considerably: although Chinese television continues to be controlled by the state it is also open to private investment in some areas, including entertainment and advertising,[29] and enjoys considerable autonomy in terms of finance and management, especially at the subnational level.[30] Chinese television is markedly Western-oriented, has modelled management practices on those found in Western commercial television, and has imported Western production values, technologies, and skills.[31] Finally, Chinese television, similarly to Yugoslav television, has ambitions to act as a core and influence other television cultures, a tendency evident in the expansion over the past decade of China's international broadcasting capacity,[32] as well as in the push for the increased quantity and quality of television exports.[33] Differences should be noted as well. The presence of market forces is even more pronounced than in the Yugoslav case: Chinese television is considerably more reliant on advertising revenues than Yugoslav television ever was and is open not only to domestic but also to foreign private investment. At the same time, the party-state is continually finding ways to retain control over the medium, seeking to ensure that both the market and foreign borrowing ultimately work to the benefit of the communist agenda. Among other things, the production of news and that of drama are subjected to detailed regulation of a kind unseen in Yugoslavia, and the party-state also limits the proportion of imported content.[34]

At the level of television culture, too, similarities can be found. A handful of illustrative examples should suffice. Much like Yugoslav serial fiction, contemporary Chinese dramas are often set in domestic settings or focus on private plots: the 1990s saw a boom in serials with domestic themes, including dramas focused on the lives of modern Chinese families in contemporary urban environments, family sagas set in the Republican era, and the so-called 'pink dramas' and 'idol dramas' that focus on the romantic lives of young urbanites and are targeted at

[28] Lewis et al. (2016), p. 27. [29] Zhao (2008). [30] Zhang (2009), p. 11.
[31] Ibid. pp. 11–13. [32] Rawnsley (2015). [33] Hong and Liu (2015), pp. 438–440.
[34] Zhu (2008), pp. 11–12.

students and young professionals.[35] A recent quantitative study of serial dramas broadcast on the two most widely watched channels in China, CCTV-1 and Hunan TV, between 1992 and 2015, found the love theme to be by far the most prominent on both channels and registered a clear trend of growth in serials focused on romantic plots from the early 1990s.[36] Although differences in methodology preclude a direct comparison with our data, these results nonetheless suggest that privatized serial fiction is similarly prominent on Chinese television, as it was on Yugoslav screens. As far as its engagement with the public realm is concerned, Chinese television likewise fits the patterns found in Yugoslavia. From its early years, television has been expected to function as an 'electronic bridge' between the communist elites and the general population, and a 'people's medium' enabling mass participation.[37] In line with this, Chinese officials cautiously endorse media criticism, which has allowed journalists to engage in critical reporting, as long as they frame their work as constructive interventions aimed at aiding the party agenda.[38] Popular television genres such as serial drama also occasionally serve as means of social critique, most notably in the case of anti-corruption dramas that had their heyday during the early 2000s.[39]

In terms of transnationalism, a more varied picture emerges: while Chinese television culture is broadly similar to its Yugoslav predecessor in terms of openness to imported content,[40] it is somewhat less dependent on Western imports, especially in recent years. Trends in entertainment and drama are particularly telling: during the 1980s and the 1990s, the majority of TV drama came from the United States, followed by Western Europe and Latin America, while recent decades have seen a surge in imports from Taiwan, Hong Kong, and South Korea.[41] This suggests that China is more successful at crafting its own distinct version of socialist transnationalism: while, as we have seen, Yugoslav TV professionals raised concerns over the reliance on Western imports and wanted to encourage a greater diversity of foreign content, these concerns and wishes never had much of an impact on actual programme flows. By contrast, the greater presence of state intervention in the Chinese

[35] Ibid. pp. 81–98. [36] Wang (2017). [37] Lull (1991), p. 88. [38] Repnikova (2017).

[39] Zhu (2008), pp. 36–41.

[40] Given that China currently limits the overall imported content to 25%, we can estimate that the share of foreign programming is roughly similar to the one found in Yugoslavia, where the average proportion stood at 27.8%.

[41] Zhu (2008), pp. 99–100.

context appears to be having the desired effect on television culture, at least as far as its transnational features are concerned.

Sources on Vietnam and Cuba are more limited, but here, too, similar patterns emerge. In Vietnam, television remains owned by the party-state, but is financially independent, with most of its revenue coming from advertising.[42] In line with the commercial imperative, programming features a large proportion of entertainment genres and fiction, including serial drama, game shows, and talk shows based on global formats. Nonetheless, communist ideals are still espoused in programming, and individual preferences and achievements are still framed in the context of the common good, albeit often with nationalist rather than specifically socialist undertones. While popular entertainment promotes a consumerist lifestyle and individual entrepreneurship, it also emphasizes the need for individuals to take care of the community and endorses 'the old socialist ethos' where individuals can rely on state support for housing, education, and healthcare.[43] In fictional programming, too, communal concerns remain paramount, and TV serials are treated, by both producers and viewers, as 'pedagogical tools', with their educational significance seen as equally important as their entertainment value.[44] In line with the market state socialist template, Vietnamese television is also rather open on imports, but much as in China, foreign programming raised concerns about 'cultural pollution' coming from abroad, and the majority of foreign programming comes from countries in relative proximity such as China and South Korea, rather than from the West.[45]

In sum, the market state socialist model is clearly useful for the analysis of television systems and cultures in the surviving state socialist countries. Further comparisons with the historical experience of Yugoslav television, but possibly also with television in Hungary, where elements of market socialism were likewise relatively pronounced, could produce interesting results and serve as a basis for reflecting on the contribution of market socialist television culture to the longevity of communist rule.

Understanding Non-Democratic Media: The Value of Comparison and Cultural Analysis

In general terms, our analysis has arguably illustrated the benefits of comparison, particularly when studying non-democratic media. One can

[42] Nguyen-Thu (2016), p. 88. [43] Ibid. [44] Drummond (2003), p. 156.
[45] Thomas (2004).

be tempted to generalise from a single-country study also when analysing the media under democratic rule, but this tendency is even more pronounced when looking at non-democratic contexts and when focusing on media cultures, as opposed to media systems. Totalitarian politics is certainly not renowned for its openness to cultural creativity, and it is all too easy to assume that political systems hostile to dissent would tend to give rise to near-identical media cultures. Yet, as our analysis has shown, state socialist television cultures differed significantly on most of the dimensions examined here, which enabled us to consider why certain cultural features arose prominently in one context but were less pronounced or absent in another. As a result, we were able to identify several systemic and contextual features that can help explain the diversity of television cultures under communist rule, such as the transnational orientation and relative core-periphery positions of television systems, as well as contextual factors such as gender relations, the extent of secularization, the forms of ethnocultural diversity, and the trajectories of state- and nation-building. These factors can also serve as a starting point for explaining the diversity of non-democratic media cultures more generally.

Second, our analysis also highlights the importance of considering cultural aspects of mediated communication when studying non-democratic media. This may seem an obvious point by now: although work on non-democratic media still tends to privilege systemic as opposed to cultural aspects, research on cultural dimensions has certainly grown considerably in recent decades. In working on this book, we were struck repeatedly by the value of cultural analysis to understanding the societal impact of mediated communication. What proved particularly productive was the analysis of the most mundane aspects of media culture, those taken for granted, such as the organization of schedules and everyday viewing patterns, the proportions of different genres, the relative prominence of historical content, or the nature of fictional settings and plots. It is through studying and comparing these seemingly banal aspects, rather than the more obviously ideological messages engrained in the programmes, that we could isolate the distinctive elements of media culture under communist rule and identify its impact on everyday life.

Particularly useful in this respect was the parallel investigation of practices and beliefs (or routines and meanings) evident at the level of production, scheduling, and programming and at the level of audience reception and use. As we have shown, state socialist broadcasters may not have been particularly effective in inculcating audiences with communist beliefs, but they achieved remarkable successes in instituting new routines and rituals and thereby in aligning viewers' everyday lives with the communist agenda. Of course, this disjunction between practices and beliefs arises in every political context, whether democratic or not, but it is arguably particularly pronounced in non-democratic systems, where the opportunities for popular participation in setting the public agenda and influencing elite decisions are restricted. A key advantage of a parallel investigation of practices and beliefs, routines and meanings – especially in the context of everyday life – is the ability to eschew the dichotomies that often plague discussions about the media and audiences in non-democratic contexts: obedience and resistance, manipulation and dissidence, public quiescence and private resistance. By attending to the patterns of both practices and beliefs, and routines and meanings of media cultures, we should be in a better position to understand how the media in non-democratic contexts help create compliance and reproduce existing structures of power, while also contributing to their fragility.

Analytical Tools: Typologies and Dimensions

In comparative media research, it has become common to advance the comparative endeavour by developing typologies. In this book, we have developed a typology of state socialist media systems, and as shown previously, this typology can serve as a useful tool for the analysis of media systems in the surviving communist states. We would also hope that, read in conjunction with the bourgeoning literature on media systems beyond the Western world, our discussion of state socialist television systems and entangled varieties of modernity can help advance the mapping of media systems globally. In particular, we believe there is considerable mileage in approaching the global diversity of media systems from the vantage point of different forms of structural and functional differentiation, anchored in entangled varieties of modernity. As explained in Chapter 4, some of these varieties emphasize the autonomy of the media vis-à-vis the state or give primacy to their independence from the broader political field, and others stress their independence from the field of the economy or privilege freedom from religious authority. It is also important to acknowledge that different visions of modernity, and hence different media systems and cultures, should not be seen as isolated, but as mutually constitutive. To acknowledge these mutual influences, two further, interrelated dimensions of variation between media systems must be considered: their transnational orientation and their core-periphery position. Finally, local conditions and historical legacies should be taken into consideration, too, including technological and infrastructural developments, gender relations, ethnocultural composition, and others.

At several points in the process of writing, we considered the option of developing a typology of state socialist television cultures, but for various reasons, this proved counter-productive. First, the seven dimensions of comparison examined in the book did not map neatly onto one another: television cultures that appeared reasonably similar with respect to their involvement with public and private realms and their transnational orientation featured at opposite ends of the spectrum with regard to secularization and gendering. Of course, as one would expect based on the features of its hard-line television system, Soviet television culture was more suspicious of entertainment, imposed more restrictions on public deliberation, was somewhat less privatized and less open to influence from the West, and was more decidedly oriented towards the past. In contrast, Yugoslav television culture stood at the opposite end on many dimensions: it was somewhat more receptive to entertainment, more tolerant of public deliberation, more open to privatization, less prone to idealised depictions of community and family life, more dependent on imports, more open to transnational programming, and more present-oriented. Polish, Romanian, and East German TV culture mostly featured somewhere on the spectrum between the two extremes marked by the Soviet Union and Yugoslavia.

However, when looking at other dimensions, the patterns of variation were different. With regards to secularization, Yugoslav television was similar to Soviet and Romanian television and secularized to a greater degree than Polish and East German television. Likewise, with regards to gender, East German television appeared more liberal in its fictional representations than did Yugoslav television. Finally, due to the multinational character of their polities and the federalised broadcasting systems in both Yugoslavia and the Soviet Union, the television cultures in both countries shared traits that set them apart from the rest of the region: the conception of the public mission conceived of television as a means of transnational integration, the programmes and scheduling patterns included content from a range of republics, and the depictions of history varied as well. Our inability to construct clear-cut models of state socialist media cultures of course results in part from the high number of dimensions of variation examined in the book. Had we reduced our analysis from seven to four and only studied publicness, privatization, transnationalism, and temporal orientation, constructing a typology would have been more straightforward. But we felt such an approach would omit dimensions that were rather important for understanding the peculiarities of state socialist television cultures – and it would also leave us ill-equipped for studying the diversity of media cultures globally.

Due to this, we argue that dimensions of variation offer much more versatile analytical tools for global comparisons, as well as for examining change over time.[46] Our discussion of continuities and discontinuities between the state socialist and post-socialist television cultures in Eastern Europe provides an example of how these dimensions of variation can be applied in a longitudinal analysis. A quick look at some of the recent comparative literature on media cultures globally confirms that the dimensions travel well beyond Eastern Europe, too. Let us briefly illustrate this by looking at secularization. As noted in Chapter 2, several aspects of television culture can be considered when estimating the extent of secularization, from the amount and nature of explicitly religious programming to the temporal arrangements of TV schedules and viewing patterns. One particularly interesting area of comparison concerns the nature of authority as represented on television, and specifically the extent to which such authority is secular in character. In their comparative study of lifestyle television in Taiwan, India, China, and Singapore, Tania Lewis, Frank Martin, and Wanning Sun examine the phenomenon of 'spiritual advice TV', ranging from shows featuring astrologers to programmes on yoga, feng shui, meditation, and alternative medicine. This category of programming is particularly prominent in India and Taiwan but conspicuously absent in China where – in line with the country's secular politics – popular advice programmes are largely led by secular authorities such as health specialists, career advisors, marriage counsellors, but also fashion specialists and travel guides.[47] Spiritual advice programming also emerged as a prominent feature of Soviet television during the late 1980s, where Anatoly Kashpirovsky became a national celebrity thanks to

[46] This applies also in the analysis of media systems: while scholars using Hallin and Mancini's typology of Western media systems had only limited success in transporting the three models to other socio-historical contexts, the four dimensions appeared to travel better. See Hallin and Mancini (2012b).

[47] Lewis et al. (2016), pp. 126–195.

his 'TV seances', broadcast on state television, during which he purportedly healed and hypnotised his audience at a distance.[48] Arguably, in a context where traditional hierarchies of power and authority were crumbling as a result of changes initiated by Gorbachev's *perestroika*, television screens became open to a wide range of experts, including those whose authority was religious or spiritual in nature. The relative secularization of cultural authority on the small screen can thus be seen as a measure of the democratization of television cultures, but it also signals important shifts in the medium's relationship with truth – an aspect that is likely to attract greater scholarly scrutiny in the context of the changing status of truth in media landscapes globally.

Television Cultures, Digital Cultures, or Hybrid Media Cultures?

In the title of the book we intentionally refer to *media* cultures: even though our empirical focus was on television, the analytical framework we developed in the book is applicable to other media. This is most obvious in the case or television's elder broadcast sibling, radio, which in many ways provided a template for the development of television both in terms of its institutional development and with respect to its cultural forms and audience uses. But other media cultures, too – from those associated with film and print publications to those linked to mobile and digital media – can also be analysed and compared along the same dimensions of variation as television. The precise conceptualization of each dimension in relation to a specific medium, and the methods employed for analysis, will of course need adapting, but we hope that our initial discussion of each dimension as it pertains to television offers a sufficient basis for such adaptations to begin.

The current digital and mobile media environment offers a particularly interesting testing ground for our comparative framework. With the fast pace of change in this area, visions of epochal transformations provoked by the ubiquity of digital, mobile, and 'smart' devices abound. Most recently, the fast growing 'internet of things' – a network of everyday 'smart' objects able to send and receive data over the internet – has been credited with bringing about nothing less than a 'fourth revolution', one in which communication technologies act as powerful environmental forces capable of transforming reality, with profound consequences for both the private and the public domains.[49] This new media world has been

[48] Huxtable (2017). [49] Froldi (2014).

associated with the potential for empowering citizens and making governments more transparent but also has prompted concerns about privacy intrusion, commercial exploitation, and political manipulation.[50] In many ways, what we are witnessing is a yet another wave of captivating visions and fantasies that accompany the rise of every new technology and play an important role in shaping both the technology's public regulation and commercial applications, as well as its use in the context of everyday life, over the whole of its life-cycle.[51] Yet, it is important to resist the lure of these fantasies and in particular the temptation of seeing them either as accurate descriptions of the media world we live in or as reliable predictions of where current developments are heading. An empirical and comparative examination of actual media cultures that are shaping up around us can help ground these captivating visions and consider the extent to which they relate to reality.

In line with this, we argue that it is too early to abandon the analysis of television cultures. Internet penetration has of course been increasing rapidly around the world, along with video-on-demand services and the use of screen devices capable of transmitting television content, from smart phones to tablets. These changes have certainly dislodged traditional modes of television viewing and opened up opportunities for consuming television content in a variety of public and private contexts, at different times. In this sense, as Milly Buonanno argued, television viewing has become more like reading a book: people can watch it whenever and wherever they want.[52] Yet the extent to which media cultures have changed as a result of these technological changes or indeed seen a decisive shift from television to other types of digitally mediated content varies considerably both within and across countries. As Lewis, Martin, and Sun point out in the aforementioned study of television in Asia, narratives centred on the West often present television as 'a heritage form', but in many countries of South and East Asia the medium remains 'the most powerful and ubiquitous media form'.[53] Even in the West, television viewing time has continued to increase in the new millennium despite the parallel proliferation of digital and mobile media use.[54]

[50] Howard (2015).

[51] See Marvin (1999); Natale and Balbi (2014). For an application to domestic media technologies, including television, see Chambers (2016).

[52] Buonanno (2008), p. 69. [53] Lewis et al. (2016), p. 3.

[54] Donders, et al. (2016), p. 51.

It is possible, of course, that the demise of television – and especially traditional television viewing – is only a matter of time, not least because surveys among younger generations frequently highlight their eagerness to embrace new technological developments and abandon traditional television viewing – or even television as such – to a greater extent than older generations. Yet it is still early to ascertain with certainty whether these patterns among youth are an effect of generation or age: will the young 'digital natives' or even 'mobile natives' of today retain their media habits in the future, as they progress through the life cycle, move into a separate household, or establish a family? There are also clear signs that television is adapting fast, and rather successfully, to the new environment both by exploiting the new opportunities opened by digital technologies and by capitalising on its established strengths, including its audiovisual nature and its ability to broadcast events live to large and dispersed audiences. In the realm of television entertainment, content produced by traditional broadcasters still plays an important role but is often reaching audiences in video-on-demand form, either through catch-up TV services offered by broadcasters themselves or, increasingly, via subscription-based providers.[55] In the context of political communication, the televised coverage of elections as well as televised presidential candidate debates retain their position as key reference points in the communicative landscape, even though their significance cannot be understood without attending to the many forms of online communication that evolve in parallel through the 'second screen'.[56] Increasingly, then, television cannot be confined to the 'box in the corner', but operates as a 'non-site-specific medium' that spreads across a range of devices and platforms from the traditional TV set to mobile phones and tablets.[57]

In this sense, what we are witnessing is perhaps not so much a wholesale transition from television cultures to digital cultures, but rather the rise of a new kind of 'hybrid' media culture, which combines elements of both traditional, analogue broadcasting, and the newer digital and mobile technologies. By analogy with the hybrid media system as theorized by Andrew Chadwick,[58] this hybrid media culture arises from the competition and conflict between different media logics and is characterized by patterns of ideas and practice that are informed by both. For instance, while the accessibility of television content via a variety of screens has contributed to a partial 'de-domestication' of television

[55] Lotz (2014); Robinson (2017). [56] Vaccari et al. (2015).
[57] Bennett and Strange (2011). [58] Chadwick (2017).

viewing, the association between television and the safety and comfort of the home environment seems to persist, at least for some viewers.[59] Likewise, although the temporal arrangements of everyday television viewing have certainly changed as a result of technologies that allow audiences to customise their viewing rhythms depending on their own preferences and schedules, the traditional mode of viewing of broadcast content according to a pre-scheduled flow retains its attractions as well.[60] Another example of hybridization is provided by the seemingly endless opportunities for the rebroadcasting, adaptation, and reassembly of television content on-line – a trend reliant on the capacity of the internet to serve as a quasi-archive, with important consequences for the temporal orientation of contemporary media cultures.[61] More importantly, even if this hybrid media culture is merely transitory in nature and will eventually give way to a world of more fully fledged digital media cultures in which the notion of television becomes obsolete, the same questions will apply about the embeddedness of new communication devices in everyday practices, the temporal and spatial organization of their use, the provenance of content accessible through them, or the nature of depictions of history available therein. The dimensions of comparison introduced in this book should therefore retain their relevance for the comparative analysis of media cultures globally, regardless of technological infrastructure.

In sum, while much of this book concerns a media age and a media world that may seem far removed from contemporary media landscapes, both the substantive findings and the analytical approach we introduced remain relevant in the present. As we have seen, the market state socialist television system, as well as the distinct television culture it gave rise to – initially found in the context of socialist Yugoslavia – outlived the Cold War and offers a template for understanding the specificity of television in most of the surviving communist-led states. As one would expect, traces of state socialist television cultures also persist in post-socialist countries, despite the far-reaching transformation that the broadcast media have undergone since 1989. By analogy, we can also assume that Cold War legacies continue to shape media cultures in the West.[62] Above all, the analytical framework we developed in the book has, we believe, the capacity to travel well not only

[59] Tsekleves et al. (2011). [60] Gentikow (2010).
[61] E.g. Ernst (2012); Garde-Hansen et al. (2009).
[62] For a recent discussion of Cold War legacies in US journalism see Zelizer (2016).

across different social and historical contexts but also across different media forms. As such, it offers a good starting point for the comparative analysis of contemporary media cultures globally, including the distinctly hybrid media cultures arising in the wake of the most recent technological changes.

Methodological Appendix

Each of the seven dimensions of television cultures was analysed using a combination of sources and methods, as outlined in Chapter 2. This Methodological Appendix provides further detail on the procedures used for life-story interviews, schedule analysis, and serial fiction analysis.

LIFE-STORY INTERVIEWS

Sampling

A total of 161 interviews were conducted, between thirty and forty for each of the five countries covered in the analysis. In the case of former socialist federations which have disintegrated following the end of communist rule (Soviet Union and Yugoslavia), interviews were conducted in at least two successor countries (Russia, Ukraine, and Estonia; Croatia and Serbia). Interview participants were recruited using snowball sampling, starting with a diverse set of initial informants identified by the interviewers, all of whom had local contacts in respective countries. Efforts were made for the initial informants to be as diverse as possible to counteract selection biases. Nonetheless, the sample is skewed in favour of participants who are female, younger (born after 1945), and better educated (secondary education or more). All participants were based in urban centres at the time of the interview, although several of them were originally born in rural regions or provincial towns and migrated to urban centres in early adulthood. These sample characteristics were taken into account in the process of analysis and interpretation.

TABLE A.1 *Life-story interviews: sample structure*

	COHORT 1 Pre-socialist/ radio generation, born before 1945	COHORT 2 First socialist/ first TV generation, born 1945–1964	COHORT 3 Last socialist/ colour TV generation, born 1965–1975	TOTAL
East Germany	4 women 6 men	9 women 1 man	3 women 7 men	16 women 14 men
Poland	7 women 2 men	6 women 7 men	7 women 2 men	20 women 11 men
Romania	3 women 3 men	7 women 2 men	7 women 7 men	17 women 12 men
Soviet Union (Russia)	1 woman 1 man	7 women 2 men	2 women 2 men	10 women 5 men
Soviet Union (Estonia)	1 women 0 men	3 women 0 men	1 woman 0 men	5 women 0 men
Soviet Union (Ukraine)	0 women 1 man	1 woman 7 men	0 women 1 man	1 woman 9 men
Yugoslavia (Croatia)	4 women 1 man	3 women 3 men	4 women 4 men	11 women 8 men
Yugoslavia (Serbia)	5 women 3 men	3 women 3 men	3 women 5 men	11 women 11 men
TOTAL	25 women 17 men	39 women 25 men	27 women 28 men	91 women 70 men

Interview Protocol

Each interview lasted for an hour on average, took place in a private or semi-private location, and was audio-recorded. Each participant was interviewed individually, with three exceptions. In two cases, one of the participants recruited (from the oldest cohort) requested to be interviewed together with another family member, and in one case, a group of four particularly valuable participants had to be interviewed together due to lack of time. In all cases the added value of including these participants was deemed sufficient to outweigh the cost incurred in terms of representativeness. The interview protocol was divided into two parts, outlined as follows, preceded by an introduction and a brief set of biographical questions.

1. ***Introduction***: Brief introduction of the project, outline of the protocol, and informed consent.
2. ***Biographical Information***: Full name and year and place of birth; subsequent places of residence, if different; profession and educational background; parents and their professions.
3. ***Part One: Life-Story Component***
   a. What are your earliest memories of television? (Prompts: Can you remember when you first watched television? Can you remember your first television set? Did your family own a television set? When did you first acquire your own television set?
   b. Did you watch television alone or with others?
   c. How often did you watch television? At what time of day did you watch?
   d. Did you have any favourite programmes? (Prompts: Can you describe x to me? / What sort of programme was that? What was it about x that you liked? And in general did you prefer x kind of programmes?)
   e. What about your parents, what did they watch?
   f. Did your viewing habits change as you got older [went to university/started work/had a family]? Repeat questions as above for different life stages.
   g. Can you remember any major events you remember finding out about from television?
   h. Can you remember any of the 'stars' of television during socialism? (Prompt: Mention some of the actors that were popular)
   i. Did you watch or listen to any foreign media?
   j. Did you watch television on festive occasions [e.g. New Year, Labour Day, etc.]?
   k. Were there any changes in TV coverage after xxx [insert key event linked with the fall of communism]? (Prompts if yes: What sort of changes? Did you change your viewing habits because of that? Did you watch different things because of that? Prompts if no: Ask for clarification.)
   l. And how about in the early 1990s and later? Did you notice any changes then? (Prompts as above.)
4. ***Part Two: Clips***: In this part, several short clips of TV programmes were shown, one each for each of the following categories of programmes: news bulletin, popular children's programme, popular domestic series, popular imported series, popular historical

series, and popular programme from the late 1980s. For each clip, the interviewees were asked whether they remembered the show, and if they did remember, what they thought about it.

Interview Analysis

All interviews were transcribed and in some cases (Poland and Romania) also translated to facilitate comparative analysis. The qualitative data analysis software package QDA Miner was used to facilitate analysis. Interviews for each country were first analysed by individual researchers who were experts for the country concerned and fluent in the local language. The analysis followed a shared set of research questions aligned with the comparative analytical framework and specifically the dimensions of variation between television cultures identified in Chapter 2. Based on this, individual country reports were produced, which included several excerpts from interviews to illustrate characteristic patterns with respect to each of the research questions. The reports were then exchanged and served as the basis for comparative analysis. Where further questions arose as result of comparative analysis, a subsequent analysis of interview materials was conducted and incorporated into the final comparative overview.

TV SCHEDULES

Most of the schedule analysis featured in the book was based on a sample of schedules collected at five-year intervals, starting in 1960 and finishing in 1990. For each of the sampled years, the sample included the first full week in October (Monday to Sunday) and two major holidays celebrated across all five countries: 1 May (Labour Day) and 31 December (New Year's Eve). In addition, a smaller sample of TV schedules linked to selected disruptive media events was analysed (see Chapter 10). Sampled schedules were mostly derived from published TV guides. For cases where actual TV schedules departed from published versions – most notably in the case of disruptive events – other archival and secondary sources were used to ascertain the nature of actual TV programming at the time.

The schedules were analysed in a variety of ways and drawing on both qualitative and quantitative techniques. Qualitative techniques were used to identify characteristic scheduling techniques used for everyday programming as opposed to festive programming, as well as to establish the ways in which schedules were adapted during disruptive events (Chapters 8 and 10). Quantitative analysis was applied to the sample of schedules for a week in October, collected at five-year intervals. This was used to illustrate the growth of broadcast hours over time (Chapter 3) as well as to investigate the relative prominence of imported programming (Chapter 7) and the relative proportions of information, educational, cultural, and entertainment content (Chapter 5). For this purpose, the analysis recorded each scheduled TV programme and its duration, and coded its origin and genre, using the following coding scheme:

Programme origin:

- Domestic
- Imported from other socialist countries
- Imported from Western countries: Western Europe and North America, but also Australia and New Zealand
- Imported from elsewhere
- Unknown

Programme genre:

- Information and propaganda: All news and current affairs programming, including sports news and cultural news programmes (if they are explicitly marked as 'news' and form part of a news block), parades, political speeches;
- Education: Education programming including language education, 'TV school', most of children's and youth programming (except when explicitly marked as entertainment or fiction), documentary programming;
- Entertainment: Serial fiction, film, children's programming of an entertaining character (e.g. children's film, quiz, cartoon etc.), game shows and similar, variety shows, lotto, sports, popular and folk music;
- Culture: TV drama, opera, ballet, classical music and any other music programmes not explicitly marked as popular or folk, literary, poetry recitals and similar, TV drama, cultural magazines;
- Other: Programme announcements, advertising, rebroadcasting of foreign programming (unless detail of genre provided).

The schedules for each country were analysed by a coder proficient in the local language and closely familiar with the nature of historical programming for that country. To ensure the robustness of coding, intracoder reliability tests were conducted for a selection of countries (Yugoslavia, East Germany, and the Soviet Union) by the same coders, several months after the initial coding was completed, using a subset of fifty programmes for each country. Cohen's Kappa and Krippendorff's Alfa were chosen as indices, and the online tool ReCal was used to assist with the calculation. The scores were nearly perfect across the board, with only one score lower than 100 per cent, namely for genre for Yugoslavia (96%, κ=0.968, α=0.968). Given that the same coding protocol was applied for all countries it was decided that the initial coding results can be considered sufficiently reliable.

SERIAL FICTION

Serial fiction was analysed using a combination of quantitative and qualitative analysis. In the first step, all serial fiction broadcast in the five countries between 1960 and 1990 was recorded, using published or archival TV schedules. This covered all programmes broadcast by two main channels in each country. For the two federal countries, the analysis was limited to a selection of channels judged to be viewed by most of the population (the two main channels of Central Television in the Soviet Union, the two main channels of TV Belgrade, and TV Zagreb in Yugoslavia). For each serial programme broadcast, details were recorded about its scheduling, duration (in number of episodes), and origin, as specified in the TV schedules. For domestically produced programmes, aspects of content were coded as well, including social setting, plot type, and historical period. Information about these aspects was derived from programme descriptions available in TV guides, complemented by archival and secondary sources. For programme origin, the country of origin was initially recorded, and the data was then recoded relying on the coding scheme used for schedule analysis (detailed earlier) to enable comparison. Social setting, plot type, and historical period were coded using the following scheme:

Social setting

- Domestic settings: apartments and houses, holiday houses, peasant dwellings, collective apartments;
- Public settings: party organs, security organs, assemblies, courts, workplaces, battlefields, universities and schools, parks, concert halls, restaurants, pubs and cafes.

Plot type:

- Personal plots: narratives focused on love and intimate relationships, family themes, and relationships with friends and neighbours;
- Public plots: fighting internal or external enemies, labour, and student life.

Historical period:

- Historical: Early modern period and nineteenth century, pre-communist period, revolution to 1941 (Soviet Union only), World War I, World War II, post-World War II, historical progression (covering several historical periods)
- Contemporary
- Future (e.g. science fiction)

To acknowledge the multiplicity of settings and plots in serial fiction, two most prominent settings and two most prominent plots were identified for each series.

As with schedule analysis, serial dramas were analysed by a coder proficient in the local language and familiar with historical serial fiction for that country. An inter-coder reliability test was conducted based on randomly selected subsets of series (all twenty-eight series for Romania, fifty for other countries), coded by five reliability coders. The results indicate a good level agreement for all four variables. For programme origin, tests showed 100 per cent agreement for East Germany, Romania, Yugoslavia, and the Soviet Union, with Poland only slightly below (97%, κ=0.942, α=0.942). Solid results with coefficients above 0.80 were obtained also for setting for all five countries (East Germany 94%, κ=0.86, α=0.86; Poland 94%, κ=0.89, α=0.90; Romania 93%, κ=0.88, α=0.88; Soviet Union 88%, κ=0.83, α=0.83; Yugoslavia 90%, κ=0.83, α=0.83), for plot for four countries (East Germany 98%, κ=0.96, α=0.96; Poland 92%, κ=0.86, α=0.86; Romania 93%, κ=0.88, α=0.88; Yugoslavia 86%, κ=0.80, α=0.80) and for historical period for all five countries (East Germany 100%, κ=1, α=1; Poland 90%, κ=0.87, α=0.87; Romania 93%, κ=0.88, α=0.88; Soviet Union 88%, κ=0.85, α=0.85; Yugoslavia 96%, κ=0.94, α=0.94). The only lower level of agreement was for plot for the Soviet Union (84%, κ=0.72, α=0.72). The latter was due to misunderstandings arising from the second coder's lack of specialist knowledge. The results obtained by the first coder were therefore judged to be sufficiently reliable.

For qualitative analysis, a small subset of serial dramas was chosen for each country. To examine representations of privacy (Chapter 6), a selection of series set exclusively in domestic settings was chosen, from different periods. To investigate depictions of history (Chapter 9), five prominent series set during World War II were selected. The chosen programmes were examined using narrative analysis techniques, focussing on the plot and characters, as well as the choice and depiction of different settings.

References

Primary Sources – Archives (for abbreviations, see List of Abbreviations of Archival Sources)

Archive of Croatian Radiotelevision, Zagreb, Croatia
Archives of Yugoslavia, Belgrade, Serbia
Romanian Television Media Archive, Bucharest, Romania
The National Archives of Romania, Bucharest, Romania
German Broadcasting Archive, Potsdam-Babelsberg, Germany
Photo Collection of the National Film Archive, Warsaw, Poland
Fortepan Online Photo Archive, Hungary
State Archive of the Russian Federation
Croatian State Archives, Zagreb, Croatia
National Digital Archives, Poland
National Archives and Records Administration, Washington, DC, USA
Russian State Archive of Literature and Art
Russian State Archive of Contemporary History
Radio Television of Serbia, Center for Public Opinion, Programme and Audience Research, Belgrade, Serbia
Radio Television of Serbia, Programme Archives of Television Belgrade, Belgrade, Serbia
Foundation Archives of Parties and Mass Organizations of the GDR in the Federal Archives, Berlin, Germany
Center for Preservation of Records of Socio-Political History of Moscow – Holdings from the former Central Archive of Social-Political History of Moscow, Moscow, Russia
Archive of Reports, Center for Public Opinion and Broadcasting Research, Warsaw, Poland.

Primary Sources – Periodicals

Antena
Govorit i pokazyvaet Moskva

Kommunist
Radio i Telewizja
Sovetskoe radio i televidenie
Studio
Tsentral'noe televidenie
TV Novosti
Godišnjak Jugoslovenske radiotelevizije

Primary Sources – Other

Alekseev, S. S. 1954. *Inter'er zhilogo doma. Sbornik statei.* Moscow: Gosudarstvennoe izdatel'stvo literatury po stroitel'stvu i arkhitekture.

Ceauşescu, Nicolae. 1984. *Romania pe Drumul Constructiei Societatii Socialiste Multilateral Dezvoltate. Rapoarte, Cuvintari, Interviuri, Articole. Vol. 26: May 1971–Februarie 1972.* Bucharest: Ed. Politica.

Lenin, Vladimir Ilyich. 1961. *Collected Works.* Moscow: Progress Publishers.

Merzhanov, B. M., and K. F. Sorokin. 1966. *Eto nuzhno novoselam.* Moscow: Ekonomika.

Mikulicz, Sergiusz. 1971. 'Współpraca z Zagranicą,' in *Z Anteny PR i Ekranu TV.* Warsaw: Wydawnictwa Radia i Telewizji.

Pijanowski, Lech. 1968. *Telewizja na co dzień.* Warsaw: Wydawnictwo Związkowe CRZZ.

Secondary Sources

Abelman, Robert, and Stewart M. Hoover, eds. 1990. *Religious Television: Controversies and Conclusions.* Norwood: Ablex Publishing.

Abramson, Albert. 1987. *The History of Television, 1880–1941.* Jefferson: McFarland.

Abramson, Albert. 1995. *Zworykin, Pioneer of Television.* Champaign: University of Illinois Press.

Abu-Lughod, Lila. 2005. *Dramas of Nationhood: The Politics of Television in Egypt.* Chicago: The University of Chicago Press.

Alexandru, Anca. 2009. 'The Role of Romanian Movies and Education in the "Genesis" of the New Man.' *Sfera Politicii* 135 (2009): 68–74.

Allen, Robert C. 1989. 'Bursting Bubbles: "Soap Opera", Audiences, and the Limits of a Genre.' In *Remote Control: Television, Audiences, and Cultural Power*, edited by Ellen Seiter, Hans Borchers, Gabriele Kreutzner, and Eva-Maria Warth, 44–55. London: Routledge.

Allen, Robert C., ed. 1995. *To Be Continued ... Soap Operas around the World.* London: Routledge.

Ames, Melissa, ed. 2012. *Time in Television Narrative: Exploring Temporality in Twenty-First-Century Programming.* Jackson: University Press of Mississippi.

Ang, Ien. 2005 [1982]. *Watching Dallas: Soap Opera and the Melodramatic Imagination.* Translated by Della Couling. London: Routledge.

Arnason, Johann P. 2000. 'Communism and Modernity.' *Daedalus* 129 (1): 61–90.

Arnason, Johann P. 2003. 'Entangled Communisms: Imperial Revolutions in Russia and China.' *European Journal of Social Theory* 6 (3): 307–325.

Arnason, Johann P. 2005. 'Alternating Modernities: The Case of Czechoslovakia.' *European Journal of Social Theory* 8 (4): 435–451.

Badenoch, Alec W., Andreas Fickers, and Christian Heinrich-Franke, eds. 2013. *Airy Curtains in the European Ether: Broadcasting and the Cold War*. Baden Baden: Nomos Verlag.

Baiburin, Albert, and Alexandra Piir. 2011. 'When We Were Happy: Remembering Soviet Holidays.' In *Petrified Utopia. Happiness Soviet Style*, edited by Maria Balina and Evgeny Dobrenko, 161–186. London: Anthem Press.

Bajomi-Lázár, Péter. 2014. *Party Colonisation of the Media in Central and Eastern Europe*. Budapest: CEU University Press.

Balina, Marina, and Evgeny Dobrenko, eds. 2011. *Petrified Utopia: Happiness Soviet Style*. London: Anthem Press.

Bardan, Alice. 2013. 'Big Brother and Little Brothers: National Identity in Recent Romanian Adaptations of Global Formats.' In *Popular Television in Eastern Europe during and since Socialism*, edited by Anikó Imre, Timothy Havens, and Katalin Lustyik, 177–198. London: Routledge.

Barker, Martin, and Ernest Mathijs. 2008. *Watching 'The Lord of the Rings': Tolkien's World Audiences*. New York: Peter Lang.

Barnhurst, Kevin G., and Diana C. Mutz. 1997. 'American Journalism and the Decline on Event-Centered Reporting.' *Journal of Communication* 47 (4): 27–53.

Bashkirova, Elena I. 2010. 'The Foreign Radio Audience in the USSR during the Cold War: An Internal perspective.' In *Cold War Broadcasting: Impact on the Soviet Union and Eastern Europe: A Collection of Studies and Documents*, edited by A. Ross Johnson and R. Eugene Parta, 103–141. Budapest: Central European University Press.

Bathrick, David. 1995. *The Powers of Speech: The Politics of Culture in the GDR*. Lincoln: University of Nebraska Press.

Bauman, Zygmunt. 1989. *Modernity and the Holocaust*. Ithaca: Cornell University Press.

Beck, Ulrich, and Daniel Levy. 2013. 'Cosmopolitanized Nations: Re-Imagining Collectivity in World Risk Society.' *Theory, Culture & Society* 30 (2): 3–31.

Bell, Erin, and Ann Gray, eds. 2010. *Televising History: Mediating the Past in Postwar Europe*. Basingstoke: Palgrave Macmillan.

Ben-Ghiat, Ruth. 2004. *Fascist Modernities: Italy, 1922–1945*. Berkeley: University of California Press.

Bennett, Andrew, and Colin Elman. 2006. 'Complex Causal Relations and Case Study Methods: The Example of Path Dependence.' *Political Analysis* 14 (3): 250–267.

Bennett, James, and Niki Strange, eds. 2011. *Television as Digital Media*. Durham: Duke University Press.

Berendt, Ivan T. 2009. *From the Soviet Bloc to the European Union: The Economic and Social Transformation of Central and Eastern Europe since 1973*. Cambridge: Cambridge University Press.

Bernhard, Michael, and Jan Kubik, eds. 2014. *Twenty Years after Communism: The Politics of Memory and Commemoration*. Oxford: Oxford University Press.

Berry, David. 2004. *The Romanian Mass Media and Cultural Development*. London: Routledge.

Betts, Paul. 2010. *Within Walls: Private Life in the German Democratic Republic*. Oxford: Oxford University Press.

Bloch, Kinga. 2013. 'The Life and Afterlife of a Socialist Media Friend: On the Long-Term Cultural Relevance of the Polish TV Series *Czterdziestolatek*.' *VIEW: Journal of European Television History and Culture* 2 (3): 88–98.

Blumler, Jay. 1992. *Television and the Public Interest: Vulnerable Values in Western European Broadcasting*. London: Sage.

Blumler, Jay G., and Michael Gurevitch. 1995 [1975]. *The Crisis of Public Communication*. London: Routledge.

Bobbio, Norberto. 1992. *Democracy and Dictatorship: The Nature and Limits of State Power*. Cambridge: Polity.

Boddy, William. 2004. *New Media and Popular Imagination: Launching Radio, Television, and Digital Media in the United States*. Oxford: Oxford University Press.

Boia, Lucian. 2001. *History and Myth in Romanian Consciousness*. Budapest: Central European University Press.

Bondebjerg, Ib, Tomasz Goban Klas, Michele Hilmes, Dana Mustata, Helle Strandgaard-Jensen, Isabelle Veyrat-Masson, and Susanne Vollber. 2008. 'American Television: Point of Reference or European Nightmare?' In *A European Television History*, edited by Jonathan Bignell and Andreas Fickers, 154–183. Oxford: Wiley-Blackwell.

Bönker, Kirsten, Julia Obertreis, and Sven Grampp, eds. 2016. *Television Beyond and Across the Iron Curtain*. Newcastle: Cambridge Scholars Publishing.

Bošnjaković, Mate. 1984. *Kulturna funcija televizije*. Zagreb: Zavod za kulturu Hrvatske

Bourdieu, Pierre. 1984. *Distinction: A Social Critique of the Judgement of Taste*. Translated by Richard Nice. Cambridge: Harvard University Press.

Bourdon, Jérôme. 2000. 'Live Television is Still Live: On Television as an Unfulfilled Promise.' *Media, Culture & Society* 22 (5): 531–665.

Bourdon, Jérôme. 2003. 'Some Sense of Time: Remembering Television.' *History and Memory* 15 (2): 5–35.

Bourdon, Jérôme. 2011. *Du service public à la télé-réalité: Une histoire culturelle des télévisions européennes*. Paris: INA.

Brabazon. Tara. 2008. 'Christmas and the Media.' In *Christmas, Ideology and Popular Culture*, edited by Sheila Whiteley, 149–163. Edinburgh: Edinburgh University Press.

Bracke, Maud Anne, and James Mark, eds. 2015. 'Between Decolonisation and the Cold War: Transnational Activism and Its Limits in Europe 1950s–1990s,' special issue, *Journal of Contemporary History* 50 (3): 3–17.

Brants, Kees, and Els De Bens. 2000. 'The Status of TV Broadcasting in Europe.' In *Television across Europe*, edited by Jan Wieten, Graham Murdock, and Peter Dahlgren, 7–22. London: Sage.

Bren, Paulina. 2010. *The Greengrocer and His TV: The Culture of Communism after the 1968 Prague Spring*. Ithaca: Cornell University Press.

Bringa, Tone. 2004. 'The Death of Tito and the End of Yugoslavia.' In *Death of the Father: An Anthropology of the End in Political Authority*, edited by John Borneman, 148–200. New York and Oxford: Berghahn, pp. 148–200.

Brkljačić, Maja. 2003. 'Tito's Bodies in Word and Image.' *Narodna umjetnost* 40 (1): 99–127.

Browning, Cristopher S. 2002. 'Coming Home or Moving Home? 'Westernizing' Narratives in Finnish Foreign Policy and the Reinterpretation of Past Identities.' *Cooperation and Conflict: Journal of the Nordic International Studies Association* 37 (1): 47–72.

Brunsdon, Charlotte. 1997. *Screen Tastes: Soap Opera to Satellite Dishes*. London: Routledge.

Buck-Morss, Susan. 2002. *Dreamworld and Catastrophe: The Passing of Mass Utopia in East and West*. Cambridge: MIT Press.

Bucur, Maria. 2006. 'Women's Stories as Sites of Memory: Gender and Remembering Romania's World Wars.' In *Gender and War in Twentieth Century Eastern Europe*, edited by Nancy M. Wingfield and Maria Bucur, 171–192. Bloomington: Indiana University Press.

Bucur, Maria. 2009. *Heroes and Victims: Remembering War in Twentieth-Century Romania*. Bloomington: Indiana University Press.

Buonanno, Milly. 2008. *The Age of Television: Experiences and Theories*. Bristol: Intellect.

Burbank, Jane. 1995. 'Lenin and the Law in Revolutionary Russia.' *Slavic Review* 54 (1): 23–44.

Burns, Russell W. 1998. *Television: An International History of the Formative Years*. London: Institution of Electrical Engineers.

Butler Breese, Elizabeth. 2011. 'Mapping the Variety of Public Spheres.' *Communication Theory* 21 (2): 130–149.

Chadwick, Andrew. 2017. *The Hybrid Media System: Politics and Power*, 2nd edn. Oxford: Oxford University Press.

Chakars, Melissa. 2015. 'Flowers, Steppe Fires, and Communists: Images of Modernity and Identity on TV Shows from Soviet Buryatia in the Brezhnev Era.' In *Modernization, Nation-Building, and Television History*, edited by Stewart Anderson and Melissa Chakars, 147–164. London: Routledge.

Chalaby, Jean K. 1996. 'Journalism as an Anglo-American Invention: A Comparison of the Development of French and Anglo-American Journalism, 1830s–1920s.' *European Journal of Communication* 11 (3): 303–326.

Chalaby, Jean K., ed. 2005. *Transnational Television Worldwide: Towards a New Media Order*. London: I. B. Tauris.

Chambers, Deborah. 2011. 'The Material Form of the Television Set: A Cultural History.' *Media History* 17 (4): 359–375.

Chambers, Deborah. 2016. *Changing Media, Homes and Households: Culture, Technologies and Meanings*. London: Routledge.

Chen, Guo-Ming. 2007. 'Asian Communication Studies: What and Where to Now.' *Review of Communication* 6 (4): 259–311.

Cheng, Yinghong. 2009. *Creating the New Man: From Enlightenment Ideals to Socialist Realities*. Honolulu: University of Hawai'i Press.

Ciontu, Andrei and Mihai Gheorghe. 2012. '50 de ani de la fabricarea primului televizor in Romania.' Noema 11 (3): 289–291.

Clark-Ibáñez, Marisol. 2004. 'Framing the Social World with Photo-Elicitation Interviews.' *American Behavioral Scientist* 47 (12): 1507–1527.

Collier, David. 1993. 'The Comparative Method.' In *Political Science: The State of the Discipline II*, edited by Ada W. Finifter, 105–119. Washington, DC: American Political Science Association.

Collins, Richard. 1992. *Satellite Television in Western Europe*, London: John Libbey.

Corin, Chris, ed. 1992. *Superwomen and the Double Burden: Women's Experience of Change in Central and Eastern Europe and the former Soviet Union*. London: Scarlet Press.

Corner, John. 2000. *Critical Ideas in Television Studies*. Oxford: Oxford University Press.

Cottle, Simon. 2006. 'Mediatized Rituals: Beyond Manufacturing Consent.' *Media, Culture & Society* 28 (3): 411–432.

Couldry, Nick. 2003. *Media Rituals: A Critical Approach*. London: Routledge.

Couldry, Nick, and Andreas Hepp. 2012. 'Comparing Media Cultures.' In *The Handbook of Comparative Communication Research*, edited by Frank Esser and Thomas Hanitzsch, 249–261. London: Routledge.

Couldry, Nick, and Andreas Hepp. 2013. 'Conceptualizing Mediatization: Context, Traditions, Arguments.' *Communication Theory* 23 (3): 191–202.

Creeber, Glen. 2001. '"Taking our Personal Lives Seriously": Intimacy, Continuity and Memory in the Television Drama Serial.' *Media, Culture & Society* 23 (4): 439–455.

Creeber, Glen. 2004. *Serial Television: Big Drama on the Small Screen*. London: British Film Institute.

Cretu, Virginia. 1980. *Educatia elevilor prin film si pentru film*. Bucharest: Editura Didactica si Pedagogica.

Crisell, Andrew. 1997. *An Introductory History of British Broadcasting*. London: Routledge.

Cronquist, Marie. 2014. 'Entangled Television Histories: Sweden and the GDR, 1969–1989.' Paper presented at the conference 'Media and the Cold War, 1975–1991,' Volda, Norway, 20–22 November 2014.

Cucu-Oancea, Ozana. 2005. 'Anihilarea unei sarbatori, 'faurirea' unei festivitati. Sarbatorile de iarna reflectate in presa vremii (1945–1989).' *Sociologie Romaneasca* 3 (3): 158–174.

Čulík, Jan. 2013. 'The Construction of Reality in Communist and Post-Communist Czech TV Serials.' In *National Mythologies in Central European TV Series: How J. R. Won the Cold War*, edited by Jan Čulík, 110–154. Brighton: Sussex Academic Press.

Curran, James, and Myung-Jin Park, eds. 2000. *De-Westernizing Media Studies*. London: Routledge.

Curry, Jane. 1990. *Poland's Journalists: Professionalism and Politics*. Cambridge: Cambridge University Press.

Daković, Nevena, and Aleksandra Milovanović. 2016. 'The Socialist Family Sitcom: Theatre at Home (Socialist Federal Republic of Yugoslavia, 1974 – Republic of Serbia, 2007).' In *Television beyond and across the Iron Curtain*, edited by Kirsten Bönker, Julia Obertreis, and Sven Grampp, 124–147. Newcastle: Cambridge Scholars Publishing.

David-Fox, Michael. 2012. *Showcasing the Great Experiment: Cultural Diplomacy and Western Visitors to the Soviet Union, 1921–1941*. Oxford: Oxford University Press.

David-Fox, Michael. 2015. *Crossing Borders: Modernity, Ideology, and Culture in Soviet Russia*. Pittsburgh: University of Pittsburgh Press.

David-Fox, Michael, Peter Holquist, and Alexander Martin, eds. 2012. *Fascination and Enmity: Russia and Germany as Entangled Histories, 1914–1945*. Pittsburgh: University of Pittsburgh Press.

Dawson, Charles C. 1989. 'TV Programming Trends in Europe in the Mid-1980s: The Beginnings of East-West Exchange.' In *Europe Speaks to Europe: International Information Flows between Eastern and Western Europe*, edited by Jörg Becker and Tamás Szecskö, 57–69. Oxford: Pergamon.

Dayan, Daniel, and Elihu Katz. 1992. *Media Events: The Live Broadcasting of History*. Cambridge: Harvard University Press.

de Albuquerque, Afonso. 2012. 'On Models and Margins: Comparative Media Models Viewed from a Brazilian Perspective.' In *Comparing Media Systems beyond the Western World*, edited by Daniel Hallin and Paolo Mancini, 72–95. Cambridge: Cambridge University Press.

de Vreese, Claes H., Jochen Peter, and Holli A. Semetko. 2001. 'Framing Politics at the Launch of the Euro: A Cross-National Comparative Study of Frames in the News.' *Political Communication* 18 (2): 107–122.

Deacon, David, and James Stanyer. 2014. 'Mediatization: Key Concept or Conceptual Bandwagon?' *Media, Culture & Society* 36 (7): 1032–1044.

Deacon, David, Michael Pickering, Graham Murdock, and Peter Golding. 2007. *Researching Communications: A Practical Guide to Methods in Media and Cultural Analysis*, 2nd edn. London: Bloomsbury Academic.

Delanty, Gerard. 2016. 'Multiple Europes, Multiple Modernities: Conceptualising the Plurality of Europe.' *Comparative European Politics* 14 (4): 398–416.

Deletant, Dennis. 1995. *Ceauşescu and the Securitate: Coercion and Dissent in Romania, 1965–1989*. Armonk: M. E. Sharpe.

Dhoest, Alexander. 2015. 'Audience Retrospection as a Source of Historiography: Oral History Interviews on Early Television Experiences.' *European Journal of Communication* 30 (1): 64–78.

Dillon, Robert. 2010. *History on British Television: Constructing Nation, Nationality and Collective Memory*. Manchester: Manchester University Press.

Dirlik, Arif. 2003. 'Global Modernity? Modernity in an Age of Global Capitalism.' *European Journal of Social Theory* 6 (3): 275–292.

Dittmar, Claudia. 2004. 'GDR Television in Competition with West German Programming.' *Historical Journal of Film, Radio and Television* 24 (3): 327–343.

Dittmar, Claudia. 2005. 'Television and Politics in the Former East Germany.' *CLCWeb: Comparative Literature and Culture* 7 (4): 1–9.

Dittmar, Claudia. 2007. 'Ostdeutsches 'Westfernsehen': Das Projekt 'Deutschland-Fernsehen' in der DDR 1958 bis 1964.' In *Zwischen Experiment und Etablierung. Die Programmentwicklung des DDR-Fernsehens 1958 bis 1963*, edited by Claudia Dittmar and Susanne Vollberg, 215–271. Leipzig: Leipziger Universitätsverlag.

Dittmar, Claudia. 2010. Feindliches Fernsehen: Das DDR-Fernsehen und seine Strategien in Umgang mit dem westdeutschen Fernsehen. Bielefeld: Transcript.

Dizard, Wilson P. 1966. *Television: A World View*. Syracuse: Syracuse University Press.

Dobbs, Michael. 1996. *Down with Big Brother: The Fall of the Soviet Empire*. London: Bloomsbury.

Dobek-Ostrowska, Bogusława. 2015. '25 Years after Communism: Four Models of Media and Politics in Central and Eastern Europe.' In *Democracy and Media in Central and Eastern Europe 25 Years On*, edited by Bogusława Dobek Ostrowska and Michał Głovacki, 11–46. Frankfurt: Peter Lang.

Dobek-Ostrowska, Bogusława, Karol Jakubowicz, Michal Głowacki, and Miklós Sükösd. 2010. *Media Systems East and West: How Different, How Similar*. Budapest: Central University Press.

Donders, Karen, Caroline Pauwels, and Jan Losen, eds. 2016. *Private Television in Western Europe: Contents, Markets, Policies*. Basingstoke: Palgrave.

Dönninghaus, Victor, and Andrei Savin. 2014. 'Leonid Brezhnev: Public Display Versus the Sacrality of Power.' *Russian Studies in History* 52 (4): 71–93.

Downey, John, and Sabina Mihelj, eds. 2012. *Central and Eastern European Media in Comparative Perspective: Politics, Economy Culture*. Aldershot: Ashgate.

Downey, John, Sabina Mihelj, and Thomas König. 2012. 'Comparing Public Spheres: Normative Models and Empirical Measurements.' *European Journal of Communication* 27 (4): 337–353.

Drummond, Lisa B. W. 2003. 'Popular Television and Images of Urban Life.' In *Consuming Urban Culture in Contemporary Vietnam*, edited by Lisa B.W. Drummond and Mandy Thomas, 155–169. London Routledge Curzon.

Duda, Igor. 2015. *Danas kada postajem pionir: Djetinjstvo i ideologija jugoslavenskoga socijalizma*. Zagreb: Srednja Europa.

Duda, Igor. 2016. 'When Capitalism and Socialism Get Along Best: Tourism, Consumer Culture, and the Idea of Progress in *Malo misto*.' In *Social Inequalities and Discontent in Yugoslav Socialism*, edited by Rory Archer, Igor Duda, and Paul Stubbs, 173–192. London: Routledge.

Dupagne, Michel, and David Waterman. 1998. 'Determinants of U.S. Television Fiction Imports in Western Europe.' *Journal of Broadcasting & Electronic Media*, 42 (2): 208–220.

Durkheim, Émile. 1984 [1893]. *The Division of Labour in Society*. Translated by W. D. Halls. Basingstoke: Palgrave Macmillan.

Dushechkina, Elena. 2003. 'Ded Moroz i Snegurochka.' *Otechestvennye zapiski* 1. Available online: http://magazines.russ.ru/oz/2003/1/2003_01_31.html.

Edelman, Robert. 2013. 'Playing Catch-Up: Soviet Media and Soccer Hooliganism, 1965–1975.' In *The Socialist Sixties: Crossing Borders in the Second World*, edited by Anne Gorsuch and Diane Koenker, 268–286. Bloomington: Indiana University Press.

Edgerton, Gary R., and Peter C. Rollins, eds. 2001.*Television Histories: Shaping Collective Memory in the Media Age*. Lexington: University Press of Kentucky.

Egorov, V., and V. Kisun'ko. 2001. 'Razvitie i stagnatsiia sovetskogo televideniia, 1970–1985 g.g.' in *TVMuseum.ru*. Available online: www.tvmuseum.ru/catalog.asp?ob_no=4624.

Eisenstadt, Shmuel N. 1974. 'Studies of Modernization and Sociological Theory.' *History and Theory* 13 (13): 225–52.

Eisenstadt, Shmuel N. 2000. 'Multiple Modernities.' *Daedalus* 129 (1): 1–29.

Eisenstein, Elizabeth L. 1979. *The Printing Press and an Agent of Change: Communications and Cultural Transformations in Early Modern Europe*. Cambridge: Cambridge University Press.

Ellis, John. 1982. *Visible Fictions: Cinema, Television*. Video. London: Routledge.

Ellis, John. 2000. *Seeing Things: Television in the Age of Uncertainty*. London: I. B. Tauris.

Engelmann-del Mestre, Frank. 2013. 'Agitprop Gone Wrong: Der Schwarze Kanal.' In *Popular Television in Authoritarian Europe*, edited by Peter Goddard, 159–175. Manchester: Manchester University Press.

Erdei, Ildiko. 2015. 'Kombinovana soba.' In *Made in YU*, edited by Tanja Petrović and Jernej Mlekuž, 107–117. Ljubljana: Založba ZRC.

Erdei, Ildiko. 2017. 'Fragmenti jugosloveske socijalističke modernosti 1970-ih u TV seriji "Pozorište u kući".' *Issues in Ethnology and Anthropology* 12 (2): 537–563.

Ernst, Wolfgang. 2012. *Digital Memory and the Archive*. Minneapolis: University of Minnesota Press.

Esser, Frank. 1999. ' "Tabloidization" of News: A Comparative Analysis of Anglo-American and German Press Journalism.' *European Journal of Communication* 14 (3): 291–324.

Esser, Frank. 2013. 'The Emerging Paradigm of Comparative Communication Enquiry: Advancing Cross-National Research in Times of Globalization.' *International Journal of Communication* 7: 113–128.

Esser, Frank, and Thomas Hanitzsch, eds. 2012. *The Handbook of Comparative Communication Research*. London: Routledge.

Estrin, Saul. 1991. 'Yugoslavia: The Case of Self-Managing Market Socialism.' *Journal of Economic Perspectives* 5 (4): 187–194.

Eugster, Ernest. 1983. *Television Programming across National Boundaries: The EBU and OIRT Experience*. Dedham: Artech House.

Evans, Christine. 2016. *Between Truth and Time: A History of Soviet Central Television*. New Haven: Yale University Press.

Ferree, Myra M., William A. Gamson, Jürgen Gerhards, and Dieter Rucht. 2002. 'Four Models of the Public Sphere in Modern Democracies.' *Theory and Society* 31 (3):289–324.

Fickers, Andreas. 2013. 'Cold War Techno-Diplomacy: Selling French Colour Television to the Eastern Bloc.' In *Airy Curtains in the European Ether: Broadcasting and the Cold War*, edited by Alexander Badenoch, Andreas Fickers, and Christian Heinrich-Franke, 77–100. Baden-Baden: Nomos Verlag.

Fickers, Andreas, and Catherine Johnson, eds. 2012. *Transnational Television History: A Comparative Approach*. London: Routledge.

Fiedler, Anke, and Michael Meyen. 2015. 'The Totalitarian Destruction of the Public Sphere? Newspapers and Structures of Public Communication in Socialist Countries: The Example of the German Democratic Republic.' *Media, Culture & Society* 37 (6): 834–849.

Field, Deborah A. 2007. *Private Life and Communist Morality in Khrushchev's Russia*. New York: Peter Lang.

Field, Deborah. 2015. 'Everyday Life and the Problem of Conceptualizing Public and Private during the Khrushchev Era.' In *Everyday Life in Russia Past and Present*, edited by Choi Chatterjee, David Ransel, Mary Cavender, and Karen Petrone, 163–180. Bloomington: Indiana University Press.

Figes, Orlando. 2007. *The Whisperers: Private Life in Stalin's Russia*. Harmondsworth: Penguin.

Filimon, Monica Elena. 2011. *Divide, Conquer, Entertain: Film Melodrama and Authoritarianism in Europe*. Unpublished PhD Thesis, the State University of New Jersey.

Fischer, Joerg-Uwe. 2001. 'Fernsehzentrum Berlin/Deutscher Fernsehfunk/ Fernsehen der DDR 1952–1991.' In *Das Schriftgut des DDR-Fernsehens: Eine Bestandsübersicht*, 13–20. Frankfurt: Deutsches Runfunksarchiv.

Fitzpatrick, Sheila. 1992. *The Cultural Front: Power and Culture in Revolutionary Russia*. Ithaca: Cornell University Press.

Fitzpatrick, Sheila. 1996. 'Supplicants and Citizens: Public Letter-Writing in Soviet Russia in the 1930s.' *Slavic Review* 55 (1): 78–105.

Fleischauer, Alexander. 2010. *Die Enkel fechten's besser aus: Thomas Müntzer und die Frühbürgerliche Revolution – Geschichtspolitik und Erinnerungskultur in der DDR*. Münster: Ascheundorff.

Froldi, Luciano. 2014. *The Fourth Revolution: How the Infosphere Is Transforming Human Reality*. Oxford: Oxford University Press.

Fulbrook, Mary. 2005. *The People's State: East German Society from Hitler to Honecker*. New Haven: Yale University Press.

Furet, François. 1999. *The Passing of an Illusion: The Idea of Communism in the Twentieth Century*. Translated by Deborah Furet. Chicago: The University of Chicago Press.

Furnham, Adrian, and Twiggy Mak. 1999. 'Sex-Role Stereotyping in Television Commercials: A Review and Comparison of Fourteen Studies Done on Five Continents Over 25 Years.' *Sex Roles* 41 (5): 413–437.

Gabrič, Aleš. 1995. *Socialistična kulturna revolucija: Slovenska kulturna politika, 1953–1962*. Ljubljana: Cankarjeva založba.

Galić, Roman. 1986. *Tehnički razvoj radija i televizije u Jugoslaviji, 1926–1986*. Zagreb: Školska knjiga.

Garcelon, Marc. 1997. 'The Shadow of the Leviathan: Public and Private in Communist and Post-Communist Society.' In *Public and Private in Thought and Practice*, edited by Jeff Weintraub and Krishan Kumar, 303–332. Chicago: Chicago University Press.

Garde-Hansen, Joanne, Andrew Hoskins, and Anna Reading, eds. 2009. *Save As … Digital Memories*. Basingstoke: Palgrave.

Gassert, Philipp. and Alan E. Steinweis, eds. 2006. *Coping with the Nazi Past: West German Debates on Nazism and Generational Conflict, 1955–1975*. Oxford: Berghahn.

Gaus, Günter. 1983. *Wo Deutschland liegt: Ein Ortebestimmung*. Hamburg: Hoffman und Campe.

Genette, Gerard. 1997. *Paratexts: Thresholds of Interpretation*. Cambridge: Cambridge University Press.

Gentikow, Barbara. 2010. 'Television Use in New Media Environments.' In *Relocating Television: Television in the Digital Context*, edited by Jostein Gripsrud, 141–155. London: Routledge.

Geraghty, Christine. 1981. 'Continuous Serial: A Definition.' In *Coronation Street*, edited by Richard Dyer, Christine Geraghty, Marion Jordan, Terry Lovell, Richard Paterson, and John Stewart, 9–26. London: British Film institute.

Geraghty, Christine. 1991. *Women and Soap Opera: A Study of Prime Time Soaps*. Cambridge: Polity.

Gerasimova, Ekaterina. 2002. 'Public Privacy in the Soviet Communal Apartment.' In *Socialist Spaces: Sites of Everyday Life in the Eastern Bloc*, edited by David Crowley and Susan E. Reid, 207–230. Oxford: Berg.

Giddens, Anthony. 1990. *The Consequences of Modernity*. Cambridge: Polity.

Gilman, Nils. 2007. *Mandarins of the Future: Modernization Theory in Cold War America*. Baltimore: Johns Hopkins University Press.

Gillespie, Nick, and Matt Welch. 2008. 'How Dallas Won the Cold War.' *The Washington Post*, 27 April 2008, www.washingtonpost.com.

Glennie, Paul, and Nigel Thrift. 2009. *Shaping the Day: A History of Timekeeping in England and Wales, 1300–1800*. Oxford: Oxford University Press.

Goddard, Peter, ed. 2013. Popular Television in Authoritarian Europe. Manchester: Manchester University Press.

Golding, Peter, and Phil Harris, eds. 1996. *Beyond Cultural Imperialism: Globalization, Communication and the New International Order*. London: Sage.

Golubev, Alexey, and Olga Smolyak. 2013. 'Making Selves through Making Things: Soviet Do-It-Yourself Culture and Practices of Late Soviet Subjectivation.' *Cahiers du monde Russe* 54 (3–4): 517–541.

Goluža, Lazo, and Darko Novaković. 1990. *Kviskoteka: igra kvizova*. Zagreb: Grafički zavod Hrvatske.

Goody, Jack, and Ian Watt. 1963. 'The Consequences of Literacy.' *Comparative Studies in Society and History* 5 (3): 304–345.

Gorsuch, Anne, and Diane Koenker, eds. 2013. *The Socialist Sixties: Crossing Borders in the Second World*. Bloomington: Indiana University Press.

Gradišnik, Ingrid. 2015. 'A Festive Bricolage: The Holiday Calendar in Slovenia over the Last Century.' *Folklore: Electronic Journal of Folklore* 60: 29–50.

Gray, Ann, and Erin Bell. 2013. *History on Television*. London: Routledge.

Green, Nicola. 2002. 'On the Move: Technology, Mobility, and the Mediation of Social Time and Space.' *The Information Society* 18 (4): 281–292.

Griffin, Roger. 2007. *Modernism and Fascism: The Sense of a Beginning under Mussolini and Hitler*. Basingstoke: Palgrave Macmillan.

Großmann, Thomas. 2015. *Fernsehen, Revolution und das Ende der DDR*. Göttingen: Wallstein.

Grzelewska, Danuta, Rafal Habielski, Andrzej Koziel, Janusz Osica, Lidia Piwonska-Pukalo. 2001. *Prasa, Radio i telewizja w Polsce: Zarys Dziejow*. Warszawa: Elipsa.

Gudykunst, William B., and Bella Mody, eds. 2002. *Handbook of International and Intercultural Communication*. London: Sage.

Guerrero, Manuel Alejandro, and Mireya Márquez-Ramírez, eds. 2014. *Media Systems and Communication Policies in Latin America*. Basingstoke: Palgrave Macmillan.

Gumbert, Heather L. 2006. 'Split Screens? Television in East Germany, 1952–1989.' In *Mass Media, Culture and Society in Twentieth-Century Germany*, edited by Karl Christian Führer and Corey Ross, 146–164. Basingstoke: Palgrave Macmillan.

Gumbert, Heather L. 2014. *Envisioning Socialism: Television and the Cold War in the German Democratic Republic*. Ann Arbor: University of Michigan Press.

Gunter, Barrie, and Michael Svennevig. 1987. *Behind and in Front of the Screen: Television's Involvement with Family Life*. London: John Libbey and Co.

Habermas, Jürgen. 1989. *The Structural Transformation of the Public Sphere: An Inquiry into a Category of Bourgeois Society*. Translated by Thomas Burger with the assistance of Frederick Lawrence. Cambridge: MIT Press.

Hallin, Daniel C., and Paolo Mancini. 2004. *Comparing Media Systems: Three Models of Media and Politics*. Cambridge: Cambridge University Press.

Hallin, Daniel C., and Paolo Mancini, eds. 2012a. *Comparing Media Systems beyond the Western World*. Cambridge: Cambridge University Press.

Hallin, Daniel C., and Paolo Mancini. 2012b. 'Conclusion.' In *Comparing Media Systems beyond the Western World*, edited by Daniel Hallin and Paolo Mancini, 278–304. Cambridge: Cambridge University Press.

Haltof, Marek. 2002. *Polish National Cinema*. Oxford: Berghahn.

Hanitzsch, Thomas. 2007. 'Deconstructing Journalism Culture: Toward a Universal Theory.' *Communication Theory* 17 (4): 367–385.

Hanitzsch, Thomas, and Frank Esser. 2012. 'Challenges and Perspectives of Comparative Communication Inquiry.' In *The Handbook of Comparative Communication Research*, edited by Frank Esser and Thomas Hanitzsch, 501–516. London: Routledge.

Hannerz, Ulf. 2004. *Foreign News: Exploring the World of Foreign Correspondents*. Chicago: University of Chicago Press.

Hanot, Muriel. 2003. ' "La télévision, c'était mieux avant!": Premier TV, premiers usages.' *Médiatiques: Récit et société* 33 (2003): 36–38.

Hanson, Philip. 1974. *Advertising and Socialism: The Nature and Extent of Consumer Advertising in the Soviet Union, Poland, Hungary and Yugoslavia*. London: Palgrave Macmillan.

Haralovich, Mary Beth. 1988. 'Suburban Family Sitcoms and Consumer Product Design: Addressing the Social Subjectivity of Homemakers.' In *Television and Its Audience: International Research Perspectives*, edited by Philip Drummond and Richard Paterson, 38–60. London: British Film Institute.

Hardy, Jonathan. 2012. 'Comparing Media Systems.' In *The Handbook of Comparative Communication Research*, edited by Frank Esser and Thomas Hanitzsch, 185–296. London Routledge.
Harris, Steven E. 2013. *Communism on Tomorrow Street: Mass Housing and Everyday Life after Stalin*. Baltimore: Johns Hopkins University Press and Washington, DC: Woodrow Wilson Center.
Harsch, Donna. 2008. *Revenge of the Domestic: Women, the Family, and Communism in the German Democratic Republic*. Princeton: Princeton University Press.
Hartog, François. 2015. *Regimes of Historicity: Presentism and Experiences of Time*. Translated by Saskia Brown. New York: Columbia University Press.
Harvey, David. 1989. *The Condition of Postmodernity: An Inquiry into the Origins of Cultural Change*, Oxford: Blackwell.
Havens, Timothy. 2006. *Global Television Marketplace*. London: BFI Publishing.
Heinrich-Franke, Christian, and Regina Immel. 2013. 'Making Holes in the Iron Curtain? The Television Programme Exchange across the Iron Curtain in the 1960s and 1970s.' In *Airy Curtains in the European Ether: Broadcasting and the Cold War*, edited by Alexander Badenoch, Andreas Fickers, and Christian Heinrich-Franke, 177–214. Baden-Baden: Nomos Verlag.
Herf, Jeffrey. 1986. *Reactionary Modernisms: Technology, Culture and Politics in Weimar and the Third Reich*. Cambridge: Cambridge University Press.
Hérnandez Corchete, Sira. 2008. *La historia contada en television: El documental televisivo de divulgación histórica en España*. Barcelona: Gedisa.
Hertle, Hans-Hermann. 2009. *Der Fall der Mauer: Die Unbeabsichtigte Selbstauflösung des SED-Staates*. Opladen: Westdeutcher Verlag.
Hesse, Kurt. 1988. *Westmedien in der DDR: Nutzung, Image und Auswirkungen bundesrepublikanischen Hörfunks und Fernsehens*. Cologne: Wissenschaft und Politik.
Hickethier, Knut. 1998. *Geschichte des deutschen Fernsehens*. Berlin: Springer.
Hilmes, Michelle. 2011. *Network Nations: A Transnational History of British and American Broadcasting*. London: Routledge.
Hobson, Dorothy. 1982. *Crossroads: The Drama of a Soap Opera*. London: Methuen.
Hoff, Peter. 2002. *Protokoll eines Laborversuchs: Kommentar zur ersten Programmschrift des DDR-Fernsehens 1955*. Leipzig: Leipziger Universität.
Hoffmann, David L. 2003. *Stalinist Values: The Cultural Norms of Soviet Modernity, 1917–1941*. Ithaca: Cornell University Press.
Holquist, Peter. 1997. ' "Information is the Alpha and Omega of Our Work": Bolshevik Surveillance in Its Pan-European Context.' *Journal of Modern History* 69 (3): 415–450.
Holzweißig, Gunter. 2002. *Die schärfste Waffe der Partei: Eine Mediengeschichte der DDR*. Cologne: Böhlau.
Hong, Yunhao, and Youling Liu. 2015. 'Internationalization of China's Television: History, Development and New Trends.' In *Routledge Handbook on Chinese Media*, edited by Gary D. Rawnsley and Ming-yeh T. Rawnsley, 427–445. London: Routledge.

Honsberger, Laura. 2016. 'Playing Socialist Games: East German Game Shows and an Alternative Model of Consumption.' In *The Cold War and Entertainment Television*, edited by Lori Maguire, 83–96. Cambridge: Cambridge Scholars Publishing.

Hoover, Stewart M. 1998. *Religion in the News: Faith and Journalism and American Public Discourse*. London: Sage.

Hoover, Stewart M., and Lynn Schofield Clark, eds. 2002. *Practicing Religion in the Age of the Media*. New York: Columbia University Press.

Hörning, Karl H., Daniela Ahrens, and Anette Gerhard. 1999. 'Do Technologies Have Time? New Practices of Time and the Transformation of Communication Technologies.' *Time & Society* 8 (2): 293–308.

Hornsby, Robert. 2013. *Protest, Reform and Repression in Khrushchev's Soviet Union*. Cambridge: Cambridge University Press.

Hoskins, Andrew. 2001. 'New Memory: Mediating History.' *Historical Journal of Film, Radio and Television* 21 (4): 333–346.

Hoskins, Andrew. 2004. 'Television and the Collapse of Memory.' *Time & Society* 13 (1): 109–127.

Hutchings, Stephen, and Natalia Rulyova. 2009. *Television and Culture in Putin's Russia: Remote Control*. London: Routledge.

Hutchings, Stephen, and Vera Tolz. 2015. *Nation, Ethnicity and Race on Russian Television: Mediating Post-Soviet Difference*. London: Routledge.

Howard, Philip N. 2015. *Pax Technica: How the Internet of Things May Set Us Free or Lock Us Up*. New Haven: Yale University Press.

Huxtable, Simon. 2017. 'Remembering a Problematic Past: TV Mystics, Perestroika and the 1990s in Post-Soviet Cultural Memory.' *European Journal of Cultural Studies* 20 (3):307–323.

Huyssens, Andreas. 1995. *Twilight Memories: Marking Time in a Culture of Amnesia*. London: Routledge.

Imre, Anikó. 2011. 'Love to Hate: National Celebrity and Racial Intimacy on Reality TV in the New Europe.' *Television & New Media* 16 (2): 103–130.

Imre, Anikó. 2016. *TV Socialism*. Durham: Duke University Press.

Imre, Anikó, Timothy Havens, and Katalin Lustyik, eds. 2013. *Popular Television in Eastern Europe during and since Socialism*. London: Routledge

Innis, Harold A. 2007 [1950]. *Empire and Communications*. Lanham: Rowman & Littlefield.

Innis, Harold A. 2008 [1951]. *The Bias of Communication*. Toronto: University of Toronto Press.

Iurovskii, A. Ia. 1998. 'Istoriia telezhurnalistiki v Rossii.' In *Televizionnaia zhurnalistika: Uchebnik*, edited by G.V. Kuznetsov, 54–90. Moscow: MGU.

Jakubowicz, Karol. 2004. 'Ideas in Our heads: The Introduction of PBS as Part of Media Systems Change in Central and Eastern Europe.' *European Journal of Communication* 19 (1): 53–74

Jameson, Frederic. 1985. 'Postmodernism and Consumer Society.' In *Postmodern Culture*, edited by Hal Foster, 111–125. London: Pluto Press.

Johnson, A. Ross, and R. Eugene Parta, eds. 2010. *Cold War Broadcasting: Impact on the Soviet Union and Eastern Europe: A Collection of Studies and Documents*. Budapest: Central European University Press.

Johnston, Derek. 2015. *Haunted Seasons: Television Ghost Stories for Christmas and Horror for Halloween*. Basingstoke: Palgrave Macmillan.

Johnston, William B. 1991. 'Global Work Force 2000: The New World Labor Market.' *Harvard Business Review* March–April 1991, 115–126.

Kansteiner, Wulf. 2006. *In Pursuit of German Memory: History, Television, and Politics after Auschwitz*. Athens: Ohio University Press.

Katz, Elihu, and Tamar Liebes. 2007. 'No More Peace! How Disaster, Terror and Wars Have Upstaged Media Events.' *International Journal of Communication* 1: 157–166.

Keightley, Emily. 2013. 'From Immediacy to Intermediacy: The Mediation of Lived Time.' *Time & Society* 22 (1): 55–75.

Keilbach, Judith. 2010. *Geschichtsbilder und Zeitzeugen: Zur Darstellung des Nationalsozialismus im bundesdeutschen Fernsehen*. Münster: Lit Verlag.

Kellner, Douglas. 1995. *Media Culture: Cultural Studies, Identity and Politics between the Modrn and the Postmodern*. London: Routledge.

Kelly, Catriona. 2014. *St. Petersburg: Shadows of the Past*. New Haven: Yale University Press.

Kemp-Welch, Anthony. 2008. *Poland under Communism: A Cold War History*. Cambridge: Cambridge University Press.

Kenez, Peter. 1985. *The Birth of the Propaganda State: Soviet Methods of Mass Mobilization, 1917–1929*. Cambridge: Cambridge University Press.

Kern, Holger Lutz, and Jens Hainmueller. 2009. 'Opium for the Masses: How Foreign Free Media Can Stabilize Authoritarian Regimes.' *Political Analysis* 17 (4): 377–399.

Kharkhordin, Oleg. 1999. *The Collective and the Individual in Russia: A Study of Practices*. Oakland: University of California Press.

Khiabany, Gholam. 2009. *Iranian Media: The Paradox of Modernity*. New York: Routledge.

Killingsworth, Matt. 2007. 'Opposition and Dissent in Soviet Type Regimes: Civil Society and Its Limitations.' *Journal of Civil Society* 3 (1): 59–79.

Kim, Young Yun. 2012. 'Comparing Intercultural Communication.' In *The Handbook of Comparative Communication Research*, edited by Frank Esser and Thomas Hanitzsch, 119–133. London: Routledge.

Kisielewska, Alicja. 2013. 'Polish TV Serials: A World of Mythologized Images.' In *National Mythologies in Central European TV Series: How J.R. Won the Cold War*, edited by Jan Čulík, 84–109. Brighton: Sussex Academic Press.

Kleinecke-Bates, Iris. 2014. *Victorians on Screen: The Nineteenth Century on British Television, 1994–2005*. Basingstoke: Palgrave Macmillan.

Knott, Kim, Elizabeth Poole, and Teemu Taira. 2013. *Media Portrayals of Religion and the Secular Sacred: Representation and Change*. Farnham: Ashgate.

Kochanowski, Katja, Sascha Trültzsch, and Reinhold Viehoff. 2013. 'An Evening with Friends and Enemies: Political Indoctrination in Popular East German Family Series.' In *Popular Television in Eastern Europe during and since Socialism*, edited by Anikó Imre, Timothy Havens, and Katalin Lustyik, 81–101. London: Routledge.

Konczak, Jaroslaw. 2008. *Od Tele-Echa do Polskiego Zoo: Ewolucja Programu TVP*. Warszawa: Wydawnictwa Akademickie i Profesjonalne.

Kornai, János. 1992. *The Socialist System: The Political Economy of Communism*. Oxford: Oxford University Press.

Koselleck, Reinhart. 2004. *Futures Past: On the Semantics of Historical Time*. New York: Columbia University Press.

Kotański, Janusz. 2004. 'Obraz Historii Polski w Kinie i Telewizji PRL.' In *Media w PRL, PRL w Mediach*, edited by Marek Malinowski, Piotr Niwiński, and Tadeusz Dmochowski, 47–57. Gdańsk: Uniwersytet Gdański.

Kotkin, Stephen. 1995. *Magnetic Mountain: Stalinism and Civilisation*. Berkeley: University of California Press.

Kotsonis, Yanni. 2000. 'Introduction: A Modern paradox: Subject and Citizen in Nineteenth- and Twentieth-Century Russia.' In *Russian Modernity: Politics, Knowledge and Practices, 1800–1950*, edited by David L. Hoffmann and Yanni Kotsonis, 1–16. Basingstoke: Palgrave Macmillan.

Kozlov, Denis. 2013. *The Readers of Novyi Mir: Coming to Terms with the Stalinist Past*. Cambridge: Harvard University Press.

Kraidy, Marwan. 2010. *Reality Television and Arab Politics: Contention and Public Life*. Cambridge: Cambridge University Press.

Lapidus, Gail W., ed. 1982. *Women, Work and Family in the Soviet Union*. Armonk: M.E. Sharpe.

Lašas, Ainius. 2015. 'Daily Democracy: Politics, Media and Democratic Culture.' In *Media and Politics in New Democracies: Europe in Comparative Perspective*, edited by Jan Zielonka, 137–153. Oxford: Oxford University Press.

Lau, Jenny Kwok Wah. 2002. *Multiple Modernities: Cinemas and Popular Media in Transcultural East Asia*. Philadelphia: Temple University Press.

Leal, Ondina Faschel. 1990. 'Popular Tastes and Erudite Repertoire: The Place and Space of Television in Brazil.' *Cultural Studies* 4 (1): 19–29.

Leandrov, Igor. 1986. Pre početka: Sećanja na pripreme za uvodenje televizijskog programa u Beogradu. Belgrade: Television Belgrade.

Lee, Woo-Seung. 2003. Das Fernsehen in geteilten Deutschland (1952–1989): Ideologische Konkurrenz und programmliche Kooperation. Potsdam: Verlag für Berlin-Brandenburg.

Lenoe, Matthew. 2004. *Closer to the Masses: Stalinist Culture, Social Revolution, and Soviet Newspapers*. Cambridge: Harvard University Press.

Lepp, Annika, and Mervi Pantti. 2013. 'Window to the West: Memories of Watching Finnish Television in Estonia during the Soviet Period.' *VIEW: Journal of European Television History and Culture* 2 (3): 77–87.

Lerner, Daniel. 1958. *The Passing of Traditional Society: Modernizing the Middle East*. New York: Free Press.

Levitsky, Daniel. 2012. *Soviet History in Thaw Cinema: The Making of New Myths and Truths*. Unpublished PhD Thesis, University College London.

Lewis, Tania, Fran Martin, and Wanning Sun. 2016. *Telemodernities: Television and Transforming Lives in Asia*. Duke University Press.

Liebes, Tamar, and Elihu Katz.1990. *The Export of Meaning: Cross-Cultural Readings of Dallas*. Oxford: Oxford University Press.

Liebes, Tamar. 1998. 'Television's Disaster Marathons: A Danger for Democratic Processes?' In *Media, Identity and Ritual*, edited by Tamar Liebes and James Curran, 71–86. London: Routledge.

Livingstone, Sonia. 2003. 'On the Challenges of Cross-National Comparative Media Research.' *European Journal of Communication* 18 (4): 477–500.

Livingstone, Sonia. 2012. 'Challenges to Comparative Research in a Globalizing Media Landscape.' In *The Handbook of Comparative Communication Research*, edited by Frank Esser and Thomas Hanitzsch, 415–429. London: Routledge.

Livingstone, Sonia, and Moira Bovill, eds. 2013. *Children and Their Changing Media Environment: A European Comparative Study*. Mahwah: Lawrence Erlbaum.

Łobodzínska, Barbara. 1995. 'Family and Working Women during and after Socialist Industrialization and Ideology.' In *Family, Women and Employment in Central-Eastern Europe*, edited by Barbara Łobodzínska, 4–40. Westport: Greenwood Publishing.

Lorimer, Rowland. 1994. *Mass Communications: A Comparative Introduction*. Manchester: Manchester University Press.

Lotz, Amanda. 2014. *Television Will Be Revolutionized*, 2nd edn. New York: New York University Press.

Lovejoy, Alice. 2013. ' "Video Knows no Borders": Samizdat Television and the Unofficial Public Sphere in "Normalized" Czechoslovakia.' In *Samizdat, Tamizdat & Beyond: Transnational media during and after Socialism*, edited by Friederike Kind-Kovács and Jessie Labov, 206–220. Oxford: Berghahn.

Lovell, Stephen. 2013. 'In Search of an Ending: *Seventeen Moments* and the Seventies.' In *The Socialist Sixties: Crossing Borders in the Second World*, edited by Anne Gorsuch and Diane Koenker, 303–321. Bloomington: Indiana University Press.

Lovell, Stephen. 2015. *Russia in the Microphone Age: A History of Soviet Radio, 1919–1970*. Oxford: Oxford University Press.

Lull, James. 1991. *China Turned On: Television, Reform and Resistance*. London: Routledge.

Lundby, Knut, ed. 2009. *Mediatization: Concept, Challenger, Consequences*. New York: Peter Lang.

Lundgren, Lars. 2012. 'Live from Moscow: The Celebration of Yuri Gagarin and Transnational Television in Europe.' *VIEW: Journal of European Television History and Culture* 1 (2): 45–55.

Lundgren, Lars. 2015. 'The Forerunners of a New Era.' *Media History* 21 (2): 178–191.

Lundgren, Lars, and Christine Evans. 2017. 'Producing Global Media Memories: Media Events and the Power Dynamics of Transnational Television History.' *European Journal of Cultural Studies* 20 (3): 252–270.

Mahoney, James, and P. Larkin Terrie. 2008. 'Comparative-Historical Analysis in Contemporary Political Science.' In *Oxford Handbook of Political Methodology*, edited by Henry Brady, Janet M. Box-Steffenmeier, and David Collier, 737–755. Oxford: Oxford University Press.

Maierean, Andreea. 2006. 'The Media Coverage of the Romanian Revolution.' *CEU Political Science Journal* 1 (1): 25–44.

Majer, Artur. 2005. '*Czterej Pancerni* i *Czterdziestolatek*, czyli o małżeństwie romantyzmu z małą stabilizacją.' In *30 Najważniejszych Programów TV w Polsce*, edited by Wiesław Godzic, 215–223. Warszawa: Wydawnictwo Trio TVN S.A.

Mäkikalli, Maija. 2016. 'Television in Hiding.' Paper presented at the conference 'Material Cultures of Television,' Hull, UK, 21–22 March 2016.

Mancini, Paolo. 2015. 'The News Media between Volatility and Hybridization.' In *Media and Politics in New Democracies: Europe in Comparative Perspective*, edited by Jan Zielonka, 25–37. Oxford: Oxford University Press.

Mankekar, Purnima. 1999. *Screening Culture, Viewing Politics: An Ethnography of Television, Womanhood and Nation in Postcolonial India*. Durham: Duke University Press.

Mansell, Gerard. 1982. *Let the Truth Be Told: 50 Years of BBC External Broadcasting*. London: Weidenfeld and Nicolson.

Marriott, Stephanie. 2007. *Live Television: Time, Space and the Broadcast Event*. London: Sage.

Marvin, Carloyn. 1999. *When Old Media Were New: Thinking about Electrical Communication in the Late Nineteenth Century*. Oxford: Oxford University Press.

Matei, Alexandru. 2013. *O tribună captivantă: Televiziune, ideologie, societate în România socialist, 1965–1983*. Bucureşti: Curtea Veche.

Mazzoleni, Gianpietro, and Winfried Schulz. 1999. ' "Mediatization" of Politics: A Challenge for Democracy?' *Political Communication* 16 (3): 247–261.

McArthur, Colin. 1976. *Television and History*. London: BFI.

McCarthy, Anna. 2001. *Ambient Television: Visual Culture and Public Space*. Durham: Duke University Press.

McGuigan, Jim. 2005. 'The Cultural Public Sphere.' *European Journal of Cultural Studies* 8 (4): 427–443.

McLuhan, Marshall. 1994 [1964]. *Understanding Media: The Extensions of Man*. Boston: MIT Press.

Merkel, Ina. 2000. *'Wir sind doch nicht die Meckerecke der Nation': Briefe an das Fernsehen der DDR*. Cologne: Schwarzkopf und Schwarzkopf.

Mevius, Martin. 2010. *The Hungarian Communist Party and the Origins of Socialist Patriotism, 1941–1953*. Oxford: Clarendon Press.

Meyen, Michael. 2001. 'Haben die Westmedien die DDR stabilisiert?' *Siegener Periodicum zur internationalen empirischen Literaturwissenschaft (SPIEL)* 20 (1): 117–133.

Meyen, Michael. 2003a. *Denver Clan und Neues Deutschland: Mediennutzung in der DDR*. Berlon: Christoph Links.

Meyen, Michael. 2003b. *Einschalten, Umschalten, Ausschalten? Das Fernsehen im DDR-Alltag*. Leipzig: Leipziger Universitätsverlag.

Meyrowitz, Joshua. 1985. *No Sense of Place: The Impact of Electronic Media on Social Behaviour*. Oxford: Oxford University Press.

Miasoedov, Boris Alekseevich. 1982. *Strana chitaet, slushaet, smotrit: statisticheskiĭ obzor*. Moscow: Financi i statistika.

Mickiewicz, Ellen. 1997. *Changing Channels: Television and the Struggle for Power in Russia*. Oxford: Oxford University Press.

Mihalcea, Eugenia. 2004. 'Censurat de trei ori.' *Jurnalul*, 23 Feb 2004. http://jurnalul.ro/special-jurnalul/cenzurat-de-trei-ori-72550.html.

Mihelj, Sabina. 2011a. *Media Nations: Communicating Belonging and Exclusion in the Modern World*. Basingstoke: Palgrave Macmillan.

Mihelj, Sabina. 2011b. 'Negotiating Culture at the Crossroads of East and West: Uplifting the Working People, Entertaining the Masses, Cultivating the Nation.' *Comparative Studies in Society and History* 53 (3): 509–39.

Mihelj, Sabina. 2012. 'Between Segmentation and Integration: Media Systems and Ethno-Cultural Diversity in Central and Eastern Europe.' In *Central and Eastern European Media in Comparative Perspective: Politics, Economy Culture*, edited by John Downey and Sabina Mihelj, 63–89. Aldershot: Ashgate.

Mihelj, Sabina. 2013. 'The Politics of Privatization: Television Entertainment and the Yugoslav Sixties.' In *The Socialist Sixties: Crossing Borders in the Second World*, edited by Anne Gorsuch and Diane Koenker, 251–267. Bloomington: Indiana University Press.

Mihelj, Sabina, and Simon Huxtable. 2016a. 'The Challenge of Flow: State Socialist Television between Revolutionary Time and Everyday Time.' *Media, Culture & Society* 38 (3): 332–348.

Mihelj, Sabina, and Simon Huxtable. 2016b. 'The Politics of Privacy on State Socialist Television.' *International Journal of Communication* 10: 2238–2257.

Mihelj, Sabina, Veronika Bajt, and Miloš Pankov. 2009. 'Reorganising the Identification Matrix: Televisual Construction of Identity in the Early Phase of Yugoslav Disintegration.' In *Media Discourse and the Yugoslav Conflicts: Representations of Self and Other*, edited by Pål Kølsto, 39–59. Aldershot: Ashgate.

Miike, Yoshitaka. 2007. 'An Asiacentric Reflection on Eurocentric Research Bias in Communication Theory.' *Communication Monographs* 74 (2): 272–278.

Miller, Barbara. 1999. *Guilt and Compliance in Unified Germany: Stasi Informers and Their Impact on Society*. London: Routledge.

Miller, David. 1990. *Market, State, and Community: Theoretical Foundations of Market Socialism*. Oxford: Clarendon Press.

Milošević, Vlado. 1984. 'Razvoj ekonomske osnove Televizije Beograd.' In *Iz istorije Televizije Beograd*, edited by Vasilije Popović, Slobodan Novaković, Srđan Barić, Slobodan Habić, Vlado Milošević, Ivko Pustišek, and Bojana Andrić, 97–184. Belgrade: Television Belgrade.

Milton, Andrew K. 1997. 'New Media Reform in Eastern Europe: A Cross-National Comparison.' In *Post-Communism and the Media in Eastern Europe*, edited by Patrick O'Neill, 7–23. London: Frank Cass.

Mitchell, Brian R. 2007. *International Historical Statistics: Europe, 1750–2005*, 6th edn. Basingstoke: Palgrave Macmillan.

Mitu, Bianca, and Stamatis Poulakidakos, eds. 2016. *Media Events: A Critical Contemporary Approach*. Basingstoke: Palgrave Macmillan.

Mojzes, Paul. 1992. *Religious Liberty in Eastern Europe and the USSR: Before and After the Great Transformation*. Boulder, CO: East European Monographs.

Mond, George, and R. Richter. 1966. 'Writers and Journalists: A Pressure Group in East European Politics.' *Journalism & Mass Communication Quarterly* 43 (1): 95–109.

Monteleone, Franco. 2006. *Storia della radio e della televisione in Italia*. Venice: Tascabili Marsilio.

Moore, Barrington. 1993 [1966]. *Social Origins of Dictatorship and Democracy: Lord and Peasant in the Making of the Modern World*. Boston: Beacon Press.

Moores, Shaun. 2000. *Media and Everyday Life*. Edinburgh: Edinburgh University Press.

Morley, David. 1986. *Family Television: Cultural Power and Domestic Leisure*, London: Rutledge.

Morley, David. 2007. *Media, Modernity and Technology: The Geography of the New*. London: Routledge.

Moseley, Rachel, and Jacinda Read. 2002. ' "Having it Ally": Popular Television (Post)Feminism.' *Feminist Media Studies* 2(2): 231–249.

Murdock, Graham. 1992. 'Citizens, Consumers and Public Culture.' In *Media Cultures: Reappraising Transnational Media*, edited by Michael Skovmand and Kim Christian Schroeder, 34–48. London: Routledge.

Mustata, Dana. 2006. 'Tracing the Unseen in Post-Communist Romanian Television.' *Tijdschrift voor Mediageschiedenis* 9 (1): 123–149.

Mustata, Dana. 2011. *The Power of Television: Including the Historicizing of the Live Romanian Revolution*. Unpublished PhD Thesis, Utrecht University.

Mustata, Dana. 2012. 'The Revolution Has Been Televised: Television as a Historical Agent in the Romanian Revolution.' *Journal of Modern European History* 10 (1): 76–97.

Mustata, Dana. 2013a. 'Television in the Age of (Post-)Communism: The Case of Romania.' In *Popular Television in Eastern Europe during and since Socialism*, edited by Anikó Imre, Timothy Havens, and Katalin Lustyik, 47–64. London: Routledge.

Mustata, Dana. 2013b. 'Geographies of Power: The Case of Foreign Broadcasting in Dictatorial Romania.' In *Airy Curtains in the European Ether: Broadcasting and the Cold War*, edited by Alexander Badenoch, Andreas Fickers, and Christian Heinrich-Franke, 149–174. Baden-Baden: Namos Verlag.

Neiger, Motti and Keren Tenenboim-Weinblatt. 2016. 'Understanding Journalism through a Nuanced Deconstruction of Temporal Layers in News Narratives.' *Journal of Communication* 66 (2): 139–160.

Nansen, Bjorn, Michael Arnold, Martin R. Gibbs, and Hilary Davis. 2009. 'Domestic Orchestration: Rhythms in the Mediated Home.' *Time & Society* 2/3: 181–207.

Natale, Simone, and Gabriele Balbi. 2014. 'Media and the Imaginary in History: The Role of the Fantastic in Different Stages of Media Change.' *Media History* 20 (2): 203–218.

Nelson, Daniel N. 1988. *Romanian Politics in the Ceausescu Era*. New York: Gordon and Breach Science Publishers.

Nelson, Michael. 1997. *War of the Black Heavens: The Battles of Western Broadcasting in the Cold War*. Syracuse: Syracuse University Press.

Nguyen-Thu, Giang. 2016. 'Personal Wealth, National Pride: Vietnamese Television and Commercial Nationalism.' In *Commercial Nationalism: Selling the Nation and Nationalizing the Sell*, edited by Zala Volčič and Mark Andrejevic, 86–105. Basingstoke: Palgrave.

Nordenstreng, Kaarle, and Tapio Varis. 1974. 'Television Traffic: A One Way Street? A Survey and Analysis of the International Flow of Television Materials.' *Reports and Papers on Mass Communication*, no. 70. Paris: Unesco.

Norris, Pippa, and Ronald Inglehart. 2009. *Cosmopolitan Communications: Cultural Diversity in a Globalized World*. Cambridge: Cambridge University Press.

Novak, Božidar. 2005. *Hrvatsko novinarstvo u 20. stoljeću*. Zagreb: Golden Marketing – Tehnička knjiga.

Novaković, Slobodan. 1984. 'Kad je vladala komedija ili četvrt veka beogradske humotističke škole.' In *Iz istorije Televizije Beograd*, edited by Vasilije Popović, Slobodan Novaković, Srđan Barić, Slobodan Habić, Vlado Milošević, Ivko Pustišek, and Bojana Anrić, 35–60.Belgrade: Television Belgrade.

Oberg, James E. 1989. *Uncovering Soviet Disasters: Exploring the Limits of Glasnost*. London: Robert Hale.

Ong, Walter J. 1982. *Orality and Literacy: The Technologizing of the Word*. New York: Methuen.

Oren, Tasha, and Sharon Shahaf, eds. 2013. *Global Television Formats: Understanding Television across Borders*. London: Routledge.

Örnebring, Henrik. 2007. 'Writing the History of Television Audiences: The Coronation in the Mass Observation Archives.' In *Re-Viewing Television History: Critical Issues in Television Historiography*, edited by Helen Wheatley, 170–183. London: I. B. Tauris.

OSI/EUMAP. 2005a. *Television across Europe: Regulation, Policy and Independence*, 4 vols. Budapest: Open Society Institute.

OSI/EUMAP. 2005b. *Summary*, vol. 1 of *Television across Europe: Regulation, Policy and Independence*. Budapest: Open Society Institute.

OSI/EUMAP. 2008. *Television across Europe: More Channels, Less Independence*. Budapest: Open Society Institute.

Ostrowska, Dorota. 2013. 'The Carnival of The Absurd: Stanisław Bareja's Alternatywy 4 and Polish Television in The 1980s Series.' In *Popular Television in Eastern Europe during and since Socialism*, edited by Anikó Imre, Timothy Havens, and Katalin Lustyik, 65–80. London: Routledge.

O'Sullivan, Tim. 1991. 'Television Memories and Cultures of Viewing 1950–1965.' In *Popular Television in Britain: Studies in Cultural History*, edited by John Corner, 159–182. London: British Film Institute.

Ouellette, Laurie. 2002. *Viewers Like You? How Public TV Failed the People*. New York: Columbia University Press.

Oushakine, Serguei. 2001. 'The Terrifying Mimicry of Samizdat.' *Public Culture* 13 (2): 194–214.

Paczkowski, Andrzej, and Malcolm Byrne, eds. 2007. *From Solidarity to Martial Law: The Polish Crisis of 1980–1981: A Documentary History*. Budapest: Central European University Press.

Pajala, Mari. 2013. 'Intervision Song Contests and Finnish Television between East and West.' In *Airy Curtains in the European Ether: Broadcasting and the Cold War*, edited by Alexander Badenoch, Andreas Fickers, and Christian Heinrich-Franke, 215–239. Baden-Baden: Namos Verlag.

Pajala, Mari. 2017. 'Long Live the Friendship between the Soviet Union and Finland!' Irony, Nostalgia, and Melodrama in Finnish Historical Television Drama and Documentary Series.' *European Journal of Cultural Studies* 20 (3): 271–284.

Pajnik, Mojca. 2012. 'Gender (In)equity in Post-Socialist Media.' In *Central and Eastern European Media in Comparative Perspective: Politics, Economy and Culture*, edited by John Downey and Sabina Mihelj, 89–112. Farnham: Ashgate.

Palmowski, Jan. 2009. *Inventing a Socialist Nation: Heimat and the Politics of Everyday Life in the GDR, 1945–1990*. Cambridge: Cambridge University Press

Parkin, Frank. 1969. 'Class Stratification in Socialist Societies.' *The British Journal of Sociology* 20 (4): 355–374.

Parks, Lisa. 2000. 'Cracking Open the Set: Television Repair and Tinkering with Gender, 1949–1955.' *Television and New Media* 1 (3): 257–278.

Parsons, Talcott. 1971. *The System of Modern Societies*. Englewood Cliffs: Prentice Hall.

Paterson, Richard. 1980. 'Planning the Family: The Art of the Television Schedule.' *Screen Education* 35: 79–85.

Patterson, Patrick Hyder. 2011. *Bought and Sold: Living and Losing the Good Life in Socialist Yugoslavia*. Ithaca: Cornell University Press.

Paulu, Burton. 1974. *Broadcasting in Eastern Europe*. Minneapolis: University of Minnesota Press.

Pehe, Veronika. 2014. 'Retro Reappropriations: Responses to The Thirty Cases of Major Zeman in the Czech Republic.' *VIEW: Journal of European Television History and Culture* 3 (5): 100–107.

Penati, Cecilia. 2013. *Il focolare elettronico: Televisione italiana delle origini e culture di visione.Televisione italiana delle origini e culture di visione*. Milan: Vita e pensiero.

Perica, Vjekoslav. 2002. *Balkan Idols: Religion and Nationalism in Yugoslav States*. Oxford: Oxford University Press.

Perry, Joseph B. 2001. *The Private Life of the Nation: Christmas and the Invention of Modern Germany*. Unpublished PhD Thesis, University of Illinois at Urbana-Champaign.

Pertierra, Anna C., and Graeme Turner. 2013. *Locating Television: Zones of Consumption*. London: Routledge.

Peruško, Zrinjka, and Antonija Čuvalo. 2014. 'Comparing Socialist and Post-Socialist Television Culture: Fifty Years of Television in Croatia.' *View: Journal of European Television History and Culture* 3 (3): 131–150

Petrescu, Dragoş. 2007. 'Communist Legacies in the 'New Europe': History, Ethnicity, and the Creation of a 'Socialist' Nation in Romania, 1945–1989.' In *Conflicted Memories: Europeanizing Contemporary Histories*, edited by Konrad Hugo Jarausch, Thomas Lindenberger, and Annelie Ramsbrock, 37–54. Oxford: Berghahn.

Petrone, John. 2010. 'Did Dallas Bring Down the Soviet Union?' *Baltic Reports*, 07 June 2010, http://balticreports.com.

Pfau, Sebastian. 2002. 'Unterhaltende Ideologie? – Die Familienserie *Die lieben Mitmenschen*.' In *Die Überwinddung der Langeweile? Zur Programmentwicklung des DDR-Fernsehens 1968 bis 1974*, edited by Claudia Dittmar and Susanne Vollberg, 299–314. Leipzig: Leipziger Universitätsverlag.

Pfau, Sebastian, and Sascha Trültzsch with Katja Kochanowski, and Tanja Rüdinger. 2010. *Von der Krügers bis zur Feuerwache: Vademekum der Familenserien des DDR-Fernsehens*. Leipzig: Leipziger Universitätsverlag.

Picard, Robert G. 2011. 'Broadcast Economics, Challenges of Scale, and Country Size.' In *Small among Giants: Television Broadcasting in Smaller Countries*, edited by Gregory Ferrell Lowe and Christian S. Nissen, 43–56. Gothenburg: Nordicom.

Pickering, Michael. 2001. *Stereotyping: The Politics of Representation*. Basingstoke: Palgrave Macmillan.

Pikulski, Tadeusz. 2002. Prywatna Historia Telewizji Publicznej. Warszawa: Muza

Poe, Marshall. 2003. *The Russian Moment in World History*. Princeton: Princeton University Press.

Pokorna-Ignatowicz, Katarzyna. 2003. Telewizja w systemie politycznym i medialnym PRL: Miedzy Polityka a Widzem. Kraków: Wydawnictwo Uniwersytetu Jagiellonskiego.

Preutu, Cristina. 2017. *Propaganda politică în România socialist: Practici instituţionale şi tehnici de comunicare, 1965–1974*. Iaşi: Alexandru Ioan Cuza University Press.

Prokhorova, Elena. 2003. *Fragmented Mythologies: Soviet TV Mini-Series of the 1970s*. Unpublished PhD Thesis, University of Pittsburgh.

Prokhorova, Elena, and Alexander M. Prokhorov. 2017. *Film and Television Genres of the Late Soviet Era*. London: Bloomsbury Academic.

Pustišek, Ivko. 1987. *Istorija zakonodavstva o radio-difuziji u Jugoslaviji: Međunarodna regulativa i jugoslovensko zakonodavstvo, 1907–1986*. Belgrade: Savremena administracija.

Putnam, Robert. 1995. 'Tuning In, Tuning Out: The Strange Disappearance of Social Capital in America.' *PS: Political Science and Politics*, 28 (4): 664–683.

Pye, Lucien W., ed. 1963. *Communications and Political Development*. Princeton: Princeton University Press.

Rajagopal, Arvind. 2001. *Politics after Television: Hindu Nationalism and the Reshaping of the Public in India*. Cambridge: Cambridge University Press.

Ramet, Pedro. 1984. 'The Interplay of Religious Policy and Nationalities Policy in the Soviet Union and Eastern Europe.' In *Religion and Nationalism in Soviet and East European Politics*, edited by Pedro Ramet, 3-41. Durham: Duke University Press.

Raundalen, Jon. 2014. 'East German Television Series in the 1980s.' Paper presented at the conference 'Media and the Cold War, 1975–1991,' Volda, Norway, 20–22 November 2014.

Rawnsley, Gary. 1996. Radio Diplomacy and Propaganda: The BBC and VOA in International Politics, 1956–64. London: Macmillan.

Rawnsley, Gary. 2015. 'Chinese International Broadcasting, Public Diplomacy, and Soft Power.' In *Routledge Handbook on Chinese Media*, edited by Gary D. Rawnsley and Ming-yeh T. Rawnsley, 460–475. London: Routledge.

Reid, Susan E. 2002. 'Cold War in the Kitchen: Gender and the De-Stalinization of Consumer Taste in the Soviet Union under Khrushchev.' *Slavic Review* 61 (2): 211–252.

Reifova, Irena. 2015. 'A Study in the History of Meaning-Making: Watching Socialist Television Serials in the Former Czechoslovakia.' *European Journal of Communication* 30 (1): 79–94.

Reifova, Irena, Petr Bednařík, and Šimon Dominik. 2013. 'Between Politics and Soap: The Articulation of Ideology and Melodrama in Czechoslovak Communist Television.' In *Popular Television in Authoritarian Europe*, edited by Peter Goddard, 91–106. Manchester: Manchester University Press.

Repnikova, Maria. 2017. *Media Politics in China: Improvising Power under Authoritarianism*. Cambridge: Cambridge University Press.

Riedel, Heide, ed. 1994. *Mit uns sieht die neue Zeit ... 40 Jahre DDR-Medien*. Berlin: Vistas.

Rittersporn, Gábor, Matt Rolf, and Jan C. Behrends. 2003. 'Exploring Public Spheres in Regimes of the Soviet Type.' In *Sphären von Öffentlichkeit in Gesellschaften sowjetischen Typs: Zwischen partei-staatlicher Selbstinszenierung und kirchlichen Gegenwelten*, edited by Rolf Rittersporn and Jan C. Behrends, 23–35. Frankfurt: Peter Lang.

Robinson, Gertrude Joch. 1977. Tito's Maverick Media: The Politics of Mass Communications in Yugoslavia. Urbana: University of Illinois Press.

Robinson, John P., and Philip E. Converse. 1972. 'The Impact of Television on Mass Media Usages: A Cross-national Comparison.' In *The Use of Time: Daily Activities of Urban and Suburban Populations in Twelve Countries*, edited by Alexander Szalai, 197–212. The Hague: Mouton.

Robinson, John P., Philip E. Converse, and Alexandre Szalai. 1972. 'Everyday Life in Twelve Countries.' In *The Use of Time: Daily Activities of Urban and Suburban Populations in Twelve Countries*, edited by Alexander Szalai, 113–144. The Hague: Mouton.

Robinson, M. J. 2017. *Television on Demand: Curatorial Culture and the Transformation of TV*. London: Bloomsbury.

Rosa, Hartmut. 2013. *Social Acceleration: A New Theory of Modernity*. New York: Columbia University Press.

Roth-Ey, Kristin. 2007. 'Finding a Place for Soviet Television.' Slavic Review 66 (2): 278–306.

Roth-Ey, Kristin. 2011. *Moscow Prime Time: How the Soviet Union Build the Media Empire that Lost the Cold War*. Ithaca: Cornell University Press.

Roudakova, Natalia. 2017. *Losing Pravda: Ethics and the Press in Post-Truth Russia*. Cambridge: Cambridge University Press.

Roy, Martin. 2000. *Luther in der DDR: Zum Wandel des Lutherbildes in der DDR-Geschichtsschreibung*. Bochum: Winkler.

Sa Martino, Louis Mauro. 2013. *The Mediatization of Religion: When Faith Rocks*. Farnham: Ashgate.

Scannell, Paddy. 1996. *Radio, Television and Modern Life: A Phenomenological Approach*. Oxford: Blackwell.

Scannell, Paddy. 2013. *Television and the Meaning of 'Live': An Inquiry into the Human Situation*. Cambridge: Polity.

Scannell, Paddy, and David Cardiff. 1991. *1922–1939: Serving the Nation, Vol. 1 of A Social History of British Broadcasting*. Oxford: Basil Blackwell.

Schiller, Herbert. 1992 [1969]. *Mass Communication and American Empire*, 2nd edn, updated. Westview Press. Boulder: Westview Press.

Schmidt, Volker H. 2006. 'Multiple Modernities or Varieties of Modernity?' *Current Sociology* 54 (1): 77–97.

Schramm, Wilbur. 1964. *Mass Media and National Development: The Role of Information in Developing Countries*. Stanford: Stanford University Press and Paris: UNESCO.

Schulz, Winfried. 2014. 'Political Communication in Long-Term Perspective.' In *Political Communication*, edited by C. Reinemann, 63–85. Berlin: de Gruyter Mouton.

Schwoch, James. 2009. *Global TV: New Media and the Cold War, 1946–69*. Champaign: University of Illinois Press.

Sheller, Mimi, and John Urry. 2003. 'Mobile Transformations of "Public" and "Private" Life.' *Theory, Culture & Society* 20 (3): 107–125.

Shleifer, Andrei, and Robert W. Vishny. 1994. 'The Politics of Market Socialism.' *Journal of Economic Perspectives* 8 (2): 165–176.

Siebert, Fredrick S., Theodore Peterson, and Wilbur Schramm. 1969 [1956]. *Four Theories of the Press: The Authoritarian, Libertarian, Social Responsibility and Soviet Communist Concepts of What the Press Should Be and Do*. Urbana: University of Illinois Press.

Silverstone, Roger. 1994. *Television and Everyday Life*. London: Routledge.

Skórzyński, Zygmunt. 1972. 'The Use of Free Time in Toruń, Maribor, and Jackson.' In *The Use of Time: Daily Activities of Urban and Suburban Populations in Twelve Countries*, edited by Alexander Szalai, 265–290. The Hague: Mouton.

Snyder, Jack. 2002. *From Voting to Violence: Democratization and Nationalist Conflict*. New York: Norton.

Sonnevend, Julia. 2016. *Stories without Borders: The Berlin Wall and the Making of a Global Iconic Event*. Oxford: Oxford University Press.

Sorescu-Marinković, Annemarie. 2010. 'Serbian Language Acquisition in Communist Romania.' *Balcanica* 41: 7–31.

Sorescu-Marinković, Annemarie. 2012. 'The World through the TV Screen: Everyday Life under Communism on the Western Romanian Border.' *Martor: The Museum of the Romanian Peasant Anthropology Review* 17: 173–88.

Spasovska, Ljubica. 2017. *The Last Yugoslav Generation: The Rethinking of Youth Politics and Cultures in Late Socialism*. Manchester: Manchester University Press.

Spigel, Lynn. 1992. *Make Room for TV: Television and the Family Ideal in Post-war America*, Chicago: The University of Chicago Press.

Standley, Michelle. 2011. 'The Cold War, Mass Tourism, and the Drive to Meet World Standards at Berlin's T.V. Tower Information Center.' In *Touring beyond the Nation: A Transnational Approach to European Tourism History*, edited by Eric G. E. Zuelow, 215–240. Farnham: Ashgate.

Steinmetz, Rüdiger, and Reinhold Viehoff. 2004. 'The Program History of Genres of Entertainment on GDR Television.' *Historical Journal of Film, Radio and Television* 24 (3): 317–325.

Steinmetz, Rüdiger, and Reinhold Viehoff. 2008. *Deutsches Fernsehen Ost. Eine Programmgeschichte des DDR-Fernsehens*. Berlin: VBB.

Štětka, Václav. 2012a. 'From Global to (G)local: Changing Patterns of Television Program Flows and Audience Preferences in Central and Eastern Europe.' *Journal of Popular Film and Television* 40 (3): 109–118.

Štětka, Václav. 2012b. 'Back to the Local? Transnational Media Flows and Audience Consumption Patterns in Central and Eastern Europe.' In *Central and Eastern European Media in Comparative Perspective: Politics, Economy and Culture*, edited by John Downey and Sabina Mihelj, 157–188. Farnham: Ashgate.

Stevens, Nick. 2002. *Understanding Media Cultures: Social Theory and Mass Communication*, 2nd edn. London: Sage.

Stites, Richard. 1988. *Revolutionary Dreams: Utopian Vision and Experimental Life in the Russian Revolution.* Oxford: Oxford University Press.

Štoll, Martin. 2018. *Television and Totalitarianism in Czechoslovakia: From the First Democratic Republic to the Fall of Communism.* London: Bloomsbury.

Strandgaard Jensen, Helle. 2015. 'Doing Media History in a Digital Age: Change and Continuity in Historiographical Practices.' *Media, Culture & Society* 38 (1): 119–128.

Straubhaar, Joseph D. 1991. 'Beyond Media Imperialism: Asymmetrical Independence and Cultural Proximity.' *Critical Studies in Mass Communication* 8 (1): 39–59.

Stupan, Ana, Blaž Mesec, and Stane Obranovič. 1967. *Televizija in kulturne aktivnosti: Mednarodna raziskava.* Ljubljana: Inštitut za sociologijo in filozofijo pri Univerzi v Ljubljani.

Suny, Ronald Grigor. 1993. *The Revenge of the Past: Nationalism, Revolution, and the Collapse of the Soviet Union.* Stanford: Stanford University Press.

Szekfü, András. 1989. 'Intruders Welcome? The Beginnings of Satellite Television in Hungary.' *European Journal of Communication* 20 (5): 15–35.

Szelényi, Szonja. 1999. *Equality by Design: The Grand Experiment in Destratification in Socialist Hungary.* Stanford: Stanford University Press.

Szostak, Sylwia. 2013. 'Post-Transitional Continuity and Change: Polish Broadcasting Flow and American TV Series.' In *Popular Television in Eastern Europe during and since Socialism*, edited by Anikó Imre, Timothy Havens, and Katalin Lustyik, 159–176. London: Routledge.

Szostak, Sylwia and Sabina Mihelj. 2017. 'Coming to Terms with Communist Propaganda: Post-Communism, Memory and Generation.' *European Journal of Cultural Studies* 20 (3): 324–340.

Sztompka, Piotr. 1993. *The Sociology of Social Change.* Oxford: Wiley-Blackwell.

Taylor, Ella. 1989. *Prime Time Families: Television Culture in Postwar America.* Berkeley: University of California Press.

Tenenboim-Weinblatt, Keren, and Motti Neiger. 2015. 'Print Is Future, Online Is Past: Cross-Media Analysis of Temporal Orientations in the News.' *Communication Research* 42 (8): 1047–1067.

Therborn, Göran. 2003. 'Entangled Modernities.' *European Journal of Social Theory* 6 (3): 293–305.

Thomas, Mandy. 2004. 'East Asian Cultural Traces in Post-Socialist Vietnam.' In *Rogue Flows: Trans-Asian Cultural Traffic*, edited by Koichi Iwabuchi, Stephen Muecke, and Nabdt Thomas, 177–196. Hong Kong: Hong Kong University Press.

Thompson, John B. 1995. *The Media and Modernity: A Social Theory of the Media*. Cambridge: Polity Press.

Thussu, Dayan Kishan, ed. 2009. *Internationalizing Media Studies*. London: Routledge.

Ting-Toomey, Stella, and Leeva Chung. 2012. *Understanding Intercultural Communication*, 2nd edn. Oxford: Oxford University Press.

Tomlinson, John. 1991. *Cultural Imperialism: A Critical Introduction*. London: Continuum.

Tomlinson, John. 2007. *The Culture of Speed: The Coming of Immediacy*. London: Sage.

Tracey, Michael. 1998. *The Decline and Fall of Public Broadcasting*. Oxford: Oxford University Press.

Trültzsch, Sascha, and Reinhold Viehoff. 2013. 'An Evening with Friends and Enemies: Political Indoctrination in Popular East German Family Series.' In *Popular Television in Eastern Europe during and since Socialism*, edited by Anikó Imre, Timothy Havens, and Katalin Lustyik, 81–101. London: Routledge.

Tsekleves, Emmanuel, Riger Witham, Koko Kondo, and Annette Hill. 2011. 'Investigating Media Use and the Television User Experience in the Home.' *Entertainment Computing* 2 (3): 151–161,

Tunstall, Jeremy. 1977. *The Media Are American*. London: Constable.

Tunstall, Jeremy. 2008. *The Media Were American: U.S. Mass Media in Decline*. Oxford: Oxford University Press.

UNESCO. 1980. *Communication and Society Today and Tomorrow, Many Voices One World, Towards a New More Just and More Efficient World Information and communication Order*. Paris: UNESCO.

Uricchio, William. 1990. 'Introduction to the History of German Television, 1935–1944.' *Historical Journal of Film, Radio and Television* 10 (2): 115–122.

Utekhin, Ilia. 2001. *Ocherki kommunal'nogo byta*. Moscow: OGI.

Vaccari, Cristiano, Andrew Chadwick, and Ben O'Loughlin. 2015. 'Dual Screening the Political: Media Events, Social Media, and Citizen Engagement.' *Journal of Communication* 65 (6): 1041–1061.

Vaizey, Hester. 2014, *Born in the GDR: Living in the Shadow of the Wall*. Oxford: Oxford University Press.

van Gennep, Arnold. 2010 [1909]. *The Rites of Passage*. London: Routledge.

van Keulen, Jolien, and Tonny Krijnen. 2014. 'The Limitations of Localization: A Cross-Cultural Comparative Study of "Farmer Wants a Wife".' *International Journal of Cultural Studies* 17 (3): 277–292.

Varis, Tapio. 1984. 'The International Flow of Television Programmes.' *Journal of Communication* 34 (1): 143–152.

Vartanova, Elena. 2012. 'The Russian Media Model in the Context of Post-Soviet Dynamics.' In *Comparing Media Systems beyond the Western World*, edited by Daniel Hallin and Paolo Mancini, 119–142. Cambridge: Cambridge University Press.

Verdery, Katherine. 1995. *National Ideology under Socialism: Identity and Cultural Politics in Ceauşescu's Romania*. Berkeley: University of California Press.

Verdery, Katherine. 2014. *Secrets and Truths: Ethnography in the Archive of Romania's Secret Police*. Budapest: Central European University Press.

Viney, Rachel. 1999. 'Religious Broadcasting on UK Television: Policy, Public Perception and Programmes.' *Cultural Trends* 9 (36): 1–28.

Virilio, Paul. 2006. *Speed and Politics*. Massachusetts: MIT Press.

Volčič, Zala, and Karmen Erjavec. 2015. 'Watching Pink Reality TV.' *Feminist Media Studies* 15 (1): 74–91.

Voltmer, Katrin. 2013. *The Media in Transitional Democracies*. Cambridge: Polity.

Vončina, Nikola. 1999. *TV osvaja Hrvatsku: Prilozi za povijest radija i televizije u Hrvatskoj III, 1954–1958*. Zagreb: Hrvatski radio.

Vučetić, Radina. 2012. *Koka-kola socijalizam: Amerikanizacija jugoslovenske popularne culture šezdesetih godina XX veka*. Belgrade: Službeni glasnik.

Vučetić, Radina. 2016. *Monopol na istinu: Partija, kultura u cenzura u Srbiji šezdesetih godina XX veka*. Belgrade: Clio.

Vuletić, Dean. 2007. 'The Socialist Star: Yugoslavia, Cold War Politics and the Eurovision Song Contest.' In *A Song for Europe. Popular Music and Politics in the Eurovision Song Contest*, edited by Ivan Raykoff and Robert Dean Tobin, 83–97. Aldershot: Ashgate.

Wachtel, Andrew Baruch. 1998. *Making a Nation, Breaking a Nation: Literature and Cultural Politics in Yugoslavia*. Stanford: Stanford University Press.

Wagner, Peter. 2012. *Modernity: Understanding the Present*. Cambridge: Polity.

Wang, Georgette. 2011. *De-Westernizing Communication Research: Altering Questions and Changing Frameworks*. London: Routledge.

Wang, Yingzi. 2017. 'Prime-Time Chinese TV Dramas in the Era of Entertainment: Key Themes and Trends.' Paper presented as part of the Centre for Research on Communication and Culture seminar series, Loughborough University, May.

Wasiak, Patryk. 2012. 'The Video Boom in Socialist Poland.' *Zeitschrift für Ostmitteleuropa-Forschung* 61 (1): 27–50.

Weintraub, Jeff. 1997. 'The Theory and Politics of the Private/Public Distinction.' In *Public and Private in Thought and Practice: Perspectives on a Grand Dichotomy*, edited by Jeff Weintraub and Krishan Kumar, 1–43, Chicago: Chicago University Press.

Werner, Michael, and Bénédicte Zimmermann. 2006. 'Beyond Comparison: Histoire Croisée and the Challenge of Reflexivity.' *History and Theory* 45 (1): 30–50.

Werts, Diane. 2006. *Christmas on Television*. Westport: Praeger.

White, Stephen. 1983. 'Political Communications in the USSR: Letters to Party, State and Press.' *Political Studies* 31 (1): 43–60.

Wierling, Dorothee. 1994. 'Die Jugend als Inner Feind: Konflikte in der Erziehungsdiktatur der sechziger Jahre.' In *Sozialgeschichte der DDR*, edited by Hartmut Kaelble, Jürgen Kocka, and Hartmut Zwahr, 404–425. Stuttgart: Klett-Cotta.

Williams, Raymond. 2007 [1974]. *Television: Technology and Cultural Form*. London: Routledge.

Wolff, Franca. 2002. *Glasnost erst kurz vor Sendeschluss: Die letzten Jahre des DDR-Fernsehens (1985–1989/90)*. Köln: Böhlau.

Wolle, Stefan. 2013. *Der große Plan: Alltag und Herrschaft in der DDR (1949–1961)*. Berlin: Christoph Links.

Yesil, Bilge. 2015. Transnationalization of Turkish Dramas: Exploring the Convergence of Local and Global Market Imperatives.' *Global Media and Communication* 11 (1): 43–60.

Youngblood, Denise. 2007. *Russian War Films: On the Cinema Front, 1914–2005*. Lawrence: University of Kansas Press.

Yurchak, Alexei. 2006. *Everything Was Forever, until It Was No More: The Last Soviet Generation*. Princeton: Princeton University Press.

Zelizer, Barbie. 2016. 'Journalism's Deep Memory: Cold War Mindedness and the Coverage of the Islamic State.' *International Journal of Communication* 10: 6060–6089.

Zerubavel, Eviatar. 1982. 'The Standardization of Time: A Sociohistorical Perspective.' *The American Journal of Sociology* 88 (1): 1–23.

Zhang, Hong. 2009. 'The Globalization of Chinese Television: The Role of the Party State.' *Media@LSE Electronic Working Papers*, No. 16.

Zhao, Yuezhi. 2008. *Communication in China: Political Economy, Power, and Conflict*. Lanham: Rowman and Littlefield.

Zhao, Yuezhi. 2012. 'Understanding China's Media System in a World Historical Context.' In *Comparing Media Systems beyond the Western World*, edited by Daniel Hallin and Paolo Mancini, 143–176. Cambridge: Cambridge University Press.

Zhu, Ying. 2008. *Television in Post-Reform China: Serial Dramas, Confucian Leadership, and the Global Television Market*. London: Routledge.

Index

Other Books in the Series (*continued from page ii*)

Richard Gunther and Anthony Mughan, eds., *Democracy and the Media: A Comparative Perspective*
Daniel C. Hallin and Paolo Mancini, *Comparing Media Systems: Three Models of Media and Politics*
Daniel C. Hallin and Paolo Mancini, eds., *Comparing Media Systems Beyond the Western World*
Roderick P. Hart, *Civic Hope: How Ordinary Citizens Keep Democracy Alive*
Robert B. Horwitz, *Communication and Democratic Reform in South Africa*
Philip N. Howard, *New Media Campaigns and the Managed Citizen*
Ruud Koopmans and Paul Statham, eds., *The Making of a European Public Sphere: Media Discourse and Political Contention*
L. Sandy Maisel, Darrell M. West, and Brett M. Clifton, *Evaluating Campaign Quality: Can the Electoral Process Be Improved?*
Douglas M. McLeod and Dhavan V. Shah, *News Frames and National Security*
Pippa Norris, *Digital Divide: Civic Engagement, Information Poverty, and the Internet Worldwide*
Pippa Norris, *A Virtuous Circle: Political Communications in Postindustrial Society*
Victor Pickard, *How America Lost the Battle for Media Democracy: Corporate Libertarianism and the Future of Media Reform*
Sue Robinson, *Networked News, Racial Divides: How Power & Privilege Shape Public Discourse in Progressive Communities*
Margaret Scammell, *Consumer Democracy: The Marketing of Politics*
Adam F. Simon, *The Winning Message: Candidate Behavior, Campaign Discourse*
Daniela Stockmann, *Media Commercialization and Authoritarian Rule in China*
Bruce A. Williams and Michael X. Delli Carpini, *After Broadcast News: Media Regimes, Democracy, and the New Information Environment*
Gadi Wolfsfeld, *Media and the Path to Peace*